Asymptotic Theory for Econometricians

This is a volume in
ECONOMIC THEORY, ECONOMETRICS, AND MATHEMATICAL ECONOMICS
A Series of Monographs and Textbooks
Consulting Editor: KARL SHELL
A complete list of titles in this series is available from the Publishers upon request.

Asymptotic Theory for Econometricians

Halbert White
DEPARTMENT OF ECONOMICS
UNIVERSITY OF CALIFORNIA, SAN DIEGO
LA JOLLA, CALIFORNIA

1984

ACADEMIC PRESS
A Division of Harcourt Brace & Company
San Diego New York Boston
London Sydney Tokyo Toronto

ACADEMIC PRESS, INC.
525 B Street, Suite 1900
San Diego, California 92101-4495

United Kingdom Edition published by
ACADEMIC PRESS, INC. (LONDON) LTD.
24/28 Oval Road, London NW1 7DX

Library of Congress Cataloging in Publication Data

White, Halbert.
Asymptotic theory for econometricians.

(Economic theory, econometrics, and mathematical economics)
Includes index.
1. Econometrics--Asymptotic theory. I. Title.
II. Series.
HB139.W5 1983 330'.028 83-10010
ISBN 0-12-746650-9

PRINTED IN THE UNITED STATES OF AMERICA

94 95 96 QW 9 8 7 6 5 4

This book is dedicated to my parents

Contents

Preface

Within the framework of the classical linear model it is a fairly straightforward matter to establish the properties of the ordinary least squares (OLS) and generalized least squares (GLS) estimators for samples of any size. Although the classical linear model is an excellent framework for developing a feel for the statistical techniques of estimation and inference that are central to econometrics, it is not particularly well adapted to the study of economic phenomena, because economists usually cannot conduct controlled experiments. Instead, the data usually exist as the outcome of a stochastic process outside the control of the investigator. For this reason, both the dependent and the explanatory variables may be stochastic, and equation disturbances may exhibit nonnormality or heteroskedasticity and serial correlation of unknown form, so that the classical assumptions are violated. Over the years a variety of useful techniques has evolved to deal with these difficulties. Many of these amount to straightforward modifications or extensions of the OLS techniques (e.g., the Cochrane–Orcutt technique, two-stage least squares, and three-stage least squares). However, the finite sample properties of these statistics are rarely easy to establish outside of somewhat limited special cases. Instead, their usefulness is justified primarily on the basis of their properties in large samples, because these properties can be fairly easily established using the powerful tools provided by laws of large numbers and central limit theory.

Despite the importance of large sample theory, it has usually received fairly cursory treatment in even the best econometrics textbooks. This is really no fault of the textbooks, however, because the field of asymptotic theory has been developing rapidly. It is only recently that econometricians have discovered or established methods for treating adequately and comprehensively the many different techniques available for dealing with the difficulties posed by economic data.

This book is intended to provide a somewhat more comprehensive and unified treatment of large sample theory than has been available previously and to relate the fundamental tools of asymptotic theory directly to many of the estimators of interest to econometricians. In addition, because economic data are generated in a variety of different contexts (time series, cross sections, time series–cross sections), we pay particular attention to the similarities and differences in the techniques appropriate to each of these contexts.

That it is possible to present our results in a fairly unified manner highlights the similarities among a variety of different techniques. It also allows us in specific instances to establish results that are somewhat more general than those previously available. We thus include some new results in addition to those that are better known.

This book is intended for use both as a reference and as a textbook for graduate students taking courses in econometrics beyond the introductory level. It is therefore assumed that the reader is familiar with the basic concepts of probability and statistics as well as with calculus and linear algebra and that the reader also has a good understanding of the classical linear model.

Because our goal here is to deal primarily with asymptotic theory, we do not consider in detail the meaning and scope of econometric models per se. Therefore, the material in this book can be usefully supplemented by standard econometrics texts, particularly any of those listed at the end of Chapter I.

I would like to express my appreciation to all those who have helped in the evolution of this work. In particular, I would like to thank Charles Bates, Ian Domowitz, Rob Engle, Clive Granger, Lars Hansen, David Hendry, and Murray Rosenblatt. Particular thanks are due Jeff Wooldridge for his work in producing the solution set for the exercises. I also thank the students in various graduate classes at UCSD, who have served as unwitting and indispensable guinea pigs in the development of this material. I am deeply grateful to Annetta Whiteman, who typed this difficult manuscript with incredible swiftness and accuracy. Finally, I would like to thank the National Science Foundation for providing financial support for this work under grant SES81–07552.

CHAPTER I

The Linear Model and Instrumental Variables Estimators

The purpose of this book is to provide the reader with the tools and concepts needed to study the behavior of econometric estimators and test statistics in large samples. Throughout, attention will be directed to estimation and inference in the framework of a linear model such as

$$\mathbf{y}_t = \mathbf{X}_t \boldsymbol{\beta}_o + \boldsymbol{\epsilon}_t, \qquad t = 1, \ldots, n,$$

where we have n observations on the dependent variable $\mathbf{y}_t$ and the explanatory variables $\mathbf{X}_t = (\mathbf{X}_{t1}, \mathbf{X}_{t2}, \ldots, \mathbf{X}_{tk})$. The stochastic disturbance $\boldsymbol{\epsilon}_t$ is unobserved, and $\boldsymbol{\beta}_o$ is an unknown $k \times 1$ vector of parameters that we are interested in learning about, either through estimation or through hypothesis testing. In matrix notation this model is written as

$$\mathbf{y} = \mathbf{X}\boldsymbol{\beta}_o + \boldsymbol{\epsilon},$$

where $\mathbf{y}$ is an $n \times 1$ vector, $\mathbf{X}$ an $n \times k$ matrix, $\boldsymbol{\beta}_o$ a $k \times 1$ vector, and $\boldsymbol{\epsilon}$ an $n \times 1$ vector.

Almost all econometric estimators can be viewed as solutions to an optimization problem. For example, the ordinary least squares estimator is the value for $\boldsymbol{\beta}$ that minimizes the sum of squared residuals

$$\begin{aligned} \mathrm{SSR}(\boldsymbol{\beta}) &= (\mathbf{y} - \mathbf{X}\boldsymbol{\beta})'(\mathbf{y} - \mathbf{X}\boldsymbol{\beta}) \\ &= \sum_{t=1}^{n} (\mathbf{y}_t - \mathbf{X}_t\boldsymbol{\beta})^2. \end{aligned}$$

The first-order conditions for a minimum are

$$\begin{aligned}\mathrm{SSR}(\boldsymbol{\beta})/\boldsymbol{\beta} &= -2\mathbf{X}'(\mathbf{y}-\mathbf{X}\boldsymbol{\beta})\\ &= -2\sum_{t=1}^{n}\mathbf{X}_t'(\mathbf{y}_t-\mathbf{X}_t\boldsymbol{\beta}) = \mathbf{0}.\end{aligned}$$

If $\mathbf{X}'\mathbf{X} = \Sigma_{t=1}^{n} \mathbf{X}_t'\mathbf{X}_t$ is nonsingular, this system of k equations in k unknowns can be uniquely solved for the *ordinary least squares* (OLS) estimator

$$\begin{aligned}\hat{\boldsymbol{\beta}}_n &= (\mathbf{X}'\mathbf{X})^{-1}\mathbf{X}'\mathbf{y}\\ &= \left(\sum_{t=1}^{n}\mathbf{X}_t'\mathbf{X}_t\right)^{-1}\sum_{t=1}^{n}\mathbf{X}_t'\mathbf{y}_t.\end{aligned}$$

Our interest centers on the behavior of estimators such as $\hat{\boldsymbol{\beta}}_n$ as n grows larger and larger. We seek conditions that will allow us to draw conclusions about the behavior of $\hat{\boldsymbol{\beta}}_n$; for example, that $\hat{\boldsymbol{\beta}}_n$ has a particular distribution or certain first and second moments.

The assumptions of the *classical linear model* allow us to draw such conclusions for any n. These conditions and results can be formally stated as the following theorem.

THEOREM 1.1: The following are the assumptions of the classical linear model.

(i) The model is known to be $\mathbf{y} = \mathbf{X}\boldsymbol{\beta}_0 + \boldsymbol{\epsilon}$, $\boldsymbol{\beta}_o < \infty$.
(ii) $\mathbf{X}$ is a nonstochastic and finite $n \times k$ matrix.
(iii) $\mathbf{X}'\mathbf{X}$ is nonsingular for all $n \geq k$.
(iv) $E(\boldsymbol{\epsilon}) = \mathbf{0}$.
(v) $\boldsymbol{\epsilon} \sim \mathrm{N}(\mathbf{0}, \sigma_o^2\mathbf{I})$, $\sigma_o^2 < \infty$.
  (a) (Existence) Given (i)–(iii), $\hat{\boldsymbol{\beta}}_n$ exists for all $n \geq k$ and is unique.
  (b) (Unbiasedness) Given (i)–(iv), $E(\hat{\boldsymbol{\beta}}_n) = \boldsymbol{\beta}_o$.
  (c) (Normality) Given (i)–(v), $\hat{\boldsymbol{\beta}}_n \sim \mathrm{N}(\boldsymbol{\beta}_o, \sigma_o^2(\mathbf{X}'\mathbf{X})^{-1})$.
  (d) (Efficiency) Given (i)–(v), $\hat{\boldsymbol{\beta}}_n$ is the maximum likelihood estimator and is the best unbiased estimator in the sense that the variance–covariance matrix of any other unbiased estimator exceeds that of $\hat{\boldsymbol{\beta}}_n$ by a positive semi-definite matrix, regardless of the value of $\boldsymbol{\beta}_o$.

Proof: See Theil [1971, Ch. 3].

In the statement of the assumptions above, $E(\cdot)$ denotes the expected value operator, and $\boldsymbol{\epsilon} \sim \mathbf{N}(\mathbf{0}, \sigma_o^2\mathbf{I})$ means that $\boldsymbol{\epsilon}$ is distributed as $(\sim)$ multivariate normal with mean vector zero and covariance matrix $\sigma_o^2\mathbf{I}$.

The properties of existence, unbiasedness, normality, and efficiency of an estimator are the small sample analogs of the properties that will be the focus of interest here. Unbiasedness tells us that the distribution of $\hat{\boldsymbol{\beta}}_n$ is centered around the unknown true value $\boldsymbol{\beta}_o$, whereas the normality property allows us to construct confidence intervals and test hypotheses using the t- or F-distributions (see Theil [1971, pp. 130–146]). The efficiency property guarantees that our estimator has the greatest possible precision within a given class of estimators and also helps ensure that tests of hypotheses have high power.

Of course, the classical assumptions are rather stringent and can easily fail in situations faced by economists. Since failures of assumptions (iii) and (iv) are easily remedied (exclude linearly dependent regressors if (iii) fails, include a constant in the model if (iv) fails), we will concern ourselves primarily with the failure of assumptions (ii) and (v). The possible failure of assumption (i) is a subject that requires a book in itself and will not be considered here. Nevertheless, the tools developed in this book will be essential to understanding and treating the consequences of the failure of assumption (i).

Let us briefly examine the consequences of various failures of assumptions (ii) or (v). First, suppose that $\boldsymbol{\epsilon}$ exhibits heteroskedasticity or serial correlation, so that $E(\boldsymbol{\epsilon\epsilon}') = \boldsymbol{\Omega} \neq \sigma_o^2\mathbf{I}$. We have the following result for the OLS estimator.

THEOREM 1.2: Suppose the classical assumptions (i)–(iv) hold but replace (v) with

(v′) $\boldsymbol{\epsilon} \sim \mathbf{N}(\mathbf{0}, \boldsymbol{\Omega}), \boldsymbol{\Omega} < \infty$.

Then (a) and (b) hold as before, (c) is replaced by

(c′) (Normality) Given (i)–(v′),

$$\hat{\boldsymbol{\beta}}_n \sim \mathbf{N}(\boldsymbol{\beta}_o, (\mathbf{X}'\mathbf{X})^{-1}\, \mathbf{X}'\boldsymbol{\Omega}\mathbf{X}\, (\mathbf{X}'\mathbf{X})^{-1}),$$

and (d) does not hold, that is, $\hat{\boldsymbol{\beta}}_n$ is no longer the best unbiased estimator.

Proof: By definition, $\hat{\boldsymbol{\beta}}_n = (\mathbf{X}'\mathbf{X})^{-1}\mathbf{X}'\mathbf{y}$. Given (i),

$$\hat{\boldsymbol{\beta}}_n = \boldsymbol{\beta}_o + (\mathbf{X}'\mathbf{X})^{-1}\mathbf{X}'\boldsymbol{\epsilon},$$

where $(\mathbf{X}'\mathbf{X})^{-1}\mathbf{X}'\boldsymbol{\epsilon}$ is a linear combination of jointly normal random variables and is therefore jointly normal with

$$E((\mathbf{X}'\mathbf{X})^{-1}\mathbf{X}'\boldsymbol{\epsilon}) = (\mathbf{X}'\mathbf{X})^{-1}\mathbf{X}'E(\boldsymbol{\epsilon}) = \mathbf{0},$$

given (ii) and (iv) and

$$\begin{aligned}\operatorname{var}(\mathbf{X}'\mathbf{X})^{-1}\mathbf{X}'\boldsymbol{\epsilon} &= E((\mathbf{X}'\mathbf{X})^{-1}\mathbf{X}'\boldsymbol{\epsilon\epsilon}'\mathbf{X}(\mathbf{X}'\mathbf{X})^{-1}) \\ &= (\mathbf{X}'\mathbf{X})^{-1}\mathbf{X}'E(\boldsymbol{\epsilon\epsilon}')\mathbf{X}(\mathbf{X}'\mathbf{X})^{-1} \\ &= (\mathbf{X}'\mathbf{X})^{-1}\mathbf{X}'\boldsymbol{\Omega}\mathbf{X}(\mathbf{X}'\mathbf{X})^{-1},\end{aligned}$$

given (ii) and (v′). Hence $\hat{\boldsymbol{\beta}}_n \sim N(\boldsymbol{\beta}_o, (\mathbf{X}'\mathbf{X})^{-1}\mathbf{X}'\boldsymbol{\Omega}\mathbf{X}(\mathbf{X}'\mathbf{X})^{-1})$. That (d) does not hold follows because there exists an unbiased estimator with smaller covariance matrix than $\hat{\boldsymbol{\beta}}_n$, namely, $\boldsymbol{\beta}_n^* = (\mathbf{X}'\boldsymbol{\Omega}^{-1}\mathbf{X})^{-1}\mathbf{X}'\boldsymbol{\Omega}^{-1}\mathbf{y}$. We examine its properties next.

As long as $\boldsymbol{\Omega}$ is known, the presence of serial correlation or heteroskedasticity does not render us incapable of testing hypotheses or constructing confidence intervals. This can still be done using (c′), although the failure of (d) indicates that the OLS estimator may not be best for these purposes. However, if $\boldsymbol{\Omega}$ is unknown (apart from a factor of proportionality), testing hypotheses and constructing confidence intervals is no longer a simple matter. One might be able to construct tests based on estimates of $\boldsymbol{\Omega}$, but the resulting statistics may have very complicated distributions. As we shall see in Chapter VI, this difficulty is lessened in large samples by the availability of convenient approximations based on the central limit theorem and laws of large numbers.

If $\boldsymbol{\Omega}$ is known, efficiency can be regained by applying OLS to a linear transformation of the original model, i.e.,

$$\mathbf{C}^{-1}\mathbf{y} = \mathbf{C}^{-1}\mathbf{X}\boldsymbol{\beta}_o + \mathbf{C}^{-1}\boldsymbol{\epsilon}$$

or

$$\mathbf{y}^* = \mathbf{X}^*\boldsymbol{\beta}_o + \boldsymbol{\epsilon}^*,$$

where $\mathbf{y}^* = \mathbf{C}^{-1}\mathbf{y}$, $\mathbf{X}^* = \mathbf{C}^{-1}\mathbf{X}$, $\boldsymbol{\epsilon}^* = \mathbf{C}^{-1}\boldsymbol{\epsilon}$ and $\mathbf{C}$ is a nonsingular factorization of $\boldsymbol{\Omega}$ such that $\mathbf{CC}' = \boldsymbol{\Omega}$ and $\mathbf{C}^{-1}\boldsymbol{\Omega}\mathbf{C}^{-1\prime} = \mathbf{I}$. This transformation ensures that $E(\boldsymbol{\epsilon}^*\boldsymbol{\epsilon}^{*\prime}) = E(\mathbf{C}^{-1}\boldsymbol{\epsilon\epsilon}'\mathbf{C}^{-1\prime}) = \mathbf{C}^{-1}E(\boldsymbol{\epsilon\epsilon}')\mathbf{C}^{-1\prime} = \mathbf{C}^{-1}\boldsymbol{\Omega}\mathbf{C}^{-1\prime} = \mathbf{I}$, so that assumption (v) once again holds. The least squares estimator for the transformed model is

$$\begin{aligned}\boldsymbol{\beta}_n^* &= (\mathbf{X}^{*\prime}\mathbf{X}^*)^{-1}\mathbf{X}^{*\prime}\mathbf{y}^* \\ &= (\mathbf{X}'\mathbf{C}^{-1\prime}\mathbf{C}^{-1}\mathbf{X})^{-1}\mathbf{X}'\mathbf{C}^{-1\prime}\mathbf{C}^{-1}\mathbf{y} \\ &= (\mathbf{X}'\boldsymbol{\Omega}^{-1}\mathbf{X})^{-1}\mathbf{X}'\boldsymbol{\Omega}^{-1}\mathbf{y}.\end{aligned}$$

The estimator $\boldsymbol{\beta}_n^*$ is called the *generalized least squares* (GLS) estimator and its properties are given by the following result.

THEOREM 1.3: The following are the "generalized" classical assumptions.

(i) The model is known to be $\mathbf{y} = \mathbf{X}\boldsymbol{\beta}_o + \boldsymbol{\epsilon}$, $\boldsymbol{\beta}_o < \infty$.
(ii) $\mathbf{X}$ is a finite nonstochastic $n \times k$ matrix.
(iii*) $\mathbf{X}'\boldsymbol{\Omega}^{-1}\mathbf{X}$ is nonsingular for all $n \geq k$ and $\boldsymbol{\Omega}$.
(iv) $E(\boldsymbol{\epsilon}) = \mathbf{0}$.
(v*) $\boldsymbol{\epsilon} \sim N(\mathbf{0},\boldsymbol{\Omega})$ is finite and nonsingular.

- (a) (Existence) Given (i)–(iii*), $\boldsymbol{\beta}_n^*$ exists for all $n \geq k$ and is unique.
- (b) (Unbiasedness) Given (i)–(iv), $E(\boldsymbol{\beta}_n^*) = \boldsymbol{\beta}_o$.
- (c) (Normality) Given (i)–(v*), $\boldsymbol{\beta}_n^* \sim N(\boldsymbol{\beta}_o, (\mathbf{X}\boldsymbol{\Omega}^{-1}\mathbf{X})^{-1})$.
- (d) (Efficiency) Given (i)–(v*), $\boldsymbol{\beta}_n^*$ is the maximum likelihood estimator and is the best unbiased estimator.

Proof: Apply Theorem 1.1 to the model $\mathbf{y}^* = \mathbf{X}^*\boldsymbol{\beta}_o + \boldsymbol{\epsilon}^*$.

If $\boldsymbol{\Omega}$ is known, we obtain efficiency by transforming the model "back" to a form in which OLS gives the efficient estimator. However, if $\boldsymbol{\Omega}$ is unknown, this transformation is not immediately available. It might be possible to estimate $\boldsymbol{\Omega}$, say by $\hat{\boldsymbol{\Omega}}$, but $\hat{\boldsymbol{\Omega}}$ is then random and so is the factorization $\hat{\mathbf{C}}$. Theorem 1.1 no longer applies. Nevertheless, we shall see in Chapter VII that in large samples we can often proceed by replacing $\boldsymbol{\Omega}$ with a suitable estimator $\hat{\boldsymbol{\Omega}}$.

Hypothesis testing in the classical linear model relies heavily on being able to make use of the t- and F-distributions. However, it is quite possible that the normality assumption of assumption (v) or (v*) may fail. When this happens, the classical t- and F-statistics generally no longer have the t- and F-distributions. Nevertheless, the central limit theorem can be applied when n is large to guarantee that $\hat{\boldsymbol{\beta}}_n$ or $\boldsymbol{\beta}_n^*$ is distributed approximately as normal, as we shall see in Chapters IV and V.

Now consider what happens when assumption (ii) fails, so that the explanatory variables $\mathbf{X}$ are stochastic. In some cases, this causes no real problems because we can examine the properties of our estimators "conditional" on $\mathbf{X}$. For example, consider the unbiasedness property. To demonstrate unbiasedness we use (i) to write

$$\hat{\boldsymbol{\beta}}_n = \boldsymbol{\beta}_o + (\mathbf{X}'\mathbf{X})^{-1}\mathbf{X}'\boldsymbol{\epsilon}.$$

If $\mathbf{X}$ is random, we can no longer write $E((\mathbf{X}'\mathbf{X})^{-1}\mathbf{X}'\boldsymbol{\epsilon}) = (\mathbf{X}'\mathbf{X})^{-1}\mathbf{X}'E(\boldsymbol{\epsilon})$ However, by taking conditional expectations, we can treat $\mathbf{X}$ as "fixed," so we have

$$\begin{aligned} E(\hat{\boldsymbol{\beta}}_n|\mathbf{X}) &= \boldsymbol{\beta}_o + E((\mathbf{X}'\mathbf{X})^{-1}\mathbf{X}'\boldsymbol{\epsilon}|\mathbf{X}). \\ &= \boldsymbol{\beta}_o + (\mathbf{X}'\mathbf{X})^{-1}\mathbf{X}'E(\boldsymbol{\epsilon}|\mathbf{X}). \end{aligned}$$

If we are willing to assume $E(\boldsymbol{\epsilon}|\mathbf{X}) = \mathbf{0}$, then conditional unbiasedness follows, i.e.,

$$E(\hat{\boldsymbol{\beta}}_n|\mathbf{X}) = \boldsymbol{\beta}_o.$$

Unconditional unbiasedness also holds as a consequence of the law of iterated expectations (given in Chapter III), i.e.,

$$E(\hat{\boldsymbol{\beta}}_n) = E[E(\hat{\boldsymbol{\beta}}_n|\mathbf{X})] = E(\boldsymbol{\beta}_o) = \boldsymbol{\beta}_o.$$

The other properties can be similarly considered. However, the assumption that $E(\boldsymbol{\epsilon}|\mathbf{X}) = \mathbf{0}$ is crucial. If $E(\boldsymbol{\epsilon}|\mathbf{X}) \neq \mathbf{0}$, $\hat{\boldsymbol{\beta}}_n$ need not be unbiased, either conditionally or unconditionally.

Situations in which $E(\boldsymbol{\epsilon}|\mathbf{X}) \neq 0$ can arise easily in economics. For example, $\mathbf{X}_t$ may contain *errors of measurement*. Suppose the model is

$$\mathrm{y}_t = \mathbf{W}_t\boldsymbol{\beta}_o + v_t, \qquad E(\mathbf{W}_t'v_t) = \mathbf{0},$$

but we measure $\mathbf{W}_t$ subject to errors $\boldsymbol{\eta}_t$ as $\mathbf{X}_t = \mathbf{W}_t + \boldsymbol{\eta}_t$, $E(\mathbf{W}_t'\boldsymbol{\eta}_t) = \mathbf{0}$, $E(\boldsymbol{\eta}_t'\boldsymbol{\eta}_t) \neq \mathbf{0}$, $E(\boldsymbol{\eta}_t'v_t) = \mathbf{0}$. Then

$$\mathrm{y}_t = \mathbf{X}_t\boldsymbol{\beta}_o + v_t - \boldsymbol{\eta}_t\boldsymbol{\beta}_o = \mathbf{X}_t\boldsymbol{\beta}_o + \epsilon_t.$$

With $\epsilon_t = v_t - \boldsymbol{\eta}_t\boldsymbol{\beta}_o$, we have $E(\mathbf{X}_t'\epsilon_t) = E[(\mathbf{W}_t' + \boldsymbol{\eta}_t')(v_t - \boldsymbol{\eta}_t\boldsymbol{\beta}_o)] = E(\boldsymbol{\eta}_t'\boldsymbol{\eta}_t)\boldsymbol{\beta}_o \neq \mathbf{0}$. Now $E(\boldsymbol{\epsilon}|\mathbf{X}) = 0$ implies that for all t, $E(\mathbf{X}_t'\epsilon_t) = \mathbf{0}$, since $E(\mathbf{X}_t'\epsilon_t) = E[E(\mathbf{X}_t'\epsilon_t|\mathbf{X})] = E[\mathbf{X}_t'E(\epsilon_t|\mathbf{X})] = 0$. Hence $E(\mathbf{X}_t'\epsilon_t) \neq \mathbf{0}$ implies $E(\boldsymbol{\epsilon}|\mathbf{X}) \neq 0$. The OLS estimator will not be unbiased in the presence of measurement errors.

As another example, consider the model

$$\mathbf{y}_t = \mathbf{y}_{t-1}\alpha_o + \mathbf{W}_t\boldsymbol{\delta}_o + \epsilon_t, \qquad E(\mathbf{W}_t'\epsilon_t) = \mathbf{0};$$

$$\epsilon_t = \rho_o\epsilon_{t-1} + \nu_t, \qquad E(\epsilon_{t-1}\nu_t) = 0.$$

This is the case of *serially correlated errors in the presence of a lagged dependent variable* $\mathbf{y}_{t-1}$. Let $\mathbf{X}_t = (\mathbf{y}_{t-1}, \mathbf{W}_t)$ and $\boldsymbol{\beta}_o' = (\alpha_o, \boldsymbol{\delta}_o')$. Again, the model is

$$\mathbf{y}_t = \mathbf{X}_t\boldsymbol{\beta}_o + \epsilon_t,$$

but we have $E(\mathbf{X}_t'\epsilon_t) = E((\mathbf{y}_{t-1}, \mathbf{W}_t)'\epsilon_t) = (E(\mathbf{y}_{t-1}\epsilon_t),\mathbf{0})'$. If we also assume $E(\mathbf{y}_{t-1}\nu_t) = 0$, $E(\mathbf{y}_{t-1}\epsilon_{t-1}) = E(\mathbf{y}_t\epsilon_t)$, and $E(\epsilon_t^2) = \sigma_o^2$, it can be shown that

$$E(\mathbf{y}_{t-1}\epsilon_t) = \sigma_o^2\rho_o/(1-\rho_o\alpha_o).$$

Thus $E(\mathbf{X}_t'\epsilon_t) \neq \mathbf{0}$ so that $E(\boldsymbol{\epsilon}|\mathbf{X}) \neq \mathbf{0}$ and OLS is not generally unbiased.

As a final example, consider a system of *simultaneous equations*

$$\mathbf{y}_{t1} = \mathbf{y}_{t2}\alpha_o + \mathbf{W}_{t1}\boldsymbol{\delta}_o + \epsilon_{t1}, \qquad E(\mathbf{W}_{t1}'\epsilon_{t1}) = \mathbf{0},$$

$$\mathbf{y}_{t2} = \mathbf{W}_{t2}\boldsymbol{\gamma}_o + \epsilon_{t2}, \qquad E(\mathbf{W}_{t2}'\epsilon_{t2}) = \mathbf{0}.$$

Suppose we are only interested in the first equation, but we know $E(\epsilon_{t1}\epsilon_{t2}) = \sigma_{12} \neq 0$. Let $\mathbf{X}_{t1} = (\mathbf{y}_{t2}, \mathbf{W}_{t1})$ and $\boldsymbol{\beta}_o' = (\alpha_o, \boldsymbol{\delta}_o')$. The equation of interest is now

$$\mathbf{y}_{t1} = \mathbf{X}_{t1}\boldsymbol{\beta}_o + \epsilon_{t1}.$$

In this case $E(\mathbf{X}_{t1}'\epsilon_{t1}) = E((\mathbf{y}_{t2}, \mathbf{W}_{t1})'\epsilon_{t1}) = (E(\mathbf{y}_{t2}\epsilon_{t1}),\mathbf{0})'$. Now $E(\mathbf{y}_{t2}\epsilon_{t1}) = E((\mathbf{W}_{t2}\boldsymbol{\gamma}_o + \epsilon_{t2})\epsilon_{t1}) = E(\epsilon_{t1}\epsilon_{t2}) = \sigma_{12} \neq 0$, assuming $E(\mathbf{W}_{t2}\epsilon_{t1}) = \mathbf{0}$. Thus $E(\mathbf{X}_{t1}'\epsilon_{t1}) = (\sigma_{12},\mathbf{0})' \neq \mathbf{0}$, so again OLS is not generally unbiased, either conditionally or unconditionally.

Not only is the OLS estimator generally biased in these circumstances, but it can be shown that this bias does not get smaller as n gets larger. Fortunately, there is an alternative to least squares that is better behaved, at least in large samples. This alternative exploits the fact that even when $E(\mathbf{X}_t'\epsilon_t) \neq \mathbf{0}$, it is often possible to use economic theory to find other variables that are uncorrelated with the errors ϵ_t. Without such variables, correlations between the observables and unobservables (the errors ϵ_t) persistently contaminate our estimators, making it impossible to learn anything about $\boldsymbol{\beta}_o$. Hence, these variables are instrumental in allowing us to estimate $\boldsymbol{\beta}_o$, and we shall denote these "instrumental variables" as a $1 \times l$ vector $\mathbf{Z}_t$. The $n \times l$ matrix $\mathbf{Z}$ has rows $\mathbf{Z}_t$.

To be useful, the instrumental variables must also be closely enough related to $\mathbf{X}_t$ so that $\mathbf{Z}'\mathbf{X}$ has full column rank. If we know from economic theory that $E(\mathbf{X}_t'\boldsymbol{\epsilon}_t) = \mathbf{0}$, then $\mathbf{X}_t$ can serve directly as the set of instrumental variables. As we saw previously, $\mathbf{X}_t$ may be correlated with $\boldsymbol{\epsilon}_t$, so we cannot always choose $\mathbf{Z}_t = \mathbf{X}_t$. Nevertheless, in each of those examples, the structure of the model suggests some reasonable choices for $\mathbf{Z}$. In the case of errors of measurement, a useful set of instrumental variables would be another set of measurements on $\mathbf{W}_t$ subject to errors $\boldsymbol{\xi}_t$ uncorrelated with $\boldsymbol{\eta}_t$ and v_t, say $\mathbf{Z}_t = \mathbf{W}_t + \boldsymbol{\xi}_t$. Then $E(\mathbf{Z}_t'\boldsymbol{\epsilon}_t) = E[(\mathbf{W}_t' + \boldsymbol{\xi}_t')(v_t - \boldsymbol{\eta}_t\boldsymbol{\beta}_o)] = \mathbf{0}$. In the case of serial correlation in the presence of lagged dependent variables, a useful choice is $\mathbf{Z}_t = (\mathbf{W}_t, \mathbf{W}_{t-1})$, provided $E(\mathbf{W}_{t-1}'\boldsymbol{\epsilon}_t) = 0$, which is not unreasonable. Note that the relation $\mathbf{y}_{t-1} = \mathbf{y}_{t-2}\boldsymbol{\alpha}_o + \mathbf{W}_{t-1}\boldsymbol{\delta}_o + \boldsymbol{\epsilon}_{t-1}$ ensures that $\mathbf{W}_{t-1}$ will be related to $\mathbf{y}_{t-1}$. In the case of simultaneous equations, a useful choice is $\mathbf{Z}_t = (\mathbf{W}_{t1}, \mathbf{W}_{t2})$. The relation $\mathbf{y}_{t2} = \mathbf{W}_{t2}\boldsymbol{\gamma}_o + \boldsymbol{\epsilon}_{t2}$ ensures that $\mathbf{W}_{t2}$ will be related to $\mathbf{y}_{t2}$.

In what follows, we shall simply assume that such instrumental variables are available. However, in Chapter IV we shall be able to specify precisely how best to choose the instrumental variables.

Earlier, we stated the important fact that almost all econometric estimators can be viewed as solutions to an optimization problem. In the present context, the zero correlation property $E(\mathbf{Z}_t'\boldsymbol{\epsilon}_t) = \mathbf{0}$ provides the fundamental basis for estimating $\boldsymbol{\beta}_o$. Because $\boldsymbol{\epsilon}_t = \mathbf{y}_t - \mathbf{X}_t\boldsymbol{\beta}_o$, $\boldsymbol{\beta}_o$ is a solution of the equations $E(\mathbf{Z}_t'(\mathbf{y}_t - \mathbf{X}_t\boldsymbol{\beta})) = \mathbf{0}$. However, we usually do not know the expectations $E(\mathbf{Z}_t'\mathbf{y}_t)$ and $E(\mathbf{Z}_t'\mathbf{X}_t)$ needed to find a solution to these equations, so we replace expectations with sample averages, which we hope will provide a close enough approximation. Thus, consider finding a solution to the equations

$$n^{-1}\sum_{t=1}^{n}\mathbf{Z}_t'(\mathbf{y}_t - \mathbf{X}_t\boldsymbol{\beta}) = \mathbf{Z}'(\mathbf{y} - \mathbf{X}\boldsymbol{\beta})/n = \mathbf{0}.$$

This is a system of l equations in k unknowns. If $l < k$, there is a multiplicity of solutions; if $l = k$, the unique solution is $\tilde{\boldsymbol{\beta}}_n = (\mathbf{Z}'\mathbf{X})^{-1}\mathbf{Z}'\mathbf{y}$, provided that $\mathbf{Z}'\mathbf{X}$ is nonsingular; and if $l > k$, these equations need have no solution, although there may be a value for $\boldsymbol{\beta}$ that makes $\mathbf{Z}'(\mathbf{y} - \mathbf{X}\boldsymbol{\beta})$ "closest" to zero.

This provides the basis for solving an optimization problem. Because economic theory typically leads to situations in which $l \geq k$, we can estimate $\boldsymbol{\beta}_o$ by finding that value of $\boldsymbol{\beta}$ which minimizes the quadratic distance from zero of $\mathbf{Z}'(\mathbf{y}-\mathbf{X}\boldsymbol{\beta})$,

$$d_n(\boldsymbol{\beta}) = (\mathbf{y}-\mathbf{X}\boldsymbol{\beta})'\mathbf{Z}\hat{\mathbf{P}}_n\mathbf{Z}'(\mathbf{y}-\mathbf{X}\boldsymbol{\beta}),$$

where $\hat{\mathbf{P}}_n$ is a symmetric $l \times l$ positive definite norming matrix which may be stochastic. For now, $\hat{\mathbf{P}}_n$ can be any symmetric positive definite matrix. In Chapter IV we shall see how the choice of $\hat{\mathbf{P}}_n$ affects the properties of our estimator and how $\hat{\mathbf{P}}_n$ can best be chosen.

We choose the quadratic distance measure because this minimization problem (minimize $d_n(\boldsymbol{\beta})$ with respect to $\boldsymbol{\beta}$) has a convenient linear solution and yields many well-known econometric estimators. Other distance measures yield other families of estimators which we will not consider here.

The first-order conditions for a minimum are

$$d_n(\boldsymbol{\beta})/\boldsymbol{\beta} = -2\mathbf{X}'\mathbf{Z}\hat{\mathbf{P}}_n\mathbf{Z}'(\mathbf{y}-\mathbf{X}\boldsymbol{\beta}) = \mathbf{0}.$$

Provided that $\mathbf{X}'\mathbf{Z}\hat{\mathbf{P}}_n\mathbf{Z}'\mathbf{X}$ is nonsingular (for which it is necessary that $\mathbf{Z}'\mathbf{X}$ have full column rank), the resulting solution is the *instrumental variables* (IV) estimator (also known as the "method of moments" estimator)

$$\tilde{\boldsymbol{\beta}}_n = (\mathbf{X}'\mathbf{Z}\hat{\mathbf{P}}_n\mathbf{Z}'\mathbf{X})^{-1}\mathbf{X}'\mathbf{Z}\hat{\mathbf{P}}_n\mathbf{Z}'\mathbf{y}.$$

All of the estimators considered in this book have this form, and by choosing $\mathbf{Z}$ or $\hat{\mathbf{P}}_n$ appropriately, we can obtain a large number of the estimators of interest to econometricians. For example, with $\mathbf{Z}=\mathbf{X}$ and $\hat{\mathbf{P}}_n = (\mathbf{X}'\mathbf{X}/n)^{-1}$, $\tilde{\boldsymbol{\beta}}_n = \hat{\boldsymbol{\beta}}_n$, that is, the IV estimator equals the OLS estimator. Given any $\mathbf{Z}$, choosing $\hat{\mathbf{P}}_n = (\mathbf{Z}'\mathbf{Z}/n)^{-1}$ gives an estimator known as *two-stage least squares* (2SLS). The tools developed in the following chapters will allow us to pick $\mathbf{Z}$ and $\hat{\mathbf{P}}_n$ in ways appropriate to most of the situations encountered in economics.

Now consider the problem of determining whether $\tilde{\boldsymbol{\beta}}_n$ is unbiased. If the model is $\mathbf{y} = \mathbf{X}\boldsymbol{\beta}_o + \boldsymbol{\epsilon}$, we have

$$\begin{aligned}\tilde{\boldsymbol{\beta}}_n &= (\mathbf{X}'\mathbf{Z}\hat{\mathbf{P}}_n\mathbf{Z}'\mathbf{X})^{-1}\mathbf{X}'\mathbf{Z}\hat{\mathbf{P}}_n\mathbf{Z}'\mathbf{y}\\ &= (\mathbf{X}'\mathbf{Z}\hat{\mathbf{P}}_n\mathbf{Z}'\mathbf{X})^{-1}\mathbf{X}'\mathbf{Z}\hat{\mathbf{P}}_n\mathbf{Z}'(\mathbf{X}\boldsymbol{\beta}_o+\boldsymbol{\epsilon})\\ &= \boldsymbol{\beta}_o + (\mathbf{X}'\mathbf{Z}\hat{\mathbf{P}}_n\mathbf{Z}'\mathbf{X})^{-1}\mathbf{X}'\mathbf{Z}\hat{\mathbf{P}}_n\mathbf{Z}'\boldsymbol{\epsilon},\end{aligned}$$

so that

$$E(\tilde{\boldsymbol{\beta}}_n) = \boldsymbol{\beta}_o + E[(\mathbf{X}'\mathbf{Z}\hat{\mathbf{P}}_n\mathbf{Z}'\mathbf{X})^{-1}\mathbf{X}'\mathbf{Z}\hat{\mathbf{P}}_n\mathbf{Z}'\boldsymbol{\epsilon}].$$

In general, it is not possible to guarantee that the second term above vanishes, even when $E(\boldsymbol{\epsilon}|\mathbf{Z}) = \mathbf{0}$. In fact, the expectation in the second term above may not even be defined. For this reason, the concept of unbiasedness is not particularly relevant to the study of IV estimators. Instead, we shall make use of the weaker concept of consistency. Loosely speaking, an estimator is "consistent" for $\boldsymbol{\beta}_o$ if it gets closer and closer to $\boldsymbol{\beta}_o$ as n grows. In Chapters II and III we make this concept precise and explore the consistency properties of OLS and IV estimators. For the examples above in which $E(\boldsymbol{\epsilon}|\mathbf{X}) \neq \mathbf{0}$, it turns out that OLS is not consistent, while consistent IV estimators are available under general conditions.

Although we only consider linear models in this book, this still covers a wide range of situations. For example, suppose we have several equations that describe demand for a group of p commodities:

$$\begin{aligned}
\mathbf{y}_{t1} &= \mathbf{X}_{t1}\boldsymbol{\beta}_1 + \boldsymbol{\epsilon}_{t1},\\
\mathbf{y}_{t2} &= \mathbf{X}_{t2}\boldsymbol{\beta}_2 + \boldsymbol{\epsilon}_{t2},\\
&\ \ \vdots\\
\mathbf{y}_{tp} &= \mathbf{X}_{tp}\boldsymbol{\beta}_p + \boldsymbol{\epsilon}_{tp}, \qquad t = 1, \ldots, n.
\end{aligned}$$

Now let $\mathbf{y}_t$ be a $p \times 1$ vector, $\mathbf{y}_t' = (\mathbf{y}_{t1}, \mathbf{y}_{t2}, \ldots, \mathbf{y}_{tp})$, let $\boldsymbol{\epsilon}_t' = (\boldsymbol{\epsilon}_{t1}, \boldsymbol{\epsilon}_{t2}, \ldots, \boldsymbol{\epsilon}_{tp})$, let $\boldsymbol{\beta}_o' = (\boldsymbol{\beta}_1', \boldsymbol{\beta}_2', \ldots, \boldsymbol{\beta}_p')$, and let

$$\mathbf{X}_t = \begin{bmatrix} \mathbf{X}_{t1} & \mathbf{0} & \cdots & \mathbf{0} \\ \mathbf{0} & \mathbf{X}_{t2} & \cdots & \mathbf{0} \\ \vdots & \vdots & \ddots & \vdots \\ \mathbf{0} & \mathbf{0} & \cdots & \mathbf{X}_{tp} \end{bmatrix}.$$

Now $\mathbf{X}_t$ is a $p \times k$ matrix, where $k = \Sigma_{i=1}^p k_i$ and $\mathbf{X}_{ti}$ is a $1 \times k_i$ vector. The system of equations can be written as

$$\begin{bmatrix} \mathbf{y}_{t1} \\ \mathbf{y}_{t2} \\ \vdots \\ \mathbf{y}_{tp} \end{bmatrix} = \begin{bmatrix} \mathbf{X}_{t1} & \mathbf{0} & \cdots & \mathbf{0} \\ \mathbf{0} & \mathbf{X}_{t2} & \cdots & \mathbf{0} \\ \vdots & \vdots & \ddots & \vdots \\ \mathbf{0} & \mathbf{0} & \cdots & \mathbf{X}_{tp} \end{bmatrix} \begin{bmatrix} \boldsymbol{\beta}_1 \\ \boldsymbol{\beta}_2 \\ \vdots \\ \boldsymbol{\beta}_p \end{bmatrix} + \begin{bmatrix} \boldsymbol{\epsilon}_{t1} \\ \boldsymbol{\epsilon}_{t2} \\ \vdots \\ \boldsymbol{\epsilon}_{tp} \end{bmatrix}$$

or

$$\mathbf{y}_t = \mathbf{X}_t\boldsymbol{\beta}_o + \boldsymbol{\epsilon}_t.$$

Letting $\mathbf{y}' = (\mathbf{y}_1', \mathbf{y}_2', \ldots, \mathbf{y}_n')$, $\mathbf{X}' = (\mathbf{X}_1', \mathbf{X}_2', \ldots, \mathbf{X}_n')$, and $\boldsymbol{\epsilon}' = (\boldsymbol{\epsilon}_1', \boldsymbol{\epsilon}_2', \ldots, \boldsymbol{\epsilon}_n')$, we can write this system as

$$\mathbf{y} = \mathbf{X}\boldsymbol{\beta}_o + \boldsymbol{\epsilon}.$$

Now $\mathbf{y}$ is $pn \times 1$, $\boldsymbol{\epsilon}$ $pn \times 1$, and $\mathbf{X}$ $pn \times k$. This allows us to consider simultaneous systems of equations in the present framework.

Alternatively, suppose that we have observations on an individual t in each of p time periods,

$$\begin{aligned} y_{t1} &= \mathbf{X}_{t1}\boldsymbol{\beta}_o + \epsilon_{t1}, \\ y_{t2} &= \mathbf{X}_{t2}\boldsymbol{\beta}_o + \epsilon_{t2}, \\ y_{tp} &= \mathbf{X}_{tp}\boldsymbol{\beta}_o + \epsilon_{tp}, \qquad t = 1, \ldots, n. \end{aligned}$$

Define $\mathbf{y}_t$ and $\boldsymbol{\epsilon}_t$ as above, and let

$$\mathbf{X}_t = \begin{bmatrix} \mathbf{X}_{t1} \\ \mathbf{X}_{t2} \\ \cdot \\ \cdot \\ \cdot \\ \mathbf{X}_{tp} \end{bmatrix}$$

be a $p \times k$ matrix. The observations can now be written as

$$\mathbf{y}_t = \mathbf{X}_t\boldsymbol{\beta}_o + \boldsymbol{\epsilon}_t,$$

or equivalently as

$$\mathbf{y} = \mathbf{X}\boldsymbol{\beta}_o + \boldsymbol{\epsilon},$$

with $\mathbf{y}$, $\mathbf{X}$, and $\boldsymbol{\epsilon}$ as defined above. This allows us to consider panel data in the present framework. Further, by adopting appropriate definitions, the case of simultaneous systems of equations for panel data can also be considered.

Recall that the GLS estimator was obtained from a linear transformation of a linear model, i.e.,

$$\mathbf{y}^* = \mathbf{X}^*\boldsymbol{\beta}_o + \boldsymbol{\epsilon}^*,$$

where $\mathbf{y}^* = \mathbf{C}^{-1}\mathbf{y}$, $\mathbf{X}^* = \mathbf{C}^{-1}\mathbf{X}$, and $\boldsymbol{\epsilon}^* = \mathbf{C}^{-1}\boldsymbol{\epsilon}$ for some nonsingular matrix $\mathbf{C}$. It follows that any such linear transformation can be considered within the present framework.

The reason for restricting our attention to linear models and IV estimators is to provide clear motivation for the concepts and techniques introduced while also maintaining a relatively simple focus for the discussion. Nevertheless, the tools presented have a much wider applicability and are directly relevant to many other models and estimation techniques.

References

Theil, H. [1971]. "Principles of Econometrics." New York: Wiley.

For Further Reading

The references given below provide useful background and detailed discussion of many of the issues touched upon in this chapter.

Chow, G. C. [1983], "Econometrics," Chapters 1, 2. New York: McGraw-Hill.

Dhrymes, P. [1978]. "Introductory Econometrics," Chapters 1–3, 6.1–6.3. New York: Springer-Verlag.

Goldberger, A. S. [1964]. "Econometric Theory," Chapters 4, 5.1–5.4, 7.1–7.4. New York: Wiley.

Harvey, A. C. [1981]. "The Econometric Analysis of Time Series," Chapters 1.2, 1.3, 1.5, 1.6, 2.1–2.4, 2.7–2.10, 7.1–7.2, 8.1, 9.1–9.2. New York: Wiley.

Intrilligator, M. [1978]. "Econometric Models, Techniques and Applications," Chapters 2, 4, 5, 6.1–6.5, 10. Englewood Cliffs, New Jersey: Prentice-Hall.

Johnston, J. [1972]. "Econometric Methods," Chapters 5–8. New York: McGraw-Hill.

Kmenta, J. [1971]. "Elements of Econometrics," Chapters 7, 8, 10.1–10.3. New York: Macmillan.

Maddala, G. S. [1977]. "Econometrics," Chapters 7, 8, 11.1–11.4, 14, 16.1–16.3. New York: McGraw-Hill.

Malinvaud, E. [1970]. "Statistical Methods of Econometrics," Chapters 1–5, 6.1–6.7). Amsterdam: North-Holland.

Theil, H. [1971]. "Principles of Econometrics," Chapters 3, 6, 7.1–7.2, 9. New York: Wiley.

CHAPTER II

Consistency

In this chapter we introduce the concepts needed to determine the behavior of $\tilde{\beta}_n$ as $n \to \infty$.

II.1 Limits

The most fundamental concept is that of a limit.

DEFINITION 2.1: Let $\{b_n\}$ be a sequence of real numbers. If there exists a real number b and if for every real $\delta > 0$ there exists an integer $N(\delta)$ such that for all $n \geq N(\delta)$, $|b_n - b| < \delta$, then b is the *limit* of the sequence $\{b_n\}$.

In this definition the constant δ can take on any real value, but it is the very small values of δ that provide the definition with its impact. By choosing δ very small, we ensure that b_n gets arbitrarily close to its limit b for all n sufficiently large. When a limit exists we say that the sequence $\{b_n\}$ *converges to b* as n tends to infinity, written $b_n \to b$ as $n \to \infty$. When no ambiguity is possible, we simply write $b_n \to b$.

EXAMPLE 2.2: (i) Let $b_n = 1 - 1/n$. Then $b_n \to 1$. (ii) Let $b_n = (1 + a/n)^n$. Then $b_n \to e^a$. (iii) Let $b_n = n^2$. Then $b_n \to \infty$. (iv) Let $b_n = (-1)^n$. Then no limit exists.

The concept of a limit extends directly to sequences of real vectors. Let b_n be a $k \times 1$ vector with real elements b_{ni}, $i = 1, \ldots, k$. If

$b_{ni} \to b_i$, $i = 1, \ldots, k$, then $b_n \to b$, where b has elements b_i, $i = 1, \ldots, k$. An analogous extension applies to matrices.

Often we wish to consider the limit of a continuous function of a sequence. For this, either of the following equivalent definitions of continuity suffices.

DEFINITION 2.3: Given $g\colon \mathbb{R}^k \to \mathbb{R}^l$ $(k, l < \infty)$ and $b \in \mathbb{R}^k$, (i) the function g is *continuous at* b if and only if for any sequence $\{b_n\}$ such that $b_n \to b$, $g(b_n) \to g(b)$; or equivalently (ii) the function g is *continuous at* b if and only if for every $\epsilon > 0$ there exists $\delta(\epsilon) > 0$ such that if $a \in \mathbb{R}^k$ and $|a_i - b_i| < \delta(\epsilon)$, $i = 1, \ldots, k$, then $|g_j(a) - g_j(b)| < \epsilon$, $j = 1, \ldots, l$. Further, if $B \subset \mathbb{R}^k$, then g is *continuous on* B if it is continuous at every point of B.

EXAMPLE 2.4: (i) From this it follows that if $a_n \to a$ and $b_n \to b$, then $a_n + b_n \to a + b$ and $a_n b_n \to ab$. (ii) The matrix inverse function is continuous at every point that represents a nonsingular matrix, so that if $\mathbf{X}'\mathbf{X}/n \to \mathbf{M}$, a finite nonsingular matrix, then $(\mathbf{X}'\mathbf{X}/n)^{-1} \to \mathbf{M}^{-1}$.

Often it is useful to have a measure of the order of magnitude of a particular sequence without particularly worrying about its convergence. The following definition compares the behavior of a sequence $\{b_n\}$ with the behavior of a power of n, say n^λ, where λ is chosen so that $\{b_n\}$ and $\{n^\lambda\}$ behave similarly.

DEFINITION 2.5: (i) The sequence $\{b_n\}$ is *at most of order* n^λ, denoted $O(n^\lambda)$, if and only if for *some* real number Δ, $0 < \Delta < \infty$, there exists a finite integer N such that for all $n \geq N$, $|n^{-\lambda} b_n| < \Delta$. (ii) The sequence $\{b_n\}$ is of *order smaller than* n^λ, denoted $o(n^\lambda)$, if and only if for *every* real number $\delta > 0$ there exists a finite integer $N(\delta)$ such that for all $n \geq N(\delta)$, $|n^{-\lambda} b_n| < \delta$.

In this definition we adopt a convention that we utilize repeatedly in the material to follow; specifically, we let Δ represent a real positive constant that we may take to be as large as necessary, and we let δ (and similarly ϵ) represent a real positive constant that we may take to be as small as necessary. In any two different places Δ (or δ) need not represent the same value, although there is no loss of generality in supposing that it does. (Why?)

As we have defined these notions, $\{b_n\}$ is $O(n^\lambda)$ if $\{n^{-\lambda} b_n\}$ is eventually bounded, whereas $\{b_n\}$ is $o(n^\lambda)$ if $n^{-\lambda} b_n \to 0$. Obviously, if $\{b_n\}$ is

$o(n^\lambda)$, then $\{b_n\}$ is $O(n^\lambda)$. Further, if $\{b_n\}$ is $O(n^\lambda)$, then for every $\delta > 0$, $\{b_n\}$ is $o(n^{\lambda+\delta})$. When $\{b_n\}$ is $O(n^0)$, it is simply (eventually) bounded and may or may not have a limit. We often write $O(1)$ in place of $O(n^0)$. Similarly, $\{b_n\}$ being $o(1)$ means $b_n \to 0$.

EXAMPLE 2.6: (i) Let $b_n = 4 + 2n + 6n^2$. Then $\{b_n\}$ is $O(n^2)$ and $o(n^{2+\delta})$ for every $\delta > 0$. (ii) Let $b_n = (-1)^n$. Then $\{b_n\}$ is $O(1)$ and $o(n^\delta)$ for every $\delta > 0$. (iii) Let $b_n = \exp(-n)$. Then $\{b_n\}$ is $o(n^{-\delta})$ for every $\delta > 0$ and also $O(n^{-\delta})$.

If each element of a vector or matrix is $O(n^\lambda)$ or $o(n^\lambda)$, then that vector or matrix is $O(n^\lambda)$ or $o(n^\lambda)$.

Some elementary facts about the orders of magnitude of sums and products of sequence are given by the next result.

PROPOSITION 2.7: Let a_n and b_n be scalars. (i) If $\{a_n\}$ is $O(n^\lambda)$ and $\{b_n\}$ is $O(n^\mu)$, then $\{a_n b_n\}$ is $O(n^{\lambda+\mu})$ and $\{a_n + b_n\}$ is $O(n^\kappa)$, where $\kappa = \max[\lambda, \mu]$. (ii) If $\{a_n\}$ is $o(n^\lambda)$ and $\{b_n\}$ is $o(n^\mu)$, then $\{a_n b_n\}$ is $o(n^{\lambda+\mu})$ and $\{a_n + b_n\}$ is $o(n^\kappa)$. (iii) If $\{a_n\}$ is $O(n^\lambda)$ and b_n is $o(n^\mu)$, then $\{a_n b_n\}$ is $o(n^{\lambda+\mu})$ and $\{a_n + b_n\}$ is $O(n^\kappa)$.

Proof: (i) Since $\{a_n\}$ is $O(n^\lambda)$ and $\{b_n\}$ is $O(n^\mu)$, there exist a Δ, $0 < \Delta < \infty$, and an N such that, for all $n \geq N$, $|n^{-\lambda}a_n| < \Delta$ and $|n^{-\mu}b_n| < \Delta$. Consider $\{a_n b_n\}$. Now $|n^{-\lambda-\mu}a_n b_n| = |n^{-\lambda}a_n n^{-\mu}b_n| = |n^{-\lambda}a_n||n^{-\mu}b_n| < \Delta^2$ for all $n \geq N$. Hence $\{a_n b_n\}$ is $O(n^{\lambda+\mu})$. Consider $\{a_n + b_n\}$. Now $|n^{-\kappa}(a_n + b_n)| = |n^{-\kappa}a_n + n^{-\kappa}b_n| \leq |n^{-\kappa}a_n| + |n^{-\kappa}b_n|$ by the triangle inequality. Since $\kappa \geq \lambda$ and $\kappa \geq \mu$, $|n^{-\kappa}(a_n + b_n)| \leq |n^{-\kappa}a_n| + |n^{-\kappa}b_n| \leq |n^{-\lambda}a_n| + |n^{-\mu}b_n| < 2\Delta$ for all $n \geq N$. Hence $\{a_n + b_n\}$ is $O(n^\kappa)$, $\kappa = \max[\lambda, \mu]$. (ii) The proof is identical to that of (i), replacing Δ with every $\delta > 0$ and N with $N(\delta)$. (iii) Since $\{a_n\}$ is $O(n^\lambda)$, there exist a Δ, $0 < \Delta < \infty$, and an N such that for all $n \geq N$, $|n^{-\lambda}a_n| < \Delta$. Since $\{b_n\}$ is $o(n^\mu)$, for every $\delta > 0$ there exists $N(\delta)$ such that, for all $n \geq N(\delta)$, $|n^{-\lambda}b_n| < \delta$. Let $N'(\delta) = \max[N, N(\delta)]$. Consider $\{a_n b_n\}$. Now $|n^{-\lambda-\mu}a_n b_n| = |n^{-\lambda}a_n n^{-\mu}b_n| = |n^{-\lambda}a_n||n^{-\mu}b_n| < \Delta\delta$ for all $n \geq N'(\delta)$. Hence, for every $\delta' = \Delta\delta$ there exists $N''(\delta') = N'(\delta'/\Delta) = N'(\delta)$ such that $|n^{-\lambda-\mu}a_n b_n| < \delta'$, for all $n \geq N''(\delta')$. Hence $\{a_n b_n\}$ is $o(n^{\lambda+\mu})$. Since $\{b_n\}$ is $o(n^\mu)$, it is also $O(n^\mu)$. That $\{a_n + b_n\}$ is $O(n^\kappa)$ follows from (i).

A particularly important special case is illustrated by the following exercise.

EXERCISE 2.8: Let A_n be a $k \times k$ matrix and let b_n be a $k \times 1$ vector. If $\{A_n\}$ is $o(1)$ and $\{b_n\}$ is $O(1)$, verify that $\{A_n b_n\}$ is $o(1)$.

For the most part, econometrics is concerned not simply with sequences of real numbers, but rather with sequences of real-valued *random* scalars or vectors. In almost every case these are either averages, for example, $\bar{Z}_n \equiv \sum_{t=1}^n Z_t/n$, or functions of averages, such as $\bar{Z}_n^2$, where $\{Z_t\}$ is, for example, a sequence of random scalars. Since the Z_t's are random variables, we have to allow for a possibility which would not otherwise occur, that is, that different realizations of the sequence $\{Z_t\}$ can lead to different limits for $\bar{Z}_n$. Convergence to a particular value must now be considered as a random event and our interest centers on cases in which nonconvergence occurs only rarely in some appropriately defined sense.

II.2 Almost Sure Convergence

The stochastic convergence concept most closely related to the limit notions previously discussed is that of *almost sure convergence.* Sequences that converge almost surely can be manipulated in almost exactly the same ways as nonrandom sequences.

Let ω represent the entire random sequence $\{Z_t\}$. Interest typically centers on averages such as

$$b_n(\omega) = n^{-1} \sum_{t=1}^{n} Z_t.$$

DEFINITION 2.9: Let $\{b_n(\omega)\}$ be a sequence of real-valued random variables. We say that $b_n(\omega)$ converges *almost surely* to b, written $b_n(\omega) \xrightarrow{\text{a.s.}} b$ if and only if there exists a real number b such that $P[\omega: b_n(\omega) \to b] = 1$.

The probability measure P describes the distribution of ω and determines the joint distribution function of the entire sequence $\{Z_t\}$. A sequence $b_n(\omega)$ converges almost surely if the probability of obtaining a realization of the sequence $\{Z_t\}$ for which convergence to b occurs is unity. Equivalently, the probability of observing a realization of $\{Z_t\}$ for which convergence to b does not occur is zero. Failure to converge is possible but will almost never happen under this definition. Obviously, then, nonstochastic convergence implies almost sure convergence.

Since a realization of ω can be regarded as a point in an infinite-dimensional space, $b_n(\omega)$ is sometimes said to converge *almost everywhere* (a.e.) in that space. Other common terminology is that $b_n(\omega)$ converges to b *with probability* 1, (w.p.1) or that $b_n(\omega)$ is *strongly consistent* for b. When no ambiguity is possible, we drop ω and simply write $b_n \xrightarrow{\text{a.s.}} b$.

EXAMPLE 2.10: Let $\bar{Z}_n \equiv n^{-1} \Sigma_{t=1}^n Z_t$, where $\{Z_t\}$ is a sequence of independent identically distributed (i.i.d.) random variables with $E(Z_t) = \mu < \infty$. Then $\bar{Z}_n \xrightarrow{\text{a.s.}} \mu$, by the Komolgorov strong law of large numbers (Theorem 3.1).

The almost sure convergence of the sample mean illustrated by this example occurs under a wide variety of conditions on the sequence $\{Z_t\}$. A discussion of these conditions is the subject of the next chapter.

As with nonstochastic limits, the almost sure convergence concept extends immediately to vectors and matrices of finite dimension. Almost sure convergence element by element suffices for almost sure convergence of vectors and matrices.

The behavior of continuous functions of almost surely convergent sequences is analogous to the nonstochastic case.

PROPOSITION 2.11: Given $g: \mathbb{R}^k \to \mathbb{R}^l$ $(k, l < \infty)$ and any sequence $\{b_n\}$ such that $b_n \xrightarrow{\text{a.s.}} b$, where b_n and b are $k \times 1$ vectors, if g is continuous at b, then $g(b_n) \xrightarrow{\text{a.s.}} g(b)$.

Proof: Since $b_n(\omega) \to b$ implies $g(b_n(\omega)) \to g(b)$, $[\omega: b_n(\omega) \to b] \subset [\omega: g(b_n(\omega)) \to g(b)]$. Hence $1 = P[\omega: b_n(\omega) \to b] \le P[\omega: g(b_n(\omega)) \to g(b)] \le 1$, so that $g(b_n) \xrightarrow{\text{a.s.}} g(b)$.

This result is one of the most important in this book, since consistency results for many of our estimators follow by simply applying Proposition 2.11.

THEOREM 2.12: Suppose

(i) $\mathbf{y} = \mathbf{X}\boldsymbol{\beta}_o + \boldsymbol{\epsilon}$;
(ii) $\mathbf{X}'\boldsymbol{\epsilon}/n \xrightarrow{\text{a.s.}} \mathbf{0}$;
(iii) $\mathbf{X}'\mathbf{X}/n \xrightarrow{\text{a.s.}} \mathbf{M}$, finite and positive definite.

Then $\hat{\boldsymbol{\beta}}_n$ exists a.s. for all n sufficiently large, and $\hat{\boldsymbol{\beta}}_n \xrightarrow{\text{a.s.}} \boldsymbol{\beta}_o$.

Proof: Since $\mathbf{X}'\mathbf{X}/n \xrightarrow{\text{a.s.}} \mathbf{M}$, it follows from Proposition 2.11 that $\det(\mathbf{X}'\mathbf{X}/n) \xrightarrow{\text{a.s.}} \det \mathbf{M}$. Because $\mathbf{M}$ is positive definite by (iii), det

$\mathbf{M} > 0$. It follows that $\det(\mathbf{X}'\mathbf{X}/n) > 0$ a.s. for all n sufficiently large, so $(\mathbf{X}'\mathbf{X}/n)^{-1}$ exists a.s. for all n sufficiently large. Hence $\hat{\boldsymbol{\beta}}_n \equiv (\mathbf{X}'\mathbf{X}/n)^{-1}\,\mathbf{X}'\mathbf{y}/n$ exists a.s. for all n sufficiently large.

Now $\hat{\boldsymbol{\beta}}_n = \boldsymbol{\beta}_o + (\mathbf{X}'\mathbf{X}/n)^{-1}\,\mathbf{X}'\boldsymbol{\epsilon}/n$ by (i). It follows from Proposition 2.11 that $\hat{\boldsymbol{\beta}}_n \xrightarrow{\text{a.s.}} \boldsymbol{\beta}_o + \mathbf{M}^{-1}\cdot\mathbf{0} = \boldsymbol{\beta}_o$, given (ii) and (iii).

Theorem 2.12 is a fundamental consistency result for least squares estimation in many commonly encountered situations. Whether this result applies in a given situation depends on the nature of the data. For example, if our observations are randomly drawn from a population, as in a pure cross section, they may be taken to be i.i.d. The conditions of Theorem 2.12 hold for i.i.d. observations provided $E(\mathbf{X}_t'\mathbf{X}_t) = \mathbf{M}$, finite and positive definite, and $E(\mathbf{X}_t'\boldsymbol{\epsilon}_t) = \mathbf{0}$, since Komolgorov's strong law of large numbers (Example 2.10) ensures that $\mathbf{X}'\mathbf{X}/n = n^{-1}\sum_{t=1}^{n}\mathbf{X}_t'\mathbf{X}_t \xrightarrow{\text{a.s.}} \mathbf{M}$ and $\mathbf{X}'\boldsymbol{\epsilon}/n = n^{-1}\sum_{t=1}^{n}\mathbf{X}_t'\boldsymbol{\epsilon}_t \xrightarrow{\text{a.s.}} \mathbf{0}$. If the observations are dependent (as in a time series), different laws of large numbers must be applied to guarantee that the appropriate conditions hold. These are given in the next chapter.

A result for the IV estimator can be proven analogously.

EXERCISE 2.13: Prove the following result. Suppose

(i) $\mathbf{y} = \mathbf{X}\boldsymbol{\beta}_o + \boldsymbol{\epsilon}$;
(ii) $\mathbf{Z}'\boldsymbol{\epsilon}/n \xrightarrow{\text{a.s.}} \mathbf{0}$;
(iii) (a) $\mathbf{Z}'\mathbf{X}/n \xrightarrow{\text{a.s.}} \mathbf{Q}$, finite with full column rank;
(b) $\hat{\mathbf{P}}_n \xrightarrow{\text{a.s.}} \mathbf{P}$, finite and positive definite.

Then $\tilde{\boldsymbol{\beta}}_n$ exists a.s. for all n sufficiently large, and $\tilde{\boldsymbol{\beta}}_n \xrightarrow{\text{a.s.}} \boldsymbol{\beta}_o$.

This consistency result for the IV estimator precisely specifies the conditions that must be satisfied for a sequence of random vectors $\{\mathbf{Z}_t\}$ to act as a set of instrumental variables. They must be unrelated to the errors, as specified by assumption (ii), and they must be closely enough related to the explanatory variables so that $\mathbf{Z}'\mathbf{X}/n$ converges to a matrix with full column rank, as required by assumption (iiia). Note that a necessary condition for this is that the order condition for identification holds (see Fisher [1966, ch. 2]), that is, that $l \geq k$. (Recall that $\mathbf{Z}$ is $pn \times l$ and $\mathbf{X}$ is $pn \times k$.) For now, we simply treat the instrumental variables as given. In Chapter IV we see how the instrumental variables may be chosen optimally.

A potentially restrictive aspect of the consistency results just given for the least squares and IV estimators is that the matrices $\mathbf{X}'\mathbf{X}/n$,

$\mathbf{Z}'\mathbf{X}/n$, and $\hat{\mathbf{P}}_n$ are each required to converge to a fixed limiting value. When the observations are not identically distributed (as in a stratified cross section, a panel, or certain time-series cases), these matrices need not converge, and the results of Theorem 2.12 and Exercise 2.13 do not necessarily apply.

Nevertheless, it is possible to obtain more general versions of these results that do not require the convergence of $\mathbf{X}'\mathbf{X}/n$, $\mathbf{Z}'\mathbf{X}/n$, or $\hat{\mathbf{P}}_n$ by generalizing Proposition 2.11. To do this we make use of the notion of uniform continuity.

DEFINITION 2.14: Given $g: \mathbb{R}^k \to \mathbb{R}^l$ $(k, l < \infty)$, we say that g is *uniformly continuous* on a set $B \subset \mathbb{R}^k$ if and only if for each $\epsilon > 0$ there is a $\delta(\epsilon) > 0$ such that if a and b belong to B and $|a_i\text{-}b_i| < \delta(\epsilon)$, $i = 1, \ldots, k$, then $|g_j(a) - g_j(b)| < \epsilon$, $j = 1, \ldots, l$.

Note that uniform continuity implies continuity on B but that continuity on B does not imply uniform continuity. The essential aspect of uniform continuity that distinguishes it from continuity is that δ depends only on ϵ and not on b. However, when B is compact, continuity does imply uniform continuity, as formally stated in the next result.

THEOREM 2.15 (*Uniform continuity theorem*): Suppose $g: \mathbb{R}^k \to \mathbb{R}^l$ is a continuous function on $C \subset \mathbb{R}^k$. If C is compact, then g is uniformly continuous on C.

Proof: See Bartle [1976, p. 160].

Now we extend Proposition 2.11 to cover situations where $b_n(\omega) - c_n \xrightarrow{\text{a. s.}} 0$, but the sequence of real numbers $\{c_n\}$ does not necessarily converge.

PROPOSITION 2.16: Let $g: \mathbb{R}^k \to \mathbb{R}^l$ be continuous on a compact set $C \subset \mathbb{R}^k$. Suppose that $b_n(\omega)$ and c_n are $k \times 1$ vectors such that $b_n(\omega) - c_n \xrightarrow{\text{a. s.}} 0$ and there exists $\eta > 0$ such that for all n sufficiently large $[c: |c - c_n| < \eta] \subset C$, i.e., for all n sufficiently large c_n is interior to C uniformly in n. Then $g(b_n(\omega)) - g(c_n) \xrightarrow{\text{a. s.}} 0$.

Proof: Let g_j be the jth element of g. Since C is compact, g_j is uniformly continuous on C by Theorem 2.15. Choose ω such that $b_n(\omega) - c_n \to 0$ as $n \to \infty$. Since c_n is interior to C for all n sufficiently large uniformly in n and $b_n(\omega) - c_n \to 0$, $b_n(\omega)$ is also interior to C for all n sufficiently large. By uniform continuity, for any $\epsilon > 0$ there exists $\delta(\epsilon) > 0$ such that if $|b_{ni}(\omega) - c_{ni}| < \delta(\epsilon)$, $i = 1, \ldots, k$, then $|g_j(b_n(\omega)) - g_j(c_n)| < \epsilon$. Since $|b_{ni}(\omega) - c_{ni}| < \delta(\epsilon)$ for all n sufficiently large and almost every ω, then $|g_j(b_n(\omega)) - g_j(c_n)| < \epsilon$ for all n sufficiently large and almost every ω. Hence $g(b_n(\omega)) - g(c_n) \xrightarrow{\text{a.s.}} 0$.

To state the results for the OLS and IV estimators below concisely, we define the following concepts, as given by White [1982, pp 484–485].

DEFINITION 2.17: A sequence of $k \times k$ matrices $\{\mathbf{A}_n\}$ is said to be *uniformly nonsingular* if and only if for some $\delta > 0$ and all n sufficiently large $|\det \mathbf{A}_n| > \delta$. If $\{\mathbf{A}_n\}$ is a sequence of positive semidefinite matrices, then $\{\mathbf{A}_n\}$ is *uniformly positive definite* if and only if $\{\mathbf{A}_n\}$ is uniformly nonsingular. If $\{\mathbf{A}_n\}$ is a sequence of $l \times k$ matrices, then $\{\mathbf{A}_n\}$ has *uniformly full column rank* if and only if there exists a sequence of $k \times k$ submatrices $\{\mathbf{A}_n^*\}$ which is uniformly nonsingular.

If a sequence of matrices is uniformly nonsingular, the elements of the sequence are prevented from getting "too close" to singularity. Similarity, if a sequence of matrices has uniformly full column rank, the elements of the sequence are prevented from getting "too close" to a matrix with less than full column rank.

Next we state the desired extensions of Theorem 2.12 and Exercise 2.13.

THEOREM 2.18: Suppose

(i) $\mathbf{y} = \mathbf{X}\boldsymbol{\beta}_o + \boldsymbol{\epsilon}$;
(ii) $\mathbf{X}'\boldsymbol{\epsilon}/n \xrightarrow{\text{a.s.}} \mathbf{0}$;
(iii) $\mathbf{X}'\mathbf{X}/n - \mathbf{M}_n \xrightarrow{\text{a.s.}} \mathbf{0}$, where $\{\mathbf{M}_n\}$ is O(1) and uniformly positive definite.

Then $\hat{\boldsymbol{\beta}}_n$ exists a.s. for all n sufficient by large and $\hat{\boldsymbol{\beta}}_n \xrightarrow{\text{a.s.}} \boldsymbol{\beta}_o$.

Proof: Because $\mathbf{M}_n$ is O(1) for all n sufficiently large, it follows from Proposition 2.16 that $\det(\mathbf{X}'\mathbf{X}/n) - \det \mathbf{M}_n \xrightarrow{\text{a.s.}} \mathbf{0}$. Since $\det \mathbf{M}_n > \delta > 0$ for all n sufficiently large by Definition 2.17, it follows that $\det(\mathbf{X}'\mathbf{X}/n) > \delta/2 > 0$ for all n sufficiently large almost surely, so that $(\mathbf{X}'\mathbf{X}/n)^{-1}$ exists a.s. for all n sufficiently large. Hence $\hat{\boldsymbol{\beta}}_n \equiv (\mathbf{X}'\mathbf{X}/n)^{-1}\mathbf{X}'\mathbf{y}/n$ exists a.s. for all n sufficiently large.

Now $\hat{\boldsymbol{\beta}}_n = \boldsymbol{\beta}_o + (\mathbf{X}'\mathbf{X}/n)^{-1}\mathbf{X}'\boldsymbol{\epsilon}/n$ by (i). It follows from Proposition 2.16 that $\hat{\boldsymbol{\beta}}_n - (\boldsymbol{\beta}_o + \mathbf{M}_n^{-1}\cdot\mathbf{0}) \xrightarrow{\text{a.s.}} \mathbf{0}$ or $\hat{\boldsymbol{\beta}}_n \xrightarrow{\text{a.s.}} \boldsymbol{\beta}_o$, given (ii) and (iii).

Compared with Theorem 2.12, the present result relaxes the requirement that $\mathbf{X}'\mathbf{X}/n \xrightarrow{\text{a.s.}} \mathbf{M}$ and instead requires that $\mathbf{X}'\mathbf{X}/n - \mathbf{M}_n \xrightarrow{\text{a.s.}} \mathbf{0}$, allowing for the possibility that $\mathbf{X}'\mathbf{X}/n$ may not converge to a fixed limit. Note that the requirement $\det \mathbf{M}_n > \delta > 0$ ensures the uniform continuity of the matrix inverse function.

The proof of the IV result requires a demonstration that $\{\mathbf{Q}_n'\mathbf{P}_n\mathbf{Q}_n\}$ is uniformly positive definite under appropriate conditions. These conditions are provided by the following result.

LEMMA 2.19: If $\{\mathbf{A}_n\}$ is a O(1) sequence of $l \times k$ matrices with uniformly full column rank and $\{\mathbf{B}_n\}$ is a O(1) sequence of uniformly positive definite $l \times l$ matrices, then $\{\mathbf{A}_n'\mathbf{B}_n\mathbf{A}_n\}$ and $\{\mathbf{A}_n'\mathbf{B}_n^{-1}\mathbf{A}_n\}$ are O(1) sequences of uniformly positive definite $k \times k$ matrices.

Proof: See White [1982, Lemma A.3].

EXERCISE 2.20: Prove the following result. Suppose

(i) $\mathbf{y} = \mathbf{X}\boldsymbol{\beta}_o + \boldsymbol{\epsilon}$;
(ii) $\mathbf{Z}'\boldsymbol{\epsilon}/n \xrightarrow{\text{a.s.}} \mathbf{0}$;
(iii) (a) $\mathbf{Z}'\mathbf{X}/n - \mathbf{Q}_n \xrightarrow{\text{a.s.}} \mathbf{0}$, where $\{\mathbf{Q}_n\}$ is O(1) and has uniformly full column rank;
(b) $\hat{\mathbf{P}}_n - \mathbf{P}_n \xrightarrow{\text{a.s.}} 0$, where $\{\mathbf{P}_n\}$ is O(1) and uniformly positive definite

Then $\tilde{\boldsymbol{\beta}}_n$ exists a.s. for all n sufficiently large, and $\tilde{\boldsymbol{\beta}}_n \xrightarrow{\text{a.s.}} \boldsymbol{\beta}_o$.

The notion of orders of magnitude extends to almost surely convergent sequences in a straightforward way.

DEFINITION 2.21: (i) The sequence $\{b_n(\omega)\}$ is *at most of order n^λ almost surely*, denoted $O_{a.s.}(n^\lambda)$, if there exists a O(1) nonstochastic sequence $\{a_n\}$ such that $n^{-\lambda}b_n(\omega) - a_n \xrightarrow{\text{a.s.}} 0$. (ii) The sequence $\{b_n(\omega)\}$ is of *order smaller than n^λ almost surely*, denoted $o_{a.s.}(n^\lambda)$, if $n^{-\lambda}b_n(\omega) \xrightarrow{\text{a.s.}} 0$.

Proposition 2.7 remains valid when $O(n^\lambda)$ and $o(n^\lambda)$ are replaced by $O_{a.s.}(n^\lambda)$ and $o_{a.s.}(n^\lambda)$, as the following result shows.

EXERCISE 2.22: Prove the following. Let a_n and b_n be random scalars. (i) If $\{a_n\}$ is $O_{a.s.}(n^\lambda)$ and $\{b_n\}$ is $O_{a.s.}(n^\mu)$, then $\{a_nb_n\}$ is $O_{a.s.}(n^{\lambda+\mu})$ and $\{a_n + b_n\}$ is $O_{a.s.}(n^\kappa)$, $\kappa = \max[\lambda, \mu]$. (ii) If $\{a_n\}$ is $o_{a.s.}(n^\lambda)$ and $\{b_n\}$ is $o_{a.s.}(n^\mu)$, then $\{a_nb_n\}$ is $o_{a.s.}(n^{\lambda+\mu})$ and $\{a_n + b_n\}$ is

$o_{a.s.}(n^{\kappa})$. (iii) If $\{a_n\}$ is $O_{a.s.}(n^{\lambda})$ and $\{b_n\}$ is $o_{a.s.}(n^{\mu})$, then $\{a_n b_n\}$ is $o_{a.s.}(n^{\lambda+\mu})$ and $\{a_n + b_n\}$ is $O_{a.s.}(n^{\kappa})$. (*Hint:* Since $\{a_n\}$ is $O_{a.s.}(n^{\lambda})$, there exists a $O(1)$ nonstochastic sequence $\{c_n\}$ such that $n^{-\lambda}a_n(\omega) - c_n \xrightarrow{a.s.} 0$, and c_n lies interior to a compact set $C = [-\Delta, \Delta]$ for all n sufficiently large uniformly in n. Apply Proposition 2.16.)

II.3 Convergence in Probability

A weaker stochastic convergence concept is that of convergence in probability, which is now defined.

DEFINITION 2.23: Let $\{b_n(\omega)\}$ be a sequence of real-valued random variables. If there exists a real number b such that for every $\epsilon > 0$, $P[\omega: |b_n(\omega) - b| < \epsilon] \to 1$ as $n \to \infty$, then $b_n(\omega)$ converges *in probability* to b, written $b_n(\omega) \xrightarrow{p} b$.

With almost sure convergence the probability measure P takes into account the joint distribution of the entire sequence $\{Z_t\}$, but with convergence in probability, we only need concern ourselves sequentially with the joint distribution of the elements of $\{Z_t\}$ that actually appear in $b_n(\omega)$, typically the first n. When a sequence converges in probability, it becomes less and less likely that an element of the sequence lies beyond any specified distance ϵ from b as n increases. The constant b is called the *probability limit of* b_n.

Convergence in probability is also referred to as *weak consistency*, and since this has been the most familiar stochastic convergence concept in econometrics, the word "weak" is often simply dropped.

The relationship between convergence in probability and almost sure convergence is specified by the following result.

THEOREM 2.24: Let $\{b_n\}$ be a sequence of random variables. If $b_n \xrightarrow{a.s.} b$, then $b_n \xrightarrow{p} b$. If $b_n \xrightarrow{p} b$, then there exists a subsequence $\{b_{n_j}\}$ such that $b_{n_j} \xrightarrow{a.s.} b$.

Proof: See Lukacs [1975, p. 48].

Thus almost sure convergence implies convergence in probability, but the converse does not hold. Nevertheless, a sequence that converges in probability always contains a *sub*sequence that converges almost surely. Essentially, convergence in probability allows more erratic behavior in the converging sequence than almost sure convergence, and by simply disregarding the erratic elements of the sequence we can obtain an almost surely convergent subsequence. For an example of a sequence that converges in probability but not almost surely, see Lukacs [1975, pp. 34–35].

EXAMPLE 2.25: Let $\bar{Z}_n = n^{-1} \sum_{t=1}^{n} Z_t$, where $\{Z_t\}$ is a sequence of random variables such that $E(Z_t) = \mu$, var $Z_t = \sigma^2 < \infty$ for all t and cov $(Z_t, Z_\tau) = 0$ for $t \neq \tau$. Then $\bar{Z}_n \xrightarrow{p} \mu$ by the Chebyshev weak law of large numbers (Rao [1973, p. 112]).

Note that, in contrast to Example 2.10, the random variables here are not assumed either to be independent (simply uncorrelated) or identically distributed (except for having identical mean and variance). However, second moments are restricted by the present result, whereas they are completely unrestricted in Example 2.10.

Note also that, under the conditions of Example 2.10, convergence in probability follows immediately from the almost sure convergence.

In general, most weak consistency results have strong consistency analogs that hold under identical or closely related conditions. For example, strong consistency also obtains under the conditions of Example 2.25. These analogs typically require somewhat more sophisticated techniques for their proof.

Vectors and matrices are said to converge in probability provided each element converges in probability.

To show that continuous functions of weakly consistent sequences converge to the functions evaluated at the probability limit, we use the following result.

PROPOSITION 2.26 (*The implication rule*): Consider events E and F_i, $i = 1, \ldots, k$, such that $E \supset \bigcap_{i=1}^{k} F_i$. Then $P[E^c] \leq \sum_{i=1}^{k} P[F_i^c]$.

Proof: See Lukacs [1975, p. 7].

PROPOSITION 2.27: Given $g: \mathbb{R}^k \to \mathbb{R}^l$ and any sequence $\{b_n\}$ such that $b_n \xrightarrow{p} b$, where b_n and b are $k \times 1$ vectors, if g is continuous at b, then $g(b_n) \xrightarrow{p} g(b)$.

Proof: Let g_j be an element of g. For every $\epsilon > 0$, the continuity of g implies that there exists $\delta(\epsilon) > 0$ such that if $|b_{ni}(\omega) - b_i| < \delta(\epsilon)$, $i = 1, \ldots, k$, then $|g_j(b_n(\omega)) - g_j(b)| < \epsilon$. Define the events $F_i \equiv [\omega: |b_{ni}(\omega) - b_i| < \delta(\epsilon)]$ and $E \equiv [\omega: |g_j(b_n(\omega)) - g_j(b)| < \epsilon]$. Then

$E \supset \bigcap_{i=1}^{k} F_i$. By the implication rule, $P[E^c] \leq \Sigma_{i=1}^{k} P[F_i^c]$. Since $b_n \xrightarrow{p} b$, for arbitrary $\eta > 0$, and all n sufficiently large, $P[F_i^c] \leq \eta$. Hence $P[E^c] \leq k\eta$, or $P[E] \geq 1 - k\eta$. Since $P[E] \leq 1$ and η is arbitrary, $P[E] \to 1$ as $n \to \infty$, hence $g_j(b_n(\omega)) \xrightarrow{p} g_j(b)$. Since this holds for all $j = 1, \ldots, l$, $g(b_n(\omega)) \xrightarrow{p} g(b)$.

This result allows us to establish direct analogs of Theorem 2.12 and Exercise 2.13.

THEOREM 2.28: Suppose

(i) $\mathbf{y} = \mathbf{X}\boldsymbol{\beta}_o + \boldsymbol{\epsilon}$;
(ii) $\mathbf{X}'\boldsymbol{\epsilon}/n \xrightarrow{p} \mathbf{0}$;
(iii) $\mathbf{X}'\mathbf{X}/n \xrightarrow{p} \mathbf{M}$, finite and positive definite.

Then $\hat{\boldsymbol{\beta}}_n$ exists in probability, and $\hat{\boldsymbol{\beta}}_n \xrightarrow{p} \boldsymbol{\beta}_o$.

Proof: The proof is identical to that of Theorem 2.12 except that Proposition 2.27 is used instead of Proposition 2.11 and convergence in probability replaces convergence almost surely.

The statement that $\hat{\boldsymbol{\beta}}_n$ exists in probability can be understood to imply that there exists a subsequence $\{\hat{\boldsymbol{\beta}}_{n_j}\}$ such that $\hat{\boldsymbol{\beta}}_{n_j}$ exists almost surely for all n_j sufficiently large, by Theorem 2.24. In other words, $\mathbf{X}'\mathbf{X}/n$ can converge to $\mathbf{M}$ in such a way that $\mathbf{X}'\mathbf{X}/n$ does not have an inverse for each n, so that $\hat{\boldsymbol{\beta}}_n$ may fail to exist for particular values of n. However, a subsequence of $\{\mathbf{X}'\mathbf{X}/n\}$ converges almost surely, and for that subsequence, $\hat{\boldsymbol{\beta}}_{n_j}$ will exist for all n_j sufficiently large.

EXERCISE 2.29: Prove the following result. Suppose

(i) $\mathbf{y} = \mathbf{X}\boldsymbol{\beta}_o + \boldsymbol{\epsilon}$;
(ii) $\mathbf{Z}'\boldsymbol{\epsilon}/n \xrightarrow{p} \mathbf{0}$;
(iii) (a) $\mathbf{Z}'\mathbf{X}/n \xrightarrow{p} \mathbf{Q}$, finite with full column rank;
(b) $\hat{\mathbf{P}}_n \xrightarrow{p} \mathbf{P}$, finite and positive definite.

Then $\tilde{\boldsymbol{\beta}}_n$ exists in probability, and $\tilde{\boldsymbol{\beta}}_n \xrightarrow{p} \boldsymbol{\beta}_o$.

Whether or not these results apply in particular situations depends on the nature of the data. As we mentioned before, for certain kinds of data it is restrictive to assume that $\mathbf{X}'\mathbf{X}/n$, $\mathbf{Z}'\mathbf{X}/n$, and $\hat{\mathbf{P}}_n$ converge to constant limits. We can relax this restriction by using an analog of Proposition 2.16. This result is also used heavily in later chapters.

PROPOSITION 2.30: Let $g: \mathbb{R}^k \to \mathbb{R}^l$ be continuous on a compact set $C \subset \mathbb{R}^k$. Suppose that $b_n(\omega)$ and c_n are $k \times 1$ vectors such that $b_n(\omega) - c_n \xrightarrow{p} 0$, and for all n sufficiently large, c_n is interior to C, uniformly in n. Then $g(b_n(\omega)) - g(c_n) \xrightarrow{p} 0$.

Proof: Let g_j be an element of g. Since C is compact, g_j is uniformly continuous by Theorem 2.15, so that for every $\epsilon > 0$ there exists $\delta(\epsilon) > 0$ such that if $|b_{ni}(\omega) - c_{ni}| < \delta(\epsilon)$, $i = 1, \ldots, k$, then $|g_j(b_n(\omega)) - g_j(c_n)| < \epsilon$. Define the events $F_i \equiv [\omega: |b_{ni}(\omega) - c_{ni}| < \delta(\epsilon)]$ and $E \equiv [\omega: |g_j(b_n(\omega)) - g_j(c_n)| < \epsilon]$. Then $E \supset \bigcap_{i=1}^k F_i$. By the implication rule, $P[E^c] \leq \sum_{i=1}^k P[F_i^c]$. Since $b_n(\omega) - c_n \xrightarrow{p} 0$, for arbitrary $\eta > 0$ and all n sufficiently large, $P[F_i^c] \leq \eta$. Hence $P[E^c] \leq k\eta$, or $P[E] \geq 1 - k\eta$. Since $P[E] \leq 1$ and η is arbitrary, $P[E] \to 1$ as $n \to \infty$, hence $g_j(b_n(\omega)) - g_j(c_n) \xrightarrow{p} 0$. Since this holds for all $j = 1, \ldots, l$, $g(b_n(\omega)) - g(c_n) \xrightarrow{p} 0$.

THEOREM 2.31: Suppose

(i) $\mathbf{y} = \mathbf{X}\boldsymbol{\beta}_o + \boldsymbol{\epsilon}$;
(ii) $\mathbf{X}'\boldsymbol{\epsilon}/n \xrightarrow{p} \mathbf{0}$;
(iii) $\mathbf{X}'\mathbf{X}/n - \mathbf{M}_n \xrightarrow{p} 0$, where $\{\mathbf{M}_n\}$ is O(1) and uniformly positive definite.

Then $\hat{\boldsymbol{\beta}}_n$ exists in probability, and $\hat{\boldsymbol{\beta}}_n \xrightarrow{p} \boldsymbol{\beta}_o$.

Proof: The proof is identical to that of Theorem 2.18 except that Proposition 2.30 is used instead of Proposition 2.16 and convergence in probability replaces convergence almost surely.

EXERCISE 2.32: Prove the following result. Suppose

(i) $\mathbf{y} = \mathbf{X}\boldsymbol{\beta}_o + \boldsymbol{\epsilon}$;
(ii) $\mathbf{Z}'\boldsymbol{\epsilon}/n \xrightarrow{p} \mathbf{0}$;
(iii) (a) $\mathbf{Z}'\mathbf{X}/n - \mathbf{Q}_n \xrightarrow{p} 0$, where $\{\mathbf{Q}_n\}$ is O(1) and has uniformly full column rank;
(b) $\hat{\mathbf{P}}_n - \mathbf{P}_n \xrightarrow{p} \mathbf{0}$, where $\{\mathbf{P}_n\}$ is O(1) and uniformly positive definite.

Then $\tilde{\boldsymbol{\beta}}_n$ exists in probability, and $\tilde{\boldsymbol{\beta}}_n \xrightarrow{p} \boldsymbol{\beta}_o$.

As with convergence almost surely, the notion of orders of magnitude extends directly to convergence in probability.

DEFINITION 2.33: (i) The sequence $\{b_n(\omega)\}$ is *at most of order n^λ in probability*, denoted $O_p(n^\lambda)$, if there exists an $O(1)$ nonstochastic sequence $\{a_n\}$ such that $n^{-\lambda}b_n(\omega) - a_n \xrightarrow{p} 0$. (ii) The sequence $\{b_n(\omega)\}$ is *of order smaller than n^λ in probability*, denoted $o_p(n^\lambda)$, if $n^{-\lambda}b_n(\omega) \xrightarrow{p} 0$.

When a sequence $\{b_n(\omega)\}$ is $O_p(1)$, we say it is *bounded in probability*, which is equivalent to the statement that for any arbitrarily small $\delta > 0$ there exists $\Delta < \infty$ and an integer N sufficiently large such that $P[\omega : |b_n(\omega)| > \Delta] < \delta$, for all $n \geq N$.

EXAMPLE 2.34: Let $b_n(\omega) = Z_n$, where $\{Z_t\}$ is a sequence of identically distributed $N(0, 1)$ random variables. Then $P[\omega : |b_n(\omega)| > \Delta] = P[|Z_n| > \Delta] = 2\Phi(-\Delta)$ for all $n \geq 1$, where Φ is the standard normal cumulative distribution function (c.d.f.). By making Δ sufficiently large, we have $2\Phi(-\Delta) < \delta$ for arbitrary $\delta > 0$. Hence, $b_n(\omega) = Z_n$ is $O_p(1)$.

Note that Φ in this example can be replaced by any c.d.f. F and the result still holds, i.e., any random variable Z with c.d.f. F is $O_p(1)$.

EXERCISE 2.35: Prove the following. Let a_n and b_n be random scalars. (i) If $\{a_n\}$ is $O_p(n^\lambda)$ and $\{b_n\}$ is $O_p(n^\mu)$, then $\{a_n b_n\}$ is $O_p(n^{\lambda+\mu})$ and $\{a_n + b_n\}$ is $O_p(n^\kappa)$, $\kappa = \max[\lambda, \mu]$. (ii) If $\{a_n\}$ is $o_p(n^\lambda)$ and $\{b_n\}$ is $o_p(n^\mu)$, then $\{a_n b_n\}$ is $o_p(n^{\lambda+\mu})$ and $\{a_n + b_n\}$ is $o_p(n^\kappa)$. (iii) If $\{a_n\}$ is $O_p(n^\lambda)$ and $\{b_n\}$ is $o_p(n^\mu)$, then $\{a_n b_n\}$ is $o_p(n^{\lambda+\mu})$ and $\{a_n + b_n\}$ is $O(n^\kappa)$. (*Hint*: Apply Proposition 2.30.)

One of the most useful results in this chapter is the following corollary to this exercise, which is applied frequently in obtaining the asymptotic normality results of Chapter IV.

COROLLARY 2.36 (*Product rule*): Let A_n be $k \times k$ and let b_n be $k \times 1$. If $\{A_n\}$ is $o_p(1)$ and b_n is $O_p(1)$, then $\{A_n b_n\}$ is $o_p(1)$.

Proof: Let $a_n \equiv A_n b_n$ and $A_n = [A_{nij}]$. Then $a_{ni} = \Sigma_{j=1}^k A_{nij} b_{nj}$. Since $\{A_{nij}\}$ is $o_p(1)$ and $\{b_{nj}\}$ is $O_p(1)$, $\{A_{nij} b_{nj}\}$ is $o_p(1)$ by Exercise 2.35(iii). Hence, $\{a_{ni}\}$ is $o_p(1)$, since it is the sum of k terms each of which is $o_p(1)$. It follows that $\{a_n \equiv A_n b_n\}$ is $o_p(1)$.

II.4 Convergence in rth Mean

The convergence notions of limits, almost sure limits, and probability limits are those most frequently encountered in econometrics, and most of the results in the literature are stated in these terms. Another convergence concept often encountered in the context of time series data is that of convergence in the rth mean.

DEFINITION 2.37: Let $b_n(\omega)$ be a sequence of real-valued random variables. If there exists a real number b such that $E(|b_n(\omega) - b|^r) \to 0$ as $n \to \infty$ for some $r > 0$, then $b_n(\omega)$ *converges in the rth mean* to b, written $b_n(\omega) \xrightarrow{\text{r. m.}} b$.

The most commonly encountered occurrence is that in which $r = 2$, in which case convergence is said to occur *in quadratic mean*, denoted $b_n(\omega) \xrightarrow{\text{q. m.}} b$. Alternatively, b is said to be the *limit in mean square* of $b_n(\omega)$, denoted l.i.m. $b_n(\omega) = b$.

A useful property of convergence in the rth mean is that it implies convergence in the sth mean for $s < r$. To prove this, we use Jensen's inequality, which we now state for convenience.

PROPOSITION 2.38 (*Jensen's inequality*): Let $g: \mathbb{R}^1 \to \mathbb{R}^1$ be a convex function on an interval $B \subset \mathbb{R}^1$ and let Z be a random variable such that $P[Z \in B] = 1$. Then $g(E(Z)) \leq E(g(Z))$. If g is concave on B, then $g(E(Z)) \geq E(g(Z))$.

Proof: See Rao [1973, pp. 57–58].

EXAMPLE 2.39: Let $g(z) = |z|$. It follows from Jensen's inequality that $|E(Z)| \leq E|Z|$. Let $g(z) = z^2$. It follows from Jensen's inequality that $E(Z)^2 \leq E(Z^2)$.

THEOREM 2.40: If $b_n(\omega) \xrightarrow{\text{r. m.}} b$ and $r > s$, then $b_n(\omega) \xrightarrow{\text{s. m.}} b$.

Proof: Let $g(z) = z^q$, $q < 1$, $z \geq 0$. Then g is concave. Set $z = |b_n(\omega) - b|^r$ and $q = s/r$. From Jensen's inequality,

$$\begin{aligned} E(|b_n(\omega) - b|^s) &= E(\{|b_n(\omega) - b|^r\}^{s/r}) \\ &\leq \{E(|b_n(\omega) - b|^r)\}^{s/r}. \end{aligned}$$

Since $E(|b_n(\omega) - b|^r) \to 0$, it follows that $E(|b_n(\omega) - b|^s) \to 0$, $b_n(\omega) \xrightarrow{\text{s. m.}} b$.

Convergence in the rth mean is a stronger convergence concept than convergence in probability, and in fact implies convergence in probability. To show this, we use the generalized Chebyshev inequality.

PROPOSITION 2.41 (*Generalized Chebyshev inequality*): Let Z be a random variable such that $E|Z|^r < \infty$, $r > 0$. Then for every $\epsilon > 0$,

$$P[|Z| \geq \epsilon] \leq E(|Z|^r)/\epsilon^r.$$

Proof: See Lukacs [1975, pp. 8–9].

Setting $r = 2$ gives the familiar Chebyshev inequality.

THEOREM 2.42: If $b_n(\omega) \xrightarrow{\text{r. m.}} b$ for some $r > 0$, then $b_n(\omega) \xrightarrow{\text{p}} b$.

Proof: Since $E(|b_n(\omega) - b|^r) \to 0$ as $n \to \infty$, $E(|b_n(\omega) - b|^r) < \infty$ for all n sufficiently large. It follows from the generalized Chebyshev inequality that, for every $\epsilon > 0$,

$$P[\omega : |b_n(\omega) - b| \geq \epsilon] \leq E(|b_n(\omega) - b|^r)/\epsilon^r.$$

Hence $P[\omega : |b_n(\omega) - b| < \epsilon] \geq 1 - E(|b_n(\omega) - b|^r)/\epsilon^r \to 1$ as $n \to \infty$, since $b_n(\omega) \xrightarrow{\text{r. m.}} b$. It follows that $b_n(\omega) \xrightarrow{\text{p}} b$.

Without further conditions, no necessary relationship holds between convergence in the rth mean and almost sure convergence. For further discussion, see Lukacs [1975, ch. 2].

Since convergence in the rth mean will be used primarily in specifying conditions for later results rather than in stating their conclusions, we provide no analogs to the previous consistency results for the least squares or IV estimators.

References

Bartle, R. G. [1976]. "The Elements of Real Analysis." New York: Wiley.

Fisher, F. M. [1966]. "The Identification Problem in Econometrics." New York: McGraw-Hill.

Lukacs, E. [1975]. "Stochastic Convergence." New York: Academic Press.

Rao, C. R. [1973]. "Linear Statistical Inference and Its Applications." New York: Wiley.

White, H. [1982]. Instrumental variables regression with independent observations, *Econometrica* **50**:483–500.

CHAPTER III

Laws of Large Numbers

In this chapter we study laws of large numbers, which provide conditions guaranteeing the stochastic convergence (e.g., of $\mathbf{Z}'\mathbf{X}/n$ and $\mathbf{Z}'\boldsymbol{\epsilon}/n$, required for the consistency results of the previous chapter. Since different conditions will apply to different kinds of economic data (e.g., time series or cross section), we shall pay particular attention to the kinds of data these conditions allow. Only strong consistency results will be stated explicitly, since strong consistency implies convergence in probability (by Theorem 2.24).

The laws of large numbers we consider are all of the following form.

PROPOSITION 3.0: Given restrictions on the dependence, heterogeneity, and moments of a sequence of random variables $\{Z_t\}$, $\bar{Z}_n - \bar{\mu}_n \xrightarrow{\text{a. s.}} 0$, where $\bar{Z}_n \equiv n^{-1} \sum_{t=1}^{n} Z_t$ and $\bar{\mu}_n \equiv E(\bar{Z}_n)$.

The results that follow specify precisely which restrictions on the dependence, heterogeneity (i.e., the extent to which the distributions of the Z_t may differ across t), and moments are sufficient to allow the conclusion $\bar{Z}_n - E(\bar{Z}_n) \xrightarrow{\text{a. s.}} 0$ to hold. As we shall see, there are sometimes trade-offs among these restrictions; for example, relaxing dependence or heterogeneity restrictions may require strengthening moment restrictions.

III.1 Independent Identically Distributed Observations

The simplest case is that of independent identically distributed (i.i.d.) random variables.

THEOREM 3.1 (*Komolgorov*): Let $\{Z_t\}$ be a sequence of i.i.d. random variables. Then $\bar{Z}_n \xrightarrow{a.s.} \mu$ if and only if $E|Z_t| < \infty$ and $E(Z_t) = \mu$

Proof: See Rao [1973, p. 115].

An interesting feature of this result is that the condition given is sufficient as well as necessary for $\bar{Z}_n \xrightarrow{a.s.} \mu$. Also note that since $\{Z_t\}$ is i.i.d., $E(\bar{Z}_n) = \mu$.

To apply this result to econometric estimators we have to know that the summands of $\mathbf{Z}'\mathbf{X}/n = n^{-1} \sum_{t=1}^n \mathbf{Z}_t'\mathbf{X}_t$ and $\mathbf{Z}'\boldsymbol{\epsilon}/n = n^{-1} \sum_{t=1}^n \mathbf{Z}_t'\epsilon_t$ are i.i.d. This occurs when the elements of $\{(\mathbf{Z}_t, \mathbf{X}_t, \epsilon_t)'\}$ are i.i.d. To prove this, we use the following result.

PROPOSITION 3.2: Let $g: \mathbb{R}^k \to \mathbb{R}^\ell$ be a continuous† function. (i) Let Z_t and Z_τ be identically distributed. Then $g(Z_t)$ and $g(Z_\tau)$ are identically distributed. (ii) Let Z_t and Z_τ be independent. Then $g(Z_t)$ and $g(Z_\tau)$ are independent.

Proof: (i) Let $\mathcal{Y}_t = g(Z_t)$, $\mathcal{Y}_\tau = g(Z_\tau)$. Let $A = [z: g(z) \leq a]$. Then $F_t(a) \equiv P[\mathcal{Y}_t \leq a] = P[Z_t \in A] = P[Z_\tau \in A] = P[\mathcal{Y}_\tau \leq a] \equiv F_\tau(a)$ for all $a \in \mathbb{R}^k$. Hence $g(Z_t)$ and $g(Z_\tau)$ are identically distributed. (ii) Let $A_1 = [z: g(z) \leq a_1]$, $A_2 = [z: g(z) \leq a_2]$. Then $F_{t\tau}(a_1, a_2) \equiv P[\mathcal{Y}_t \leq a_1, \mathcal{Y}_\tau \leq a_2] = P[Z_t \in A_1, Z_\tau \in A_2] = P[Z_t \in A_1]P[Z_\tau \in A_2] = P[\mathcal{Y}_t \leq a_1]P[\mathcal{Y}_\tau \leq a_2] = F_t(a_1)F_\tau(a_2)$ for all $a_1, a_2 \in \mathbb{R}^k$. Hence $g(Z_t)$ and $g(Z_\tau)$ are independent.

PROPOSITION 3.3: If $\{(\mathbf{Z}_t, \mathbf{X}_t, \epsilon_t)'\}$ is an i.i.d. random sequence, then $\{\mathbf{X}_t'\mathbf{X}_t\}$, $\{\mathbf{X}_t'\epsilon_t\}$, $\{\mathbf{Z}_t'\mathbf{X}_t\}$, $\{\mathbf{Z}_t'\epsilon_t\}$, and $\{\mathbf{Z}_t'\mathbf{Z}_t\}$ are i.i.d. sequences.

Proof: Immediate from Proposition 3.2(i) and (ii).

To write the moment conditions on the explanatory variables in compact form, we make use of the Cauchy–Schwartz inequality, which follows as a corollary to the following result.

PROPOSITION 3.4 (*Hölder's inequality*): If $p > 1$ and $1/p + 1/q = 1$ and if $E|\mathcal{Y}|^p < \infty$ and $E|Z|^q < \infty$, then $E|\mathcal{Y}Z| \leq [E|\mathcal{Y}|^p]^{1/p} [E|Z|^q]^{1/q}$.

Proof: See Lukacs [1975, p. 11].

† This result also holds for measurable functions, defined in Definition 3.21.

If $p = q = 2$, we have the Cauchy–Schwartz inequality,

$$E|\mathcal{Y}\mathcal{Z}| \le E(\mathcal{Y}^2)^{1/2}\, E(\mathcal{Z}^2)^{1/2}.$$

The i, jth element of $\mathbf{X}_t'\mathbf{X}_t$ is given by $\Sigma_{h=1}^p \mathbf{X}_{thi}\mathbf{X}_{thj}$, and it follows from the triangle inequality that

$$\left|\sum_{h=1}^p \mathbf{X}_{thi}\mathbf{X}_{thj}\right| \le \sum_{h=1}^p |\mathbf{X}_{thi}\mathbf{X}_{thj}|.$$

Hence,

$$\begin{aligned} E\left|\sum_{h=1}^p \mathbf{X}_{thi}\mathbf{X}_{thj}\right| &\le \sum_{h=1}^p E|\mathbf{X}_{thi}\mathbf{X}_{thj}| \\ &\le \sum_{h=1}^p (E|\mathbf{X}_{thi}|^2)^{1/2}(E|\mathbf{X}_{thj}|^2)^{1/2} \end{aligned}$$

by the Cauchy–Schwartz inequality. It follows that the elements of $\mathbf{X}_t'\mathbf{X}_t$ will have $E|\Sigma_{h=1}^p \mathbf{X}_{thi}\mathbf{X}_{thj}| < \infty$ (as we require to apply Komolgorov's law of large numbers), provided simply that $E|\mathbf{X}_{thi}|^2 < \infty$ for all h and i.

Combining Theorems 3.1 and 2.12, we have the following OLS consistency result for i.i.d. observations.

THEOREM 3.5: Suppose

(i) $\mathbf{y} = \mathbf{X}\boldsymbol{\beta}_o + \boldsymbol{\epsilon}$;
(ii) $\{(\mathbf{X}_t, \boldsymbol{\epsilon}_t)'\}$ is an i.i.d. sequence;
(iii) (a) $E(\mathbf{X}_t'\boldsymbol{\epsilon}_t) = \mathbf{0}$;
(b) $E|\mathbf{X}_{thi}\boldsymbol{\epsilon}_{th}| < \infty$, $h = 1, \ldots, p$, $i = 1, \ldots, k$;
(iv) (a) $E|\mathbf{X}_{thi}|^2 < \infty$, $h = 1, \ldots, p$, $i = 1, \ldots, k$;
(b) $\mathbf{M} \equiv E(\mathbf{X}_t'\mathbf{X}_t)$ is positive definite.

Then $\hat{\boldsymbol{\beta}}_n$ exists a.s. for all n sufficiently large, and $\hat{\boldsymbol{\beta}}_n \xrightarrow{\text{a.s.}} \boldsymbol{\beta}_o$.

Proof: Given (ii), $\{\mathbf{X}_t'\boldsymbol{\epsilon}_t\}$ and $\{\mathbf{X}_t'\mathbf{X}_t\}$ are i.i.d. sequences. The elements of $\mathbf{X}_t'\boldsymbol{\epsilon}_t$ and $\mathbf{X}_t'\mathbf{X}_t$ have finite expected absolute values, given (iii) and (iv) and applying the Cauchy–Schwartz inequality as above. By Theorem 3.1, $\mathbf{X}'\boldsymbol{\epsilon}/n = n^{-1}\,\Sigma_{t=1}^n \mathbf{X}_t'\boldsymbol{\epsilon}_t \xrightarrow{\text{a.s.}} \mathbf{0}$, and $\mathbf{X}'\mathbf{X}/n = n^{-1}\,\Sigma_{t=1}^n \mathbf{X}_t'\mathbf{X}_t \xrightarrow{\text{a.s.}} \mathbf{M}$, finite and positive definite, so the conditions of Theorem 2.12 are satisfied and the result follows.

This result is useful in situations in which we have observations from a random sample, as in a simple cross section. The result does not apply to stratified cross sections since there the observations are not identically distributed across strata and generally will not apply to time-series data, since there the observations $(\mathbf{X}_t, \boldsymbol{\epsilon}_t)$ generally are not independent. For these situations, we need laws of large numbers that do not impose the i.i.d. assumption.

Since (i) is assumed, we could equally well have specified (ii) as requiring that $\{(\mathbf{X}_t, \mathbf{y}_t)'\}$ is an i.i.d. sequence and then applied Proposition 3.2, which implies that $\{(\mathbf{X}_t, \boldsymbol{\epsilon}_t)'\}$ is an i.i.d. sequence. Next, note that conditions sufficient to ensure $E(\mathbf{X}_t'\boldsymbol{\epsilon}_t) = \mathbf{0}$ would be $\mathbf{X}_t$ independent of $\boldsymbol{\epsilon}_t$ for all t and $E(\boldsymbol{\epsilon}_t) = \mathbf{0}$; alternatively, it would suffice that $E(\boldsymbol{\epsilon}_t|\mathbf{X}_t) = \mathbf{0}$. This latter condition follows if $E(\mathbf{y}_t|\mathbf{X}_t) = \mathbf{X}_t\boldsymbol{\beta}_o$ and we define $\boldsymbol{\epsilon}_t$ as $\boldsymbol{\epsilon}_t \equiv \mathbf{y}_t - E(\mathbf{y}_t|\mathbf{X}_t) = \mathbf{y}_t - \mathbf{X}_t\boldsymbol{\beta}_o$. Both of these alternatives to (iii) are stronger than the simple requirement that $E(\mathbf{X}_t'\boldsymbol{\epsilon}_t) = \mathbf{0}$. Note that no restrictions are placed on the second moment of $\boldsymbol{\epsilon}_t$ in obtaining consistency for $\hat{\boldsymbol{\beta}}_n$. In fact, $\boldsymbol{\epsilon}_t$ can have infinite variance without affecting the consistency of $\hat{\boldsymbol{\beta}}_n$ for $\boldsymbol{\beta}_o$.

The result for the IV estimator is analogous.

EXERCISE 3.6: Prove the following result. Given

(i) $\mathbf{y} = \mathbf{X}\boldsymbol{\beta}_o + \boldsymbol{\epsilon}$;

(ii) $\{(\mathbf{Z}_t, \mathbf{X}_t, \boldsymbol{\epsilon}_t)'\}$ an i.i.d. sequence;

(iii) (a) $E(\mathbf{Z}_t'\boldsymbol{\epsilon}_t) = \mathbf{0}$;

(b) $E|\mathbf{Z}_{thi}\boldsymbol{\epsilon}_{th}| < \infty$, $h = 1, \ldots, p$, $i = 1, \ldots, l$;

(iv) (a) $E|\mathbf{Z}_{thi}\mathbf{X}_{thj}| < \infty$, $h = 1, \ldots, p$, $i = 1, \ldots, l$, and $j = 1, \ldots, k$;

(b) $\mathbf{Q} \equiv E(\mathbf{Z}_t'\mathbf{X}_t)$ has full column rank;

(c) $\hat{\mathbf{P}}_n \xrightarrow{\text{a.s.}} \mathbf{P}$, finite and positive definite.

Then $\tilde{\boldsymbol{\beta}}_n$ exists a.s. for all n sufficiently large, and $\tilde{\boldsymbol{\beta}}_n \xrightarrow{\text{a.s.}} \boldsymbol{\beta}_o$.

III.2 Independent Heterogeneously Distributed Observations

For cross-sectional data, it is often appropriate to assume that the observations are independent but not identically distributed. The failure of the identical distribution assumption results from stratifying (grouping) the population in some way. The independence assumption remains valid provided that sampling within and across the strata is random. A law of large numbers useful in these situations is the following.

THEOREM 3.7 (*Markov*): Let $\{Z_t\}$ be a sequence of independent random variables, with finite means $\mu_t \equiv E(Z_t)$. If for some $\delta > 0$, $\sum_{t=1}^{\infty} (E|Z_t - \mu_t|^{1+\delta})/t^{1+\delta} < \infty$, then $\bar{Z}_n - \bar{\mu}_n \xrightarrow{\text{a.s.}} 0$.

Proof: See Chung [1974, pp. 125–126].

In this result the random variables are allowed to be heterogeneous (i.e., not identically distributed), but the moments are restricted by the condition that $\sum_{t=1}^{\infty} E|Z_t - \mu_t|^{1+\delta}/t^{1+\delta} < \infty$, known as Markov's condition. If $\delta = 1$, we have a law of large numbers due to Komolgorov (e.g., see Rao [1973, p. 114]). But Markov's condition allows us to choose δ arbitrarily small, thus reducing the restrictions imposed on Z_t.

By making use of Jensen's inequality and the following useful inequality, it is possible to state a corollary with a simpler moment condition.

PROPOSITION 3.8 (*The c_r inequality*): Let $\mathcal{Y}$ and Z be random variables with $E|\mathcal{Y}|^r < \infty$ and $E|Z|^r < \infty$ for some $r > 0$. Then

$$E|\mathcal{Y} + Z|^r \le c_r(E|\mathcal{Y}|^r + E|Z|^r),$$

where $c_r = 1$ if $r \le 1$ and $c_r = 2^{r-1}$ if $r > 1$.

Proof: See Lukacs [1975, p. 13].

COROLLARY 3.9: Let $\{Z_t\}$ be a sequence of independent random variables such that $E|Z_t|^{1+\delta} < \Delta < \infty$ for some $\delta > 0$ and all t. Then $\bar{Z}_n - \bar{\mu}_n \xrightarrow{\text{a.s.}} 0$.

Proof: By Proposition 3.8,

$$E|Z_t - \mu_t|^{1+\delta} \le 2^{\delta}(E|Z_t|^{1+\delta} + |\mu_t|^{1+\delta}).$$

By assuming that $E|Z_t|^{1+\delta} < \Delta$ and using Jensen's inequality,

$$|\mu_t| \le E|Z_t| \le (E|Z_t|^{1+\delta})^{1/(1+\delta)}.$$

It follows that for all t,

$$|\mu_t|^{1+\delta} < \Delta.$$

Hence, for all t, $E|Z_t - \mu_t|^{1+\delta} < 2^{1+\delta}\Delta$. Verifying the moment condition of Theorem 3.7, we have

$$\sum_{t=1}^{\infty} E|Z_t - \mu_t|^{1+\delta}/t^{1+\delta} < 2^{1+\delta}\,\Delta \sum_{t=1}^{\infty} 1/t^{1+\delta} < \infty,$$

since $\Sigma_{t=1}^{\infty} 1/t^{1+\delta} < \infty$ for any $\delta > 0$. Hence the conditions of Theorem 3.7 are satisfied and the result follows.

Compared with Theorem 3.1, this corollary imposes slightly more in the way of moment restrictions but allows the observations to be rather heterogeneous.

It is useful to point out that a nonstochastic sequence can be viewed as a sequence of independent, not identically distributed, random variables where the distribution function of these random variables places probability one at the observed value. Hence, Corollary 3.9 can be applied to situations in which we have fixed regressors, provided they are uniformly bounded, as the condition $E|Z_t|^{1+\delta} < \Delta < \infty$ requires. Situations with unbounded fixed regressors can be treated using Theorem 3.7.

To apply Corollary 3.9 to the linear model, we use the following fact.

Proposition 3.10: If $\{(\mathbf{Z}_t, \mathbf{X}_t, \boldsymbol{\epsilon}_t)'\}$ is an independent sequence, then $\{\mathbf{X}_t'\mathbf{X}_t\}$, $\{\mathbf{X}_t'\boldsymbol{\epsilon}_t\}$, $\{\mathbf{Z}_t'\mathbf{X}_t\}$, $\{\mathbf{Z}_t'\boldsymbol{\epsilon}_t\}$, and $\{\mathbf{Z}_t'\mathbf{Z}_t\}$ are independent sequences.

Proof: Immediate from Proposition 3.2(ii).

To simplify the moment conditions that we impose, we use the following consequence of Hölder's inequality.

Proposition 3.11 (*Minkowski's inequality*): If $q \geq 1$ and $E|\mathcal{Y}|^q < \infty$ and $E|Z|^q < \infty$, then

$$E|\mathcal{Y} + Z|^q \leq [(E|\mathcal{Y}|^q)^{1/q} + (E|Z|^q)^{1/q}]^q.$$

Proof: See Lukacs [1975, p. 11].

To apply Corollary 3.9 to $\mathbf{X}_t'\mathbf{X}_t$, we need to ensure that $E|\Sigma_{h=1}^{p} \mathbf{X}_{thi}\mathbf{X}_{thj}|^{1+\delta}$ is bounded uniformly in t. This is accomplished by the following corollary.

Corollary 3.12: Suppose $E|\mathbf{X}_{thi}^2|^{1+\delta} < \Delta < \infty$ for some $\delta > 0$, all $h = 1, \ldots, p$, $i = 1, \ldots, k$, and all t. Then each element of $\mathbf{X}_t'\mathbf{X}_t$ satisfies $E|\Sigma_{h=1}^{p} \mathbf{X}_{thi}\mathbf{X}_{thj}|^{1+\delta} < \Delta' < \infty$ for some $\delta > 0$, all $i, j = 1, \ldots, k$, and all t, where $\Delta' \equiv p^{1+\delta}\Delta$.

Proof: By Minkowski's inequality,

$$E\left|\sum_{h=1}^{p} \mathbf{X}_{thi}\mathbf{X}_{thj}\right|^{1+\delta} \leq \left[\sum_{h=1}^{p} (E|\mathbf{X}_{thi}\mathbf{X}_{thj}|^{1+\delta})^{1/(1+\delta)}\right]^{1+\delta}$$

By the Cauchy–Schwartz inequality,

$$E|\mathbf{X}_{thi}\mathbf{X}_{thj}|^{1+\delta} \leq [E|\mathbf{X}_{thi}^2|^{1+\delta}]^{1/2}[E|\mathbf{X}_{thj}^2|^{1+\delta}]^{1/2}.$$

Since $E|\mathbf{X}_{thi}^2|^{1+\delta} < \Delta < \infty$, $h = 1, \ldots, p$, $i = 1, \ldots, k$, it follows that for all $h = 1, \ldots, p$ and $i, j = 1, \ldots, k$,

$$E|\mathbf{X}_{thi}\mathbf{X}_{thj}|^{1+\delta} \leq \Delta^{1/2}\Delta^{1/2} = \Delta,$$

so that

$$E\left|\sum_{h=1}^{p} \mathbf{X}_{thi}\mathbf{X}_{thj}\right|^{1+\delta} \leq \left[\sum_{h=1}^{p} \Delta^{1/(1+\delta)}\right]^{1+\delta}$$

$$= p^{1+\delta}\Delta = \Delta'.$$

The requirement that $E|\mathbf{X}_{thi}^2|^{1+\delta} < \Delta < \infty$ means that all the explanatory variables have moments slightly greater than 2 uniformly bounded. A similar requirement is imposed on the elements of $\mathbf{X}_t'\boldsymbol{\epsilon}_t$.

EXERCISE 3.13: Show that if $E|\mathbf{X}_{thi}\boldsymbol{\epsilon}_{th}|^{1+\delta} < \Delta < \infty$ for some $\delta > 0$, all $h = 1, \ldots, p$, $i = 1, \ldots, k$, and all t, then each element of $\mathbf{X}_t'\boldsymbol{\epsilon}_t$ satisfies $E|\Sigma_{h=1}^{p} \mathbf{X}_{thi}\boldsymbol{\epsilon}_{th}|^{1+\delta} < \Delta' < \infty$ for some $\delta > 0$, all $i = 1, \ldots, k$, and all t, where $\Delta' = p^{1+\delta}\Delta$.

We now have all the needed results to obtain a consistency theorem for the ordinary least squares estimator. Since the argument is analogous to that of Theorem 3.5 we state the result as an exercise.

EXERCISE 3.14: Prove the following result. Suppose

(i) $\mathbf{y} = \mathbf{X}\boldsymbol{\beta}_o + \boldsymbol{\epsilon}$;
(ii) $\{(\mathbf{X}_t, \boldsymbol{\epsilon}_t)'\}$ is an independent sequence;
(iii) (a) $E(\mathbf{X}_t'\boldsymbol{\epsilon}_t) = \mathbf{0}$;
 (b) $E|\mathbf{X}_{thi}\boldsymbol{\epsilon}_{th}|^{1+\delta} < \Delta < \infty$ for some $\delta > 0$, all $h = 1, \ldots, p$, $i = 1, \ldots, k$, and all t;
(iv) (a) $E|\mathbf{X}_{thi}^2|^{1+\delta} < \Delta < \infty$ for some $\delta > 0$, all $h = 1, \ldots, p$, $i = 1, \ldots, k$, and all t;
 (b) $\mathbf{M}_n \equiv E(\mathbf{X}'\mathbf{X}/n)$ is uniformly positive definite.

Then $\hat{\boldsymbol{\beta}}_n$ exists a.s. for all n sufficiently large, and $\hat{\boldsymbol{\beta}}_n \xrightarrow{\text{a.s.}} \boldsymbol{\beta}_o$.

Compared with Theorem 3.5, we have relaxed the identical distribution assumption at the expense of imposing slightly greater moment restrictions in (iiib) and (iva). Also note that (iva) implies that $\mathbf{M}_n$ is $O(1)$. (Why?)

The extra generality we have gained now allows treatment of situations with fixed regressors, or observations from a stratified cross section, and also applies to models with heteroskedastic errors. None of these cases is covered by Theorem 3.5.

The result for the IV estimator is analogous.

THEOREM 3.15: Suppose

(i) $\mathbf{y} = \mathbf{X}\boldsymbol{\beta}_o + \boldsymbol{\epsilon}$;
(ii) $\{(\mathbf{Z}_t, \mathbf{X}_t, \boldsymbol{\epsilon}_t)'\}$ is an independent sequence;
(iii) (a) $E(\mathbf{Z}_t'\boldsymbol{\epsilon}_t) = \mathbf{0}$;
(b) $E|\mathbf{Z}_{thi}\boldsymbol{\epsilon}_{th}|^{1+\delta} < \Delta < \infty$ for some $\delta > 0$, all $h = 1, \ldots, p$, $i = 1, \ldots, l$, and all t;
(iv) (a) $E|\mathbf{Z}_{thi}\mathbf{X}_{thj}|^{1+\delta} < \Delta < \infty$ for some $\delta > 0$, all $h = 1, \ldots, p$, $i = 1, \ldots, l$, $j = 1, \ldots, k$, and all t;
(b) $\mathbf{Q}_n \equiv E(\mathbf{Z}'\mathbf{X}/n)$ has uniformly full column rank;
(c) $\hat{\mathbf{P}}_n - \mathbf{P}_n \xrightarrow{a.s.} \mathbf{0}$, where $\{\mathbf{P}_n\}$ is $O(1)$ and uniformly positive definite.

Then $\tilde{\boldsymbol{\beta}}_n$ exists a.s. for all n sufficiently large, and $\hat{\boldsymbol{\beta}}_n \xrightarrow{a.s.} \boldsymbol{\beta}_0$.

Proof: By Proposition 3.9, $\{\mathbf{Z}_t'\boldsymbol{\epsilon}_t\}$ and $\{\mathbf{Z}_t'\mathbf{X}_t\}$ are independent sequences with elements satisfying the moment condition of Corollary 3.8, given (iiib) and (iva), by arguments analogous to those of Corollary 3.12 and Exercise 3.13. It follows from Corollary 3.9 that $\mathbf{Z}'\boldsymbol{\epsilon}/n \xrightarrow{a.s.} \mathbf{0}$ and $\mathbf{Z}'\mathbf{X}/n - \mathbf{Q}_n \xrightarrow{a.s.} \mathbf{0}$, where $\mathbf{Q}_n$ is $O(1)$ given (iva) as a consequence of Jensen's inequality. Hence, the conditions of Exercise 2.20 are satisfied and the results follow.

III.3 Dependent Identically Distributed Observations

The assumption of independence is often inappropriate for economic time series, which typically exhibit considerable dependence. To cover these cases, we need laws of large numbers that allow the random variables of our model to be dependent. To speak precisely about the kinds of dependence allowed, we need to make explicit some fundamental notions of probability theory that we have so far used implicitly.

DEFINITION 3.16: A family (collection) $\mathfrak{F}$ of subsets of a set Ω is a *σ-field* (*σ-algebra*) provided

(i) $\varnothing$ and Ω belong to $\mathfrak{F}$;
(ii) if F belongs to $\mathfrak{F}$, then F^c (the complement of F in Ω) belongs to $\mathfrak{F}$;
(iii) if $\{F_i\}$ is a sequence of sets in $\mathfrak{F}$, then $\bigcup_{i=1}^{\infty} F_i$ belongs to $\mathcal{F}$.

EXAMPLE 3.17: (i) Let Ω be any set, and let $\mathfrak{F}$ be the family of all subsets of Ω. (ii) Let $\mathfrak{F}$ be the family consisting of the following two subsets of Ω: Ω and $\varnothing$.

EXAMPLE 3.18: The *Borel field* $\mathcal{B}$ is the smallest collection of sets (called the *Borel sets*) that includes

(i) all intervals $\{z: -\infty < z \leq a\}$, $a \in \mathbb{R}$;
(ii) the complement B^c of any set B in $\mathcal{B}$;
(iii) the union $\bigcup_{i=1}^{\infty} B_i$ of any sequence $\{B_i\}$ in $\mathcal{B}$.

The Borel sets of $\mathbb{R}$ just defined are said to be *generated* by all the closed half-lines of $\mathbb{R}$ in (i). The same Borel sets would be generated by all the open half-lines of $\mathbb{R}$, all the open intervals of $\mathbb{R}$, or all the closed intervals of $\mathbb{R}$. These Borel sets have the property that if P is a probability measure and $B \in \mathcal{B}$, then $P[B]$ is well defined. There do exist subsets of the real line not in $\mathcal{B}$ for which probabilities are not defined, but constructing such sets is very complicated. Thus we can think of the Borel field as consisting of all the events on the real line to which we can assign a probability. Sets not in $\mathcal{B}$ will not define events.

The Borel field just defined relates to real-valued random variables. A simple extension covers vector-valued random variables.

DEFINITION 3.19: The *Borel field* $\mathcal{B}^q$, $q < \infty$, is the smallest collection of sets that includes

(i) all intervals $\{z: -\infty < z \leq a\}$ where z is a $q \times 1$ vector and $a \in \mathbb{R}^q$;
(ii) the complement B^c of any set B in $\mathcal{B}^q$;
(iii) the union $\bigcup_{i=1}^{\infty} B_i$ of any sequence $\{B_i\}$ in $\mathcal{B}^q$.

The same collection of sets $\mathcal{B}^q$ is also generated by all the open (or closed) sets of $\mathbb{R}^q$, as well as by all the open intervals of $\mathbb{R}^q$. In this notation, $\mathcal{B}$ and $\mathcal{B}^1$ mean the same thing.

Recall that in the previous chapter we let a point ω correspond to an infinite sequence of random variables $\{Z_t\}$. Generally, we are interested in infinite sequences $\{(\mathbf{Z}_t, \mathbf{X}_t, \boldsymbol{\epsilon}_t)'\}$. If $p = 1$, this is a sequence of random $(l + k + 1) \times 1$ vectors, whereas if $p > 1$, this is a sequence of $(l + k + 1) \times p$ matrices. Nevertheless, we can convert these matrices into vectors by simply stacking the columns of a matrix, one on top of the other, to yield a $p(l + k + 1) \times 1$ vector, denoted $\text{vec}(\mathbf{Z}_t, \mathbf{X}_t, \boldsymbol{\epsilon}_t)'$. (In what follows, we drop the vec operator and understand that it is implicit in this context.) Generally, then, we are interested in infinite *sequences* of q-dimensional random vectors, where $q = p(l + k + 1)$. Corresponding to these are the Borel sets of $\mathbb{R}^q_\infty$, defined as the Cartesian product of a countable infinity of copies of $\mathbb{R}^q$, $\mathbb{R}^q_\infty \equiv \mathbb{R}^q \times \mathbb{R}^q \times \ldots$. In what follows we can think of ω taking its values in $\Omega = \mathbb{R}^q_\infty$. The events in which we are interested are the Borel sets of $\mathbb{R}^q_\infty$, which we define as follows.

DEFINITION 3.20: The Borel sets of $\mathbb{R}^q_\infty$, denoted $\mathfrak{F}$, are the smallest collection of sets that includes

(i) all sets of the form $\times_{i=1}^{\infty} B_i$, where each $B_i \in \mathcal{B}^q$ and $B_i = \mathbb{R}^q$ except for finitely many i;
(ii) the complement F^c of any set F in $\mathfrak{F}$;
(iii) the union $\cup_{i=1}^{\infty} F_i$ of any sequence $\{F_i\}$ in $\mathfrak{F}$.

A set of the form specified by (i) is called a *measurable finite-dimensional product cylinder,* so $\mathfrak{F}$ is the Borel σ-field generated by all the measurable finite-dimensional product cylinders. The events to which we shall assign probabilities are the Borel sets of $\mathbb{R}^q_\infty$, i.e., those in $\mathfrak{F}$. A *probability space* consists of the triple $(\Omega, \mathfrak{F}, P)$, where P is the probability function for ω that will determine the joint p.d.f. of $\{Z_t\}$.

When $q = 1$, the elements of the sequence $\{Z_t\}$ can be thought of as functions from $\Omega = \mathbb{R}^1_\infty$ to the real line $\mathbb{R}$ that simply pick off the tth coordinate of ω. This is made explicit by writing $Z_t(\omega)$ in place of Z_t. When $q > 1$, $Z_t(\omega)$ maps $\mathbb{R}^q_\infty$ into $\mathbb{R}^q$.

DEFINITION 3.21: A function g on Ω to $\mathbb{R}$ is $\mathfrak{F}$-*measurable* if for every real number a the set $[\omega : g(\omega) \leq a] \in \mathfrak{F}$.

EXAMPLE 3.22: Set $q = 1$. Then $Z_t(\omega)$ as just defined is $\mathfrak{F}$-measurable since $[\omega: Z_t(\omega) \leq a] = [z_1, \ldots, z_{t-1}, z_t, z_{t+1}, \ldots : z_1 < \infty, \ldots, z_{t-1} < \infty, z_t \leq a, z_{t+1} < \infty, \ldots] \in \mathfrak{F}$ for any a.

When a function is $\mathfrak{F}$-measurable, it means that we can express the probability of an event, say, $[Z_t \leq a]$, in terms of the probability of an event in $\mathfrak{F}$, say, $[\omega: Z_t(\omega) \leq a]$. In fact, a random variable is precisely an $\mathfrak{F}$-measurable function from Ω to $\mathbb{R}$.

In Definition 3.21 the σ-field $\mathfrak{F}$ can be replaced by any σ-field $\mathcal{G}$, in which case we say that the function of g is $\mathcal{G}$-measurable. When the σ-field is taken to be $\mathfrak{F}$, the Borel sets of $\mathbb{R}^q_\infty$, we shall drop explicit reference to $\mathfrak{F}$ and simply say that the function g is measurable. Otherwise, the relevant σ-field will be explicitly identified.

PROPOSITION 3.23: Let f and g be $\mathcal{G}$-measurable real-valued functions, and let c be a real number. Then the functions cf, $f + g$, fg, and $|f|$ are also $\mathcal{G}$-measurable.

Proof: See Bartle [1966, Lemma 2.6].

EXAMPLE 3.24: If $Z_t(\omega)$ is measurable, then $Z_t(\omega)/n$ is measurable, so that $\bar{Z}_n(\omega) = \Sigma_{t=1}^n Z_t(\omega)/n$ is measurable.

A function from Ω to $\mathbb{R}^q$ is measurable if and only if each component of the vector valued function is measurable. The notion of measurability extends to transformations from Ω to Ω in the following way.

DEFINITION 3.25: A one-to-one transformation† $T: \Omega \rightarrow \Omega$ defined on $(\Omega, \mathfrak{F}, P)$ is *measurable* provided that $T^{-1}(\mathfrak{F}) \subset \mathfrak{F}$.

In other words, the transformation T is measurable provided that any set taken by the transformation (or its inverse) into $\mathfrak{F}$ is itself a set in $\mathfrak{F}$. This ensures that sets that are not events cannot be transformed into events, nor can events be transformed into sets that are not events.

EXAMPLE 3.26: For any $\omega = (\ldots, z_{t-2}, z_{t-1}, z_t, z_{t+1}, z_{t+2}, \ldots)$ let $\omega' = T\omega = (\ldots, z_{t-1}, z_t, z_{t+1}, z_{t+2}, z_{t+3}, \ldots)$, so that T transforms ω by shifting each of its coordinates back one location. Then T is measurable since $T\omega$ is in $\mathfrak{F}$ and $T^{-1}\omega$ is in $\mathfrak{F}$.

† The transformation T maps a point of Ω, say ω, into another point of Ω, say $\omega' = T\omega$. When T operates on a set F, it should be understood as operating on each element of F. Similarly, when T operates on a family $\mathfrak{F}$, it should be understood as operating on each set in the family.

The transformation of this example is often called the *shift,* or the *backshift operator.* By using such transformations, it is possible to define a corresponding transformation of a random variable. For example, set $Z_1(\omega) = Z(\omega)$, where Z is a measurable function from Ω to $\mathbb{R}$; then we can define the random variables $Z_2(\omega) = Z(T\omega)$, $Z_3(\omega) = Z(T^2\omega)$, and so on, provided that T is a measurable transformation. The random variables constructed in this way are said to be random variables *induced* by a measurable transformation.

Definition 3.27: A transformation T from Ω to Ω is *measure preserving* if it is measurable and if $P(T^{-1}F) = P(F)$ for *all* F in $\mathfrak{F}$.

The random variables induced by *measure-preserving* transformations then have the property that $P[Z_1 \leq a] = P[\omega : Z(\omega) \leq a] = P[\omega : Z(T\omega) \leq a] = P[Z_2 \leq a]$. In fact, such random variables have an even stronger property. We use the following definition.

Definition 3.28: Let G_1 be the joint distribution function of the sequence $\{Z_1, Z_2, \ldots\}$, where Z_t is a $q \times 1$ vector, and let $G_{\tau+1}$ be the joint distribution function of the sequence $\{Z_{\tau+1}, Z_{\tau+2}, \ldots\}$. The sequence $\{Z_t\}$ is *stationary* if and only if $G_1 = G_{\tau+1}$ for each $\tau \geq 1$.

In other words, a sequence is stationary if the *joint* distribution of the variables in the sequence is identical, regardless of the date of the first observation.

Proposition 3.29: Let Z be a random variable (i.e., $Z(\omega)$ is a measurable function) and T be a measure-preserving transformation. Let $Z_1(\omega) = Z(\omega)$, $Z_2(\omega) = Z(T\omega)$, . . . , $Z_n(\omega) = Z(T^{n-1}\omega)$ for each ω in Ω. Then $\{Z_t\}$ is a stationary sequence.

Proof: Stout [1974, p. 169].

A converse to this result is also available.

Proposition 3.30: Let $\{Z_t\}$ be a stationary sequence. Then there exists a measure-preserving transformation T defined on $(\Omega, \mathfrak{F}, P)$ such that $Z_1(\omega) = Z_1(\omega)$, $Z_2(\omega) = Z_1(T\omega)$, $Z_3(\omega) = Z_1(T^2\omega)$, . . . , $Z_n(\omega) = Z_1(T^{n-1}\omega)$ for all ω in Ω.

Proof: Stout [1974, p. 170].

Example 3.31: Let $\{Z_t\}$ be a sequence of i.i.d. $N(0, 1)$ random variables. Then $\{Z_t\}$ is stationary.

The independence imposed in this example is crucial. If the $\{Z_t\}$ is simply identically distributed $N(0, 1)$, the sequence is not necessarily stationary, because it is possible to construct different joint distributions that all have normal marginal distributions. By changing the joint distributions with t, we could violate the stationarity condition while preserving marginal normality. Thus stationarity is a strengthening of the identical distribution assumption, since it applies to joint and not simply marginal distributions. On the other hand, stationarity is weaker than the i.i.d. assumption, since i.i.d. sequences are stationary, but stationary sequences do not have to be independent.

Does a version of the law of large numbers, Theorem 3.1, hold if the i.i.d. assumption is simply replaced by the stationarity assumption? The answer is no, unless additional restrictions are imposed.

EXAMPLE 3.32: Let $\mathcal{U}_t$ be a sequence of i.i.d. random variables uniformly distributed on [0, 1] and let Z be $N(0, 1)$, independent of $\mathcal{U}_t$, $t = 1, 2, \ldots$. Define $\mathcal{Y}_t = Z + \mathcal{U}_t$. Then $\{\mathcal{Y}_t\}$ is stationary (why?), but $\bar{\mathcal{Y}}_n \equiv \sum_{t=1}^n \mathcal{Y}_t/n$ does not converge to $E(\mathcal{Y}_t) = \frac{1}{2}$. Instead, $\bar{\mathcal{Y}}_n - Z \xrightarrow{\text{a.s.}} \frac{1}{2}$.

In this example, $\bar{\mathcal{Y}}_n$ converges to a random variable, $Z + \frac{1}{2}$, rather than to a constant. The problem is that there is too much dependence in the sequence $\{\mathcal{Y}_t\}$. No matter how far into the future we take an observation on $\mathcal{Y}_t$, the initial value $\mathcal{Y}_1$ still determines to some extent what $\mathcal{Y}_t$ will be, as a result of the common component Z. In fact, the correlation between $\mathcal{Y}_1$ and $\mathcal{Y}_t$ is always positive for any value of t.

To obtain a law of large numbers, we have to impose a restriction on the dependence or "memory" of the sequence. One such restriction is the concept of *ergodicity*.

DEFINITION 3.33: Let $\{Z_t\}$ be a stationary sequence and let T be the measure-preserving transformation of Proposition 3.30 defined on $(\Omega, \mathfrak{F}, P)$. Then $\{Z_t\}$ is *ergodic* if and only if for any two events F and $G \in \mathfrak{F}$, $\lim_{n\to\infty} n^{-1} \sum_{t=1}^n P(F \cap T^t G) = P(F)\, P(G)$.

If F and G were independent, then $P(F \cap G) = P(F)\, P(G)$. We can think of $T^t G$ as being the event G shifted t periods into the future, and since $P(T^t G) = P(G)$ when T is measure preserving, this definition says that an ergodic process (sequence) is one such that for any events F and G, F and $T^t G$ are independent on average in the limit. Thus ergodicity can be thought of as a form of "average asymptotic independence." For more on measure-preserving transformations, stationarity, and ergodicity the reader may consult Doob [1953, pp. 167–185] and Rosenblatt [1978].

The desired law of large numbers can now be stated.

THEOREM 3.34 (*Ergodic theorem*): Let $\{Z_t\}$ be a stationary ergodic scalar sequence with $E|Z_t| < \infty$. Then $\bar{Z}_n \xrightarrow{\text{a.s.}} \mu \equiv E(Z_t)$.

Proof: See Stout [1974, p. 181].

To apply this result, we make use of the following theorem.

THEOREM 3.35: Let g be an $\mathfrak{F}$-measurable function onto $\mathbb{R}^k$ and define $\mathcal{Y}_t \equiv g(Z_t, Z_{t+1}, \ldots)$, where Z_t is $q \times 1$. (i) If $\{Z_t\}$ is stationary, then $\{\mathcal{Y}_t\}$ is stationary. (ii) If $\{Z_t\}$ is stationary and ergodic, then $\{\mathcal{Y}_t\}$ is stationary and ergodic.†

Proof: See Stout [1974, pp. 170, 182].

PROPOSITION 3.36: If $\{(\mathbf{Z}_t, \mathbf{X}_t, \boldsymbol{\epsilon}_t)'\}$ is a stationary ergodic sequence, then $\{\mathbf{X}_t'\mathbf{X}_t\}$, $\{\mathbf{X}_t'\boldsymbol{\epsilon}_t\}$, $\{\mathbf{Z}_t'\mathbf{X}_t\}$, $\{\mathbf{Z}_t'\boldsymbol{\epsilon}_t\}$, and $\{\mathbf{Z}_t'\mathbf{Z}_t\}$ are stationary ergodic sequences.

Proof: Immediate from Theorem 3.35 and Proposition 3.23.

Now we can state a result applicable to time-series data.

THEOREM 3.37: Suppose

(i) $\mathbf{y} = \mathbf{X}\boldsymbol{\beta}_o + \boldsymbol{\epsilon}$;
(ii) $\{(\mathbf{X}_t, \boldsymbol{\epsilon}_t)'\}$ is a stationary ergodic sequence;
(iii) (a) $E(\mathbf{X}_t'\boldsymbol{\epsilon}_t) = \mathbf{0}$;
(b) $E|\mathbf{X}_{thi}\boldsymbol{\epsilon}_{th}| < \infty$, $h = 1, \ldots, p$, $i = 1, \ldots, k$;
(iv) (a) $E|\mathbf{X}_{thi}|^2 < \infty$, $h = 1, \ldots, p$, $i = 1, \ldots, k$;
(b) $\mathbf{M} \equiv E(\mathbf{X}_t'\mathbf{X}_t)$ is positive definite

Then $\hat{\boldsymbol{\beta}}_n$ exists a.s. for all n sufficiently large, and $\hat{\boldsymbol{\beta}}_n \xrightarrow{\text{a.s.}} \boldsymbol{\beta}_o$.

Proof: We verify the conditions of Theorem 2.12. Given (ii), $\{\mathbf{X}_t'\boldsymbol{\epsilon}_t\}$ and $\{\mathbf{X}_t'\mathbf{X}_t\}$ are stationary ergodic sequences by Proposition 3.36, with elements having finite expected absolute values (given (iii) and (iv)). By the ergodic Theorem 3.34, $\mathbf{X}'\boldsymbol{\epsilon}/n \xrightarrow{\text{a.s.}} \mathbf{0}$ and

† The fact that g depends on the present and possibly infinite future of the sequence $\{Z_t\}$ is an interesting feature of this result. If the process $\{Z_t\}$ had an infinite past as well, g could also depend on the infinite past of $\{Z_t\}$ without affecting the validity of this result.

$\mathbf{X}'\mathbf{X}/n \xrightarrow{\text{a.s.}} \mathbf{M}$, finite and positive definite. Hence, the conditions of Theorem 2.12 hold and the results follow.

Compared with Theorem 3.5, we have replaced the i.i.d. assumption with the strictly weaker condition that the regressors and errors are stationary and ergodic. In both results, only the finiteness of second-order moments and cross moments is imposed. Thus Theorem 3.5 is a corollary of Theorem 3.37.

A direct generalization of Exercise 3.6 for the IV estimator is also available.

EXERCISE 3.38: Prove the following result. Given

(i) $\mathbf{y} = \mathbf{X}\boldsymbol{\beta}_o + \boldsymbol{\epsilon}$;
(ii) $\{(\mathbf{Z}_t, \mathbf{X}_t, \boldsymbol{\epsilon}_t)'\}$ is a stationary ergodic sequence;
(iii) (a) $E(\mathbf{Z}_t'\boldsymbol{\epsilon}_t) = \mathbf{0}$;
(b) $E|\mathbf{Z}_{thi}\boldsymbol{\epsilon}_{th}| < \infty$, $h = 1, \ldots, p$, $i = 1, \ldots, l$;
(iv) (a) $E|\mathbf{Z}_{thi}\mathbf{X}_{thj}| < \infty$, $h = 1, \ldots, p$, $i = 1, \ldots, l$, and $j = 1, \ldots, k$;
(b) $\mathbf{Q} \equiv E(\mathbf{Z}_t'\mathbf{X}_t)$ has full column rank;
(c) $\hat{\mathbf{P}}_n \xrightarrow{\text{a.s.}} \mathbf{P}$, finite and positive definite.

Then $\tilde{\boldsymbol{\beta}}_n$ exists a.s. for all n sufficiently large, and $\tilde{\boldsymbol{\beta}}_n \xrightarrow{\text{a.s.}} \boldsymbol{\beta}_0$.

Economic applications of Theorem 3.37 and Exercise 3.38 depend on whether it is reasonable to suppose that economic time series are stationary and ergodic. Ergodicity is often difficult to ascertain theoretically (although it does hold for certain Markov sequences; see Stout [1974, pp. 185–200]) and is impossible to verify empirically (since this requires an infinite sample). Stationarity, on the other hand, is a property that can be investigated empirically. However, many important economic time series seem not to be stationary but heterogeneous, exhibiting means, variances, and covariances that change over time.

III.4 Dependent Heterogeneously Distributed Observations

To apply the consistency results of the preceding chapter to dependent heterogeneously distributed observations, we need to find conditions that ensure that the law of large numbers continues to hold. This can be done by replacing the ergodicity assumption with somewhat stronger conditions on the dependence of a sequence, known as *mixing conditions.*

To specify these conditions, we use the following definition.

DEFINITION 3.39: The *Borel field generated by* $\{Z_t(\omega), t = n, \ldots, n+m\}$, denoted $\mathcal{B}_n^{n+m} = \sigma(Z_n, \ldots, Z_{n+m})$, is the smallest collection of subsets of Ω that includes

(i) all sets of the form $\times_{i=1}^{n-1} \mathbb{R}^q \times_{i=n}^{n+m} B_i \times_{i=n+m+1}^{\infty} \mathbb{R}^q$, where each $B_i \in \mathcal{B}^q$;
(ii) the complement A^c of any set A in $\mathcal{B}_n^{n+m}$;
(iii) the union $\bigcup_{i=1}^{\infty} A_i$ of any sequence $\{A_i\}$ in $\mathcal{B}_n^{n+m}$.

The σ-field $\mathcal{B}_n^{n+m}$ is the smallest σ-field of subsets of Ω with respect to which $Z_t(\omega)$, $t = n, \ldots, n+m$ are measurable. In other words, $\mathcal{B}_n^{n+m}$ is the smallest collection of events that allows us to express the probability of an event, say, $[Z_n < a_1, Z_{n+1} < a_2]$, in terms of the probability of an event in $\mathcal{B}_n^{n+m}$, say $[\omega : Z_n(\omega) < a_1, Z_{n+1}(\omega) < a_2]$. The definition of mixing is given in terms of the Borel fields generated by subsets of the history of a process extending infinitely far into both the past and future, $\{Z_t\}_{t=-\infty}^{\infty}$. For our purposes, we can think of Z_1 as representing the first observation available to us, so Z_t is unobservable for $t \leq 0$. In what follows, the fact that Z_t, $t \leq 0$ is unobservable does not matter. All that does matter is the behavior of Z_t, $t \leq 0$, if we could observe it.

DEFINITION 3.40: Let $\mathcal{B}_{-\infty}^{n} \equiv \sigma(\ldots, Z_n)$ be the smallest collection of subsets of Ω that contains the union of the σ-fields $\mathcal{B}_a^n$ as $a \to -\infty$; let $\mathcal{B}_{n+m}^{\infty} = \sigma(Z_{n+m}, \ldots)$ be the smallest collection of subsets of Ω that contains the union of the σ-fields $\mathcal{B}_{n+m}^{a}$ as $a \to \infty$.

Intuitively, we can think of $\mathcal{B}_{-\infty}^{n}$ as representing all the information contained in the past of the sequence $\{Z_t\}$ up to time n, whereas $\mathcal{B}_{n+m}^{\infty}$ represents all the information contained in the future of the sequence $\{Z_t\}$ from time $n+m$ on.

We now define two measures of dependence between σ-fields.

DEFINITION 3.41: Let $\mathcal{G}$ and $\mathcal{H}$ be σ-fields and define

$$\phi(\mathcal{G}, \mathcal{H}) \equiv \sup_{\{G \in \mathcal{G}, H \in \mathcal{H} : P(G) > 0\}} |P(H|G) - P(H)|,$$

$$\alpha(\mathcal{G}, \mathcal{H}) \equiv \sup_{\{G \in \mathcal{G}, H \in \mathcal{H}\}} |P(G \cap H) - P(G)P(H)|.$$

Intuitively, ϕ and α measure the dependence of the events in $\mathcal{H}$ on those in $\mathcal{G}$ in terms of how much the probability of the joint occurrence of an event in each σ-algebra differs from the product of the probabilities of each event occurring. The events in $\mathcal{G}$ and $\mathcal{H}$ are independent if and only if ϕ and α are zero. The function α provides an absolute measure of dependence and ϕ a relative measure of dependence

DEFINITION 3.42: For a sequence of random vectors $\{Z_t\}$, with $\mathcal{B}_{-\infty}^n$ and $\mathcal{B}_{n+m}^{\infty}$ as in Definition 3.40, define the *mixing coefficients* $\phi(m) \equiv \sup_n \phi(\mathcal{B}_{-\infty}^n, \mathcal{B}_{n+m}^{\infty})$ and $\alpha(m) \equiv \sup_n \alpha(\mathcal{B}_{-\infty}^n, \mathcal{B}_{n+m}^{\infty})$.

If, for the sequence $\{Z_t\}$, $\phi(m) \to 0$ as $m \to \infty$, $\{Z_t\}$ is called *ϕ-mixing*. If, for the sequence $\{Z_t\}$, $\alpha(m) \to 0$ as $m \to \infty$, $\{Z_t\}$ is called *α-mixing*.

The quantities $\phi(m)$ and $\alpha(m)$ measure how much dependence exists between events separated by at least m time periods. Hence, if $\phi(m) = 0$ or $\alpha(m) = 0$ for some m, events m periods apart are independent. By allowing $\phi(m)$ or $\alpha(m)$ to approach zero as $m \to \infty$, we allow consideration of situations in which events are independent asymptotically. In the probability literature, ϕ-mixing sequences are also called *uniform mixing* (see Iosifescu and Theodorescu [1969]), whereas α-mixing sequences are called *strong mixing* (see Rosenblatt [1956]). Because $\phi(m) \geq \alpha(m)$, ϕ-mixing implies α-mixing.

EXAMPLE 3.43: (i) Let $\{Z_t\}$ be a γ-independent sequence (i.e., Z_t is independent of $Z_{t-\tau}$ for all $\tau > \gamma$). Then $\phi(m) = \alpha(m) = 0$ for all $m > \gamma$. (ii) Let $\{Z_t\}$ be a nonstochastic sequence. Then it is an independent sequence, so $\phi(m) = \alpha(m) = 0$ for all $m > 0$. (iii) Let $Z_t = \rho Z_{t-1} + \epsilon_t$, $t = 1, \ldots, n$, where $|\rho| < 1$ and $\epsilon_t \sim$ i.i.d. $N(0, 1)$. (This model is called the *Gaussian AR(1) process.*) Then $\alpha(m) \to 0$ as $m \to \infty$, although $\phi(m) \not\to 0$ as $m \to \infty$ (Ibragimov and Linnik [1972, pp. 312–313]).

The concept of mixing has a meaningful physical interpretation. Imagine a dry martini initially poured so that 99% is gin and 1% is vermouth (placed in a layer at the top). The martini is steadily stirred by a swizzle stick, and we observe the proportions of gin and vermouth in any measurable set (i.e., volume of martini). If these proportions tend to 99 and 1% after many stirs, regardless of which volume we observe, then the process is mixing. In this example, the stochastic process corresponds to the position of a given particle at each point in time, which can be represented as a sequence of three-dimensional vectors $\{Z_t\}$.

The asymptotic independence notion of mixing is a stronger memory requirement than that of ergodicity, since, for a stationary sequence, mixing implies ergodicity, as the next result makes precise.

PROPOSITION 3.44: Let $\{Z_t\}$ be a stationary sequence. If $\alpha(m) \to 0$ as $m \to \infty$, then $\{Z_t\}$ is ergodic.

Proof: See Rosenblatt [1978].

Note that if $\phi(m) \to 0$ as $m \to \infty$, then $\alpha(m) \to 0$ as $m \to \infty$, so that ϕ-mixing processes are also ergodic. Ergodic processes are not necessarily mixing, however. For more on mixing and ergodicity, see Rosenblatt [1972 and 1978].

To state the law of large numbers for mixing sequences we use the following definition.

DEFINITION 3.45: Let r be a real number such that $1 \leq r \leq \infty$. (i) If $\phi(m) = O(m^{-\lambda})$ for $\lambda > r/(2r-1)$, then $\phi(m)$ is *of size* $r/(2r-1)$. (ii) If $r > 1$ and $\alpha(m) = O(m^{-\lambda})$ for $\lambda > r/(r-1)$, then $\alpha(m)$ is *of size* $r/(r-1)$.

This definition allows precise statements about the memory of a random sequence that we shall relate to moment conditions expressed in terms of r. As $r \to \infty$, the sequence exhibits more and more dependence, while as $r \to 1$, the sequence exhibits less dependence.

EXAMPLE 3.46: (i) Let $\{Z_t\}$ be independent $N(0, \sigma_t^2)$. Then $\{Z_t\}$ has $\phi(m)$ of size $r/(2r-1)$ for $r = 1$. (ii) Let Z_t be a Gaussian AR(1) process. It can be shown that $\{Z_t\}$ has $\alpha(m)$ of size $r/(r-1)$ for any $r > 1$, since $\alpha(m)$ decreases exponentially with m.

The result of this example extends to many finite autoregressive moving average (ARMA) processes. Under general conditions, finite ARMA processes have exponentially decaying memories.

Using these definitions we can state a law of large numbers, due to McLeish [1975], which applies to heterogeneous dependent sequences.

THEOREM 3.47 (*McLeish*): Let $\{Z_t\}$ be a scalar sequence with $\phi(m)$ of size $r/(2r-1)$ or $\alpha(m)$ of size $r/(r-1)$, $r > 1$, with finite means $\mu_t \equiv E(Z_t)$. If for some δ, $0 < \delta \leq r$, $\sum_{t=1}^{\infty} (E|Z_t - \mu_t|^{r+\delta}/t^{r+\delta})^{1/r} < \infty$, then $\bar{Z}_n - \bar{\mu}_n \xrightarrow{\text{a.s.}} 0$.

Proof: See McLeish [1975, Theorem 2.10].

This result generalizes the Markov law of large numbers, Theorem 3.7. (There we have $r = 1$.)

Using an argument analogous to that used in obtaining Corollary 3.9, we obtain the following corollary.

COROLLARY 3.48: Let $\{Z_t\}$ be a sequence with $\phi(m)$ of size $r/(2r-1)$ or $\alpha(m)$ of size $r/(r-1)$, $r > 1$, such that $E|Z_t|^{r+\delta} < \Delta < \infty$ for some $\delta > 0$, and all t. Then $\bar{Z}_n - \bar{\mu}_n \xrightarrow{a.s.} 0$.

Setting r arbitrarily close to unity yields a generalization of Corollary 3.9 that would apply to sequences with exponential memory decay. For sequences with longer memories, r is greater, and the moment restrictions increase accordingly. Here we have a clear trade-off between the amount of allowable dependence and the sufficient moment restrictions.

To apply this result, we use the following theorem.

THEOREM 3.49: Let g be a measurable function onto $\mathbb{R}^k$ and define $\mathcal{Y}_t \equiv g(Z_t, Z_{t+1}, \ldots, Z_{t+\tau})$, where τ is finite. If the sequence of $q \times 1$ vectors $\{Z_t\}$ is mixing such that $\phi(m)$ $(\alpha(m))$ is $O(m^{-\lambda})$ for some $\lambda > 0$, then $\{\mathcal{Y}_t\}$ is mixing such that $\phi_{\mathcal{Y}}(m)(\alpha_{\mathcal{Y}}(m))$ is $O(m^{-\lambda})$.

Proof: See White and Domowitz [1984, Lemma 2.1].

In other words, measurable functions of mixing processes are mixing and of the same size. Note that whereas functions of ergodic processes retained ergodicity for any τ, finite or infinite, mixing is guaranteed only for finite τ.

PROPOSITION 3.50: If $\{(\mathbf{Z}_t, \mathbf{X}_t, \boldsymbol{\epsilon}_t)'\}$ is a mixing sequence, then $\{\mathbf{X}_t'\mathbf{X}_t\}$, $\{\mathbf{X}_t'\boldsymbol{\epsilon}_t\}$, $\{\mathbf{Z}_t'\mathbf{X}_t\}$, $\{\mathbf{Z}_t'\boldsymbol{\epsilon}_t\}$, and $\{\mathbf{Z}_t'\mathbf{Z}_t\}$ are mixing sequences of the same size.

Proof: Immediate from Theorem 3.49 and Proposition 3.23.

Now we can generalize the results of Exercise 3.14 to allow for dependence as well as heterogeneity.

EXERCISE 3.51: Prove the following result. Suppose

(i) $\mathbf{y} = \mathbf{X}\boldsymbol{\beta}_o + \boldsymbol{\epsilon}$;
(ii) $\{(\mathbf{X}_t, \boldsymbol{\epsilon}_t)'\}$ is a mixing sequence with $\phi(m)$ of size $r/(2r-1)$, $r \geq 1$ or $\alpha(m)$ of size $r/(r-1)$, $r > 1$;
(iii) (a) $E(\mathbf{X}_t'\boldsymbol{\epsilon}_t) = \mathbf{0}$;

(b) $E|\mathbf{X}_{thi}\epsilon_{th}|^{r+\delta} < \Delta < \infty$ for some $\delta > 0$, $h = 1, \ldots, p$, $i = 1, \ldots, k$, and all t;

(iv) (a) $E|\mathbf{X}^2_{thi}|^{r+\delta} < \Delta < \infty$ for some $\delta > 0$ and all $h = 1, \ldots, p$, $i = 1, \ldots, k$ and all t;

(b) $\mathbf{M}_n \equiv E(\mathbf{X}'\mathbf{X}/n)$ is uniformly positive definite.

Then $\hat{\boldsymbol{\beta}}_n$ exists a.s. for all n sufficiently large, and $\hat{\boldsymbol{\beta}}_n \xrightarrow{a.s.} \boldsymbol{\beta}_o$.

From this result, we can obtain the result of Exercise 3.14 as a direct corollary by setting $r = 1$. Compared to our first consistency result, Theorem 3.5, we have relaxed the independence and identical distribution assumptions, but strengthened the moment requirements somewhat. Among the many different possibilities which this result allows, we can have lagged dependent variables and nonstochastic variables both appearing in the explanatory variables $\mathbf{X}_t$. The regression errors $\boldsymbol{\epsilon}_t$ may be heteroscedastic or may be serially correlated.

In fact, Exercise 3.51 is an extremely powerful result that appears applicable to a very wide range of situations faced by economists. For further discussion of linear models with mixing observations, see Domowitz [1983].

Applications of Exercise 3.51 often use the following result, which allows the interchange of expectation and infinite sums.

Proposition 3.52: Let $\{Z_t\}$ be a sequence of random variables such that $\Sigma_{t=1}^{\infty} E|Z_t| < \infty$. Then $\Sigma_{t=1}^{\infty} Z_t$ converges a.s. and $E(\Sigma_{t=1}^{\infty} Z_t) = \Sigma_{t=1}^{\infty} E(Z_t) < \infty$.

Proof: See Billingsley [1979, p. 181].

This result is useful in verifying the conditions of Exercise 3.51 for the following exercise.

Exercise 3.53: (i) State conditions that are sufficient to ensure the consistency of the OLS estimator for the model $\mathbf{y}_t = \boldsymbol{\alpha}\mathbf{y}_{t-1} + \boldsymbol{\beta}\mathbf{x}_t + \boldsymbol{\epsilon}_t$, where $\mathbf{y}_t$, $\mathbf{x}_t$, and $\boldsymbol{\epsilon}_t$ are scalars. *Hint:* The Minkowski inequality applies to infinite sums, that is, given $\{Z_t\}$ such that $\Sigma_{t=1}^{\infty} (E|Z_t|^p)^{1/p} < \infty$, then $E|\Sigma_{t=1}^{\infty} Z_t|^p \leq (\Sigma_{t=1}^{\infty} (E|Z_t|^p)^{1/p})^p$. (ii) Find a simple model to which Exercise 3.51 does not apply.

Conditions for the consistency of the IV estimator are given by the next result.

THEOREM 3.54: Suppose

(i) $\mathbf{y} = \mathbf{X}\boldsymbol{\beta}_o + \boldsymbol{\epsilon}$;
(ii) $\{(\mathbf{Z}_t, \mathbf{X}_t, \boldsymbol{\epsilon}_t)'\}$ is a mixing sequence with $\phi(m)$ of size $r/(2r-1)$, $r \geq 1$ or $\alpha(m)$ of size $r/(r-1)$, $r > 1$;
(iii) (a) $E(\mathbf{Z}_t'\boldsymbol{\epsilon}_t) = 0$;
(b) $E|\mathbf{Z}_{thi}\boldsymbol{\epsilon}_{th}|^{r+\delta} < \Delta < \infty$ for some $\delta > 0$ and all $h = 1, \ldots, p$, $i = 1, \ldots, l$, and t;
(iv) (a) $E|\mathbf{Z}_{thi}\mathbf{X}_{thj}|^{r+\delta} < \Delta < \infty$ for some $\delta > 0$ and all $h = 1, \ldots, p$, $i = 1, \ldots, l$, $j = 1, \ldots, k$, and t;
(b) $\mathbf{Q}_n \equiv E(\mathbf{Z}'\mathbf{X}/n)$ has uniformly full column rank;
(c) $\hat{\mathbf{P}}_n - \mathbf{P}_n \xrightarrow{a.s.} \mathbf{0}$, where $\{\mathbf{P}_n\}$ is $O(1)$ and uniformly positive definite.

Then $\tilde{\boldsymbol{\beta}}_n$ exists a.s. for all n sufficiently large, and $\tilde{\boldsymbol{\beta}}_n \xrightarrow{a.s.} \boldsymbol{\beta}_o$.

Proof: By Proposition 3.50, $\{\mathbf{Z}_t'\boldsymbol{\epsilon}_t\}$ and $\{\mathbf{Z}_t'\mathbf{X}_t\}$ are mixing sequences with elements satisfying the conditions of Corollary 3.48 (given (iiib) and (iva)). It follows from Corollary 3.48 that $\mathbf{Z}'\boldsymbol{\epsilon}/n \xrightarrow{a.s.} \mathbf{0}$ and $\mathbf{Z}'\mathbf{X}/n - \mathbf{Q}_n \xrightarrow{a.s.} \mathbf{0}$, where $\mathbf{Q}_n$ is $O(1)$, given (iva) as a consequence of Jensen's inequality. Hence the conditions of Exercise 2.20 are satisfied and the results follow.

Although mixing is an appealing dependence concept, it shares with ergodicity the property that it can be somewhat difficult to verify theoretically and is impossible to verify empirically. An alternative dependence concept that is easier to verify theoretically is a form of asymptotic noncorrelation.

DEFINITION 3.55: The scalar sequence $\{Z_t\}$ has *asymptotically uncorrelated* elements (or is *asymptotically uncorrelated*) if there exist constants $\{\rho_\tau, \tau \geq 0\}$ such that $0 \leq \rho_\tau \leq 1$, $\Sigma_{\tau=0}^{\infty} \rho_\tau < \infty$ and $\text{cov}(Z_t, Z_{t+\tau}) \leq \rho_\tau (\text{var } Z_t \text{ var } Z_{t+\tau})^{1/2}$ for all $\tau > 0$, where $\text{var } Z_t < \infty$ for all t.

Note that ρ_τ is only an upper bound on the correlation between Z_t and $Z_{t+\tau}$ and that actual correlation may depend on t. Further, only positive correlation matters, so that if Z_t and $Z_{t+\tau}$ are negatively correlated, we can set $\rho_\tau = 0$. Also note that for $\Sigma_{\tau=0}^{\infty} \rho_\tau < \infty$, it is necessary that $\rho_\tau \to 0$ as $\tau \to \infty$, and it is sufficient that for all τ sufficiently large, $\rho_\tau < \tau^{-1-\delta}$ for some $\delta > 0$.

EXAMPLE 3.56: Let $Z_t = \rho Z_{t-1} + \epsilon_t$, where ϵ_t is i.i.d., $E(\epsilon_t) = 0$, var $\epsilon_t = \sigma_\infty^2$, $E(Z_{t-1}\epsilon_t) = 0$. Then $\text{corr}(Z_t, Z_{t+\tau}) = \rho^\tau$. If $0 \leq \rho < 1$, $\Sigma_{\tau=0}^\infty \rho^\tau = 1/(1-\rho) < \infty$, so the sequence $\{Z_t\}$ is asymptotically uncorrelated.

If a sequence has constant variance and has covariances that depend only on the time lag between Z_t and $Z_{t+\tau}$, the sequence is said to be *covariance stationary.* (This is implied by stationarity but is weaker because a sequence can be covariance stationary without being stationary.) Verifying that a covariance stationary sequence has asymptotically uncorrelated elements is straightforward when the process has a finite ARMA representation (see Granger and Newbold [1977, Ch. 1]). In this case, ρ_τ can be determined from well-known formulas (see, e.g., Granger and Newbold [1977, Ch.1]) and the condition $\Sigma_{\tau=0}^\infty \rho_\tau < \infty$ can be directly evaluated. Thus covariance stationary sequences as well as stationary ergodic sequences can often be shown to be asymptotically uncorrelated, although an asymptotically uncorrelated sequence need not be stationary and ergodic or covariance stationary. Under general conditions on the size of $\phi(m)$ or $\alpha(m)$, mixing processes can be shown to be asymptotically uncorrelated. Asymptotically uncorrelated sequences need not be mixing, however.

A law of large numbers for asymptotically uncorrelated sequences is the following.

THEOREM 3.57: Let $\{Z_t\}$ be a scalar sequence with asymptotically uncorrelated elements with means $\mu_t \equiv E(Z_t)$ and $\sigma_t^2 \equiv \text{var } Z_t < \Delta < \infty$. Then $\bar{Z}_n - \bar{\mu}_n \xrightarrow{\text{a. s.}} 0$.

Proof: Immediate from Stout [1974, Theorem 3.7.2].

Compared with Corollary 3.48, we have relaxed the dependence restriction from asymptotic independence (mixing) to asymptotic uncorrelation, but we have altered the moment requirements from restrictions on moments of order $r + \delta$ ($r \geq 1$, $\delta > 0$) to second moments. Typically, this is a strengthening of the moment restrictions.

Since taking functions of random variables alters their correlation properties, there is no simple analog of Proposition 3.2, Theorem 3.35, or Theorem 3.49. To obtain consistency results for the OLS or IV estimators, one must directly assume that *all* the appropriate sequences are asymptotically uncorrelated so that the a.s. convergence assumed in Theorem 2.18 or Exercise 2.20 holds. Since asymptotically uncorrelated sequences will not play an important role in the rest of this book, we omit stating and proving results for such sequences.

III.5 Martingale Difference Sequences

In all of the consistency results obtained so far, there has been the explicit requirement that either $E(\mathbf{X}_t'\boldsymbol{\epsilon}_t)=\mathbf{0}$ or $E(\mathbf{Z}_t'\boldsymbol{\epsilon}_t)=\mathbf{0}$. Economic theory must play a crucial role in justifying this assumption. In fact, it often occurs that economic theory is used to justify the stronger assumption that $E(\boldsymbol{\epsilon}_t|\mathbf{X}_t)=\mathbf{0}$ or $E(\boldsymbol{\epsilon}_t|\mathbf{Z}_t)=\mathbf{0}$, which then implies $E(\mathbf{X}_t'\boldsymbol{\epsilon}_t)=\mathbf{0}$ or $E(\mathbf{Z}_t'\boldsymbol{\epsilon}_t)=\mathbf{0}$. In particular, this occurs when the regression function $\mathbf{X}_t\boldsymbol{\beta}_o$ is viewed as the value of $\mathbf{y}_t$ we expect to observe when $\mathbf{X}_t$ occurs. In other words, when $\mathbf{X}_t\boldsymbol{\beta}_o$, is the conditional expectation of $\mathbf{y}_t$ given $\mathbf{X}_t$, i.e., $E(\mathbf{y}_t|\mathbf{X}_t)= \mathbf{X}_t\boldsymbol{\beta}_o$. Then we define $\boldsymbol{\epsilon}_t \equiv \mathbf{y}_t - E(\mathbf{y}_t|\mathbf{X}_t)=\mathbf{y}_t - \mathbf{X}_t\boldsymbol{\beta}_o$. Using the algebra of conditional expectations given below, it is straight-forward to show that $E(\boldsymbol{\epsilon}_t|\mathbf{X}_t)=\mathbf{0}$.

One of the more powerful economic theories (powerful in the sense of imposing a great deal of structure on the resulting regression model) is the theory of rational expectations. Often this theory cannot only be used to justify the assumption that $E(\boldsymbol{\epsilon}_t|\mathbf{X}_t)=\mathbf{0}$ but further that $E(\boldsymbol{\epsilon}_t|\mathbf{X}_t, \mathbf{X}_{t-1}, \ldots ; \boldsymbol{\epsilon}_{t-1}, \boldsymbol{\epsilon}_{t-2}, \ldots)=\mathbf{0}$, i.e., that the conditional expectation of $\boldsymbol{\epsilon}_t$, given the entire past history of the errors $\boldsymbol{\epsilon}_t$ and the current and past values of the explanatory variables $\mathbf{X}_t$, is zero. This assumption allows us to apply laws of large numbers for martingale difference sequences, which are convenient and powerful.

To define what martingale difference sequences are and to state the associated results, we need to provide a more complete background on the properties of conditional expectations, which we draw from Doob [1953].

So far we have relied on the reader's intuitive understanding of what a conditional expectation is. A more precise definition is based on the following notion.

DEFINITION 3.58: Let $\mathcal{G}$ be a σ-field of sets in Ω, and let $\mathcal{G}'$ be the σ-field of sets in Ω that are either sets of $\mathcal{G}$ or that have the form $G \cup F$ where $G \in \mathcal{G}$ and F is a subset of a $\mathcal{G}$ set which has probability zero. We call $\mathcal{G}'$ the *completion* of $\mathcal{G}$.

DEFINITION 3.59: The *conditional expectation of a random variable* $\mathcal{Y}$ *given* $\mathcal{G}$ is defined as any function $E(\mathcal{Y}|\mathcal{G})$ from Ω to $\mathbb{R}^1$ that is measurable with respect to $\mathcal{G}'$, that has $\mathrm{E}(|\mathrm{E}(\mathcal{Y}|\mathcal{G})|) < \infty$, and that satisfies the equation

$$E(1_{[G]}E(\mathcal{Y}|\mathcal{G})) = E(1_{[G]}\mathcal{Y})$$

for all sets G in $\mathcal{G}$, where $1_{[G]}$ is the indicator function equal to unity on the set G and zero elsewhere.

Because $E(\mathcal{Y}|\mathcal{G})$ is a measurable function from Ω to $\mathbb{R}^1$, it is a random variable. As Doob [1953, p. 18] notes, this definition actually defines an entire class of random variables each of which satisfies the above definition, because any random variable with probability one equal to any function $E(\mathcal{Y}|\mathcal{G})$ satisfying this definition also satisfies this definition. Note that the conditional expectation has been defined as a function measurable with respect to $\mathcal{G}'$. This is done to rule out certain pathological possibilities that could otherwise arise. However, if a random variable is measurable with respect to $\mathcal{G}'$, it is equal with probability one to a random variable measurable with respect to $\mathcal{G}$ (see Doob [1953, p. 605]) so that there is a version of $E(\mathcal{Y}|\mathcal{G})$ measurable with respect to $\mathcal{G}$. We can think of this version as the one being utilized in any given formula, because generally any member of the class of random variables specified by the definition can be used in any expression involving a conditional expectation.

To put the conditional expectation in more familiar terms, we relate this definition to the expectation of $\mathcal{Y}_t$ conditional on other random variables Z_t, $t = a, \ldots, b$, as follows.

DEFINITION 3.60: Let $\mathcal{Y}_t$ be a random variable such that $E(|\mathcal{Y}_t|) < \infty$ and let $\mathcal{B}_a^b = \sigma(Z_a, Z_{a+1}, \ldots, Z_b)$ be the σ-algebra generated by the random vectors Z_t, $t = a, \ldots, b$. Then the *conditional expectation of* $\mathcal{Y}_t$ *given* Z_t, $t = a, \ldots, b$, is defined as

$$E(\mathcal{Y}_t|Z_a, \ldots, Z_b) \equiv E(\mathcal{Y}_t|\mathcal{B}_a^b).$$

If we let $E(\mathcal{Y}_t|\mathcal{B}_a^b)$ be measurable with respect to $\mathcal{B}_a^b$, the conditional expectation can be expressed as a function of Z_t, $t = a, \ldots, b$, as the following result shows.

PROPOSITION 3.61: Let $E(\mathcal{Y}_t|Z_a, \ldots, Z_b)$ be measurable with respect to $\mathcal{B}_a^b$. Then there exists a function $g(Z_a, \ldots, Z_b)$ measurable with respect to $\mathcal{B}_a^b$ such that

$$E(\mathcal{Y}_t|Z_a, \ldots, Z_b) = g(Z_a, \ldots, Z_b).$$

Proof: Immediate from Doob [1953, Theorem 1.5, p. 603].

EXAMPLE 3.62: Let $\mathcal{Y}$ and Z be jointly normal with $E(\mathcal{Y}) = E(Z) = 0$, var $\mathcal{Y} = \sigma^2_{\mathcal{Y}}$, var $Z = \sigma^2_Z$, cov$(\mathcal{Y}, Z) = \sigma_{\mathcal{Y}Z}$. Then

$$E(\mathcal{Y}|Z) = (\sigma_{\mathcal{Y}Z}/\sigma^2_Z)Z.$$

The role of economic theory can now be interpreted as specifying a particular form for the function g in Proposition 3.61, although, as we can see from Example 3.62, the g function is in fact a direct consequence of the form of the joint distribution of the random variables involved. For an economic theory to be completely legitimate, the g function specified by that economic theory must be identical to that implied by the joint distribution of the random variables; otherwise the economic theory provides only an approximation to the statistical relationship between the random variables of the model.

We now state some useful properties of conditional expectations.

PROPOSITION 3.63: Let $\mathcal{G}'$ and $\mathcal{H}'$ be the completions of σ-fields $\mathcal{G}$ and $\mathcal{H}$ and suppose $\mathcal{G}' \subset \mathcal{H}'$ and that some (and therefore every) version of $E(\mathcal{Y}|\mathcal{H})$ is measurable with respect to $\mathcal{G}'$. Then

$$E(\mathcal{Y}|\mathcal{H}) = E(\mathcal{Y}|\mathcal{G}),$$

with probability one.

Proof: See Doob [1953, p. 21].

In other words, conditional expectations with respect to two different σ-fields, one contained in the other, coincide *provided* that the expectation conditioned on the larger σ-field is measurable with respect to the *smaller* σ-field. Otherwise, no necessary relation holds between the two conditional expectations.

EXAMPLE 3.64: Suppose $E(\mathcal{Y}_t|\mathcal{H}_{t-1}) = 0$, where $\mathcal{H}_{t-1} = \sigma(\ldots, \mathcal{Y}_{t-2}, \mathcal{Y}_{t-1})$. Then $E(\mathcal{Y}_t|\mathcal{Y}_{t-1}) = 0$, since $E(\mathcal{Y}_t|\mathcal{Y}_{t-1}) = E(\mathcal{Y}_t|\mathcal{G}_{t-1})$, where $\mathcal{G}_{t-1} = \sigma(\mathcal{Y}_{t-1})$ satisfies $\mathcal{G}'_{t-1} \subset \mathcal{H}'_{t-1}$ and $E(\mathcal{Y}_t|\mathcal{H}_{t-1}) = 0$ is measurable with respect to $\mathcal{G}'_{t-1}$.

PROPOSITION 3.65: If $\mathcal{Y}$ is a random variable and Z is a random variable measurable with respect to $\mathcal{G}$ such that $E|\mathcal{Y}| < \infty$ and $E|Z\mathcal{Y}| < \infty$, then with probability one

$$E(Z\mathcal{Y}|\mathcal{G}) = ZE(\mathcal{Y}|\mathcal{G})$$

and

$$E([\mathcal{Y} - E(\mathcal{Y}|\mathcal{G})]Z) = 0.$$

Proof: See Doob [1953, p. 22].

EXAMPLE 3.66: Let $\mathcal{G} = \sigma(\mathbf{X}_t)$. Then $E(\mathbf{X}_t'\mathbf{y}_t|\mathbf{X}_t) = \mathbf{X}_t'E(\mathbf{y}_t|\mathbf{X}_t)$. Define $\boldsymbol{\epsilon}_t \equiv \mathbf{y}_t - E(\mathbf{y}_t|\mathbf{X}_t)$. Then $E(\mathbf{X}_t'\boldsymbol{\epsilon}_t) = E(\mathbf{X}_t'[\mathbf{y}_t - E(\mathbf{y}_t|\mathbf{X}_t)]) = \mathbf{0}$.

If we set $E(\mathbf{y}_t|\mathbf{X}_t) = \mathbf{X}_t\beta_o$, the result of this example justifies the orthogonality condition for the OLS estimator, $E(\mathbf{X}_t'\boldsymbol{\epsilon}_t) = \mathbf{0}$.

PROPOSITION 3.67 (*Linearity*): Let $a_1, \ldots, a_k$ be finite constants and suppose $\mathcal{Y}_1, \ldots, \mathcal{Y}_k$ are random variables such that $E(\sum_{j=1}^k a_j\mathcal{Y}_j) < \infty$. Then

$$E\left(\sum_{j=1}^{k} a_j\mathcal{Y}_j|\mathcal{G}\right) = \sum_{j=1}^{k} a_jE(\mathcal{Y}_j|\mathcal{G}).$$

Proof: See Doob [1953, p. 23].

A version of Jensen's inequality also holds for conditional expectations.

PROPOSITION 3.68 (*Conditional Jensen's inequality*): Let g: $\mathbb{R}^1 \to \mathbb{R}^1$ be a convex function on an interval $B \subset \mathbb{R}^1$ and let $\mathcal{Y}$ be a random variable such that $P[\mathcal{Y} \in B] = 1$. If $E|\mathcal{Y}| < \infty$ and $E|g(\mathcal{Y})| < \infty$, then

$$g[E(\mathcal{Y}|\mathcal{G})] \leq E(g(\mathcal{Y})|\mathcal{G})$$

for any Borel field $\mathcal{G}$. If g is concave, then

$$g[E(\mathcal{Y}|\mathcal{G})] \geq E(g(\mathcal{Y})|\mathcal{G}).$$

Proof: See Doob [1953, p. 33].

EXAMPLE 3.69: Let $g(y) = |y|$. It follows from the conditional Jensen's inequality that $|E(\mathcal{Y}|\mathcal{G})| \leq E(|\mathcal{Y}||\mathcal{G})$.

One of the most useful properties of the conditional expectation is given by the law of iterated expectations.

PROPOSITION 3.70 (*Law of iterated expectations*): Let $\mathcal{G}$ be a σ-field of sets in Ω. Then

$$E[E(\mathcal{Y}|\mathcal{G})] = E(\mathcal{Y}).$$

Proof: Set $G = \Omega$ in Definition 3.59.

EXAMPLE 3.71: Suppose $E(\boldsymbol{\epsilon}_t|\mathbf{X}_t) = \mathbf{0}$. Then by Proposition 3.70, $E(\boldsymbol{\epsilon}_t) = E(E(\boldsymbol{\epsilon}_t|\mathbf{X}_t)) = \mathbf{0}$.

A more general result is the following.

PROPOSITION 3.72 (*Law of iterated expectations*): Let $\mathcal{G}$ and $\mathcal{H}$ be σ-fields of sets in Ω with $\mathcal{H} \subset \mathcal{G}$, and suppose $E(|\mathcal{Y}|) < \infty$. Then

$$E[E(\mathcal{Y}|\mathcal{G})|\mathcal{H}] = E(\mathcal{Y}|\mathcal{H}).$$

Proof: See Doob [1953, p. 37].

Proposition 3.70 is the special case of Proposition 3.72 in which $\mathcal{H}$ is set equal to the trivial σ-field $\{\emptyset, \Omega\}$.

With the law of iterated expectations available, it is straightforward to show that the conditional expectation has an optimal prediction property, in the sense that in predicting a random variable $\mathcal{Y}$ the prediction mean squared error of the conditional expectation of $\mathcal{Y}$ is smaller than that of any other predictor of $\mathcal{Y}$ measurable with respect to the same σ-field.

THEOREM 3.73: Let $\mathcal{Y}$ be a random variable with $E(\mathcal{Y}^2) < \infty$ and let $\hat{\mathcal{Y}} \equiv E(\mathcal{Y}|\mathcal{G})$ be $\mathcal{G}$-measurable. Then for any other $\mathcal{G}$-measurable random variable $\tilde{\mathcal{Y}}$, $E((\mathcal{Y} - \hat{\mathcal{Y}})^2) \leq E((\mathcal{Y} - \tilde{\mathcal{Y}})^2)$.

Proof: Adding and subtracting $\hat{\mathcal{Y}}$ in $(\mathcal{Y} - \tilde{\mathcal{Y}})^2$ gives

$$\begin{aligned} E((\mathcal{Y} - \tilde{\mathcal{Y}})^2) &= E((\mathcal{Y} - \hat{\mathcal{Y}} + \hat{\mathcal{Y}} - \tilde{\mathcal{Y}})^2) \\ &= E((\mathcal{Y} - \hat{\mathcal{Y}})^2) + 2E((\mathcal{Y} - \hat{\mathcal{Y}})(\hat{\mathcal{Y}} - \tilde{\mathcal{Y}})) \\ &\quad + E((\hat{\mathcal{Y}} - \tilde{\mathcal{Y}})^2). \end{aligned}$$

By the law of iterated expectations and Proposition 3.65,

$$\begin{aligned} E((\mathcal{Y} - \hat{\mathcal{Y}})(\hat{\mathcal{Y}} - \tilde{\mathcal{Y}})) &= E[E((\mathcal{Y} - \hat{\mathcal{Y}})(\hat{\mathcal{Y}} - \tilde{\mathcal{Y}})|\mathcal{G})] \\ &= E[E(\mathcal{Y} - \hat{\mathcal{Y}}|\mathcal{G})(\hat{\mathcal{Y}} - \tilde{\mathcal{Y}})]. \end{aligned}$$

But $E(\mathcal{Y} - \hat{\mathcal{Y}}|\mathcal{G}) = 0$, so $E((\mathcal{Y} - \hat{\mathcal{Y}})(\hat{\mathcal{Y}} - \tilde{\mathcal{Y}})) = 0$ and

$$E((\mathcal{Y} - \tilde{\mathcal{Y}})^2) = E((\mathcal{Y} - \hat{\mathcal{Y}})^2) + E((\hat{\mathcal{Y}} - \tilde{\mathcal{Y}})^2),$$

and the result follows.

This result provides us with another interpretation for the conditional expectation. The conditional expectation of $\mathcal{Y}$ given $\mathcal{G}$ gives the minimum mean squared error prediction of $\mathcal{Y}$ based on a specified information set (σ-field) $\mathcal{G}$.

With the next definition (from Stout [1974, p. 30]) we will have sufficient background to define the concept of a martingale difference sequence.

DEFINITION 3.74: Let $\{\mathcal{Y}_t\}$ be a sequence of random scalars, and let $\{\mathfrak{F}_t\}$ be a sequence of σ-fields $\mathfrak{F}_t \subset \mathfrak{F}$ such that $\mathfrak{F}_{t-1} \subset \mathfrak{F}_t$ for all t (i.e., $\{\mathfrak{F}_t\}$ is an *increasing* sequence of σ-fields). If $\mathcal{Y}_t$ is measurable with respect to $\mathfrak{F}_t$, then $\{\mathfrak{F}_t\}$ is said to be *adapted* to the sequence $\{\mathcal{Y}_t\}$ and $\{\mathcal{Y}_t, \mathfrak{F}_t\}$ is called an *adapted stochastic sequence.*

One way of generating an adapted stochastic sequence is to let $\mathfrak{F}_t$ be the σ-field generated by current and past $\mathcal{Y}_t$, i.e., $\mathfrak{F}_t = \sigma(\ldots, \mathcal{Y}_{t-1}, \mathcal{Y}_t)$. Then $\{\mathfrak{F}_t\}$ is increasing and $\mathcal{Y}_t$ is always measurable with respect to $\mathfrak{F}_t$. However, $\mathfrak{F}_t$ can contain more than just the present and past of $\mathcal{Y}_t$; it can also contain the present and past of other random variables as well. For example, let $\mathcal{Y}_t = Z_{t1}$, where $Z_t' = (Z_{t1}, \ldots, Z_{tq})$, and let $\mathfrak{F}_t = \sigma(\ldots, Z_{t-1}, Z_t)$. Then $\mathfrak{F}_t$ is again increasing and $\mathcal{Y}_t$ is again measurable with respect to $\mathfrak{F}_t$, so $\{\mathcal{Y}_t, \mathfrak{F}_t\}$ is an adapted stochastic sequence. This is the situation most relevant to our purposes.

DEFINITION 3.75: Let $\{\mathcal{Y}_t, \mathfrak{F}_t\}$ be an adapted stochastic sequence. Then $\{\mathcal{Y}_t, \mathfrak{F}_t\}$ is a *martingale difference sequence* if and only if

$$E(\mathcal{Y}_t|\mathfrak{F}_{t-1}) = 0 \qquad \text{for all} \quad t \geq 2.$$

EXAMPLE 3.76: (i) Let $\{\mathcal{Y}_t\}$ be a sequence of i.i.d. random variables with $E(\mathcal{Y}_t) = 0$, and let $\mathfrak{F}_t = \sigma(\ldots, \mathcal{Y}_{t-1}, \mathcal{Y}_t)$. Then $\{\mathcal{Y}_t, \mathfrak{F}_t\}$ is a martingale difference sequence. (ii) (*The Levy device*) Let $\{\mathcal{Y}_t, \mathfrak{F}_t\}$ be any adapted stochastic sequence such that $E|\mathcal{Y}_t| < \infty$ for all t. Then

$$\{\mathcal{Y}_t - E(\mathcal{Y}_t|\mathfrak{F}_{t-1}), \mathfrak{F}_t\}$$

is a martingale difference sequence because $\mathcal{Y}_t - E(\mathcal{Y}_t|\mathfrak{F}_{t-1})$ is measurable with respect to $\mathfrak{F}_t$ and, by linearity,

$$E[\mathcal{Y}_t - E(\mathcal{Y}_t|\mathfrak{F}_{t-1})|\mathfrak{F}_{t-1}] = E(\mathcal{Y}_t|\mathfrak{F}_{t-1}) - E(\mathcal{Y}_t|\mathfrak{F}_{t-1}) = 0.$$

The device of Example 3.76 (ii) is useful in certain circumstances because it reduces the study of the behavior of an arbitrary sequence of random variables to the study of the behavior of a martingale difference sequence and a sequence of conditional expectations (Stout [1974, p. 33]).

The martingale difference assumption is often justified in economics by the efficient markets theory or rational expectations theory, e.g., Samuelson [1965]. In these theories the random variable $\mathcal{Y}_t$ is the price change of an asset or a commodity traded in a competitive market and $\mathfrak{F}_t$ is the σ-field generated by all current and past information available to market participants, $\mathfrak{F}_t = \sigma(\ldots, \mathcal{Z}_{t-1}, \mathcal{Z}_t)$, where $\mathcal{Z}_t$ is a finite-dimensional vector of observable information, including information on $\mathcal{Y}_t$. A zero profit condition then ensures that $E(\mathcal{Y}_t|\mathfrak{F}_{t-1}) = 0$. Note that if $\mathcal{G}_t = \sigma(\ldots, \mathcal{Y}_{t-1}, \mathcal{Y}_t)$, then $\{\mathcal{Y}_t, \mathcal{G}_t\}$ is also an adapted stochastic sequence, and because $\mathcal{G}_t \subset \mathfrak{F}_t$, it follows from Proposition 3.72 that

$$E(\mathcal{Y}_t|\mathcal{G}_{t-1}) = E[E(\mathcal{Y}_t|\mathfrak{F}_{t-1})|\mathcal{G}_{t-1}] = 0,$$

so $\{\mathcal{Y}_t, \mathcal{G}_t\}$ is also a martingale difference sequence.

The martingale difference assumption often arises in a regression context in the following way. Suppose we have observations on a scalar $\mathbf{y}_t$ (set $p = 1$ for now) that we are interested in explaining or forecasting on the basis of variables $\mathbf{Z}_t$ as well as on the basis of the past values of $\mathbf{y}_t$. Let $\mathfrak{F}_{t-1}$ be the σ-field containing the information used to explain or forecast $\mathbf{y}_t$, i.e., $\mathfrak{F}_{t-1} = \sigma(\ldots (\mathbf{Z}_{t-1}, \mathbf{y}_{t-2})', (\mathbf{Z}_t, \mathbf{y}_{t-1})')$. Then by Proposition 3.61,

$$E(\mathbf{y}_t|\mathfrak{F}_{t-1}) = g(\ldots, (\mathbf{Z}_{t-1}, \mathbf{y}_{t-2})', (\mathbf{Z}_t, \mathbf{y}_{t-1})'),$$

where g is some function of current and past values of $\mathbf{Z}_t$ and past values of $\mathbf{y}_t$. Let $\mathbf{X}_t$ contain a finite number of current and lagged values of $(\mathbf{Z}_t, \mathbf{y}_{t-1})$, e.g., $\mathbf{X}_t' = ((\mathbf{Z}_{t-\tau}, \mathbf{y}_{t-\tau-1})', \ldots, (\mathbf{Z}_t, \mathbf{y}_{t-1})')$ for some $\tau < \infty$. Economic theory is then often used in an attempt to justify the assumption that for some $\boldsymbol{\beta}_o < \infty$,

$$g(\ldots, (\mathbf{Z}_{t-1}, \mathbf{y}_{t-2})', (\mathbf{Z}_t, \mathbf{y}_{t-1})') = \mathbf{X}_t\boldsymbol{\beta}_o.$$

If this is legitimate, we then have

$$E(\mathbf{y}_t|\mathfrak{F}_{t-1}) = \mathbf{X}_t\boldsymbol{\beta}_o.$$

Note that by definition, $\mathbf{y}_t$ is measurable with respect to $\mathfrak{F}_t$, so that $\{\mathbf{y}_t, \mathfrak{F}_t\}$ is an adapted stochastic sequence. Hence, by Levy's device, $\{\mathbf{y}_t - E(\mathbf{y}_t|\mathfrak{F}_{t-1}), \mathfrak{F}_t\}$ is a martingale difference sequence. If we let

$$\boldsymbol{\epsilon}_t = \mathbf{y}_t - \mathbf{X}_t\boldsymbol{\beta}_o$$

and it is true that $E(\mathbf{y}_t|\mathfrak{F}_{t-1}) = \mathbf{X}_t\boldsymbol{\beta}_o$, then $\boldsymbol{\epsilon}_t = \mathbf{y}_t - E(\mathbf{y}_t|\mathfrak{F}_{t-1})$, so $\{\boldsymbol{\epsilon}_t, \mathfrak{F}_t\}$ is a martingale difference sequence. Of direct importance for least squares estimation is the fact that $\{\mathfrak{F}_t\}$ is also adapted to each sequence of cross products between regressors and errors $\{\mathbf{X}_{ti}\epsilon_t\}$, $i = 1, \ldots, k$. It is then easily shown that $\{\mathbf{X}_{ti}\epsilon_t, \mathfrak{F}_t\}$ is also a martingale difference sequence, since by Proposition 3.65

$$E(\mathbf{X}_{ti}\epsilon_t|\mathfrak{F}_{t-1}) = \mathbf{X}_{ti}E(\epsilon_t|\mathfrak{F}_{t-1}) = \mathbf{0}.$$

A law of large numbers for martingale difference sequences is the following theorem.

THEOREM 3.77 (*Chow*): Let $\{Z_t, \mathfrak{F}_t\}$ be a martingale difference sequence. If for some $r \geq 1$, $\sum_{t=1}^{\infty} (E|Z_t|^{2r})/t^{1+r} < \infty$, then $\bar{Z}_n \xrightarrow{\text{a. s.}} 0$.

Proof: See Stout [1974, p. 154–155].

Note the similarity of the present result to the Markov law of large numbers, Theorem 3.7. There the stronger assumption of independence replaces the martingale difference assumption, whereas the required moment conditions are weaker with independence than they are here. A corollary analogous to Corollary 3.9 also holds.

EXERCISE 3.78: Prove the following. Let $\{Z_t, \mathfrak{F}_t\}$ be a martingale difference sequence such that $E|Z_t|^{2r} < \Delta < \infty$ for some $r \geq 1$, and all t. Then $\bar{Z}_n \xrightarrow{\text{a. s.}} 0$.

Using this result and the law of large numbers for mixing sequences, we can state the following consistency result for the OLS estimator.

THEOREM 3.79: Suppose

(i) $\mathbf{y} = \mathbf{X}\boldsymbol{\beta}_o + \boldsymbol{\epsilon}$;

(ii) $\{\mathbf{X}_t'\}$ is a sequence of mixing random variables with $\phi(m)$ of size $r/(2r-1)$, $r \geq 1$, or $\alpha(m)$ of size $r/(r-1)$, $r > 1$;

(iii) (a) $\mathrm{E}(\mathbf{X}_{thi}\epsilon_{th}|\mathfrak{F}_{t-1}) = 0$, where $\{\mathfrak{F}_t\}$ is adapted to $\{\mathbf{X}_{thi}\epsilon_{th}\}$, $h = 1, \ldots, p$, $i = 1, \ldots, k$;

(b) $E|\mathbf{X}_{thi}\epsilon_{th}|^{2r} < \Delta < \infty$ for some $r > 1$ and all $h = 1, \ldots, p$, $i = 1, \ldots, k$, and t;

(iv) (a) $E|\mathbf{X}_{thi}^2|^{r+\delta} < \Delta < \infty$ for some $\delta > 0$ and all $h = 1, \ldots, p$, $i = 1, \ldots, k$, and t;

(b) $\mathbf{M}_n \equiv E(\mathbf{X}'\mathbf{X}/n)$ is uniformly positive definite.

Then $\hat{\boldsymbol{\beta}}_n$ exists a.s. for all n sufficiently large, and $\hat{\boldsymbol{\beta}}_n \xrightarrow{\text{a. s.}} \boldsymbol{\beta}_0$.

Proof: To verify that the conditions of Theorem 2.18 hold, we note first that $\mathbf{X}'\boldsymbol{\epsilon}/n = \Sigma_{h=1}^{p} \mathbf{X}_h'\boldsymbol{\epsilon}_h/n$. where $\mathbf{X}_h$ is the $n \times k$ matrix with rows $\mathbf{X}_{th}$ and $\boldsymbol{\epsilon}_h$ is the $n \times 1$ vector with elements ϵ_{th}. By assumption (iiia), $\{\mathbf{X}_{thi}\epsilon_{th}, \mathfrak{F}_t\}$ is a Martingale difference sequence. Because the moment conditions of Exercise 3.78 are satisfied by (iiib), we have $n^{-1} \Sigma_{t=1}^{n} \mathbf{X}_{thi}\epsilon_{th} \xrightarrow{\text{a.s.}} 0, h = 1, \ldots, p, i = 1, \ldots, k$, so $\mathbf{X}'\boldsymbol{\epsilon}/n \xrightarrow{\text{a.s.}} \mathbf{0}$ by Proposition 2.11.

Next, Proposition 3.50 ensures that $\{\mathbf{X}_t'\mathbf{X}_t\}$ is a mixing sequence (given (ii)) that satisfies the conditions of Corollary 3.48 (given (iva)). It follows that $\mathbf{X}'\mathbf{X}/n - \mathbf{M}_n \xrightarrow{\text{a.s.}} \mathbf{0}$, and $\mathbf{M}_n$ is $O(1)$ (given (iva)) by Jensen's inequality. Hence the conditions of Theorem 2.18 are satisfied and the result follows.

Note that the conditions placed on $\mathbf{X}_t$ by (ii) and (iva) ensure that $\mathbf{X}'\mathbf{X}/n - \mathbf{M}_n \xrightarrow{\text{a.s.}} \mathbf{0}$ and that these conditions can be replaced by any other conditions that ensure the same conclusion.

A result for the IV estimator can be obtained analogously.

EXERCISE 3.80: Prove the following result. Given

(i) $\mathbf{y} = \mathbf{X}\boldsymbol{\beta}_o + \boldsymbol{\epsilon}$;

(ii) $\{(\mathbf{Z}_t, \mathbf{X}_t, \boldsymbol{\epsilon}_t)\}$ is a mixing sequence with $\phi(m)$ of size $r/(2r-1)$, $r \geq 1$ or $\alpha(m)$ of size $r/(r-1)$, $r > 1$;

(iii) (a) $E(\mathbf{Z}_{thi}\epsilon_{th}|\mathfrak{F}_{t-1}) = 0$, where $\{\mathfrak{F}_t\}$ is adapted to $\{\mathbf{Z}_{thi}\epsilon_{th}\}$, $h = 1, \ldots, p$, $i = 1, \ldots, l$;
(b) $E|\mathbf{Z}_{thi}\epsilon_{th}|^{2r} < \Delta < \infty$ for some $r > 1$, and all $h = 1, \ldots, p$, $i = 1, \ldots, l$, and t;

(iv) (a) $E|\mathbf{Z}_{thi}\mathbf{X}_{thj}|^{r+\delta} < \Delta < \infty$ for some $\delta > 0$, and all $h = 1, \ldots, p$, $i = 1, \ldots, l$, $j = 1, \ldots, k$, and t;
(b) $\mathbf{Q}_n \equiv E(\mathbf{Z}'\mathbf{X}/n)$ has uniformly full column rank;
(c) $\hat{\mathbf{P}}_n - \mathbf{P}_n \xrightarrow{\text{a.s.}} \mathbf{0}$, where $\{\mathbf{P}_n\}$ is $O(1)$ and is uniformly positive definite.

Then $\tilde{\boldsymbol{\beta}}_n$ exists a.s. for all n sufficiently large and $\tilde{\boldsymbol{\beta}}_n \xrightarrow{\text{a.s.}} \boldsymbol{\beta}_o$.

As with results for the OLS estimator, (ii) and (iva) can be replaced by any other conditions that ensure $\mathbf{Z}'\mathbf{X}/n - \mathbf{Q}_n \xrightarrow{\text{a.s.}} \mathbf{0}$. Note that assumption (ii) is stronger than absolutely necessary here. Instead, it suffices that $\{(\mathbf{Z}_t, \mathbf{X}_t)'\}$ is appropriately mixing. However, assumption (ii) is needed later to ensure the consistency of estimated covariance matrices.

References

Bartle, R. G. [1966]. "The Elements of Integration." New York: Wiley.

Billingsley, P. [1979]. "Probability and Measure." New York: Wiley.

Chung, K. L. [1974]. "A Course in Probability Theory." New York: Harcourt.

Domowitz, I. [1983]. The Linear Model with Stochastic Regressors and Heteroskedastic Dependent Errors, Discussion Paper, Center for Mathematical Studies in Economics and Management Sciences, Northwestern University, Evanston, Illinois.

Doob, J. L. [1954]. "Stochastic Processes." New York: Wiley.

Granger, C. W. J. and P. Newbold [1977]. "Forecasting Economic Time Series." New York: Academic Press.

Ibragimov, I. A. and Y. V. Linnik [1977]. "Independent and Stationary Sequences of Random Variables." The Netherlands: Wolters-Noordhof.

Iosifescu, M. and R. Theodorescu [1969]. "Random Processes and Learning." Berlin and New York: Springer-Verlag.

Lukacs, E. [1975]. "Stochastic Convergence." New York: Academic Press.

McLeish, D. L. [1975]. A maximal inequality and dependent strong laws, *Ann. Probab.* **3:** 826–836.

Rao, C. R. [1973]. "Linear Statistical Inference and Its Applications." New York: Wiley.

Rosenblatt, M. [1956]. A central limit theorem and a strong mixing condition, *Proc. Nat. Acad. Sci. U.S.A.* **42,** 43–47.

Rosenblatt, M. [1972]. Uniform ergodicity and strong mixing, *Z. Wahrsch. Verw. Gebiete* **24:** 79–84.

Rosenblatt, M. [1978]. Dependence and asymptotic independence for random processes, *in* "Studies in Probability Theory" (M. Rosenblatt, ed.) Washington, D.C.: Mathematical Association of America.

Samuelson, P. [1965]. Proof that properly anticipated prices fluctuate randomly, *Industrial Management Review* **6:** 41–49.

Stout, W. F. [1974]. "Almost Sure Convergence." New York: Academic Press.

White, H. and I. Domowitz [1984]. Nonlinear regression with dependent observations, *Econometrica,* forthcoming.

CHAPTER IV

Asymptotic Normality

In the classical linear model with fixed regressors and normally distributed i.i.d. errors, the least squares estimator $\hat{\beta}_n$ is distributed as multivariate normal with $E(\hat{\beta}_n) = \beta_0$ and var $\hat{\beta}_n = \sigma_0^2 (\mathbf{X}'\mathbf{X})^{-1}$ for any sample size n. This fact forms the basis for statistical tests of hypotheses, based typically on t- and F-statistics. When the sample size is large, econometric estimators such as $\hat{\beta}_n$ have a distribution that is approximately normal under very general conditions, and this fact forms the basis for large sample statistical tests of hypotheses. In this chapter we study the tools used in determining the asymptotic distribution of $\tilde{\beta}_n$, how this asymptotic distribution can be used to test hypotheses in large samples, and how asymptotic efficiency can be obtained.

IV.1 Convergence in Distribution

The most fundamental concept is that of convergence in distribution.

DEFINITION 4.1: Let $\{b_n\}$ be a sequence of random finite-dimensional vectors with joint distribution functions $\{F_n\}$. If $F_n(z) \rightarrow F(z)$ as $n \rightarrow \infty$ for every continuity point z, where F is the distribution function of a random variable Z, then b_n *converges in distribution* to the random variable Z, denoted $b_n \xrightarrow{d} Z$.

Heuristically, the distribution of b_n gets closer and closer to that of the random variable Z, so the distribution F can be used as an approximation to the distribution of b_n. When $b_n \xrightarrow{d} Z$, we also say that b_n *converges in law* to Z (written $b_n \xrightarrow{L} Z$), or that b_n is *asymptotically distributed* as F, denoted $b_n \overset{A}{\sim} F$. Then F is called the *limiting distribution* of b_n. Note that the convergence specified by this definition is pointwise and only has to occur at points z where F is continuous.

EXAMPLE 4.2: Let $\{b_n\}$ be a sequence of i.i.d. random variables with distribution function F. Then (trivially) F is the limiting distribution of b_n.

This illustrates the fact that convergence in distribution is a very weak convergence concept and by itself implies nothing about the convergence of the sequence of random variables.

EXAMPLE 4.3: Let $\{Z_t\}$ be i.i.d. random variables with mean μ and variance $\sigma^2 < \infty$. Define $b_n \equiv (\bar{Z}_n - E(\bar{Z}_n))/(\text{var } \bar{Z}_n)^{1/2} = n^{-1/2} \sum_{t=1}^{n} (Z_t - \mu)/\sigma$. Then by the Lindeberg–Levy central limit theorem (Theorem 5.2), $b_n \overset{A}{\sim} N(0, 1)$.

In other words, the sample mean $\bar{Z}_n$, when standardized, has a distribution that approaches the standard normal distribution. This result holds under very general conditions on the sequence $\{Z_t\}$, and the conditions under which this convergence occurs are studied at length in the next chapter. In this chapter, we simply assume that such general conditions are satisfied, so convergence in distribution is guaranteed.

Convergence in distribution is meaningful even when the limiting distribution is that of a degenerate random variable.

LEMMA 4.4: Suppose $b_n \xrightarrow{p} b$ (a constant). Then $b_n \overset{A}{\sim} F_b$, where F_b is the distribution function of a random variable Z that takes the value b with probability one (i.e., $b_n \xrightarrow{d} b$). Also, if $b_n \overset{A}{\sim} F_b$, then $b_n \xrightarrow{p} b$.

Proof: See Rao [1973, p. 120].

In other words, convergence in probability to a constant implies convergence in distribution to that constant. The converse is also true.

A useful implication of convergence in distribution is the following lemma.

LEMMA 4.5: If $b_n \xrightarrow{d} Z$, then b_n is $O_p(1)$.

Proof: Recall that b_n is $O_p(1)$ if, given any $\delta > 0$, $\lim P[|b_n| > \Delta] < \delta$ for some $\Delta < \infty$. Because $b_n \xrightarrow{d} Z$, $P[|b_n| > \Delta] \rightarrow P[|Z| > \Delta]$, provided (without loss of generality) that Δ and $-\Delta$ are continuity points of the distribution of Z. Hence $\lim P[|b_n| > \Delta] = P[|Z| > \Delta] < \delta$ for any $\delta > 0$ and Δ sufficiently large.

This allows us to establish the next useful lemma.

LEMMA 4.6 (*Product rule*): Recall from Corollary 2.36 that if $\{A_n\}$ is $o_p(1)$ and $\{b_n\}$ is $O_p(1)$, then $\{A_n b_n\}$ is $o_p(1)$. Hence, if $A_n \xrightarrow{p} 0$ and $b_n \xrightarrow{d} Z$, then $A_n b_n \xrightarrow{p} 0$.

In turn, this result is often used in conjunction with the following result, which is one of the most useful of those relating convergence in probability and convergence in distribution.

LEMMA 4.7 (*Asymptotic equivalence*): Let $\{a_n\}$ and $\{b_n\}$ be sequences of random vectors. If $a_n - b_n \xrightarrow{p} 0$ and $b_n \xrightarrow{d} Z$, then $a_n \xrightarrow{d} Z$.

Proof: See Rao [1973, p. 123].

This result is helpful in situations in which we wish to find the asymptotic distribution of a_n but cannot easily do so directly. Often, however, it is easy to find a b_n that has a known asymptotic distribution and that satisfies $a_n - b_n \xrightarrow{p} 0$. Lemma 4.7 then ensures that a_n has the same limiting distribution as b_n, and we say that a_n is "asymptotically equivalent" to b_n. The joint use of Lemmas 4.6 and 4.7 is the key to the proof of the asymptotic normality results for the OLS and IV estimators.

Another useful tool in the study of convergence in distribution is the characteristic function.

DEFINITION 4.8: Let Z be a $k \times 1$ random vector with distribution function F. The *characteristic function* of Z is defined as $f(\lambda) \equiv E(\exp i\lambda' Z)$, where $i^2 = -1$ and λ is a $k \times 1$ real vector.

EXAMPLE 4.9: Let Z be a nonstochastic real number, $Z = c$. Then $f(\lambda) = E(\exp i\lambda Z) = E(\exp i\lambda c) = \exp i\lambda c$.

EXAMPLE 4.10: (i) Let $Z \sim N(\mu, \sigma^2)$. Then $f(\lambda) = \exp(i\lambda\mu - \lambda^2\sigma^2/2)$. (ii) Let $Z \sim N(\mu, V)$, where μ is $k \times 1$ and V is $k \times k$. Then $f(\lambda) = \exp(i\lambda'\mu - \lambda' V\lambda/2)$.

A useful table of characteristic functions is given by Lukacs [1970, p. 18].

Because the characteristic function is the Fourier transformation of the distribution function, it has the property that any characteristic function uniquely determines a distribution function, as formally expressed by the next result.

THEOREM 4.11 (*Uniqueness theorem*): Two distribution functions are identical if and only if their characteristic functions are identical.

Proof: See Lukacs [1974, p. 14].

Thus the behavior of a random variable can be studied either through its distribution function or its characteristic function, whichever is more convenient.

EXAMPLE 4.12: The distribution of a linear transformation of a random variable is easily found using the characteristic function. Consider $\mathcal{Y} = A'Z$, where A' is a $q \times k$ matrix. Let θ be $q \times 1$. Then $f_{\mathcal{Y}}(\theta) = E(\exp i\theta'\mathcal{Y}) = E(\exp i\theta'A'Z) = E(\exp i\lambda'Z) = f_Z(\lambda)$, defining $\lambda = A\theta$. Hence if $Z \sim N(\mu, V)$, $f_{\mathcal{Y}}(\theta) = f_Z(\lambda) = \exp(i\lambda'\mu - \lambda'V\lambda/2) = \exp(i\theta'A'\mu - \theta'A'VA\theta/2)$ so that $\mathcal{Y} \sim N(A'\mu, A'VA)$ by the uniqueness theorem.

Other useful facts regarding characteristic functions are the following.

PROPOSITION 4.13: Let $\mathcal{Y} = aZ + b$, a, $b \in \mathbb{R}$. Then $f_{\mathcal{Y}}(\lambda) = f_Z(a\lambda) \exp i\lambda b$.

Proof: $f_{\mathcal{Y}}(\lambda) = E(\exp i\lambda\mathcal{Y}) = E(\exp i\lambda(aZ + b)) = E(\exp i\lambda aZ \cdot \exp i\lambda b) = E(\exp i\lambda aZ) \exp i\lambda b = f_Z(\lambda a) \exp i\lambda b$.

PROPOSITION 4.14: Let $\mathcal{Y}$ and Z be independent. Then if $\mathcal{S} = \mathcal{Y} + Z$, $f_{\mathcal{S}}(\lambda) = f_{\mathcal{Y}}(\lambda) f_Z(\lambda)$.

Proof: $f_{\mathcal{S}}(\lambda) = E(\exp i\lambda\mathcal{S}) = E(\exp i\lambda(\mathcal{Y} + Z)) = E(\exp i\lambda\mathcal{Y} \exp i\lambda Z) = E(\exp i\lambda\mathcal{Y})E(\exp i\lambda Z)$ by independence. Hence $f_{\mathcal{S}}(\lambda) = f_{\mathcal{Y}}(\lambda) f_Z(\lambda)$.

PROPOSITION 4.15: If the kth moment μ_k of a distribution function F exists, then the characteristic function f of F can be differentiated k times and $f^{(k)}(0) = i^k \mu_k$, where $f^{(k)}$ is the kth derivative of f.

Proof: This is an immediate corollary of Lukacs [1970, Corollary 3 to Theorem 2.3.1, p. 22].

EXAMPLE 4.16: Suppose that $Z \sim N(0, \sigma^2)$. Then $f'(0) = 0$, $f''(0) = -\sigma^2, f'''(0) = 0$, etc.

The main result of use in studying convergence in distribution is the following.

THEOREM 4.17 (*Continuity theorem*): Let $\{b_n\}$ be a sequence of random $k \times 1$ vectors with characteristic functions $\{f_n(\lambda)\}$. If $b_n \xrightarrow{d} Z$, then for every $\lambda, f_n(\lambda) \rightarrow f(\lambda)$, where $f(\lambda) = E(\exp i\lambda' Z)$. Further, if for every λ, $f_n(\lambda) \rightarrow f(\lambda)$ and f is continuous at $\lambda = 0$, then $b_n \xrightarrow{d} Z$, where $f(\lambda) = E(\exp i\lambda' Z)$.

Proof: See Lukacs [1970, pp. 49–50].

This result essentially says that convergence in distribution is equivalent to convergence of characteristic functions. The usefulness of the result is that often it is much easier to study the limiting behavior of characteristic functions than distribution functions. If the sequence of characteristic functions $f_n(\lambda)$ converges to a characteristic function $f(\lambda)$ that is continuous at $\lambda = 0$, this theorem guarantees that the limiting distribution F of b_n is that corresponding to the characteristic function $f(\lambda)$.

In all the cases that follow, the limiting distribution F will either be that of a degenerate random variable (following from convergence in probability to a constant) or be a multivariate normal distribution (following from an appropriate central limit theorem). In the latter case, it is often convenient to standardize the random variables so that the asymptotic distribution is unit multivariate normal. To do this we can use the matrix square root.

EXERCISE 4.18: Prove the following. Let V be a positive (semi) definite symmetric matrix. Then there exists a positive (semi) definite symmetric matrix square root $V^{1/2}$ such that the elements of $V^{1/2}$ are continuous functions of V and $V^{1/2}V^{1/2} = V$. (*Hint:* Express V as $V = Q'DQ$ where Q is an orthogonal matrix and D is diagonal with the eigenvalues of V along the diagonal.)

EXERCISE 4.19: Show that if $Z \sim N(\mathbf{0}, V)$, then $V^{-1/2}Z \sim N(\mathbf{0}, \mathbf{I})$, provided V is positive definite, where $V^{-1/2} = (V^{1/2})^{-1}$.

DEFINITION 4.20: Let $\{b_n\}$ be a sequence of random vectors. If there exists a symmetric matrix V_n positive definite for all n sufficiently large such that $V_n^{-1/2}b_n \overset{A}{\sim} N(\mathbf{0}, \mathbf{I})$, then V_n is called the *asymptotic covariance matrix* of b_n, denoted avar b_n.

When var b_n is finite, we can usually define $V_n = \text{var } b_n$. Note that the behavior of b_n is not restricted to require that V_n converge to any limit, although it may. Generally, however, we will at least require that the smallest eigenvalues of V_n and V_n^{-1} are uniformly bounded away from zero for all n sufficiently large. Even when var b_n is not finite, the asymptotic covariance matrix can exist, although in such cases we cannot set $V_n = \text{var } b_n$.

EXAMPLE 4.21: Define $b_n = \mathcal{Z} + \mathcal{Y}/n$ where $\mathcal{Z} \sim N(0, 1)$ and $\mathcal{Y}$ is Cauchy, independent of $\mathcal{Z}$. Then var b_n is infinite for every n, but $b_n \overset{A}{\sim} N(0, 1)$ as a consequence of Lemma 4.7. Hence avar $b_n = 1$.

Given a sequence $\{V_n^{-1/2}b_n\}$ that converges in distribution, we shall often be interested in the behavior of linear combinations of b_n, say, $\{A_n b_n\}$, where A_n, like $V_n^{-1/2}$, is not required to converge to a particular limit. We can use characteristic functions to study the behavior of these sequences by making use of the following corollary to the continuity theorem.

COROLLARY 4.22: If $\lambda \in \mathbb{R}^k$ and a sequence $\{f_n(\lambda)\}$ of characteristic functions converges to a characteristic function $f(\lambda)$, then the convergence is uniform in every compact subset of $\mathbb{R}^k$.

Proof: This is a straightforward extension of Lukacs [1970, p. 50].

This result says that in any compact subset of $\mathbb{R}^k$ the distance between $f_n(\lambda)$ and $f(\lambda)$ does not depend on λ, but only on n. This fact is crucial to establishing the next result.

LEMMA 4.23: Let $\{b_n\}$ be a sequence of random $k \times 1$ vectors with characteristic functions $\{f_n(\lambda)\}$, and suppose $f_n(\lambda) \rightarrow f(\lambda)$. If $\{A_n\}$ is any sequence of $k \times q$ nonstochastic matrices such that $\{A_n\}$ is O(1), then the sequence $\{A_n' b_n\}$ has characteristic functions $\{f_n^*(\theta)\}$, where θ is $q \times 1$, such that for every $\theta, f_n^*(\theta) - f(A_n\theta) \rightarrow 0$.

Proof: From Example 4.12, $f_n^*(\theta) = f_n(A_n\theta)$. For fixed θ, $\lambda_n \equiv A_n\theta$ takes values in a compact region of $\mathbb{R}^k$, say, $\mathcal{N}_\theta$, for all n sufficiently large because $\{A_n\}$ is O(1). Because $f_n(\lambda) \to f(\lambda)$, we have $f_n(\lambda_n) - f(\lambda_n) \to 0$ uniformly for all λ_n in $\mathcal{N}_\theta$, by Corollary 4.20. Hence for fixed θ, $f_n(A_n\theta) - f(A_n\theta) = f_n^*(\theta) - f(A_n\theta) \to 0$ for any O(1) sequence $\{A_n\}$. Because θ is arbitrary, the result follows.

The following consequence of this result is used many times below.

COROLLARY 4.24: Let $\{b_n\}$ be a sequence of random $k \times 1$ vectors such that $V_n^{-1/2} b_n \overset{A}{\sim} N(\mathbf{0}, \mathbf{I})$, where $\{V_n\}$ and $\{V_n^{-1}\}$ are O(1). Let $\{A_n\}$ be a O(1) sequence of (nonstochastic) $k \times q$ matrices with full column rank q for all n sufficiently large, uniformly in n. Then the sequence $\{A_n' b_n\}$ is such that $\Gamma_n^{-1/2} A_n' b_n \overset{A}{\sim} N(\mathbf{0}, \mathbf{I})$, where $\Gamma_n \equiv A_n' V_n A_n$ and $\{\Gamma_n\}$ and $\{\Gamma_n^{-1}\}$ are O(1).

Proof: $\{\Gamma_n\}$ is O(1) by Proposition 2.30. $\{\Gamma_n^{-1}\}$ is O(1) because $\{\Gamma_n\}$ is O(1) and $\det \Gamma_n > \delta > 0$ for all n sufficiently large, given the conditions on $\{A_n\}$ and $\{V_n\}$. Let $f_n^*(\theta)$ be the characteristic function of $\Gamma_n^{-1/2} A_n' b_n = \Gamma_n^{-1/2} A_n' V_n^{1/2} V_n^{-1/2} b_n$. Because $\{\Gamma_n^{-1/2} A_n' V_n^{1/2}\}$ is O(1), Lemma 4.23 applies, implying $f_n^*(\theta) - f(V_n^{1/2} A_n \Gamma_n^{-1/2}\theta) \to 0$, where $f(\lambda) = \exp(-\lambda'\lambda/2)$, the limiting characteristic function of $V_n^{-1/2} b_n$. Now $f(V_n^{1/2} A_n \Gamma_n^{-1/2}\theta) = \exp(-\theta' \Gamma_n^{-1/2} A_n' V_n A_n \Gamma_n^{-1/2} \theta/2) = \exp(-\theta'\theta/2)$ by definition of $\Gamma_n^{-1/2}$. Hence $f_n^*(\lambda) - \exp(-\theta'\theta/2) \to 0$, so $\Gamma_n^{-1/2} A_n' b_n \overset{A}{\sim} N(\mathbf{0}, \mathbf{I})$ by the continuity theorem 4.17.

This result allows us to complete the proof of the following very general asymptotic normality result for the least squares estimator.

THEOREM 4.25: Given

(i) $\mathbf{y} = \mathbf{X}\boldsymbol{\beta}_o + \boldsymbol{\epsilon}$;
(ii) $\mathbf{V}_n^{-1/2} n^{-1/2} \mathbf{X}'\boldsymbol{\epsilon} \overset{A}{\sim} N(\mathbf{0}, \mathbf{I})$, where $\mathbf{V}_n \equiv \text{var}(n^{-1/2}\mathbf{X}'\boldsymbol{\epsilon})$ is O(1) and uniformly positive definite;
(iii) $\mathbf{X}'\mathbf{X}/n - \mathbf{M}_n \xrightarrow{p} \mathbf{0}$, where $\mathbf{M}_n \equiv E(\mathbf{X}'\mathbf{X}/n)$ is O(1) and uniformly positive definite.

Then $\mathbf{D}_n^{-1/2}\sqrt{n}(\hat{\boldsymbol{\beta}}_n - \boldsymbol{\beta}_o) \overset{A}{\sim} N(\mathbf{0}, \mathbf{I})$, where $\mathbf{D}_n \equiv \mathbf{M}_n^{-1}\mathbf{V}_n\mathbf{M}_n^{-1}$. Suppose in addition that

(iv) there exists $\hat{\mathbf{V}}_n$ positive semidefinite and symmetric such that $\hat{\mathbf{V}}_n - \mathbf{V}_n \xrightarrow{p} \mathbf{0}$. Then $\hat{\mathbf{D}}_n - \mathbf{D}_n \xrightarrow{p} \mathbf{0}$, where $\hat{\mathbf{D}}_n \equiv (\mathbf{X}'\mathbf{X}/n)^{-1} \hat{\mathbf{V}}_n (\mathbf{X}'\mathbf{X}/n)^{-1}$.

Proof: Because $\mathbf{X}'\mathbf{X}/n - \mathbf{M}_n \xrightarrow{p} \mathbf{0}$ and $\mathbf{M}_n$ is finite and nonsingular by (iii), $(\mathbf{X}'\mathbf{X}/n)^{-1}$ and $\hat{\boldsymbol{\beta}}_n$ exist in probability. Given (i) and the existence of $(\mathbf{X}'\mathbf{X}/n)^{-1}$,

$$\sqrt{n}(\boldsymbol{\beta}_n - \boldsymbol{\beta}_o) = (\mathbf{X}'\mathbf{X}/n)^{-1} n^{-1/2}\mathbf{X}'\boldsymbol{\epsilon}.$$

Hence, given (ii),

$$\sqrt{n}(\hat{\boldsymbol{\beta}}_n - \boldsymbol{\beta}_o) - \mathbf{M}_n^{-1} n^{-1/2}\mathbf{X}'\boldsymbol{\epsilon} = [(\mathbf{X}'\mathbf{X}/n)^{-1} - \mathbf{M}_n^{-1}]\mathbf{V}_n^{1/2}\mathbf{V}_n^{-1/2} n^{-1/2}\mathbf{X}'\boldsymbol{\epsilon},$$

or, premultiplying by $\mathbf{D}_n^{-1/2}$,

$$\begin{aligned}\mathbf{D}_n^{-1/2}\sqrt{n}(\hat{\boldsymbol{\beta}}_n - \boldsymbol{\beta}_o) &- \mathbf{D}_n^{-1/2}\mathbf{M}_n^{-1} n^{-1/2}\mathbf{X}'\boldsymbol{\epsilon} \\ &= \mathbf{D}_n^{-1/2}[(\mathbf{X}'\mathbf{X}/n)^{-1} - \mathbf{M}_n^{-1}]\mathbf{V}_n^{1/2}\mathbf{V}_n^{-1/2} n^{-1/2}\mathbf{X}'\boldsymbol{\epsilon}.\end{aligned}$$

The desired result will follow by applying the product rule lemma 4.6 to the line immediately above, and the asymptotic equivalence lemma 4.7 to the preceding line. Now $\mathbf{V}_n^{-1/2} n^{-1/2}\mathbf{X}'\boldsymbol{\epsilon} \overset{A}{\sim} N(\mathbf{0}, \mathbf{I})$ by (ii); further, $\mathbf{D}_n^{-1/2}[(\mathbf{X}'\mathbf{X}/n)^{-1} - \mathbf{M}_n^{-1}]\mathbf{V}_n^{1/2}$ is $o_p(1)$ because $\mathbf{D}_n^{-1/2}$ and $\mathbf{V}_n^{1/2}$ are $O(1)$ given (ii) and (iii), and $[(\mathbf{X}'\mathbf{X}/n)^{-1} - \mathbf{M}_n^{-1}]$ is $o_p(1)$ by Proposition 2.30 given (ii). Hence, by Lemma 4.5,

$$\mathbf{D}_n^{-1/2}\sqrt{n}(\boldsymbol{\beta}_n - \boldsymbol{\beta}_o) - \mathbf{D}_n^{-1/2}\mathbf{M}_n^{-1} n^{-1/2}\mathbf{X}'\boldsymbol{\epsilon} \xrightarrow{p} \mathbf{0}.$$

By Lemma 4.7, the asymptotic distribution of $\mathbf{D}_n^{-1/2}\sqrt{n}(\hat{\boldsymbol{\beta}}_n - \boldsymbol{\beta}_o)$ is the same as that of $\mathbf{D}_n^{-1/2}\mathbf{M}_n^{-1} n^{-1/2}\mathbf{X}'\boldsymbol{\epsilon}$. We find the asymptotic distribution of this random variable by applying Corollary 4.24, which immediately yields $\mathbf{D}_n^{-1/2}\mathbf{M}_n^{-1} n^{-1/2}\mathbf{X}'\boldsymbol{\epsilon} \overset{A}{\sim} N(\mathbf{0}, \mathbf{I})$.

Because (ii), (iii), and (iv) hold, $\hat{\mathbf{D}}_n - \mathbf{D}_n \xrightarrow{p} \mathbf{0}$ as an immediate consequence of Proposition 2.30.

The structure of this result is very straightforward. Given that the model is truly linear, we require only that $(\mathbf{X}'\mathbf{X}/n)$ and $(\mathbf{X}'\mathbf{X}/n)^{-1}$ are $O_p(1)$ and that $n^{-1/2}\mathbf{X}'\boldsymbol{\epsilon}$ is asymptotically unit normal after standardizing by the inverse square root of its asymptotic covariance matrix. The asymptotic covariance (dispersion) matrix of $\sqrt{n}(\hat{\boldsymbol{\beta}}_n - \boldsymbol{\beta}_o)$ is $\mathbf{D}_n$, which can be consistently estimated by $\hat{\mathbf{D}}_n$. Note that this result allows the regressors to be stochastic and imposes no restriction on the serial correlation or heteroskedasticity of $\boldsymbol{\epsilon}_t$, except that needed to ensure that (ii) holds. As we shall see in the next chapter, only mild restrictions are imposed in guaranteeing (ii).

In special cases, it may be known that $\mathbf{V}_n$ has a special form. For example, when $\boldsymbol{\epsilon}_t$ is an i.i.d. scalar with $E(\boldsymbol{\epsilon}_t) = \mathbf{0}$, $E(\boldsymbol{\epsilon}_t^2) = \sigma_o^2$, and $\mathbf{X}_t$ nonstochastic, then $\mathbf{V}_n = \sigma_o^2\mathbf{X}'\mathbf{X}/n$. Finding a consistent estimator for $\mathbf{V}_n$ then requires no more than finding a consistent estimator for σ_o^2.

In more general cases considered below it is often possible to write

$$\mathbf{V}_n = E(\mathbf{X}'\boldsymbol{\epsilon}\boldsymbol{\epsilon}'\mathbf{X}/n) = E(\mathbf{X}'\boldsymbol{\Omega}_n\mathbf{X}/n).$$

Finding a consistent estimator for $\mathbf{V}_n$ in these cases is made easier by the knowledge of the structure of $\boldsymbol{\Omega}_n$. However, even when $\boldsymbol{\Omega}_n$ is unknown, it turns out that consistent estimators for $\mathbf{V}_n$ are generally available. The conditions under which $\mathbf{V}_n$ can be consistently estimated are treated in Chapter VI.

A result analogous to Theorem 4.25 is available for instrumental variables estimators. Because the proof follows that of Theorem 4.25 very closely, proof of the following result is left as an exercise.

EXERCISE 4.26: Prove the following result. Given

(i) $\mathbf{y} = \mathbf{X}\boldsymbol{\beta}_o + \boldsymbol{\epsilon}$;

(ii) $\mathbf{V}_n^{-1/2} n^{-1/2}\mathbf{Z}'\boldsymbol{\epsilon} \overset{A}{\sim} N(\mathbf{0}, \mathbf{I})$, where $\mathbf{V}_n \equiv \text{var}(n^{-1/2}\mathbf{Z}'\boldsymbol{\epsilon})$ is $O(1)$ and uniformly positive definite;

(iii) (a) $\mathbf{Z}'\mathbf{X}/n - \mathbf{Q}_n \xrightarrow{p} \mathbf{0}$, where $\mathbf{Q}_n \equiv E(\mathbf{Z}'\mathbf{X}/n)$ is $O(1)$ with uniformly full column rank;

(b) There exists $\hat{\mathbf{P}}_n$ such that $\hat{\mathbf{P}}_n - \mathbf{P}_n \xrightarrow{p} \mathbf{0}$ and $\mathbf{P}_n$ is $O(1)$ and uniformly positive definite.

Then $\mathbf{D}_n^{-1/2}\sqrt{n}(\tilde{\boldsymbol{\beta}}_n - \boldsymbol{\beta}_o) \overset{A}{\sim} N(\mathbf{0}, \mathbf{I})$, where

$$\mathbf{D}_n \equiv (\mathbf{Q}_n'\mathbf{P}_n\mathbf{Q}_n)^{-1}\mathbf{Q}_n'\mathbf{P}_n\mathbf{V}_n\mathbf{P}_n\mathbf{Q}_n(\mathbf{Q}_n'\mathbf{P}_n\mathbf{Q}_n)^{-1}.$$

Suppose in addition that

(iv) There exists $\hat{\mathbf{V}}_n$ positive semidefinite and symmetric such that $\hat{\mathbf{V}}_n - \mathbf{V}_n \xrightarrow{p} \mathbf{0}$.

Then $\hat{\mathbf{D}}_n - \mathbf{D}_n \to \mathbf{0}$, where

$$\hat{\mathbf{D}}_n = (\mathbf{X}'\mathbf{Z}\hat{\mathbf{P}}_n\mathbf{Z}'\mathbf{X}/n^2)^{-1}(\mathbf{X}'\mathbf{Z}/n)\hat{\mathbf{P}}_n\hat{\mathbf{V}}_n\hat{\mathbf{P}}_n(\mathbf{Z}'\mathbf{X}/n)(\mathbf{X}'\mathbf{Z}\hat{\mathbf{P}}_n\mathbf{Z}'\mathbf{X}/n^2)^{-1}.$$

IV.2 Hypothesis Testing

A direct and very important use of the asymptotic normality of a given estimator is in hypothesis testing. Often, hypotheses of interest can be expressed in terms of linear combinations of the parameters as

$$\underset{(q \times k)(k \times 1)}{\mathbf{R}\boldsymbol{\beta}_o} = \underset{(q \times 1)}{\mathbf{r}},$$

where $\mathbf{R}$ and $\mathbf{r}$ are a matrix and a vector of known elements that, through $\mathbf{R}\boldsymbol{\beta}_o = \mathbf{r}$, specify the hypotheses of interest. For example, if the hypothesis is that the elements of $\boldsymbol{\beta}_o$ sum to unity, $\mathbf{R} = [1, 1, \ldots, 1]$ and $\mathbf{r} = 1$.

Several different approaches can be taken in computing a statistic to test the null hypothesis $\mathbf{R}\boldsymbol{\beta}_o = \mathbf{r}$ versus the alternative $\mathbf{R}\boldsymbol{\beta}_o \neq \mathbf{r}$. The methods that we consider here involve the use of *Wald*, *Lagrange multiplier*, and *quasi-likelihood ratio* statistics.

Although the approaches to forming the test statistics differ, the way that we determine their asymptotic distributions is the same. In each case we exploit an underlying asymptotic normality property to obtain a statistic distributed asymptotically as χ^2. To do this we use the following results.

LEMMA 4.27: Let $g: \mathbb{R}^k \to \mathbb{R}^l$ be continuous on $\mathbb{R}^k$ and let $b_n \xrightarrow{d} Z$, a $k \times 1$ random vector. Then $g(b_n) \xrightarrow{d} g(Z)$.

Proof: See Rao [1973, p. 124].

COROLLARY 4.28: Let $V_n^{-1/2} b_n \overset{A}{\sim} N(\mathbf{0}, \mathbf{I}_k)$. Then $b_n' V_n^{-1} b_n = b_n' V_n^{-1/2} V_n^{-1/2} b_n \overset{A}{\sim} \chi_k^2$.

Proof: By hypothesis, $V_n^{-1/2} b_n \xrightarrow{d} Z \sim N(\mathbf{0}, \mathbf{I}_k)$. The function $g(z) = z'z$ is continuous on $\mathbb{R}^k$. Hence $b_n' V_n^{-1} b_n = g(V_n^{-1/2} b_n) \xrightarrow{d} g(Z) = Z'Z \sim \chi_k^2$.

Typically, V_n will be unknown, but there will be a consistent estimator $\hat{V}_n$ such that $\hat{V}_n - V_n \xrightarrow{p} \mathbf{0}$. To replace V_n in Corollary 4.28 with $\hat{V}_n$, we use the following result.

LEMMA 4.29: Let g: $\mathbb{R}^k \to \mathbb{R}^l$ be continuous on $\mathbb{R}^k$. If $a_n - b_n \xrightarrow{p} 0$ and $b_n \xrightarrow{p} Z$, then $g(a_n) - g(b_n) \xrightarrow{p} 0$ and $g(a_n) \xrightarrow{p} g(Z)$.

Proof: Rao [1973, p. 124] proves that $g(a_n) - g(b_n) \xrightarrow{p} 0$. That $g(a_n) \xrightarrow{d} g(Z)$ follows from Lemmas 4.7 and 4.27.

Now we can prove the result that is the basis for finding the asymptotic distribution of the Wald, Lagrange multiplier, and quasi-likelihood ratio tests.

THEOREM 4.30: Let $V_n^{-1/2} b_n \overset{A}{\sim} N(\mathbf{0}, \mathbf{I}_k)$, and suppose there exists $\hat{V}_n$ positive semidefinite and symmetric such that $\hat{V}_n - V_n \xrightarrow{p} \mathbf{0}$, where V_n is O(1), and for all n sufficiently large, $\det V_n > \delta > 0$. Then $b_n' \hat{V}_n^{-1} b_n \overset{A}{\sim} \chi_k^2$.

Proof: We apply Lemma 4.29. Consider $\hat{V}_n^{-1/2} b_n - V_n^{-1/2} b_n$, where $\hat{V}_n^{-1/2}$ exists in probability for all n sufficiently large. Now $\hat{V}_n^{-1/2} b_n - V_n^{-1/2} b_n = (\hat{V}_n^{-1/2} V_n^{1/2} - \mathbf{I}) V_n^{-1/2} b_n$. By hypothesis, $V_n^{-1/2} b_n \overset{A}{\sim} N(\mathbf{0}, \mathbf{I}_k)$, and $\hat{V}_n^{-1/2} V_n^{1/2} - \mathrm{I} \xrightarrow{p} 0$ by Proposition 2.30. It follows from the product rule lemma 4.6 that $\hat{V}_n^{-1/2} b_n - V_n^{-1/2} b_n \xrightarrow{p} 0$. Because $V_n^{-1/2} b_n \xrightarrow{d} Z \sim N(\mathbf{0}, \mathbf{I}_k)$, it follows from Lemma 4.29 that $b_n' \hat{V}_n^{-1} b_n \overset{A}{\sim} \chi_k^2$.

The Wald statistic allows the simplest analysis, although it may or may not be the easiest statistic to compute in a given situation. The motivation for the Wald statistic is that when the null hypothesis is correct, $\mathbf{R}\hat{\boldsymbol{\beta}}_n$ should be close to $\mathbf{R}\boldsymbol{\beta}_o = \mathbf{r}$, so a value of $\mathbf{R}\hat{\boldsymbol{\beta}}_n - \mathbf{r}$ far from zero is evidence against the null hypothesis. To tell how far from zero $\mathbf{R}\hat{\boldsymbol{\beta}}_n - \mathbf{r}$ must be before we reject the null hypothesis, we need to determine its asymptotic distribution.

THEOREM 4.31 (*Wald test*): Let the conditions of Theorem 4.25 hold and let rank $\mathbf{R} = q \leq k$. Then under $H_0\!: \mathbf{R}\boldsymbol{\beta}_o = \mathbf{r}$,

(i) $\boldsymbol{\Gamma}_n^{-1/2} \sqrt{n} (\mathbf{R}\hat{\boldsymbol{\beta}}_n - \mathbf{r}) \overset{A}{\sim} N(\mathbf{0}, \mathbf{I})$, where

$$\boldsymbol{\Gamma}_n \equiv \mathbf{R}\mathbf{D}_n\mathbf{R}' = \mathbf{R}\mathbf{M}_n^{-1}\mathbf{V}_n\mathbf{M}_n^{-1}\mathbf{R}'.$$

(ii) the Wald statistic $\mathcal{W}_n \equiv n(\mathbf{R}\hat{\boldsymbol{\beta}}_n - \mathbf{r})' \hat{\boldsymbol{\Gamma}}_n^{-1} (\mathbf{R}\hat{\boldsymbol{\beta}}_n - \mathbf{r}) \overset{A}{\sim} \chi_q^2$, where

$$\hat{\boldsymbol{\Gamma}}_n \equiv \mathbf{R}\hat{\mathbf{D}}_n\mathbf{R}' = \mathbf{R}(\mathbf{X}'\mathbf{X}/n)^{-1}\hat{\mathbf{V}}_n(\mathbf{X}'\mathbf{X}/n)^{-1}\mathbf{R}'.$$

Proof: (i) Under H_0, $\mathbf{R}\hat{\boldsymbol{\beta}}_n - \mathbf{r} = \mathbf{R}(\hat{\boldsymbol{\beta}}_n - \boldsymbol{\beta}_o)$, so $\boldsymbol{\Gamma}_n^{-1/2}\sqrt{n}(\mathbf{R}\hat{\boldsymbol{\beta}}_n - \mathbf{r}) = \boldsymbol{\Gamma}_n^{-1/2}\mathbf{R}\mathbf{D}_n^{-1/2}\mathbf{D}_n^{-1/2}\sqrt{n}(\hat{\boldsymbol{\beta}}_n - \boldsymbol{\beta}_o)$. It follows from Corollary 4.24 that $\boldsymbol{\Gamma}_n^{-1/2}\sqrt{n}(\mathbf{R}\hat{\boldsymbol{\beta}}_n - \mathbf{r}) \overset{A}{\sim} N(0, \mathbf{I})$. (ii) Because $\hat{\mathbf{D}}_n - \mathbf{D}_n \xrightarrow{p} \mathbf{0}$ from Theorem 4.25, it follows that $\hat{\boldsymbol{\Gamma}}_n - \boldsymbol{\Gamma}_n \xrightarrow{p} \mathbf{0}$ by Proposition 2.30. Given the result in (i), (ii) follows from Theorem 4.30.

This version of the Wald statistic is useful regardless of the presence of heteroskedasticity or serial correlation in the error terms because a consistent estimator ($\hat{\mathbf{V}}_n$) for $\mathbf{V}_n$ is used in computing $\hat{\boldsymbol{\Gamma}}_n$. In the special case when $\mathbf{V}_n$ can be consistently estimated by $\hat{\sigma}_n^2(\mathbf{X}'\mathbf{X}/n)$, the Wald test has the form

$$\mathcal{W}_n = n(\mathbf{R}\hat{\boldsymbol{\beta}}_n - \mathbf{r})'[\mathbf{R}(\mathbf{X}'\mathbf{X}/n)^{-1}\mathbf{R}']^{-1}(\mathbf{R}\hat{\boldsymbol{\beta}}_n - \mathbf{r})/\hat{\sigma}_n^2,$$

which is simply q times the standard F-statistic for testing the hypothesis $\mathbf{R}\boldsymbol{\beta}_o = \mathbf{r}$. The validity of the asymptotic χ^2_q distribution for this statistic depends crucially on the consistency of $\hat{\mathbf{V}}_n = \hat{\sigma}^2_n(\mathbf{X}'\mathbf{X}/n)$ for $\mathbf{V}_n$; if this $\hat{\mathbf{V}}_n$ is not consistent for $\mathbf{V}_n$, the asymptotic distribution of this form for $\mathcal{W}_n$ is not χ^2_q in general.

The Wald statistic is most convenient in situations in which the restrictions $\mathbf{R}\boldsymbol{\beta}_o = \mathbf{r}$ are not easy to impose in estimating $\boldsymbol{\beta}_o$. When these restrictions are easily imposed (say, $\mathbf{R}\boldsymbol{\beta}_o = \mathbf{r}$ specifies that the last element of $\boldsymbol{\beta}_o$ is zero), the Lagrange multiplier statistic is more easily computed.

The motivation for the Lagrange multiplier statistic is that a constrained least squares estimator can be obtained by solving the problem

$$\min_{\boldsymbol{\beta}} (\mathbf{y} - \mathbf{X}\boldsymbol{\beta})'(\mathbf{y} - \mathbf{X}\boldsymbol{\beta})/n \qquad \text{s.t.} \quad \mathbf{R}\boldsymbol{\beta} = \mathbf{r},$$

which is equivalent to finding the saddle point of the Lagrangian

$$\mathcal{L} = (\mathbf{y} - \mathbf{X}\boldsymbol{\beta})'(\mathbf{y} - \mathbf{X}\boldsymbol{\beta})/n + (\mathbf{R}\boldsymbol{\beta} - \mathbf{r})'\boldsymbol{\lambda}.$$

The Lagrange multipliers $\boldsymbol{\lambda}$ can be thought of as giving the shadow price of the constraint and should therefore be small when the constraint is valid and large otherwise. (See Engle [1981] for a general discussion.) The Lagrange multiplier test can be thought of as testing the hypothesis that $\boldsymbol{\lambda} = \mathbf{0}$.

The-first order conditions are

$$\partial\mathcal{L}/\partial\boldsymbol{\beta} = 2(\mathbf{X}'\mathbf{X}/n)\boldsymbol{\beta} - 2\mathbf{X}'\mathbf{y}/n + \mathbf{R}'\boldsymbol{\lambda} = \mathbf{0}$$
$$\partial\mathcal{L}/\partial\boldsymbol{\lambda} = \mathbf{R}\boldsymbol{\beta} - \mathbf{r} = \mathbf{0}.$$

To solve for the estimate of the Lagrange multiplier, premultiply the first equation by $\mathbf{R}(\mathbf{X}'\mathbf{X}/n)^{-1}$ and set $\mathbf{R}\boldsymbol{\beta} = \mathbf{r}$. This yields

$$\ddot{\boldsymbol{\lambda}}_n = 2(\mathbf{R}(\mathbf{X}'\mathbf{X}/n)^{-1}\mathbf{R}')^{-1}(\mathbf{R}\hat{\boldsymbol{\beta}}_n - \mathbf{r})$$
$$\ddot{\boldsymbol{\beta}}_n = \hat{\boldsymbol{\beta}}_n - (\mathbf{X}'\mathbf{X}/n)^{-1}\mathbf{R}'\ddot{\boldsymbol{\lambda}}_n/2,$$

where $\ddot{\boldsymbol{\beta}}_n$ is the constrained least squares estimator (which automatically satisfies $\mathbf{R}\ddot{\boldsymbol{\beta}}_n = \mathbf{r}$). In this form, $\ddot{\boldsymbol{\lambda}}_n$ is simply a nonsingular transformation of $\mathbf{R}\hat{\boldsymbol{\beta}}_n - \mathbf{r}$. This allows the following result to be proved very simply.

THEOREM 4.32 (*Lagrange multiplier test*): Let the conditions of

Theorem 4.25 hold and let rank $\mathbf{R} = q \leq k$. Then under $H_0: \mathbf{R}\boldsymbol{\beta}_o = \mathbf{r}$,

(i) $\boldsymbol{\Lambda}_n^{-1/2}\sqrt{n}\ddot{\boldsymbol{\lambda}}_n \overset{A}{\sim} N(\mathbf{0}, \mathbf{I})$, where

$$\boldsymbol{\Lambda}_n \equiv 4(\mathbf{R}\mathbf{M}_n^{-1}\mathbf{R}')^{-1}\boldsymbol{\Gamma}_n(\mathbf{R}\mathbf{M}_n^{-1}\mathbf{R}')^{-1}$$

and $\boldsymbol{\Gamma}_n$ is as defined in Theorem 4.31.

(ii) The Lagrange multiplier statistic $\mathcal{LM}_n \equiv n\ddot{\boldsymbol{\lambda}}_n'\hat{\boldsymbol{\Lambda}}_n^{-1}\ddot{\boldsymbol{\lambda}}_n \overset{A}{\sim} \chi_q^2$, where

$$\hat{\boldsymbol{\Lambda}}_n \equiv 4(\mathbf{R}(\mathbf{X}'\mathbf{X}/n)^{-1}\mathbf{R}')^{-1}\mathbf{R}(\mathbf{X}'\mathbf{X}/n)^{-1}\ddot{\mathbf{V}}_n(\mathbf{X}'\mathbf{X}/n)^{-1}\mathbf{R}' \times (\mathbf{R}(\mathbf{X}'\mathbf{X}/n)^{-1}\mathbf{R}')^{-1}$$

and $\ddot{\mathbf{V}}_n$ is computed from the constrained regression such that $\ddot{\mathbf{V}}_n - \mathbf{V}_n \xrightarrow{p} \mathbf{0}$ under H_0.

Proof: (i) Consider the difference

$$\boldsymbol{\Lambda}_n^{-1/2}\sqrt{n}\ddot{\boldsymbol{\lambda}}_n - 2\boldsymbol{\Lambda}_n^{-1/2}(\mathbf{R}\mathbf{M}_n^{-1}\mathbf{R}')^{-1}\sqrt{n}(\mathbf{R}\hat{\boldsymbol{\beta}}_n - \mathbf{r})$$
$$= 2\boldsymbol{\Lambda}_n^{-1/2}[(\mathbf{R}(\mathbf{X}'\mathbf{X}/n)^{-1}\mathbf{R}')^{-1} - (\mathbf{R}\mathbf{M}_n^{-1}\mathbf{R}')^{-1}]\boldsymbol{\Gamma}_n^{1/2}\boldsymbol{\Gamma}_n^{-1/2}(\mathbf{R}\hat{\boldsymbol{\beta}}_n - \mathbf{r}).$$

From Theorem 4.31, $\boldsymbol{\Gamma}_n^{-1/2}(\mathbf{R}\hat{\boldsymbol{\beta}}_n - \mathbf{r}) \overset{A}{\sim} N(\mathbf{0}, \mathbf{I})$. Because $(\mathbf{X}'\mathbf{X}/n) - \mathbf{M}_n \xrightarrow{p} \mathbf{0}$, it follows from Proposition 2.30 and the fact that $\boldsymbol{\Lambda}_n^{-1/2}$ and $\boldsymbol{\Gamma}_n^{-1/2}$ are $O(1)$ that $\boldsymbol{\Lambda}_n^{-1/2}[(\mathbf{R}(\mathbf{X}'\mathbf{X}/n)^{-1}\mathbf{R}')^{-1} - (\mathbf{R}\mathbf{M}_n^{-1}\mathbf{R}')^{-1}]\boldsymbol{\Gamma}_n^{1/2} \xrightarrow{p} \mathbf{0}$. Hence by the produce rule lemma 4.6,

$$\boldsymbol{\Lambda}_n^{-1/2}\sqrt{n}\ddot{\boldsymbol{\lambda}}_n - 2\boldsymbol{\Lambda}_n^{-1/2}(\mathbf{R}\mathbf{M}_n^{-1}\mathbf{R}')^{-1}\sqrt{n}(\mathbf{R}\hat{\boldsymbol{\beta}}_n - \mathbf{r}) \xrightarrow{p} \mathbf{0}.$$

It follows from Lemma 4.7 that $\boldsymbol{\Lambda}_n^{-1/2}\sqrt{n}\ddot{\boldsymbol{\lambda}}_n$ has the same asymptotic distribution as $2\boldsymbol{\Lambda}_n^{-1/2}(\mathbf{R}\mathbf{M}_n^{-1}\mathbf{R}')^{-1}\sqrt{n}(\mathbf{R}\hat{\boldsymbol{\beta}}_n - \mathbf{r})$. It follows immediately from Corollary 4.24 that $2\boldsymbol{\Lambda}_n^{-1/2}(\mathbf{R}\mathbf{M}_n^{-1}\mathbf{R}')^{-1}\sqrt{n}(\mathbf{R}\hat{\boldsymbol{\beta}}_n - \mathbf{r}) \sim N(\mathbf{0}, \mathbf{I})$; hence $\boldsymbol{\Lambda}_n^{-1/2}\sqrt{n}\ddot{\boldsymbol{\lambda}}_n \overset{A}{\sim} N(\mathbf{0}, \mathbf{I})$.

(ii) Because $\ddot{\mathbf{V}}_n - \mathbf{V}_n \xrightarrow{p} \mathbf{0}$ by hypothesis and $(\mathbf{X}'\mathbf{X}/n) - \mathbf{M}_n \xrightarrow{p} \mathbf{0}$, $\hat{\boldsymbol{\Lambda}}_n - \boldsymbol{\Lambda}_n \xrightarrow{p} \mathbf{0}$ by Proposition 2.30. Given the result in (i), (ii) follows from Theorem 4.30.

Note that the Wald and Lagrange multiplier statistics would be identical if $\hat{\mathbf{V}}_n$ were used in place of $\ddot{\mathbf{V}}_n$. This suggests that the two statistics should be asymptotically equivalent.

EXERCISE 4.33: Prove that under the conditions of Theorems 4.31 and 4.32, $\mathcal{W}_n - \mathcal{LM}_n \xrightarrow{p} 0$.

Although the fact that $\ddot{\boldsymbol{\lambda}}_n$ is a linear combination of $\mathbf{R}\hat{\boldsymbol{\beta}}_n - \mathbf{r}$ simplifies the proof of Theorem 4.32, the whole point of using the Lagrange multiplier statistic is to avoid computing $\hat{\boldsymbol{\beta}}_n$ and to compute only the simpler $\ddot{\boldsymbol{\beta}}_n$. Computation of $\ddot{\boldsymbol{\beta}}_n$ is particularly simple when the model is $\mathbf{y} = \mathbf{X}_1\boldsymbol{\beta}_1 + \mathbf{X}_2\boldsymbol{\beta}_2 + \boldsymbol{\epsilon}$ and H_0 specifies that $\boldsymbol{\beta}_2$ (a $q \times 1$ vector) is zero. Then

$$\mathbf{R} = [\underset{(q\times k-q)}{\mathbf{0}} \; : \underset{(q\times q)}{\mathbf{I}}], \qquad \underset{(q\times 1)}{\mathbf{r}} = \mathbf{0},$$

and $\ddot{\boldsymbol{\beta}}'_n = (\ddot{\boldsymbol{\beta}}'_{1n}, \mathbf{0})$ where $\ddot{\boldsymbol{\beta}}_{1n} = (\mathbf{X}'_1\mathbf{X}_1)^{-1}\mathbf{X}'_1\mathbf{y}$.

EXERCISE 4.34: Define $\ddot{\boldsymbol{\epsilon}} = \mathbf{y} - \mathbf{X}_1\ddot{\boldsymbol{\beta}}_{1n}$. Show that under $H_0\!:\boldsymbol{\beta}_2 = \mathbf{0}$,

$$\begin{aligned}\ddot{\boldsymbol{\lambda}}_n &= 2\mathbf{X}'_2(\mathbf{I} - \mathbf{X}_1(\mathbf{X}'_1\mathbf{X}_1)^{-1}\mathbf{X}'_1)\ddot{\boldsymbol{\epsilon}}/n \\ &= 2\mathbf{X}'_2\ddot{\boldsymbol{\epsilon}}/n.\end{aligned}$$

(*Hint:* $\mathbf{R}\hat{\boldsymbol{\beta}}_n - \mathbf{r} = \mathbf{R}(\mathbf{X}'\mathbf{X}/n)^{-1}\mathbf{X}'(\mathbf{y} - \mathbf{X}\ddot{\boldsymbol{\beta}}_n)/n$).

By applying the particular form of $\mathbf{R}$ to the result of Theorem 4.32(ii), we obtain

$$\mathcal{LM}_n = n\ddot{\boldsymbol{\lambda}}'_n[(-\mathbf{X}'_2\mathbf{X}_1(\mathbf{X}'_1\mathbf{X}_1)^{-1}\!:\!\mathbf{I}_q)\ddot{\mathbf{V}}_n(-\mathbf{X}'_2\mathbf{X}_1(\mathbf{X}'_1\mathbf{X}_1)^{-1}\!:\!\mathbf{I}_q)']^{-1}\ddot{\boldsymbol{\lambda}}_n/4.$$

When $\mathbf{V}_n$ can be consistently estimated by $\ddot{\mathbf{V}}_n = \ddot{\sigma}^2_n(\mathbf{X}'\mathbf{X}/n)$, where $\ddot{\sigma}^2_n = \ddot{\boldsymbol{\epsilon}}'\ddot{\boldsymbol{\epsilon}}/n$, the $\mathcal{LM}_n$ statistic simplifies even further.

EXERCISE 4.35: If $\ddot{\sigma}^2_n(\mathbf{X}'\mathbf{X}/n) - \mathbf{V}_n \xrightarrow{p} \mathbf{0}$ and $\boldsymbol{\beta}_2 = \mathbf{0}$, show that $\mathcal{LM}_n = n\ddot{\boldsymbol{\epsilon}}'\mathbf{X}(\mathbf{X}'\mathbf{X})^{-1}\mathbf{X}'\ddot{\boldsymbol{\epsilon}}/(\ddot{\boldsymbol{\epsilon}}'\ddot{\boldsymbol{\epsilon}})$, which is n times the simple $\mathbf{R}^2$ of the regression of $\ddot{\boldsymbol{\epsilon}}$ on $\mathbf{X}$.

The result of this exercise implies a very simple procedure for testing $\boldsymbol{\beta}_2 = \mathbf{0}$ when $\mathbf{V}_n = \sigma^2_o\mathbf{M}_n$. First, regress $\mathbf{y}$ on $\mathbf{X}_1$ and form the constrained residuals $\ddot{\boldsymbol{\epsilon}}$. Then regress $\ddot{\boldsymbol{\epsilon}}$ on $\mathbf{X}$. The product of the sample size n and the simple R^2 (i.e., without adjustment for the presence of a constant in the regression) from this regression is the $\mathcal{LM}_n$ test statistic, which has the χ^2_q distribution asymptotically. As Engle [1981] showed, many interesting diagnostic statistics can be computed in this way.

When the errors ϵ_t are scalar i.i.d. $N(0, \sigma^2_o)$ random variables, the OLS estimator is also the maximum likelihood estimator (MLE) because $\hat{\boldsymbol{\beta}}_n$ solves the problem

$$\max_{\boldsymbol{\beta},\sigma} \mathcal{L}(\boldsymbol{\beta}, \sigma; \mathbf{y}) = \exp\left[-n\log\sqrt{2\pi} - n\log\sigma - \tfrac{1}{2}\sum_{t=1}^{n}(\mathbf{y}_t - \mathbf{X}_t\boldsymbol{\beta})^2/\sigma^2\right],$$

where $\mathcal{L}(\boldsymbol{\beta}, \sigma; \mathbf{y})$ is the sample likelihood based on the normality assumption. When $\boldsymbol{\epsilon}_t$ is not i.i.d. $N(\mathbf{0}, \sigma_o^2)$, $\hat{\boldsymbol{\beta}}_n$ is said to be a quasi-maximum likelihood estimator (QMLE).

When $\hat{\boldsymbol{\beta}}_n$ is the MLE, hypothesis tests can be based on the log-likelihood ratio

$$\mathcal{LR}_n = \log[\mathcal{L}(\ddot{\boldsymbol{\beta}}_n, \ddot{\boldsymbol{\sigma}}_n; \mathbf{y})/\mathcal{L}(\hat{\boldsymbol{\beta}}_n, \hat{\boldsymbol{\sigma}}_n; \mathbf{y})],$$

where $\hat{\boldsymbol{\sigma}}_n^2 = n^{-1} \Sigma_{t=1}^n (\mathbf{y}_t - \mathbf{X}_t\hat{\boldsymbol{\beta}}_n)^2$ as before and $\ddot{\boldsymbol{\beta}}_n$, $\ddot{\boldsymbol{\sigma}}_n$ solves

$$\max_{\beta,\sigma} \mathcal{L}(\boldsymbol{\beta}, \boldsymbol{\sigma}; \mathbf{y}) \qquad \text{s.t.} \quad \mathbf{R}\boldsymbol{\beta} = \mathbf{r}.$$

It is easy to show that $\ddot{\boldsymbol{\beta}}_n$ is the constrained OLS estimator and $\ddot{\boldsymbol{\sigma}}_n^2 = \ddot{\boldsymbol{\epsilon}}'\ddot{\boldsymbol{\epsilon}}/n$ as before. The likelihood ratio is nonnegative and always less than or equal to 1. Simple algebra yields

$$\mathcal{LR}_n = (n/2) \log(\hat{\boldsymbol{\sigma}}_n^2/\ddot{\boldsymbol{\sigma}}_n^2).$$

Because $\ddot{\boldsymbol{\sigma}}_n^2 = \hat{\boldsymbol{\sigma}}_n^2 + (\hat{\boldsymbol{\beta}}_n - \ddot{\boldsymbol{\beta}}_n)'(\mathbf{X}'\mathbf{X}/n)(\hat{\boldsymbol{\beta}}_n - \ddot{\boldsymbol{\beta}}_n)$ (verify this),

$$\mathcal{LR}_n = -(n/2) \log[1 + (\hat{\boldsymbol{\beta}}_n - \ddot{\boldsymbol{\beta}}_n)'(\mathbf{X}'\mathbf{X}/n)(\hat{\boldsymbol{\beta}}_n - \ddot{\boldsymbol{\beta}}_n)/\hat{\boldsymbol{\sigma}}_n^2].$$

To find the asymptotic distribution of this statistic, we make use of the mean value theorem of calculus.

THEOREM 4.36 (*Mean value theorem*): Let s: $\mathbb{R}^k \to \mathbb{R}^1$ be defined on an open convex set $\Theta \subset \mathbb{R}^k$ such that s is continuously differentiable on Θ with gradient ∇s. Then for any points θ and $\theta_o \in \Theta$ there exists $\bar{\theta}$ on the segment connecting θ and θ_o such that $s(\theta) = s(\theta_o) + \nabla s(\bar{\theta})(\theta - \theta_o)$.

Proof: See Bartle [1976, p. 365].

For the present application, we choose $s(\theta) = \log(1 + \theta)$. If we also choose $\theta_o = 0$, we have $s(\theta) = (\log 1) + (1/1 + \bar{\theta}) \cdot \theta = (1/1 + \bar{\theta}) \cdot \theta$, where $\bar{\theta}$ lies between θ and zero. Let $\theta_n = (\hat{\boldsymbol{\beta}}_n - \ddot{\boldsymbol{\beta}}_n)'(\mathbf{X}'\mathbf{X}/n)(\hat{\boldsymbol{\beta}}_n - \ddot{\boldsymbol{\beta}}_n)/\ddot{\boldsymbol{\sigma}}_n^2$ so that under H_0, $|\bar{\theta}_n| < |\theta_n| \xrightarrow{p} 0$; hence $\bar{\theta}_n \xrightarrow{p} 0$. Applying the mean value theorem now gives

$$\mathcal{LR}_n = -(n/2)(1 + \bar{\theta}_n)^{-1}(\hat{\boldsymbol{\beta}}_n - \ddot{\boldsymbol{\beta}}_n)'(\mathbf{X}'\mathbf{X}/n)(\hat{\boldsymbol{\beta}}_n - \ddot{\boldsymbol{\beta}}_n)/\ddot{\boldsymbol{\sigma}}_n^2.$$

Because $(1 + \bar{\theta}_n)^{-1} \xrightarrow{p} 1$, it follows from Lemma 4.6 that

$$-2\mathcal{LR}_n - n(\hat{\boldsymbol{\beta}}_n - \ddot{\boldsymbol{\beta}}_n)'(\mathbf{X}'\mathbf{X}/n)(\hat{\boldsymbol{\beta}}_n - \ddot{\boldsymbol{\beta}}_n)/\hat{\boldsymbol{\sigma}}_n^2 \xrightarrow{p} 0,$$

provided the second term has a limiting distribution. Now

$$\hat{\boldsymbol{\beta}}_n - \ddot{\boldsymbol{\beta}}_n = (\mathbf{X}'\mathbf{X}/n)^{-1}\mathbf{R}'(\mathbf{R}(\mathbf{X}'\mathbf{X}/n)^{-1}\mathbf{R}')^{-1}(\mathbf{R}\hat{\boldsymbol{\beta}}_n - \mathbf{r}).$$

Thus

$$-2\mathcal{LR}_n - n(\mathbf{R}\hat{\boldsymbol{\beta}}_n - \mathbf{r})'[\mathbf{R}(\mathbf{X}'\mathbf{X}/n)^{-1}\mathbf{R}']^{-1}(\mathbf{R}\hat{\boldsymbol{\beta}}_n - \mathbf{r})/\hat{\sigma}_n^2 \xrightarrow{p} 0.$$

This second term is the Wald statistic formed with $\hat{\mathbf{V}}_n = \hat{\sigma}_n^2(\mathbf{X}'\mathbf{X}/n)$, so $-2\mathcal{LR}_n$ is asymptotically equivalent to the Wald statistic and has the χ_q^2 distribution asymptotically, *provided* $\hat{\sigma}_n^2(\mathbf{X}'\mathbf{X}/n)$ is a consistent estimator for $\mathbf{V}_n$. If this is not true, then $-2\mathcal{LR}_n$ does not in general have the χ_q^2 distribution asymptotically. It does have a limiting distribution, but not a simple one that has been tabulated or is easily computable. Note that it is not violation of the normality assumption per se, but the failure of $\mathbf{V}_n$ to equal $\sigma_o^2\mathbf{M}_n$ that results in $-2\mathcal{LR}_n$ not having the χ_q^2 distribution asymptotically.

The formal statement of the result for the $\mathcal{LR}_n$ statistic is the following.

THEOREM 4.37 (*Likelihood ratio test*): Let the conditions of Theorem 4.25 hold, let rank $\mathbf{R} = q \leq k$, and let $\hat{\sigma}_n^2(\mathbf{X}'\mathbf{X}/n) - \mathbf{V}_n \xrightarrow{p} \mathbf{0}$. Then under $H_0\colon \mathbf{R}\boldsymbol{\beta}_0 = \mathbf{r}$, $-2\mathcal{LR}_n \overset{A}{\sim} \chi_q^2$.

Proof: Set $\hat{\mathbf{V}}_n$ in Theorem 4.31 to $\hat{\mathbf{V}}_n = \hat{\sigma}_n^2(\mathbf{X}'\mathbf{X}/n)$. Then from the argument preceding the theorem above $-2\mathcal{LR}_n - \mathcal{W}_n \xrightarrow{p} 0$. Because $\mathcal{W}_n \overset{A}{\sim} \chi_q^2$, it follows from Lemma 4.7 that $-2\mathcal{LR}_n \overset{A}{\sim} \chi_q^2$.

The mean value theorem just introduced provides a convenient way to find the asymptotic distribution of statistics used to test nonlinear hypotheses. In general, nonlinear hypotheses can be conveniently represented as

$$H_0\colon \mathbf{s}(\boldsymbol{\beta}_o) = \mathbf{0},$$

where $\mathbf{s}\colon \mathbb{R}^k \to \mathbb{R}^q$ is a continuously differentiable function of $\boldsymbol{\beta}$.

EXAMPLE 4.38: Suppose $\mathbf{y} = \mathbf{X}_1\beta_1 + \mathbf{X}_2\beta_2 + \mathbf{X}_3\beta_3 + \boldsymbol{\epsilon}$, where $\mathbf{X}_1$, $\mathbf{X}_2$, and $\mathbf{X}_3$ are $n \times 1$ and β_1, β_2, and β_3 are scalars. Further, suppose we hypothesize that $\beta_3 = \beta_1\beta_2$. Then $\mathbf{s}(\boldsymbol{\beta}_0) = \beta_3 - \beta_1\beta_2 = 0$ expresses the null hypothesis.

Just as with linear restrictions, we can construct a Wald test based on the asymptotic distribution of $\mathbf{s}(\hat{\boldsymbol{\beta}}_n)$; we can construct a Lagrange multiplier test based on the Lagrange multipliers derived from minimizing the least squares (or other estimation) objective function subject to the constraint; or we can form a log-likelihood ratio.

To illustrate the approach, consider the Wald test based on $\mathbf{s}(\hat{\boldsymbol{\beta}}_n)$. As before, a value of $\mathbf{s}(\hat{\boldsymbol{\beta}}_n)$ far from zero is evidence against H_0. To tell how far $\mathbf{s}(\hat{\boldsymbol{\beta}}_n)$ must be from zero to reject H_0, we need to determine its asymptotic distribution. This is provided by the next result.

THEOREM 4.39 (*Wald test*): Let the conditions of Theorem 4.25 hold and let rank $\nabla\mathbf{s}(\boldsymbol{\beta}_o) = q \leq k$. Then under $H_0: \mathbf{s}(\boldsymbol{\beta}_o) = \mathbf{0}$,

(i) $\boldsymbol{\Gamma}_n^{-1/2}\sqrt{n}\,\mathbf{s}(\hat{\boldsymbol{\beta}}_n) \overset{A}{\sim} N(\mathbf{0}, \mathbf{I})$, where

$$\boldsymbol{\Gamma}_n \equiv \nabla\mathbf{s}(\boldsymbol{\beta}_o)\mathbf{D}_n\nabla\mathbf{s}(\boldsymbol{\beta}_o)'.$$

(ii) The Wald statistic $\mathcal{W}_n \equiv n\,\mathbf{s}(\hat{\boldsymbol{\beta}}_n)'\hat{\boldsymbol{\Gamma}}_n^{-1}\mathbf{s}(\hat{\boldsymbol{\beta}}_n) \overset{A}{\sim} \chi^2_q$, where

$$\begin{aligned}\hat{\boldsymbol{\Gamma}}_n &\equiv \nabla\mathbf{s}(\hat{\boldsymbol{\beta}}_n)\hat{\mathbf{D}}_n\nabla\mathbf{s}(\hat{\boldsymbol{\beta}}_n)' \\ &= \nabla\mathbf{s}(\hat{\boldsymbol{\beta}}_n)(\mathbf{X}'\mathbf{X}/n)^{-1}\hat{\mathbf{V}}_n(\mathbf{X}'\mathbf{X}/n)^{-1}\nabla\mathbf{s}(\hat{\boldsymbol{\beta}}_n)'.\end{aligned}$$

Proof: (i) Because $\mathbf{s}(\boldsymbol{\beta})$ is a vector function, we apply the mean value theorem to each element $\mathbf{s}_i(\boldsymbol{\beta})$, $i = 1, \ldots, q$,

$$\mathbf{s}_i(\hat{\boldsymbol{\beta}}_n) = \mathbf{s}_i(\boldsymbol{\beta}_o) + \nabla\mathbf{s}_i(\bar{\boldsymbol{\beta}}_n^{(i)})(\hat{\boldsymbol{\beta}}_n - \boldsymbol{\beta}_o),$$

where $\bar{\boldsymbol{\beta}}_n^{(i)}$ is a $k \times 1$ vector lying on the segment connecting $\hat{\boldsymbol{\beta}}_n$ and $\boldsymbol{\beta}_o$. The superscript (i) reflects the fact that the mean value may be different for each element $\mathbf{s}_i(\boldsymbol{\beta})$ of $\mathbf{s}(\boldsymbol{\beta})$.

Under H_0, $\mathbf{s}_i(\boldsymbol{\beta}_o) = \mathbf{0}$, $i = 1, \ldots, q$, so

$$\sqrt{n}\mathbf{s}_i(\hat{\boldsymbol{\beta}}_n) = \nabla\mathbf{s}_i(\bar{\boldsymbol{\beta}}_n^{(i)})\sqrt{n}(\hat{\boldsymbol{\beta}}_n - \boldsymbol{\beta}_o).$$

This suggests considering the difference

$$\begin{aligned}&\sqrt{n}\mathbf{s}_i(\hat{\boldsymbol{\beta}}_n) - \nabla\mathbf{s}_i(\boldsymbol{\beta}_o)\sqrt{n}(\hat{\boldsymbol{\beta}}_n - \boldsymbol{\beta}_o) \\ &\quad = (\nabla\mathbf{s}_i(\bar{\boldsymbol{\beta}}_n^{(i)}) - \nabla\mathbf{s}_i(\boldsymbol{\beta}_o))\sqrt{n}(\hat{\boldsymbol{\beta}}_n - \boldsymbol{\beta}_o) \\ &\quad = (\nabla\mathbf{s}_i(\bar{\boldsymbol{\beta}}_n^{(i)}) - \nabla\mathbf{s}_i(\boldsymbol{\beta}_o))\mathbf{D}_n^{1/2}\mathbf{D}_n^{-1/2}\sqrt{n}(\hat{\boldsymbol{\beta}}_n - \boldsymbol{\beta}_o).\end{aligned}$$

By Theorem 4.25, $\mathbf{D}_n^{-1/2}\sqrt{n}(\hat{\boldsymbol{\beta}}_n - \boldsymbol{\beta}_o) \overset{A}{\sim} N(\mathbf{0}, \mathbf{I})$. Because $\hat{\boldsymbol{\beta}}_n \xrightarrow{p} \boldsymbol{\beta}_o$, it follows that $\bar{\boldsymbol{\beta}}_n^{(i)} \xrightarrow{p} \boldsymbol{\beta}_o$, so $\nabla\mathbf{s}_i(\bar{\boldsymbol{\beta}}_n^{(i)}) - \nabla\mathbf{s}_i(\boldsymbol{\beta}_o) \xrightarrow{p} \mathbf{0}$ by Proposition 2.27. Because $\mathbf{D}_n^{1/2}$ is $O(1)$, we have $(\nabla\mathbf{s}_i(\bar{\boldsymbol{\beta}}_n^{(i)}) - \nabla\mathbf{s}_i(\boldsymbol{\beta}_o))\mathbf{D}_n^{1/2} \xrightarrow{p} \mathbf{0}$. It follows from Lemma 4.6 that

$$\sqrt{n}\mathbf{s}_i(\hat{\boldsymbol{\beta}}_n) - \nabla\mathbf{s}_i(\boldsymbol{\beta}_o)\sqrt{n}(\hat{\boldsymbol{\beta}}_n - \boldsymbol{\beta}_o) \xrightarrow{p} \mathbf{0}, \qquad i = 1, \ldots, q.$$

In vector form this becomes

$$\sqrt{n}\mathbf{s}(\hat{\boldsymbol{\beta}}_n) - \nabla\mathbf{s}(\boldsymbol{\beta}_o)\sqrt{n}(\hat{\boldsymbol{\beta}}_n - \boldsymbol{\beta}_o) \xrightarrow{p} \mathbf{0},$$

and because $\mathbf{\Gamma}_n^{-1/2}$ is O(1),

$$\mathbf{\Gamma}_n^{-1/2}\sqrt{n}\mathbf{s}(\hat{\boldsymbol{\beta}}_n) - \mathbf{\Gamma}_n^{-1/2}\nabla\mathbf{s}(\boldsymbol{\beta}_o)\sqrt{n}(\hat{\boldsymbol{\beta}}_n - \boldsymbol{\beta}_o) \xrightarrow{p} \mathbf{0}.$$

Corollary 4.24 immediately yields $\mathbf{\Gamma}_n^{-1/2}\nabla\mathbf{s}(\boldsymbol{\beta}_o)\sqrt{n}(\hat{\boldsymbol{\beta}}_n - \boldsymbol{\beta}_o) \overset{A}{\sim} N(\mathbf{0}, \mathbf{I})$, so by Lemma 4.7, $\mathbf{\Gamma}_n^{-1/2}\sqrt{n}\mathbf{s}(\hat{\boldsymbol{\beta}}_n) \overset{A}{\sim} N(0, \mathbf{I})$.

(ii) Because $\hat{\mathbf{D}}_n - \mathbf{D}_n \xrightarrow{p} \mathbf{0}$ from Theorem 4.25 and $\nabla\mathbf{s}(\hat{\boldsymbol{\beta}}_n) - \nabla\mathbf{s}(\boldsymbol{\beta}_o) \xrightarrow{p} \mathbf{0}$ by Proposition 2.27, $\hat{\mathbf{\Gamma}}_n - \mathbf{\Gamma}_n \xrightarrow{p} \mathbf{0}$ by Proposition 2.30. Given the result in (i), (ii) follows from Theorem 4.30.

Note the similiarity of this result to Theorem 4.31 which gives the Wald test for the linear hypothesis $\mathbf{R}\boldsymbol{\beta}_o = \mathbf{r}$. In the present context, $\mathbf{s}(\boldsymbol{\beta}_o)$ plays the role of $\mathbf{R}\boldsymbol{\beta}_o - \mathbf{r}$, whereas $\nabla\mathbf{s}(\boldsymbol{\beta}_o)$ plays the role of $\mathbf{R}$ in computing the covariance matrix.

EXERCISE 4.40: Write down the Wald statistic for testing the hypothesis of Example 4.38.

EXERCISE 4.41: Give the Lagrange multiplier statistic for testing $H_0: \mathbf{s}(\boldsymbol{\beta}_o) = \mathbf{0}$ versus $H_1: \mathbf{s}(\boldsymbol{\beta}_o) \neq \mathbf{0}$, and derive its limiting distribution under the conditions of Theorem 4.25.

EXERCISE 4.42: Give the Wald and Lagrange multiplier statistics for testing the hypotheses $\mathbf{R}\boldsymbol{\beta}_o = \mathbf{r}$ and $\mathbf{s}(\boldsymbol{\beta}_o) = \mathbf{0}$ on the basis of the IV estimator $\tilde{\boldsymbol{\beta}}_n$ and derive their limiting distributions under the conditions of Exercise 4.26.

IV.3 Asymptotic Efficiency

Given a class of estimators (e.g., the class of instrumental variables estimators), it is desirable to choose that member of the class that has the smallest asymptotic covariance matrix (assuming that this member exists and can be computed). The reason for this is that such estimators are obviously more precise, and in general allow construction of more powerful test statistics. In what follows, we shall abuse notation slightly and write avar $\tilde{\boldsymbol{\beta}}_n$ instead of avar $\sqrt{n}(\tilde{\boldsymbol{\beta}}_n - \boldsymbol{\beta}_o)$.

DEFINITION 4.43: Given two consistent asymptotically normal estimators $\tilde{\boldsymbol{\beta}}_n$ and $\boldsymbol{\beta}_n^*$, $\boldsymbol{\beta}_n^*$ is said to be *asymptotically efficient relative to* $\tilde{\boldsymbol{\beta}}_n$ if and only if for all n sufficiently large, avar $\tilde{\boldsymbol{\beta}}_n$ − avar $\boldsymbol{\beta}_n^*$ is positive semidefinite for any $\boldsymbol{\beta}_o$. Given a class of estimators, a member of that class is *asymptotically efficient within the class* if and only if it is asymptotically efficient relative to every other member of its class.

The estimators we consider are the instrumental variables estimators

$$\tilde{\boldsymbol{\beta}}_n = (\mathbf{X}'\mathbf{Z}\hat{\mathbf{P}}_n\mathbf{Z}'\mathbf{X})^{-1}\mathbf{X}'\mathbf{Z}\hat{\mathbf{P}}_n\mathbf{Z}'\mathbf{y}.$$

We saw in Exercise 4.26 that the asymptotic covariance matrix of these estimators is

$$\mathbf{D}_n = (\mathbf{Q}_n'\mathbf{P}_n\mathbf{Q}_n)^{-1}\mathbf{Q}_n'\mathbf{P}_n\mathbf{V}_n\mathbf{P}_n\mathbf{Q}_n(\mathbf{Q}_n'\mathbf{P}_n\mathbf{Q}_n)^{-1}.$$

We now consider the problem of how the IV estimator can be constructed so as to make $\mathbf{D}_n$ as small as possible.

We first consider how $\hat{\mathbf{P}}_n$ can be optimally chosen. Until now, we have let $\hat{\mathbf{P}}_n$ be any positive definite matrix. It turns out, however, that by choosing $\hat{\mathbf{P}}_n = \hat{\mathbf{V}}_n^{-1}$, one obtains an asymptotically efficient estimator for the class of IV estimators with given instrumental variables $\mathbf{Z}$. To prove this, we make use of the following proposition.

PROPOSITION 4.44: Let $\mathbf{A}$ and $\mathbf{B}$ be positive definite matrices of order k. Then $\mathbf{A} - \mathbf{B}$ is positive semidefinite if and only if $\mathbf{B}^{-1} - \mathbf{A}^{-1}$ is positive semidefinite.

Proof: This follows from Goldberger [1964, Theorem 1.7.21, p. 38].

The usefulness of this result hinges on the fact that in the cases of interest to us it will often be much easier to determine whether $\mathbf{B}^{-1} - \mathbf{A}^{-1}$ is positive semidefinite than to examine the positive definiteness of $\mathbf{A} - \mathbf{B}$ directly.

PROPOSITION 4.45: Given instrumental variables $\mathbf{Z}$ and the conditions of Exercise 4.26, the choice $\hat{\mathbf{P}}_n = \hat{\mathbf{V}}_n^{-1}$ gives the IV estimator

$$\boldsymbol{\beta}_n^* = (\mathbf{X}'\mathbf{Z}\hat{\mathbf{V}}_n^{-1}\mathbf{Z}'\mathbf{X})^{-1}\mathbf{X}'\mathbf{Z}\hat{\mathbf{V}}_n^{-1}\mathbf{Z}'\mathbf{y},$$

which is asymptotically efficient within the class

$$\tilde{\boldsymbol{\beta}}_n = (\mathbf{X}'\mathbf{Z}\hat{\mathbf{P}}_n\mathbf{Z}'\mathbf{X})^{-1}\mathbf{X}'\mathbf{Z}\hat{\mathbf{P}}_n\mathbf{Z}'\mathbf{y}.$$

Proof: From Exercise 4.26, we have

$$\text{avar}\ \boldsymbol{\beta}_n^* = (\mathbf{Q}_n'\mathbf{V}_n^{-1}\mathbf{Q}_n)^{-1}.$$

From Proposition 4.44, avar $\tilde{\boldsymbol{\beta}}_n$ − avar $\boldsymbol{\beta}_n^*$ is p.s.d. if and only if (avar $\boldsymbol{\beta}_n^*)^{-1}$ − (avar $\tilde{\boldsymbol{\beta}}_n)^{-1}$ is p.s.d. Now for all n sufficiently large,

$$
\begin{aligned}
&(\operatorname{avar} \boldsymbol{\beta}_n^*)^{-1} - (\operatorname{avar} \tilde{\boldsymbol{\beta}}_n)^{-1} \\
&\quad = \mathbf{Q}_n'\mathbf{V}_n^{-1}\mathbf{Q}_n - \mathbf{Q}_n'\mathbf{P}_n\mathbf{Q}_n(\mathbf{Q}_n'\mathbf{P}_n\mathbf{V}_n\mathbf{P}_n\mathbf{Q}_n)^{-1}\mathbf{Q}_n'\mathbf{P}_n\mathbf{Q}_n \\
&\quad = \mathbf{Q}_n'\mathbf{V}_n^{-1/2}(\mathbf{I} \\
&\qquad - \mathbf{V}_n^{1/2}\mathbf{P}_n\mathbf{Q}_n(\mathbf{Q}_n'\mathbf{P}_n\mathbf{V}_n^{1/2}\mathbf{V}_n^{1/2}\mathbf{P}_n\mathbf{Q}_n)^{-1}\mathbf{Q}_n'\mathbf{P}_n\mathbf{V}_n^{1/2})\mathbf{V}_n^{-1/2}\mathbf{Q}_n \\
&\quad = \mathbf{Q}_n'\mathbf{V}_n^{-1/2}(\mathbf{I} - \mathbf{G}_n(\mathbf{G}_n'\mathbf{G}_n)^{-1}\mathbf{G}_n)\mathbf{V}_n^{-1/2}\mathbf{Q}_n,
\end{aligned}
$$

where $\mathbf{G}_n \equiv \mathbf{V}_n^{-1/2}\mathbf{P}_n\mathbf{Q}_n$. This is a quadratic form in an idempotent matrix and is therefore p.s.d. The result follows.

EXERCISE 4.46: Given instrumental variables $\mathbf{X}$, suppose that $\mathbf{V}_n^{-1/2} \Sigma_{t=1}^n \mathbf{X}_t'\boldsymbol{\epsilon}_t \overset{A}{\sim} N(\mathbf{0}, \mathbf{I})$, where $\mathbf{V}_n = \sigma_o^2\mathbf{M}_n$. Show that the asymptotically efficient estimator is $\hat{\boldsymbol{\beta}}_n$, under the conditions of Theorem 4.25.

EXERCISE 4.47: Given instrumental variables $\mathbf{Z}$, suppose that $\mathbf{V}_n^{-1/2} \Sigma_{t=1}^n \mathbf{Z}_t'\boldsymbol{\epsilon}_t \overset{A}{\sim} N(\mathbf{0}, \mathbf{I})$, where $\mathbf{V}_n = \sigma_o^2\mathbf{L}_n$ and $\mathbf{L}_n \equiv E(\mathbf{Z}'\mathbf{Z}/n)$. Show that the asymptotically efficient estimator is the two-stage least squares estimator

$$\tilde{\boldsymbol{\beta}}_{2SLS} = (\mathbf{X}'\mathbf{Z}(\mathbf{Z}'\mathbf{Z})^{-1}\mathbf{Z}'\mathbf{X})^{-1}\mathbf{X}'\mathbf{Z}(\mathbf{Z}'\mathbf{Z})^{-1}\mathbf{Z}'\mathbf{y}$$

under the conditions of Exercise 4.26.

Note that the value of σ_o^2 plays no role in either Exercise 4.46 or Exercise 4.47 as long as it is finite. In what follows, we shall simply ignore σ_o^2, and proceed as if $\sigma_o^2 = 1$.

Proposition 4.45 provides the optimal estimator for given instrumental variables $\mathbf{Z}$. The next result shows that whenever additional instrumental variables satisfying the conditions of Exercise 4.26 are available, the efficiency of the IV estimator can potentially be improved by their use. To establish this, we make use of the formula for the inverse of a partitioned matrix, which we now state for convenience.

PROPOSITION 4.48: Define the $k \times k$ nonsingular symmetric matrix

$$\mathbf{A} = \begin{bmatrix} \mathbf{B} & \mathbf{C}' \\ \mathbf{C} & \mathbf{D} \end{bmatrix},$$

where $\mathbf{B}$ is $k_1 \times k_1$, $\mathbf{C}$ is $k_2 \times k_1$ and $\mathbf{D}$ is $k_2 \times k_2$. Then, defining $\mathbf{E} \equiv \mathbf{D} - \mathbf{C}\mathbf{B}^{-1}\mathbf{C}'$,

$$\mathbf{A}^{-1} = \begin{bmatrix} \mathbf{B}^{-1}(\mathbf{I} + \mathbf{C}'\mathbf{E}^{-1}\mathbf{C}\mathbf{B}^{-1}) & -\mathbf{B}^{-1}\mathbf{C}'\mathbf{E}^{-1} \\ -\mathbf{E}^{-1}\mathbf{C}\mathbf{B}^{-1} & \mathbf{E}^{-1} \end{bmatrix}.$$

Proof: See Goldberger [1964, p. 27].

PROPOSITION 4.49: Partition $\mathbf{Z}$ as $\mathbf{Z} = (\mathbf{Z}_1, \mathbf{Z}_2)$ and suppose the conditions of Exercise 4.26 hold for both $\mathbf{Z}_1$ and $\mathbf{Z}$. Define $\mathbf{V}_{1n} = E(\mathbf{Z}_1'\boldsymbol{\epsilon\epsilon}'\mathbf{Z}_1/n)$, $\tilde{\boldsymbol{\beta}}_n = (\mathbf{X}'\mathbf{Z}_1\hat{\mathbf{V}}_{1n}^{-1}\mathbf{Z}_1'\mathbf{X})^{-1}\mathbf{X}'\mathbf{Z}_1\hat{\mathbf{V}}_{1n}^{-1}\mathbf{Z}_1'\mathbf{y}$, and $\boldsymbol{\beta}_n^* = (\mathbf{X}'\mathbf{Z}\hat{\mathbf{V}}_n^{-1}\mathbf{Z}'\mathbf{X})^{-1}\mathbf{X}'\mathbf{Z}\hat{\mathbf{V}}_n^{-1}\mathbf{Z}'\mathbf{y}$.

Then avar $\tilde{\boldsymbol{\beta}}_n -$ avar $\boldsymbol{\beta}_n^*$ is a positive semidefinite matrix for all n sufficiently large.

Proof: Partition $\mathbf{Q}_n$ as $\mathbf{Q}_n' = (\mathbf{Q}_{1n}', \mathbf{Q}_{2n}')$, where $\mathbf{Q}_{1n} = E(\mathbf{Z}_1'\mathbf{X}/n)$, $\mathbf{Q}_{2n} = E(\mathbf{Z}_2'\mathbf{X}/n)$, and partition $\mathbf{V}_n$ as

$$\mathbf{V}_n = \begin{bmatrix} \mathbf{V}_{1n} & \mathbf{V}_{12n} \\ \mathbf{V}_{21n} & \mathbf{V}_{2n} \end{bmatrix}.$$

The partitioned inverse formula gives

$$\mathbf{V}_n^{-1} = \begin{bmatrix} \mathbf{V}_{1n}^{-1}(\mathbf{I} + \mathbf{V}_{12n}\mathbf{E}_n^{-1}\mathbf{V}_{21n}\mathbf{V}_{1n}^{-1}) & -\mathbf{V}_{1n}^{-1}\mathbf{V}_{12n}\mathbf{E}_n^{-1} \\ -\mathbf{E}_n^{-1}\mathbf{V}_{21n}\mathbf{V}_{1n}^{-1} & \mathbf{E}_n^{-1} \end{bmatrix},$$

where $\mathbf{E}_n \equiv \mathbf{V}_{2n} - \mathbf{V}_{21n}\mathbf{V}_{1n}^{-1}\mathbf{V}_{12n}$. From Exercise 4.26, we have

$$\text{avar}\ \tilde{\boldsymbol{\beta}}_n = (\mathbf{Q}_{1n}'\mathbf{V}_{1n}^{-1}\mathbf{Q}_{1n})^{-1},$$
$$\text{avar}\ \boldsymbol{\beta}_n^* = (\mathbf{Q}_n'\mathbf{V}_n^{-1}\mathbf{Q}_n)^{-1}.$$

We apply Proposition 4.44 and consider

$$\begin{aligned}
&(\text{avar}\ \boldsymbol{\beta}_n^*)^{-1} - (\text{avar}\ \tilde{\boldsymbol{\beta}}_n)^{-1} \\
&= \mathbf{Q}_n'\mathbf{V}_n^{-1}\mathbf{Q}_n - \mathbf{Q}_{1n}'\mathbf{V}_{1n}^{-1}\mathbf{Q}_{1n} \\
&= [\mathbf{Q}_{1n}', \mathbf{Q}_{2n}']\mathbf{V}_n^{-1}[\mathbf{Q}_{1n}', \mathbf{Q}_{2n}']' - \mathbf{Q}_{1n}'\mathbf{V}_{1n}^{-1}\mathbf{Q}_{1n} \\
&= \mathbf{Q}_{1n}'(\mathbf{V}_{1n}^{-1} + \mathbf{V}_{1n}^{-1}\mathbf{V}_{12n}\mathbf{E}_n^{-1}\mathbf{V}_{21n}\mathbf{V}_{1n}^{-1})\mathbf{Q}_{1n} \\
&\quad - \mathbf{Q}_{2n}'\mathbf{E}_n^{-1}\mathbf{V}_{21n}\mathbf{V}_{1n}^{-1}\mathbf{Q}_{1n} - \mathbf{Q}_{1n}'\mathbf{V}_{1n}^{-1}\mathbf{V}_{12n}\mathbf{E}_n^{-1}\mathbf{Q}_{2n} \\
&\quad + \mathbf{Q}_{2n}'\mathbf{E}_n^{-1}\mathbf{Q}_{2n} - \mathbf{Q}_{1n}'\mathbf{V}_{1n}^{-1}\mathbf{Q}_{1n} \\
&= \mathbf{Q}_{1n}'\mathbf{V}_{1n}^{-1}\mathbf{V}_{12n}\mathbf{E}_n^{-1}\mathbf{V}_{21}\mathbf{V}_{1n}^{-1}\mathbf{Q}_{1n} - \mathbf{Q}_{2n}'\mathbf{E}_n^{-1}\mathbf{V}_{21n}\mathbf{V}_{1n}^{-1}\mathbf{Q}_{1n} \\
&\quad - \mathbf{Q}_{1n}'\mathbf{V}_{1n}^{-1}\mathbf{V}_{12n}\mathbf{E}_n^{-1}\mathbf{Q}_{2n} + \mathbf{Q}_{2n}'\mathbf{E}_n^{-1}\mathbf{Q}_{2n} \\
&= [\mathbf{Q}_{1n}'\mathbf{V}_{1n}^{-1}\mathbf{V}_{12n} - \mathbf{Q}_{2n}']\mathbf{E}_n^{-1}[\mathbf{V}_{21n}\mathbf{V}_{1n}^{-1}\mathbf{Q}_{1n} - \mathbf{Q}_{2n}].
\end{aligned}$$

Because $\mathbf{E}_n^{-1}$ is a symmetric positive definite matrix (why?), we can write $\mathbf{E}_n^{-1} = \mathbf{E}_n^{-1/2}\mathbf{E}_n^{-1/2}$, so that

$$\begin{aligned}
&(\text{avar}\ \boldsymbol{\beta}_n^*)^{-1} - (\text{avar}\ \tilde{\boldsymbol{\beta}}_n)^{-1} \\
&= [\mathbf{Q}_{1n}'\mathbf{V}_{1n}^{-1}\mathbf{V}_{12n} - \mathbf{Q}_{2n}']\mathbf{E}_n^{-1/2}\mathbf{E}_n^{-1/2}[\mathbf{V}_{21n}\mathbf{V}_{1n}^{-1}\mathbf{Q}_{1n} - \mathbf{Q}_{2n}].
\end{aligned}$$

Because this is the product of a matrix and its transpose, we immediately have $(\text{avar}\,\boldsymbol{\beta}_n^*)^{-1} - (\text{avar}\,\tilde{\boldsymbol{\beta}}_n)^{-1}$ is p.s.d. so that the result follows from Proposition 4.44.

This result states essentially that the asymptotic precision of the IV estimator cannot be worsened by including additional instrumental variables. We can be more specific, however, and specify situations in which $\text{avar}\,\tilde{\boldsymbol{\beta}}_n = \text{avar}\,\boldsymbol{\beta}_n^*$, so that nothing is gained by adding an extra instrumental variable.

PROPOSITION 4.50: Let the conditions of Proposition 4.49 hold. Then $\text{avar}\,\tilde{\boldsymbol{\beta}}_n = \text{avar}\,\boldsymbol{\beta}_n^*$ if and only if

$$E(\mathbf{X}'\mathbf{Z}_1/n)E(\mathbf{Z}_1'\boldsymbol{\epsilon}\boldsymbol{\epsilon}'\mathbf{Z}_1/n)^{-1}E(\mathbf{Z}_1'\boldsymbol{\epsilon}\boldsymbol{\epsilon}'\mathbf{Z}_2/n) - E(\mathbf{X}'\mathbf{Z}_2/n) = 0.$$

Proof: Immediate from the final line of the proof of Proposition 4.49.

To interpet this condition, consider the special case in which $E(\mathbf{Z}'\boldsymbol{\epsilon}\boldsymbol{\epsilon}'\mathbf{Z}/n) = E(\mathbf{Z}'\mathbf{Z}/n)$. In this case the difference in Proposition 4.50 can be consistently estimated by

$$n^{-1}(\mathbf{X}'\mathbf{Z}_1(\mathbf{Z}_1'\mathbf{Z}_1)^{-1}\mathbf{Z}_1'\mathbf{Z}_2 - \mathbf{X}'\mathbf{Z}_2) = n^{-1}\mathbf{X}(\mathbf{Z}_1(\mathbf{Z}_1'\mathbf{Z}_1)^{-1}\mathbf{Z}_1' - \mathbf{I})\mathbf{Z}_2.$$

This quantity is recognizable as the cross product of $\mathbf{Z}_2$ and the projection of $\mathbf{X}$ onto the space orthogonal to that spanned by the columns of $\mathbf{Z}_1$. If we write $\tilde{\mathbf{X}} = \mathbf{X}(\mathbf{Z}_1(\mathbf{Z}_1'\mathbf{Z}_1)^{-1}\mathbf{Z}_1' - \mathbf{I})$, the difference in Proposition 4.50 is consistently estimated by $\tilde{\mathbf{X}}'\mathbf{Z}_2/n$, so that $\text{avar}\,\tilde{\boldsymbol{\beta}}_n = \text{avar}\,\boldsymbol{\beta}_n^*$ if and only if $\tilde{\mathbf{X}}'\mathbf{Z}_2/n \xrightarrow{p} \mathbf{0}$, which can be interpreted as saying that adding $\mathbf{Z}_2$ to the list of instrumental variables is of no use if it is uncorrelated with $\tilde{\mathbf{X}}$, the matrix of residuals of the regression of $\mathbf{X}$ on $\mathbf{Z}_1$.

One of the interesting consequences of Propositions 4.49 and 4.50 is that in the presence of heteroskedasticity or serial correlation of unknown form, there may exist estimators for the linear model more efficient than OLS. This result has been obtained independently by Cragg [1983] and Chamberlain [1982]. To construct these estimators, it is necessary to find additional instrumental variables uncorrelated with $\boldsymbol{\epsilon}_t$. If $\mathbf{E}(\boldsymbol{\epsilon}_t|\mathbf{X}_t) = 0$, such instrumental variables are easily found, because any measurable function of $\mathbf{X}_t$ will be uncorrelated with $\boldsymbol{\epsilon}_t$. Hence, we can set $\mathbf{Z}_t = (\mathbf{X}_t, z(\mathbf{X}_t))$, where $z(\mathbf{X}_t)$ is a $1 \times l - k$ vector of measurable functions of $\mathbf{X}_t$.

EXAMPLE 4.51: Let $p = k = 1$ so $\mathbf{y}_t = \mathbf{X}_t\boldsymbol{\beta}_o + \boldsymbol{\epsilon}_t$, where $\mathbf{y}_t$, $\mathbf{X}_t$ and $\boldsymbol{\epsilon}_t$

are scalars. Suppose that $\mathbf{X}_t$ is nonstochastic, and for convenience suppose $\mathbf{M}_n \equiv n^{-1} \sum_{t=1}^{n} \mathbf{X}_t^2 \to 1$. Let ϵ_t be independent heterogeneously distributed such that $E(\epsilon_t) = 0$ and $E(\epsilon_t^2) = \sigma_t^2$. Further, suppose $\mathbf{X}_t > \delta > 0$ for all t, and take $z(\mathbf{X}_t) = \mathbf{X}_t^{-1}$ so that $\mathbf{Z}_t = (\mathbf{X}_t, \mathbf{X}_t^{-1})$. We consider $\hat{\boldsymbol{\beta}}_n = (\mathbf{X}'\mathbf{X})^{-1}\mathbf{X}'\mathbf{y}$ and $\boldsymbol{\beta}_n^* = (\mathbf{X}'\mathbf{Z}\hat{\mathbf{V}}_n^{-1}\mathbf{Z}\mathbf{X})^{-1}\mathbf{X}'\mathbf{Z}\hat{\mathbf{V}}_n^{-1}\mathbf{Z}\mathbf{y}$, and suppose that sufficient other assumptions guarantee that the result of Exercise 4.26 holds for both estimators.

By Propositions 4.49 and 4.50, it follows that avar $\hat{\boldsymbol{\beta}}_n >$ avar $\boldsymbol{\beta}_n^*$ if and only if

$$\left(n^{-1} \sum_{t=1}^{n} \sigma_t^2 \mathbf{X}_t^2\right)^{-1} \left(n^{-1} \sum_{t=1}^{n} \sigma_t^2\right) - 1 \neq 0$$

or equivalently, if and only if $n^{-1} \sum_{t=1}^{n} \sigma_t^2 \mathbf{X}_t^2 \neq n^{-1} \sum_{t=1}^{n} \sigma_t^2$. This would certainly occur if $\sigma_t = \mathbf{X}_n^{-1}$. (Verify this using Jensen's inequality.)

It also follows from Propositions 4.49 and 4.50 that when $\mathbf{V}_n \neq \mathbf{L}_n$, there may exist estimators more efficient than two-stage least squares. If $l > k$, additional instrumental variables are not necessarily required to improve efficiency over 2SLS (see White [1982]); but as the result of Proposition 4.49 indicates, additional instrumental variables (e.g., functions of $\mathbf{Z}_t$) can nevertheless generate further improvements.

This suggests that in the presence of serial correlation or heteroskedasticity of unknown form there may be no limit to the number of instrumental variables available for improving the efficiency of the estimator. The situation is different in the absence of heteroskedasticity or serial correlation, however. In this case it is possible to specify precisely a finite set of instrumental variables that yield the greatest possible efficiency in a sense made explicit below.

Although we have seen that instrumental variables need only be uncorrelated with the errors ϵ_t, we now restrict attention to those variables $\mathbf{W}_{th}$ such that

$$E(\epsilon_{th} | \mathbf{W}_{th}) = 0, \qquad h = 1, \ldots, p; \quad t = 1, \ldots, n,$$

and we call the row vector $\mathbf{W}_{th}$ the set of *instrumental variable candidates for* $\mathbf{X}_{th}$. $\mathbf{W}_{th}$ may be of either finite or infinite dimension, and may include past or future values of variables first observed at time period t. Because $E(\epsilon_{th} | \mathbf{W}_{th}) = 0$, any element of $\mathbf{W}_{th}$ or any function of the elements of $\mathbf{W}_{th}$ will be uncorrelated with ϵ_{th}, and we now consider how best to choose functions of $\mathbf{W}_{th}$ as instrumental variables. The result that we obtain below says essentially that in the absence of serial correlation or heteroskedasticity the best intrumental variables are those functions of $\mathbf{W}_{th}$ appearing in the conditional expectation of $\mathbf{X}_{th}$, given $\mathbf{W}_{th}$.

To state the result precisely, we extend the notion of asymptotic efficiency as follows.

DEFINITION 4.52: Given two consistent asymptotically normal estimators $\tilde{\boldsymbol{\beta}}_n$ and $\boldsymbol{\beta}_n^*$, the estimator $\boldsymbol{\beta}_n^*$ is *essentially asymptotically efficient relative to* $\tilde{\boldsymbol{\beta}}_n$ if and only if for any $\delta > 0$, there exists $N(\delta)$ such that for all $n > N(\delta)$, $(1+\delta)\text{avar}\,\tilde{\boldsymbol{\beta}}_n - \text{avar}\,\boldsymbol{\beta}_n^*$ is positive semidefinite for any $\boldsymbol{\beta}_o$. Given a class of estimators, a member is *essentially asymptotically efficient within the class* if and only if it is essentially asymptotically efficient relative to every other member of its class.

The need for Definition 4.52 arises because it is possible for two asymptotic covariance matrices to fluctuate with n is such a way that neither avar $\tilde{\boldsymbol{\beta}}_n$ − avar $\boldsymbol{\beta}_n^*$ nor avar $\boldsymbol{\beta}_n^*$ − avar $\tilde{\boldsymbol{\beta}}_n$ is ever positive semidefinite for all n. However, by considering the difference between something just slightly greater than avar $\tilde{\boldsymbol{\beta}}_n$ and avar $\boldsymbol{\beta}_n^*$, one can obtain a positive semidefinite matrix. Establishing that an estimator is essentially asymptotically efficient is a consequence of using the behavior of consistent estimates of asymptotic covariance matrices to infer the behavior of the asymptotic covariance matrices themselves. This is based on the following result.

LEMMA 4.53: Let $\hat{A}_n$, A_n, $\hat{B}_n$ and B_n be symmetric matrices such that A_n and B_n are O(1), $\det A_n > \epsilon > 0$ for all n sufficiently large, $\hat{A}_n - A_n \xrightarrow{p} \mathbf{0}$, $\hat{B}_n - B_n \xrightarrow{p} \mathbf{0}$ and $\hat{A}_n - \hat{B}_n$ is positive semidefinite for all n. Then for any $\delta > 0$, there exists $N(\delta)$ such that for all $n > N(\delta)$, $(1+\delta)A_n - B_n$ is positive semidefinite. Further, if $A_n \to A$ and $B_n \to B$, where A and B are constant matrices, then $A - B$ is positive semidefinite.

Proof: See White [1983, Lemma A.2].

This result implies that if $\hat{A}_n - \hat{B}_n$ is always positive semidefinite, where $\hat{A}_n$ and $\hat{B}_n$ are consistent estimators of asymptotic covariance matrices A_n and B_n, then the estimator with asymptotic covariance matrix B_n is essentially asymptotically efficient relative to that with asymptotic covariance matrix A_n. Further, if A_n and B_n each converges to a limit, then the qualification "essentially" can be removed. The next result is established on this basis.

THEOREM 4.54 (*Optimal instrumental variables*): Suppose there exists a unique σ-field generated by row vectors $\mathbf{W}_{th}$ such that

(i) $E(\boldsymbol{\epsilon}_{th}|\mathbf{W}_{th}) = 0$ and $E(\boldsymbol{\epsilon}_{th}|\mathcal{G}_{th}) \neq 0$ for all $\mathcal{G}_{th} \supset \sigma(\mathbf{W}_{th})$, $h = 1, \ldots, p$, $t = 1, \ldots, n$;
(ii) $E(\boldsymbol{\epsilon}_{th}^2|\mathbf{W}_{th}) = 1$, $h = 1, \ldots, p$, $t = 1, \ldots, n$;
(iii) $E(\boldsymbol{\epsilon}_{th}\boldsymbol{\epsilon}_{\tau g}|\mathbf{W}_{th}, \mathbf{W}_{\tau g}) = 0, g \neq h = 1, \ldots, p, \tau \neq t = 1, \ldots, n$;

and suppose the conditions of Exercise 4.26 hold for instrumental variables $\mathbf{Z}$ satisfying

$$E(\mathbf{X}_{th}|\mathbf{W}_{th}) = \mathbf{Z}_{th}\Pi_o, \; h = 1, \ldots, p; \; t = 1, \ldots, n,$$

where Π_o is an $l \times k$ matrix of full column rank containing no zero rows, and for $\hat{\mathbf{P}}_n = (\mathbf{Z}'\mathbf{Z}/n)^{-1}$.

Let $\tilde{\mathbf{Z}}_{th}$ be any $1 \times \tilde{l}$ vector of measurable functions of $\mathbf{W}_{th}$ not equal to $\mathbf{Z}_{th}$, and let $\tilde{\mathbf{Z}}$ be the matrix with rows $\tilde{\mathbf{Z}}_{th}$. Suppose that the conditions of Exercise 4.26 hold for $\tilde{\mathbf{Z}}$ and for $\tilde{\mathbf{P}}_n = (\tilde{\mathbf{Z}}'\tilde{\mathbf{Z}}/n)^{-1}$. Define

$$\boldsymbol{\beta}_n^* = (\mathbf{X}'\mathbf{Z}(\mathbf{Z}'\mathbf{Z})^{-1}\mathbf{Z}'\mathbf{X})^{-1}\mathbf{X}'\mathbf{Z}(\mathbf{Z}'\mathbf{Z})^{-1}\mathbf{Z}'\mathbf{y},$$
$$\tilde{\boldsymbol{\beta}}_n = (\mathbf{X}'\tilde{\mathbf{Z}}(\tilde{\mathbf{Z}}'\tilde{\mathbf{Z}})^{-1}\tilde{\mathbf{Z}}'\mathbf{X})^{-1}\mathbf{X}'\tilde{\mathbf{Z}}(\tilde{\mathbf{Z}}'\tilde{\mathbf{Z}})^{-1}\tilde{\mathbf{Z}}'\mathbf{y}.$$

Suppose $\tilde{\mathbf{Z}}'\mathbf{Z}/n - E(\tilde{\mathbf{Z}}'\mathbf{Z}/n) \xrightarrow{p} \mathbf{0}$.

Then $\boldsymbol{\beta}_n^*$ is essentially asymptotically efficient relative to $\tilde{\boldsymbol{\beta}}_n$. Further, $\boldsymbol{\beta}_n^*$ is asymptotically efficient relative to $\tilde{\boldsymbol{\beta}}_n$, provided that avar $\boldsymbol{\beta}_n^*$ and avar $\tilde{\boldsymbol{\beta}}_n$ both converge to constant matrices.

Proof: Define

$$\mathbf{V}_n \equiv \text{var}(n^{-1/2}\mathbf{Z}'\boldsymbol{\epsilon}),$$
$$\tilde{\mathbf{V}}_n \equiv \text{var}(n^{-1/2}\tilde{\mathbf{Z}}'\boldsymbol{\epsilon}).$$

Given (ii) and (iii), it follows that

$$\mathbf{V}_n = \mathbf{L}_n \equiv E(\mathbf{Z}'\mathbf{Z}/n),$$
$$\tilde{\mathbf{V}}_n = \tilde{\mathbf{L}}_n \equiv E(\tilde{\mathbf{Z}}'\tilde{\mathbf{Z}}/n).$$

To show this, we write

$$\tilde{\mathbf{V}}_n \equiv E(\tilde{\mathbf{Z}}'\boldsymbol{\epsilon}\boldsymbol{\epsilon}'\tilde{\mathbf{Z}}/n)$$
$$= n^{-1} \sum_{t=1}^{n} \sum_{\tau=1}^{n} \sum_{h=1}^{p} \sum_{g=1}^{p} E(\tilde{\mathbf{Z}}_{th}'\boldsymbol{\epsilon}_{th}\boldsymbol{\epsilon}_{\tau g}\tilde{\mathbf{Z}}_{\tau g}).$$

By the law of iterated expectations,

$$E(\tilde{\mathbf{Z}}'_{th}\boldsymbol{\epsilon}_{th}\boldsymbol{\epsilon}_{\tau g}\tilde{\mathbf{Z}}_{\tau g}) = E[E(\tilde{\mathbf{Z}}'_{th}\boldsymbol{\epsilon}_{th}\boldsymbol{\epsilon}_{\tau g}\tilde{\mathbf{Z}}_{\tau g}|\mathbf{W}_{th}, \mathbf{W}_{\tau g})]$$
$$= E[\tilde{\mathbf{Z}}'_{th}E(\boldsymbol{\epsilon}_{th}\boldsymbol{\epsilon}_{\tau g}|\mathbf{W}_{th}, \mathbf{W}_{\tau g})\tilde{\mathbf{Z}}_{\tau g}]$$

by Proposition 3.65, because $\tilde{\mathbf{Z}}_{th}$ and $\tilde{\mathbf{Z}}_{\tau g}$ are both measurable with respect to $\sigma(\mathbf{W}_{th}, \mathbf{W}_{\tau g})$. Substituting (ii) and (iii) gives

$$E(\tilde{\mathbf{Z}}'_{th}\boldsymbol{\epsilon}_{th}\boldsymbol{\epsilon}_{\tau g}\tilde{\mathbf{Z}}_{\tau g}) = 0, \qquad t \neq \tau, \quad g \neq h,$$
$$E(\tilde{\mathbf{Z}}'_{th}\boldsymbol{\epsilon}_{th}\boldsymbol{\epsilon}_{th}\tilde{\mathbf{Z}}_{th}) = E(\tilde{\mathbf{Z}}'_{th}\tilde{\mathbf{Z}}_{th}).$$

Hence

$$\tilde{\mathbf{V}}_n = n^{-1} \sum_{t=1}^{n} \sum_{h=1}^{p} E(\tilde{\mathbf{Z}}'_{th}\tilde{\mathbf{Z}}_{th})$$
$$= E(\tilde{\mathbf{Z}}'\tilde{\mathbf{Z}}/n) \equiv \tilde{\mathbf{L}}_n.$$

A similar argument with $\mathbf{Z}$ replacing $\tilde{\mathbf{Z}}$ yields

$$\mathbf{V}_n = \mathbf{L}_n.$$

Now we consider

$$(1 + \delta) \operatorname{avar} \tilde{\boldsymbol{\beta}}_n - \operatorname{avar} \boldsymbol{\beta}^*_n$$

and proceed to show that for any $\delta > 0$, there exists $N(\delta)$ sufficiently large that for all $n \geq N(\delta)$, $(1 + \delta) \operatorname{avar} \tilde{\boldsymbol{\beta}}_n - \operatorname{avar} \boldsymbol{\beta}^*_n$ is p.s.d.

First, consider

$$\operatorname{avar} \boldsymbol{\beta}^*_n = (\mathbf{Q}'_n\mathbf{L}_n^{-1}\mathbf{Q}_n)^{-1},$$

where $\mathbf{Q}_n = \mathbf{E}(\mathbf{Z}'\mathbf{X}/n)$. Because $E(\mathbf{X}_{th}|\mathbf{W}_{th}) = \mathbf{Z}_{th}\Pi_o$, we have

$$E(\mathbf{Z}'_{th}\mathbf{X}_{th}) = E[E(\mathbf{Z}'_{th}\mathbf{X}_{th}|\mathbf{W}_{th})]$$
$$= E[\mathbf{Z}'_{th}E(\mathbf{X}_{th}|\mathbf{W}_{th})]$$
$$= E(\mathbf{Z}'_{th}\mathbf{Z}_{th})\Pi_o,$$

which implies that

$$E(\mathbf{Z}'\mathbf{X}/n) = n^{-1} \sum_{t=1}^{n} \sum_{h=1}^{p} E(\mathbf{Z}'_{th}\mathbf{X}_{th})$$
$$= n^{-1} \sum_{t=1}^{n} \sum_{h=1}^{p} E(\mathbf{Z}'_{th}\mathbf{Z}_{th})\Pi_o$$
$$= E(\mathbf{Z}'\mathbf{Z}/n)\Pi_o.$$

Hence,

$$\text{avar}\,\boldsymbol{\beta}_n^* = (\Pi_o' E(\mathbf{Z}'\mathbf{Z}/n)\Pi_o)^{-1}.$$

Next, consider

$$\text{avar}\,\tilde{\boldsymbol{\beta}}_n = (\tilde{\mathbf{Q}}_n' \tilde{\mathbf{L}}_n^{-1} \tilde{\mathbf{Q}}_n)^{-1},$$

where $\tilde{\mathbf{Q}}_n = E(\tilde{\mathbf{Z}}'\mathbf{X}/n)$. Now

$$\begin{aligned} E(\tilde{\mathbf{Z}}_{th}'\mathbf{X}_{th}) &= E[E(\tilde{\mathbf{Z}}_{th}'\mathbf{X}_{th}|\mathbf{W}_{th})] \\ &= E[\tilde{\mathbf{Z}}_{th}' E(\mathbf{X}_{th}|\mathbf{W}_{th})] \\ &= E[\tilde{\mathbf{Z}}_{th}'\mathbf{Z}_{th}\Pi_o] \\ &= E(\tilde{\mathbf{Z}}_{th}'\mathbf{Z}_{th})\Pi_o, \end{aligned}$$

so that

$$\begin{aligned} E(\tilde{\mathbf{Z}}'\mathbf{X}/n) &= n^{-1} \sum_{t=1}^{n} \sum_{h=1}^{p} E(\tilde{\mathbf{Z}}_{th}'\mathbf{X}_{th}) \\ &= n^{-1} \sum_{t=1}^{n} \sum_{h=1}^{p} E(\tilde{\mathbf{Z}}_{th}'\mathbf{Z}_{th})\Pi_o \\ &= E(\tilde{\mathbf{Z}}'\mathbf{Z}/n)\Pi_o, \end{aligned}$$

so that

$$\text{avar}\,\tilde{\boldsymbol{\beta}}_n = (\Pi_o' E(\mathbf{Z}'\tilde{\mathbf{Z}}/n) E(\tilde{\mathbf{Z}}'\tilde{\mathbf{Z}}/n)^{-1} E(\tilde{\mathbf{Z}}'\mathbf{Z}/n)\Pi_o)^{-1}.$$

Applying Proposition 4.44, we have that

$$(1+\delta)\,\text{avar}\,\tilde{\boldsymbol{\beta}}_n - \text{avar}\,\boldsymbol{\beta}_n^* \qquad \text{is p.s.d.}$$

if and only if

$$(\text{avar}\,\boldsymbol{\beta}_n^*)^{-1} - (1+\delta)^{-1}(\text{avar}\,\tilde{\boldsymbol{\beta}}_n)^{-1} \qquad \text{is p.s.d.,}$$

or equivalently, if and only if

$$(1+\delta)(\text{avar}\,\boldsymbol{\beta}_n^*)^{-1} - (\text{avar}\,\tilde{\boldsymbol{\beta}}_n)^{-1} \qquad \text{is p.s.d.}$$

Note that

$$\begin{aligned} &(1+\delta)(\text{avar}\,\boldsymbol{\beta}_n^*)^{-1} - (\text{avar}\,\tilde{\boldsymbol{\beta}}_n)^{-1} \\ &\quad = (1+\delta)\Pi_o' E(\mathbf{Z}'\mathbf{Z}/n)\Pi_o \\ &\qquad - \Pi_o' E(\mathbf{Z}'\tilde{\mathbf{Z}}/n) E(\tilde{\mathbf{Z}}'\tilde{\mathbf{Z}}/n)^{-1} E(\tilde{\mathbf{Z}}'\mathbf{Z}/n)\Pi_o. \end{aligned}$$

To evaluate this expression, we apply Lemma 4.53, setting $\hat{A}_n = \Pi_o'\mathbf{Z}'\mathbf{Z}/n\Pi_o$ and $\hat{B}_n = \Pi_o'\mathbf{Z}'\tilde{\mathbf{Z}}/n(\tilde{\mathbf{Z}}'\tilde{\mathbf{Z}}/n)^{-1}\tilde{\mathbf{Z}}'\mathbf{Z}/n\Pi_o$. Under the conditions given, $\hat{A}_n - A_n \to \mathbf{0}$, where $A_n = \Pi_o' E(\mathbf{Z}'\mathbf{Z}/n)\Pi_o$ and $\hat{B}_n - B_n \xrightarrow{p} \mathbf{0}$ where $B_n = \Pi_o' E(\mathbf{Z}'\tilde{\mathbf{Z}}/n)E(\tilde{\mathbf{Z}}'\tilde{\mathbf{Z}}/n)^{-1}E(\tilde{\mathbf{Z}}'\mathbf{Z}/n)\Pi_o$. Now

$$\begin{aligned}\hat{A}_n - \hat{B}_n &= \Pi_o'(\mathbf{Z}'\mathbf{Z}/n - \mathbf{Z}'\tilde{\mathbf{Z}}/n(\tilde{\mathbf{Z}}'\tilde{\mathbf{Z}}/n)^{-1}\tilde{\mathbf{Z}}'\mathbf{Z}/n)\Pi_o \\ &= \Pi_o'[\mathbf{Z}'(\mathbf{I} - \tilde{\mathbf{Z}}(\tilde{\mathbf{Z}}'\tilde{\mathbf{Z}})^{-1}\tilde{\mathbf{Z}}')\mathbf{Z}/n]\Pi_o,\end{aligned}$$

which is p.s.d. for all n. It follows from Lemma 4.53 that for any δ, there exists $N(\delta)$ such that for all $n > N(\delta)$, $(1 + \delta)A_n - B_n$ is p.s.d. This implies that $(1 + \delta)(\text{avar}\, \boldsymbol{\beta}_n^*)^{-1} - (\text{avar}\, \tilde{\boldsymbol{\beta}}_n)^{-1}$ is p.s.d., so that by Proposition 4.44, $(1 + \delta)\text{avar}\, \tilde{\boldsymbol{\beta}}_n - \text{avar}\, \boldsymbol{\beta}_n^*$ is p.s.d. Hence, $\boldsymbol{\beta}_n^*$ is essentially asymptotically efficient relative to $\tilde{\boldsymbol{\beta}}_n$ by Definition 4.52. It also follows from Lemma 4.53 that if avar $\boldsymbol{\beta}_n^*$ and avar $\tilde{\boldsymbol{\beta}}_n$ converge to constant limits, then $\boldsymbol{\beta}_n^*$ is asymptotically efficient relative to $\tilde{\boldsymbol{\beta}}_n$.

Condition (i) states that $\sigma(\mathbf{W}_{th})$ is the largest information set such that $\boldsymbol{\epsilon}_{th}$ has conditional mean zero. Conditions (ii) and (iii) express precisely the assumption of the absence of heteroskedasticity or serial correlation.

Note that from a theoretical standpoint, it is no restriction at all to suppose that the conditional expectation has this linear form, because the elements of $\mathbf{Z}_{th}$ can be arbitrary measurable functions of $\mathbf{W}_{th}$ and we can simply set $\mathbf{Z}_{th} = \hat{\mathbf{X}}_{th}$, where $\hat{\mathbf{X}}_{th} \equiv E(\mathbf{X}_{th}|\mathbf{W}_{th})$ and then $\Pi_o = \mathbf{I}$. From a practical standpoint, however, such instrumental variables may not be available because $\hat{\mathbf{X}}_{th}$ may not be completely known (i.e., Π_o may not be known); however, if the conditional expectation is known up to a linear transformation, we can proceed without losing any efficiency in estimation.

Clearly, any variable appearing in both $\mathbf{W}_{th}$ and $\mathbf{X}_{th}$ will appear in $\mathbf{Z}_{th}$, so that when $E(\mathbf{X}_{th}|\mathbf{W}_{th}) = \mathbf{X}_{th}$, we obtain the OLS estimator as the optimal IV estimator.

The most restrictive feature of this result is that we assume the absence of heteroskedasticity, serial correlation, or even contemporaneous correlation among the components of $\boldsymbol{\epsilon}_t$. We saw earlier that if we drop this assumption, then it may or may not be possible to find a finite set of instrumental variables that yields a fully efficient estimator. This situation arises because no attempt is made to remove the serial correlation or heteroskedasticity. However, when the form of the serial correlation or heteroskedasticity is known, it may be possible to remove this "nonsphericality" using an appropriate linear transformation of the model, and thereby attain efficiency in a manner analogous to the way that GLS improves on the efficiency of the OLS estimator when heteroskedasticity or serial correlation are present.

It requires some care to show that improvements analogous to GLS over OLS exist in the IV framework. The approach that we shall take is to view a model with nonspherical errors (e.g., heteroskedasticity or serial correlation) as arising from a specific nonsingular linear transformation of an underlying spherical model, specifically a model satisfying the conditions of Theorem 4.54, and (i)–(iii) in particular. Thus, we consider models of the form

$$\tilde{\mathbf{y}} = \tilde{\mathbf{X}}\beta_o + \tilde{\boldsymbol{\epsilon}},$$

where $\tilde{\mathbf{y}} = \mathbf{C}_n\mathbf{y}$, $\tilde{\mathbf{X}} = \mathbf{C}_n\mathbf{X}$, $\tilde{\boldsymbol{\epsilon}} = \mathbf{C}_n\boldsymbol{\epsilon}$, and $\mathbf{C}_n$ is a known nonsingular $np \times np$ matrix that induces heteroskedasticity or serial correlation in $\tilde{\boldsymbol{\epsilon}}$.

To guarantee that a useful IV estimator exists for the nonspherical model just introduced, it will suffice to impose certain restrictions on $\mathbf{C}_n$. In particular, we shall seek to ensure that instrumental variable candidates $\tilde{\mathbf{W}}_{th}$ exist for $\tilde{\mathbf{X}}_{th}$.

To see what restrictions on $\mathbf{C}_n$ will suffice for this, we consider a sequence of examples. First, suppose $p = 1$ (a single equation model). Let $\mathbf{C}_n$ have typical elements $\mathbf{c}_{t\tau}$, and suppose that heteroskedasticity is induced by $\mathbf{c}_{tt} \neq \mathbf{c}_{\tau\tau}$ for some $t \neq \tau = 1, \ldots, n$. Set $\mathbf{c}_{t\tau} = 0$ if $t \neq \tau$. Then $\tilde{\boldsymbol{\epsilon}}_t = \mathbf{c}_{tt}\boldsymbol{\epsilon}_t$ and

$$E(\tilde{\boldsymbol{\epsilon}}_t|\mathbf{W}_t) = E(\mathbf{c}_{tt}\boldsymbol{\epsilon}_t|\mathbf{W}_t).$$

If $\mathbf{c}_{tt}$ is measurable with respect to $\sigma(\mathbf{W}_t)$ (i.e., if $\mathbf{c}_{tt}$ is a function *only* of $\mathbf{W}_t$), then

$$E(\tilde{\boldsymbol{\epsilon}}_t|\mathbf{W}_t) = \mathbf{c}_{tt}E(\boldsymbol{\epsilon}_t|\mathbf{W}_t) = 0,$$

so that functions of $\mathbf{W}_t$ are also available for constructing instrumental variables for $\tilde{\mathbf{X}}_t$. If $\mathbf{c}_{tt}$ were not measurable with respect to $\sigma(\mathbf{W}_t)$, then no instrumental variables need exist and indeed it can happen that $E(\tilde{\boldsymbol{\epsilon}}_t) \neq 0$.

Next, suppose that we have a system of equations ($p > 1$) with contemporaneous correlation induced by $\mathbf{c}_{tt} \neq \mathbf{I}_p$, $t = 1, \ldots, n$, and $\mathbf{c}_{t\tau} = 0$, $t \neq \tau$, where $\mathbf{c}_{t\tau}$ is now a $p \times p$ matrix with elements $\mathbf{c}_{t\tau hg}$, g, $h = 1, \ldots, p$. Then

$$\tilde{\boldsymbol{\epsilon}}_{th} = \sum_{g=1}^{p} \mathbf{c}_{tthg}\boldsymbol{\epsilon}_{tg}.$$

Now let $\tilde{\mathbf{W}}_{th}$ be an arbitrary vector. Then

$$E(\tilde{\boldsymbol{\epsilon}}_{th}|\tilde{\mathbf{W}}_{th}) = \sum_{g=1}^{p} E(\mathbf{c}_{tthg}\boldsymbol{\epsilon}_{tg}|\tilde{\mathbf{W}}_{th}).$$

If $\mathbf{c}_{tthg}$ is measurable with respect to $\sigma(\tilde{\mathbf{W}}_{th})$ and if $E(\boldsymbol{\epsilon}_{tg}|\tilde{\mathbf{W}}_{th}) = 0$ for $g = 1, \ldots, p$, then $E(\tilde{\boldsymbol{\epsilon}}_{th}|\tilde{\mathbf{W}}_{th}) = 0$. Otherwise, it may or may not be true that $E(\tilde{\boldsymbol{\epsilon}}_{th}|\tilde{\mathbf{W}}_{th}) = 0$. For example, if $\mathbf{c}_{tthg}$ is a nonstochastic constant, it will be measurable with respect to any information set. Also, if $\tilde{\mathbf{W}}_{th}$ consists of only those elements that are common to $\mathbf{W}_{tg}$, $g = 1, \ldots, p$, then $E(\tilde{\boldsymbol{\epsilon}}_{th}|\tilde{\mathbf{W}}_{th}) = 0$. The formal way of expressing the requirement that $\tilde{\mathbf{W}}_{th}$ consists of only those elements that are common to $\mathbf{W}_{tg}$ is to write

$$\sigma(\tilde{\mathbf{W}}_{th}) = \bigwedge_{g=1}^{p} \sigma(\mathbf{W}_{tg}).$$

This denotes the intersection of the σ-fields $\sigma(\mathbf{W}_{tg})$, $g = 1, \ldots, p$, which is the maximal σ-field contained in all of them.

Note that if $\sigma(\mathbf{W}_{th})$ is not a subfield of each $\sigma(\mathbf{W}_{tg})$, $g = 1, \ldots, p$, then it can happen that $E(\tilde{\boldsymbol{\epsilon}}_{th}|\mathbf{W}_{th}) \neq 0$, which implies that the instrumental variables for the transformed model cannot necessarily be constructed from the same conditioning variables as in the underlying model.

Now consider a general situation in which there is serial correlation as well as contemporaneous correlation and possibly heteroskedasticity, so that $\mathbf{c}_{tt} \neq \mathbf{I}_p$ and $\mathbf{c}_{t\tau} \neq 0$. Then

$$\tilde{\boldsymbol{\epsilon}}_t = \sum_{\tau=1}^{n} \mathbf{c}_{t\tau}\boldsymbol{\epsilon}_{\tau}.$$

In particular, a typical element of $\tilde{\boldsymbol{\epsilon}}_t$ has the form

$$\tilde{\boldsymbol{\epsilon}}_{th} = \sum_{\tau=1}^{n} \sum_{g=1}^{p} \mathbf{c}_{t\tau hg}\boldsymbol{\epsilon}_{\tau g}.$$

Again, let $\tilde{\mathbf{W}}_{th}$ be an arbitrary vector. Then

$$E(\tilde{\boldsymbol{\epsilon}}_{th}|\tilde{\mathbf{W}}_{th}) = \sum_{\tau=1}^{n} \sum_{g=1}^{p} E(\mathbf{c}_{t\tau hg}\boldsymbol{\epsilon}_{\tau g}|\tilde{\mathbf{W}}_{th}).$$

For $E(\tilde{\boldsymbol{\epsilon}}_{th}|\tilde{\mathbf{W}}_{th}) = 0$, it suffices that $\mathbf{c}_{t\tau hg}$ is measurable with respect to $\sigma(\tilde{\mathbf{W}}_{th})$, and that $E(\boldsymbol{\epsilon}_{\tau g}|\tilde{\mathbf{W}}_{th}) = 0$. For this it suffices that $\tilde{\mathbf{W}}_{th}$ is measurable with respect to $\sigma(\mathbf{W}_{\tau g})$, $\tau = 1, \ldots, n$, $g = 1, \ldots, p$; for example, let $\sigma(\tilde{\mathbf{W}}_{th}) = \bigwedge_{\tau=1}^{n} \bigwedge_{g=1}^{p} \sigma(\mathbf{W}_{\tau g})$. Now $\tilde{\mathbf{W}}_{th}$ contains only variables for which $\boldsymbol{\epsilon}_{\tau g}$ has conditional mean zero for all values of g and τ for example, variables jointly strictly exogenous with respect to $\boldsymbol{\epsilon}_{th}$.

In each case above, it was possible to find conditioning variables for the transformed model useful in constructing instrumental variables for the transformed model, provided that the elements of $\mathbf{C}_n$ were appropriately measurable and that the conditioning variables considered did not contain information on the location of the underlying errors involved in the transformation. Although we indicated how failure of these conditions can lead to the failure of appropriate instrumental variables to exist, the conditions discussed do not appear to be necessary, because appropriate cancellations may yield $E(\tilde{\boldsymbol{\epsilon}}_{th}|\tilde{\mathbf{W}}_{th}) = 0$, even though $E(\boldsymbol{\epsilon}_{\tau g}|\tilde{\mathbf{W}}_{th}) \neq 0$ for all τ and g. In fact, it can still be true that $\tilde{\mathbf{Z}}'\tilde{\boldsymbol{\epsilon}}/n \xrightarrow{\text{a. s.}} \mathbf{0}$, where the elements of $\tilde{\mathbf{Z}}_{th}$ are measurable functions of $\tilde{\mathbf{W}}_{th}$ even when $E(\tilde{\boldsymbol{\epsilon}}_{th}|\tilde{\mathbf{W}}_{th}) \neq 0$ for all t and h.

In the cases discussed above, it was assumed only that $\mathbf{C}_n$ was nonsingular. We do not require $\mathbf{C}_n$ to be lower triangular, although this is certainly possible. For any lower triangular $\mathbf{C}_n$, an upper triangular $\mathbf{C}_n$ can lead to an identical $\boldsymbol{\Omega}_n$ matrix, as well as matrices that are neither upper nor lower triangular. In the case of the general classical linear model, it makes no difference how $\boldsymbol{\Omega}_n$ is "factored." Here, however, it does matter, because the way in which $\boldsymbol{\Omega}_n$ is factored may affect the determination of what instrumental variable candidates are available for the nonspherical model, that is, what $\tilde{\mathbf{W}}_{th}$ consists of.

This is a consequence of the general condition that we adopt to ensure the efficiency of the IV analogue of the GLS estimator, namely that each row of $\mathbf{C}_n$ has elements that are measurable with respect to $\sigma(\tilde{\mathbf{W}}_{th})$, where

$$\sigma(\tilde{\mathbf{W}}_{th}) = \bigwedge_{\{1 \le \tau \le n, 1 \le g \le p:\, c_{t\tau hg} \neq 0\}} \sigma(\mathbf{W}_{\tau g}), \; h = 1, \ldots, p, \; t = 1, \ldots, n.$$

This is the natural generalization of the condition imposed in each of the special cases considered above.

Exercise 4.55: Verify that if the rows of $\mathbf{C}_n$ satisfy the condition just given, then

$$E(\tilde{\boldsymbol{\epsilon}}_{th}|\tilde{\mathbf{W}}_{th}) = 0, \; h = 1, \ldots, p; \; t = 1, \ldots, n.$$

Further, if instrumental variables $\tilde{\mathbf{Z}}_{th}$ are chosen as measurable functions of $\tilde{\mathbf{W}}_{th}$, show that

$$E(\tilde{\mathbf{Z}}'\tilde{\boldsymbol{\epsilon}}\tilde{\boldsymbol{\epsilon}}'\tilde{\mathbf{Z}}/n) = E(\tilde{\mathbf{Z}}'\boldsymbol{\Omega}_n\tilde{\mathbf{Z}}/n),$$

where $\mathbf{\Omega}_n = \mathbf{C}_n\mathbf{C}_n'$. *Hint:* Use the law of iterated expectations to write

$$E(\tilde{\mathbf{Z}}_{th}'\tilde{\boldsymbol{\epsilon}}_{th}\tilde{\boldsymbol{\epsilon}}_{\tau g}\tilde{\mathbf{Z}}_{\tau g}) = E[E(\tilde{\mathbf{Z}}_{th}'\tilde{\boldsymbol{\epsilon}}_{th}\tilde{\boldsymbol{\epsilon}}_{\tau g}\tilde{\mathbf{Z}}_{\tau g}|\tilde{\mathbf{W}}_{th}, \tilde{\mathbf{W}}_{\tau g})].$$

Let $\omega_{t\tau hg} = E(\tilde{\boldsymbol{\epsilon}}_{th}\tilde{\boldsymbol{\epsilon}}_{\tau g}|\tilde{\mathbf{W}}_{th}, \tilde{\mathbf{W}}_{\tau g})$, $\omega_{t\tau} = [\omega_{t\tau hg}]$ and $\mathbf{\Omega}_n = [\omega_{t\tau}]$.

The conditions imposed on $\tilde{\mathbf{W}}_{th}$ above imply that $\tilde{\mathbf{W}}_{th}$ contains less information than $\mathbf{W}_{th}$, so that less information is available for constructing the instrumental variables for the nonspherical model, generally speaking. For this reason, the optimal instrumental variables for the underlying model cannot generally be obtained by applying the transformation $\mathbf{C}_n^{-1}$ to $\tilde{\mathbf{Z}}$. Nor is it generally true that transformation of optimal instrumental variables $\mathbf{Z}$ for the underlying model by $\mathbf{C}_n$ yields instrumental variables for the nonspherical model that satisfy the conditions of Exercise 4.26.

Also, note that if $\mathbf{C}_n$ is upper triangular, a different set of instrumental variable candidates may be available than if $\mathbf{C}_n$ is lower triangular, as alluded to previously. This reveals the importance of a careful specification of the way in which a given conditional covariance matrix $\mathbf{\Omega}_n$ arises.

The second part of Exercise 4.55 makes clear the way in which $\mathbf{C}_n$ induces a particular form of heteroskedasticity or serial correlation, and the condition above specifies precisely what kinds of nonsphericality can be induced. In particular, any nonstochastic choice for $\mathbf{C}_n$ is always available, because the rows of a nonstochastic matrix will be measurable with respect to any σ-field. This allows the case of contemporaneous covariance, for which

$$\begin{aligned} \omega_{t\tau} &= \mathbf{\Sigma} \qquad \text{if} \quad t = \tau \\ &= \mathbf{0} \qquad \text{otherwise,} \end{aligned}$$

for some fixed matrix $\mathbf{\Sigma}$. It also allows the case of serial correlation, for which

$$\omega_{t\tau} = R_{|t-\tau|} \neq 0 \qquad \text{for} \quad \text{some } t \neq \tau.$$

Note that here $\omega_{t\tau}$ depends only on $|t - \tau|$ and not on t or τ alone.

More general situations are also admitted, because the elements of a given row of $\mathbf{C}_n$ can be stochastic. For example, let $p = 1$. Heteroskedasticity is allowed in which

$$\omega_{tt} = f(\tilde{\mathbf{W}}_t)$$

for some function f. In particular, if $\tilde{\mathbf{W}}_t$ contains $\mathbf{y}_{t-1}$ and $\mathbf{X}_{t-1}$, then the ARCH model of Engle [1982] is allowed. For the simplest form of this model,

$$\begin{aligned}\omega_{tt} &= E(\epsilon_t^2|\tilde{\mathbf{W}}_t)\\ &= \epsilon_{t-1}^2\rho_o = (\mathbf{y}_{t-1} - \mathbf{X}_{t-1}\boldsymbol{\beta}_o)^2\rho_o.\end{aligned}$$

If a GLS-like result is available for IV estimators, then we should expect to be able to show that the optimal IV estimator as given in Theorem 4.54 is asymptotically efficient with respect to the optimal IV estimator for any nonspherical model satisfying the condition just discussed and the conditions of Exercise 4.26, say,

$$\tilde{\boldsymbol{\beta}}_n = (\tilde{\mathbf{X}}'\tilde{\mathbf{Z}}\tilde{\mathbf{V}}_n^{-1}\tilde{\mathbf{Z}}'\tilde{\mathbf{X}})^{-1}\tilde{\mathbf{X}}'\tilde{\mathbf{Z}}\tilde{\mathbf{V}}_n^{-1}\tilde{\mathbf{Z}}'\mathbf{y},$$

where $\tilde{\mathbf{V}}_n = E(\tilde{\mathbf{Z}}'\tilde{\epsilon}\tilde{\epsilon}'\tilde{\mathbf{Z}}/n)$, and $\tilde{\mathbf{Z}}$ has rows $\tilde{\mathbf{Z}}_{th}$ with elements that are measurable functions of $\tilde{\mathbf{W}}_{th}$. Because we have not characterized the optimal instrumental variables for this case, it will suffice to show efficiency of $\boldsymbol{\beta}_n^*$ relative to $\tilde{\boldsymbol{\beta}}_n$ for any appropriate choice $\tilde{\mathbf{Z}}$.

It follows from Theorem 4.26 that

$$\text{avar}\,\boldsymbol{\beta}_n^* = (\mathbf{Q}_n\mathbf{L}_n^{-1}\mathbf{Q}_n)^{-1}$$

and

$$\text{avar}\,\tilde{\boldsymbol{\beta}}_n = (\tilde{\mathbf{Q}}_n'\tilde{\mathbf{V}}_n^{-1}\tilde{\mathbf{Q}}_n)^{-1},$$

where $\tilde{\mathbf{Q}}_n = E(\tilde{\mathbf{Z}}'\tilde{\mathbf{X}}/n)$. Consistent estimators for avar $\boldsymbol{\beta}_n^*$ and avar $\tilde{\boldsymbol{\beta}}_n$ are $(\mathbf{X}'\mathbf{Z}(\mathbf{Z}'\mathbf{Z})^{-1}\mathbf{Z}'\mathbf{X}/n)^{-1}$ and $(\tilde{\mathbf{X}}'\tilde{\mathbf{Z}}(\tilde{\mathbf{Z}}'\boldsymbol{\Omega}_n\tilde{\mathbf{Z}})^{-1}\tilde{\mathbf{Z}}'\tilde{\mathbf{X}}/n)^{-1}$, and we investigate asymptotic efficiency by considering a consistent estimate of the difference $(\text{avar}\,\boldsymbol{\beta}_n^*)^{-1} - (\text{avar}\,\tilde{\boldsymbol{\beta}}_n)^{-1}$, that is,

$$[\mathbf{X}'\mathbf{Z}(\mathbf{Z}'\mathbf{Z})^{-1}\mathbf{Z}'\mathbf{X} - \tilde{\mathbf{X}}'\tilde{\mathbf{Z}}(\tilde{\mathbf{Z}}'\boldsymbol{\Omega}_n\tilde{\mathbf{Z}})^{-1}\tilde{\mathbf{Z}}'\tilde{\mathbf{X}}]/n.$$

Dropping the division by n and substituting $\tilde{\mathbf{X}} = \mathbf{C}_n\mathbf{X}$ and $\boldsymbol{\Omega}_n = \mathbf{C}_n\mathbf{C}_n'$, we have

$$\mathbf{X}'\mathbf{Z}(\mathbf{Z}'\mathbf{Z})^{-1}\mathbf{Z}'\mathbf{X} - \mathbf{X}'\mathbf{C}_n'\tilde{\mathbf{Z}}(\tilde{\mathbf{Z}}'\mathbf{C}_n\mathbf{C}_n'\tilde{\mathbf{Z}})^{-1}\tilde{\mathbf{Z}}'\mathbf{C}_n\mathbf{X}.$$

Define $\mathbf{Z}^* = \mathbf{C}_n'\tilde{\mathbf{Z}}$ and substitute in the above to obtain

$$\mathbf{X}'\mathbf{Z}(\mathbf{Z}'\mathbf{Z})^{-1}\mathbf{Z}'\mathbf{X} - \mathbf{X}'\mathbf{Z}^*(\mathbf{Z}^{*\prime}\mathbf{Z}^*)^{-1}\mathbf{Z}^{*\prime}\mathbf{X}.$$

This expression is a difference between two positive semidefinite matrices, and without further information it is not possible to determine whether this difference is positive semidefinite, which would imply the result we seek.

However, further information is potentially available. Suppose $\mathbf{Z}^*$ could be adjoined to the matrix of instrumental variables $\mathbf{Z}$ without violating the conditions of Theorem 4.54. Because $\mathbf{Z}$ is optimal, $\mathbf{Z}^*$ is redundant and it can be shown that

$$E(\mathbf{Z}^{*\prime}\mathbf{X}/n) = E(\mathbf{Z}^{*\prime}\mathbf{Z}/n)E(\mathbf{Z}'\mathbf{Z}/n)^{-1}E(\mathbf{Z}'\mathbf{X}/n),$$

provided that $E(\mathbf{Z}^{*\prime}\boldsymbol{\epsilon}\boldsymbol{\epsilon}'\mathbf{Z}/n) = E(\mathbf{Z}^{*\prime}\mathbf{Z}/n)$. This fact follows either from Proposition 4.50 or the linear dependence of $\mathbf{Z}^*$ on $\mathbf{Z}$. Replacing expected values by consistent estimators and dropping a division by n yields

$$\mathbf{Z}^{*\prime}\mathbf{X} = \mathbf{Z}^{*\prime}\mathbf{Z}(\mathbf{Z}'\mathbf{Z})^{-1}\mathbf{Z}'\mathbf{X}.$$

Substituting this into the apparently indeterminate expression above yields

$$\mathbf{X}'\mathbf{Z}(\mathbf{Z}'\mathbf{Z})^{-1}\mathbf{Z}'\mathbf{X} - \mathbf{X}'\mathbf{Z}(\mathbf{Z}'\mathbf{Z})^{-1}\mathbf{Z}'\mathbf{Z}^*(\mathbf{Z}^{*\prime}\mathbf{Z}^*)^{-1}\mathbf{Z}^{*\prime}\mathbf{Z}(\mathbf{Z}'\mathbf{Z})^{-1}\mathbf{Z}'\mathbf{X}$$
$$= \mathbf{X}'\mathbf{Z}(\mathbf{Z}'\mathbf{Z})^{-1}\mathbf{Z}'(\mathbf{I} - \mathbf{Z}^*(\mathbf{Z}^{*\prime}\mathbf{Z}^*)^{-1}\mathbf{Z}^{*\prime})\mathbf{Z}(\mathbf{Z}'\mathbf{Z})^{-1}\mathbf{Z}'\mathbf{X},$$

which is readily seen to be positive semidefinite. Once certain technicalities have been disposed of, this will be sufficient to prove the superiority of $\boldsymbol{\beta}_n^*$ over $\tilde{\boldsymbol{\beta}}_n$.

The success of this approach now depends on whether $\mathbf{Z}^* = \mathbf{C}_n'\mathbf{Z}$ can indeed be harmlessly adjoined to $\mathbf{Z}$. In other words, can the matrix $\bar{\mathbf{Z}} = (\mathbf{Z}, \mathbf{Z}^*)$ be treated as a legitimate set of instrumental variables? For this, it will suffice that $\mathbf{Z}_{th}^*$ has elements measurable with respect to $\sigma(\mathbf{W}_{th})$. Because this is straightforward, we leave it as an exercise.

EXERCISE 4.56: Show that $\mathbf{Z}_{th}^*$ has elements measurable with respect to $\sigma(\mathbf{W}_{th})$, when the elements of $\tilde{\mathbf{Z}}_{th}$ are measurable with respect to $\sigma(\tilde{\mathbf{W}}_{th})$ and each row of $\mathbf{C}_n$ has elements $\mathbf{c}_{t\tau hg}$ measurable with respect to

$$\sigma(\tilde{\mathbf{W}}_{th}) = \bigwedge_{\{1\leq\tau\leq t;\ 1\leq g\leq n:\ \mathbf{c}_{t\tau hg}\neq 0\}} \sigma(\mathbf{W}_{\tau g}),\ h = 1, \ldots, p;\ t = 1, \ldots, n.$$

Hint: a typical row $\mathbf{Z}_{th}^*$ can be written

$$\mathbf{Z}_{th}^* = \sum_{\tau=1}^{n}\sum_{g=1}^{p} \mathbf{c}_{\tau tgh}\tilde{\mathbf{Z}}_{\tau g}.$$

Also let

$$\mathcal{G}_{th} = \bigvee_{\{1\leq\tau\leq n,\ 1\leq g\leq p:\ \mathbf{c}_{\tau tgh}\neq 0\}} \sigma(\tilde{\mathbf{W}}_{\tau g})$$

denote the minimal σ-field containing all of the indicated $\sigma(\tilde{\mathbf{W}}_{\tau g})$.

This result implies that any elements of $\mathbf{Z}^*$ can indeed be harmlessly adjointed to $\mathbf{Z}$, ensuring the validity of the argument sketched above. Now we can formally state and prove the efficiency result for the IV analogue of GLS.

THEOREM 4.57 (*Generalized instrumental variables*): Suppose there exists a unique σ-field generated by row vectors $\mathbf{W}_{th}$ such that

(i) $E(\boldsymbol{\epsilon}_{th}|\mathbf{W}_{th}) = 0$ and $E(\boldsymbol{\epsilon}_{th}|\mathcal{G}_{th}) \neq 0$ for all $\mathcal{G}_{th} \supset \sigma(\mathbf{W}_{th})$, $h = 1, \ldots, p$, $t = 1, \ldots, n$;
(ii) $E(\boldsymbol{\epsilon}_{th}^2|\mathbf{W}_{th}) = 1$, $h = 1, \ldots, p$, $t = 1, \ldots, n$;
(iii) $E(\boldsymbol{\epsilon}_{th}\boldsymbol{\epsilon}_{\tau g}|\mathbf{W}_{th}, \mathbf{W}_{\tau g}) = 0$, $h \neq g = 1, \ldots, p$, $t \neq \tau = 1, \ldots, n$;

and suppose that the conditions of Exercise 4.26 hold for instrumental variables $\mathbf{Z}$ satisfying

$$E(\mathbf{X}_{th}|\mathbf{W}_{th}) = \mathbf{Z}_{th}\Pi_o, \qquad h = 1, \ldots, p, \quad t = 1, \ldots, n,$$

where Π_o is an $l \times k$ matrix of full column rank containing no zero rows, and for $\hat{\mathbf{P}}_n = (\mathbf{Z}'\mathbf{Z}/n)^{-1}$.

Suppose the conditions of Exercise 4.26 hold for the model

$$\tilde{\mathbf{y}} = \tilde{\mathbf{X}}\boldsymbol{\beta}_o + \tilde{\boldsymbol{\epsilon}},$$

where $\tilde{\mathbf{y}} = \mathbf{C}_n\mathbf{y}$, $\tilde{\mathbf{X}} = \mathbf{C}_n\mathbf{X}$, $\tilde{\boldsymbol{\epsilon}} = \mathbf{C}_n\boldsymbol{\epsilon}$ and $\mathbf{C}_n$ is a given nonsingular $np \times np$ matrix with rows containing elements $\mathbf{c}_{t\tau hg}$ measurable with respect to

$$\sigma(\tilde{\mathbf{W}}_{th}) = \bigwedge_{\{1 \le \tau \le t;\, 1 \le g \le p:\, \mathbf{c}_{t\tau hg} \neq 0\}} \sigma(\mathbf{W}_{\tau g}),$$

for instrumental variables $\tilde{\mathbf{Z}}_{th}$ chosen as measurable functions of $\tilde{\mathbf{W}}_{th}$, and for $\mathbf{P}_n = \tilde{\mathbf{V}}_n^{-1} \equiv E(\tilde{\mathbf{Z}}'\tilde{\boldsymbol{\epsilon}}\tilde{\boldsymbol{\epsilon}}'\tilde{\mathbf{Z}}/n)^{-1}$, where $\tilde{\mathbf{Z}}$ has rows $\tilde{\mathbf{Z}}_{th}$.

Define $\mathbf{Z}^* = \mathbf{C}_n'\tilde{\mathbf{Z}}$, let $\mathbf{z}^* = \mathbf{Z}^* - \mathbf{Z}E(\mathbf{Z}'\mathbf{Z}/n)^{-1}E(\mathbf{Z}'\mathbf{Z}^*/n)$, let $\bar{\mathbf{z}}$ contain the nonzero columns of $\mathbf{z}^*$, and suppose that the conditions of Exercise 4.26 hold for instrumental variables $\bar{\mathbf{Z}} = (\mathbf{Z}, \bar{\mathbf{z}})$. Define

$$\boldsymbol{\beta}_n^* = (\mathbf{X}'\mathbf{Z}(\mathbf{Z}'\mathbf{Z})^{-1}\mathbf{Z}'\mathbf{X})^{-1}\mathbf{X}'\mathbf{Z}(\mathbf{Z}'\mathbf{Z})^{-1}\mathbf{Z}'\mathbf{y} \qquad \text{and}$$

$$\tilde{\boldsymbol{\beta}}_n = (\tilde{\mathbf{X}}'\tilde{\mathbf{Z}}\tilde{\mathbf{V}}_n^{-1}\tilde{\mathbf{Z}}'\tilde{\mathbf{X}})^{-1}\tilde{\mathbf{X}}'\tilde{\mathbf{Z}}\tilde{\mathbf{V}}_n^{-1}\tilde{\mathbf{Z}}'\tilde{\mathbf{y}}.$$

Then $\boldsymbol{\beta}_n^*$ is essentially asymptotically efficient relative to $\tilde{\boldsymbol{\beta}}_n$ for any choice $\mathbf{C}_n$. Further, $\boldsymbol{\beta}_n^*$ is asymptotically efficient relative to $\tilde{\boldsymbol{\beta}}_n$ provided that avar $\boldsymbol{\beta}_n^*$ and avar $\tilde{\boldsymbol{\beta}}_n$ both converge to constant matrices.

Proof: We wish to show that for any $\delta > 0$ there exists n sufficiently large such that $(1 + \delta)$ avar $\tilde{\boldsymbol{\beta}}_n -$ avar $\boldsymbol{\beta}_n^*$ is p.s.d. Given the conditions of the theorem, we have

$$\text{avar}\,\tilde{\boldsymbol{\beta}}_n = (\tilde{\mathbf{Q}}_n'\tilde{\mathbf{V}}_n^{-1}\tilde{\mathbf{Q}}_n)^{-1}$$

$$\text{avar}\,\boldsymbol{\beta}_n^* = (\mathbf{Q}_n'\mathbf{L}_n^{-1}\mathbf{Q}_n)^{-1},$$

where $\tilde{\mathbf{Q}}_n \equiv E(\tilde{\mathbf{Z}}'\tilde{\mathbf{X}}/n)$, $\mathbf{Q}_n = E(\mathbf{Z}'\mathbf{X}/n)$ and $\mathbf{L}_n = E(\mathbf{Z}'\mathbf{Z}/n)$. By Exercise 4.55 we can write

$$\begin{aligned}\text{avar}\,\tilde{\boldsymbol{\beta}}_n &= [E(\tilde{\mathbf{X}}'\tilde{\mathbf{Z}}/\mathbf{n})E(\tilde{\mathbf{Z}}'\boldsymbol{\Omega}_n\tilde{\mathbf{Z}}/n)^{-1}E(\tilde{\mathbf{Z}}'\tilde{\mathbf{X}}/n)]^{-1}\\ &= [E(\tilde{\mathbf{X}}'\tilde{\mathbf{Z}}/n)E(\tilde{\mathbf{Z}}'\mathbf{C}_n\mathbf{C}_n'\tilde{\mathbf{Z}}/n)^{-1}E(\tilde{\mathbf{Z}}'\tilde{\mathbf{X}}/n)]^{-1}\\ &= [E(\mathbf{X}'\mathbf{C}_n'\tilde{\mathbf{Z}}/n)E(\tilde{\mathbf{Z}}'\mathbf{C}_n\mathbf{C}_n'\tilde{\mathbf{Z}}/n)^{-1}E(\tilde{\mathbf{Z}}'\mathbf{C}_n\mathbf{X}/n)]^{-1}\end{aligned}$$

Because $\mathbf{Z}^* = \mathbf{C}_n'\tilde{\mathbf{Z}}$, we have

$$\text{avar}\,\tilde{\boldsymbol{\beta}}_n = [E(\mathbf{X}'\mathbf{Z}^*/n)E(\mathbf{Z}^{*\prime}\mathbf{Z}^*/n)^{-1}E(\mathbf{Z}^{*\prime}\mathbf{X}/n)]^{-1}.$$

We can also express this as

$$\begin{aligned}\text{avar}\,\tilde{\boldsymbol{\beta}}_n = [&E(\mathbf{X}'\mathbf{Z}/n)E(\mathbf{Z}'\mathbf{Z}/n)^{-1}E(\mathbf{Z}'\mathbf{Z}^*/n)E(\mathbf{Z}^{*\prime}\mathbf{Z}^*/n)^{-1}\\ &\times E(\mathbf{Z}^{*\prime}\mathbf{Z}/n)E(\mathbf{Z}'\mathbf{Z}/n)^{-1}E(\mathbf{Z}'\mathbf{Z}/n)]^{-1}\end{aligned}$$

by making use of the fact that

$$E(\mathbf{Z}^{*\prime}\mathbf{Z}/n)E(\mathbf{Z}'\mathbf{Z}/n)^{-1}E(\mathbf{Z}'\mathbf{X}/n) = E(\mathbf{Z}^{*\prime}\mathbf{X}/n).$$

To verify this equality, we note that Proposition 4.50 implies

$$E(\bar{\mathbf{z}}'\mathbf{Z}/n)E(\mathbf{Z}'\mathbf{Z}/n)^{-1}E(\mathbf{Z}'\mathbf{X}/n) - E(\bar{\mathbf{z}}'\mathbf{X}/n) = 0,$$

because $\mathbf{Z}$ is the efficient set of instrumental variables by Theorem 4.53. Because $\mathbf{z}^* = (\bar{\mathbf{z}}, 0)$, we can also write

$$E(\mathbf{z}^{*\prime}\mathbf{Z}/n)E(\mathbf{Z}'\mathbf{Z}/n)^{-1}E(\mathbf{Z}'\mathbf{X}/n) - E(\mathbf{z}^{*\prime}\mathbf{X}/n) = 0.$$

By definition, $\mathbf{z}^* = \mathbf{Z}^* - \mathbf{Z}E(\mathbf{Z}'\mathbf{Z}/n)^{-1}E(\mathbf{Z}'\mathbf{Z}^*/n)$. Substituting this expression for $\mathbf{z}^*$ gives

$$\begin{aligned}&E(\mathbf{Z}^{*\prime}\mathbf{Z}/n)E(\mathbf{Z}'\mathbf{Z}/n)^{-1}E(\mathbf{Z}'\mathbf{X}/n) - E(\mathbf{Z}^{*\prime}\mathbf{X}/n)\\ &\quad - E(\mathbf{Z}^{*\prime}\mathbf{Z}/n)E(\mathbf{Z}'\mathbf{Z}/n)^{-1}E(\mathbf{Z}'\mathbf{Z}/n)E(\mathbf{Z}'\mathbf{Z}/n)^{-1}E(\mathbf{Z}'\mathbf{X}/n)\\ &\quad + E(\mathbf{Z}^{*\prime}\mathbf{Z}/n)E(\mathbf{Z}'\mathbf{Z}/n)^{-1}E(\mathbf{Z}'\mathbf{X}/n) = 0.\end{aligned}$$

The last two terms above cancel, which leaves the desired result,

$$E(\mathbf{Z}^{*\prime}\mathbf{X}/n) = E(\mathbf{Z}^{*\prime}\mathbf{Z}/n)E(\mathbf{Z}'\mathbf{Z}/n)^{-1}E(\mathbf{Z}'\mathbf{X}/n).$$

Substituting for $\mathbf{Q}_n$ and $\mathbf{L}_n$ gives

$$\text{avar}\,\boldsymbol{\beta}_n^* = [E(\mathbf{X}'\mathbf{Z}/n)E(\mathbf{Z}'\mathbf{Z}/n)^{-1}E(\mathbf{Z}'\mathbf{X}/n)]^{-1}.$$

To show that $(1+\delta)\text{avar}\,\tilde{\boldsymbol{\beta}}_n - \text{avar}\,\boldsymbol{\beta}_n^*$ is p.s.d., we apply Proposition 4.44 and Lemma 4.53 and consider the difference between consistent estimators of $(\text{avar}\,\boldsymbol{\beta}_n^*)^{-1}$ and $(\text{avar}\,\tilde{\boldsymbol{\beta}}_n)^{-1}$,

$$\begin{aligned} &n^{-1}\mathbf{X}'\mathbf{Z}(\mathbf{Z}'\mathbf{Z})^{-1}\mathbf{Z}'\mathbf{X} - n^{-1}\mathbf{X}'\mathbf{Z}(\mathbf{Z}'\mathbf{Z})^{-1}\\ &\qquad \times \mathbf{Z}'\mathbf{Z}^*(\mathbf{Z}^{*\prime}\mathbf{Z}^*)^{-1}\mathbf{Z}^{*\prime}\mathbf{Z}(\mathbf{Z}'\mathbf{Z})^{-1}\mathbf{Z}'\mathbf{X}\\ &\quad = n^{-1}\mathbf{X}'\mathbf{Z}(\mathbf{Z}'\mathbf{Z})^{-1}\mathbf{Z}'(\mathbf{I} - \mathbf{Z}^*(\mathbf{Z}^{*\prime}\mathbf{Z}^*)^{-1}\mathbf{Z}^{*\prime})\mathbf{Z}(\mathbf{Z}'\mathbf{Z})^{-1}\mathbf{Z}'\mathbf{X}.\end{aligned}$$

This is a quadratic form in an idempotent matrix, and is therefore positive semidefinite. It follows from Lemma 4.52 that $(1+\delta)(\text{avar}\,\boldsymbol{\beta}_n^*)^{-1} - (\text{avar}\,\tilde{\boldsymbol{\beta}}_n)^{-1}$ is p.s.d. for all n sufficiently large. It then follows from Proposition 4.44 that $(1+\delta)\,\text{avar}\,\tilde{\boldsymbol{\beta}}_n - \text{avar}\,\boldsymbol{\beta}_n^*$ is p.s.d. for all n sufficiently large, and the proof is complete.

This result guarantees that no transformation of the model satisfying the conditions of the theorem and inducing heteroskedasticity or serial correlation can yield an estimator more efficient than $\boldsymbol{\beta}_n^*$, the two-stage least squares estimator for the spherical model with optimal instrumental variables. Equivalently, removing the heteroskedasticity or serial correlation induced by an appropriate transformation cannot worsen and will generally improve the efficiency of the estimator, provided optimal instrumental variables are chosen once the nonsphericality has been removed.

In other words, starting from a model with nonsphericality induced by a specific transformation $\mathbf{C}_n$, efficiency can be obtained by transforming the model

$$\tilde{\mathbf{y}} = \tilde{\mathbf{X}}\boldsymbol{\beta}_o + \tilde{\boldsymbol{\epsilon}}$$

by premultiplying by $\mathbf{C}_n^{-1}$ to give

$$\mathbf{C}_n^{-1}\tilde{\mathbf{y}} = \mathbf{C}_n^{-1}\tilde{\mathbf{X}}\boldsymbol{\beta}_o + \mathbf{C}_n^{-1}\tilde{\boldsymbol{\epsilon}},$$

or

$$\mathbf{y} = \mathbf{X}\boldsymbol{\beta}_o + \boldsymbol{\epsilon}.$$

This step is precisely analogous to the GLS transformation. Then, using the optimal instrumental variables for the spherical model, obtain the efficient (2SLS) estimator:

$$\begin{aligned}\boldsymbol{\beta}_n^* &= (\mathbf{X}'\mathbf{Z}(\mathbf{Z}'\mathbf{Z})^{-1}\mathbf{Z}'\mathbf{X})^{-1}\mathbf{X}'\mathbf{Z}(\mathbf{Z}'\mathbf{Z})^{-1}\mathbf{Z}'\mathbf{y}\\ &= (\tilde{\mathbf{X}}'\mathbf{C}_n^{-1}\mathbf{Z}(\mathbf{Z}'\mathbf{Z})^{-1}\mathbf{Z}'\mathbf{C}_n^{-1}\tilde{\mathbf{X}})^{-1}\tilde{\mathbf{X}}'\mathbf{C}_n^{-1\prime}\mathbf{Z}(\mathbf{Z}'\mathbf{Z})^{-1}\mathbf{Z}'\mathbf{C}_n^{-1}\tilde{\mathbf{y}}.\end{aligned}$$

Note that the optimal instrumental variables are not generally obtained by a transformation of instrumental variables available for the nonspherical model. However, there are at least two important special cases where it is possible to choose $\tilde{\mathbf{Z}} = \mathbf{C}_n\mathbf{Z}$ without possibly violating $\tilde{\mathbf{Z}}'\tilde{\boldsymbol{\epsilon}}/n \xrightarrow{\text{a. s.}} \mathbf{0}$. These are the cases of pure heteroskedasticity or contemporaneous correlation in a nonrecursive system. If the choice $\tilde{\mathbf{Z}} = \mathbf{C}_n\mathbf{Z}$ is available, then one can substitute $\mathbf{Z} = \mathbf{C}_n^{-1}\tilde{\mathbf{Z}}$ in the expression above. Further substitution of $\boldsymbol{\Omega}_n^{-1}$ for $\mathbf{C}_n^{-1\prime}\mathbf{C}_n^{-1}$ gives

$$\boldsymbol{\beta}_n^* = (\tilde{\mathbf{X}}'\boldsymbol{\Omega}_n^{-1}\tilde{\mathbf{Z}}(\tilde{\mathbf{Z}}'\boldsymbol{\Omega}_n^{-1}\tilde{\mathbf{Z}})^{-1}\tilde{\mathbf{Z}}'\boldsymbol{\Omega}_n^{-1}\tilde{\mathbf{X}})^{-1}\tilde{\mathbf{X}}'\boldsymbol{\Omega}_n^{-1}\tilde{\mathbf{Z}}(\tilde{\mathbf{Z}}'\boldsymbol{\Omega}_n^{-1}\tilde{\mathbf{Z}}_n)^{-1}\tilde{\mathbf{Z}}'\boldsymbol{\Omega}_n^{-1}\tilde{\mathbf{y}}.$$

As special cases this contains the SURE estimator of Zellner [1962] and the 3SLS estimator of Zellner and Theil [1962] for $\boldsymbol{\Omega}_n$ known.

In fact, it is always possible to represent $\boldsymbol{\beta}_n^*$ in this form by appropriately defining $\tilde{\mathbf{Z}}$. However, when this is done, $\tilde{\mathbf{Z}}$ may not be a legitimate choice of instrumental variables for the nonspherical model.

Although we have gained considerable insight by supposing that nonsphericality is induced by a particular transformation of a spherical model, this is not necessarily the way in which models present themselves. Often, economic theory will specify the instrumental variable candidates $\tilde{\mathbf{W}}_{th}$ for the nonspherical model, which then implies a particular form for $\boldsymbol{\Omega}_n$ when we condition on $\sigma(\tilde{\mathbf{W}}_{th}, \tilde{\mathbf{W}}_{\tau g})$. Because there is generally no unique transformation $\mathbf{B}_n$ such that $\mathbf{B}_n\boldsymbol{\Omega}_n\mathbf{B}_n' = \mathbf{I}$, one may not know $\mathbf{C}_n$. The choice of $\mathbf{B}_n$ then depends on convenience or plausibility. The question that now arises is whether it matters that $\mathbf{C}_n$ is unknown or whether it suffices simply to know (or be able to estimate) $\boldsymbol{\Omega}_n$. The next theorem provides general conditions under which no efficiency is lost by using $\mathbf{B}_n \neq \mathbf{C}_n^{-1}$.

THEOREM 4.58: Suppose the conditions of Theorem 4.57 are satisfied. For any nonsingular matrix $\mathbf{B}_n$ such that $\mathbf{B}_n\boldsymbol{\Omega}_n\mathbf{B}_n' = \mathbf{I}$, where $\mathbf{C}_n\mathbf{C}_n' = \boldsymbol{\Omega}_n$, define

$$\ddot{\mathbf{y}} = \mathbf{B}_n\tilde{\mathbf{y}}, \qquad \ddot{\mathbf{X}} = \mathbf{B}_n\tilde{\mathbf{X}}, \qquad \text{and} \qquad \ddot{\boldsymbol{\epsilon}} = \mathbf{B}_n\tilde{\boldsymbol{\epsilon}}.$$

Let $\ddot{\mathbf{W}}_{th}$ be a row vector such that $E(\ddot{\boldsymbol{\epsilon}}_{th}|\ddot{\mathbf{W}}_{th}) = 0$, and $E(\ddot{\boldsymbol{\epsilon}}_{th}|\mathcal{G}_{th}) \neq 0$ for any $\mathcal{G}_{th} \supset \sigma(\ddot{\mathbf{W}}_{th})$, and suppose that the conditions of Exercise 4.26 hold for the model $\ddot{\mathbf{y}} = \ddot{\mathbf{X}}\boldsymbol{\beta}_o + \ddot{\boldsymbol{\epsilon}}$, for instrumental variables $\ddot{\mathbf{Z}}$ satisfying

$$E(\ddot{\mathbf{X}}_{th}|\ddot{\mathbf{W}}_{th}) = \ddot{\mathbf{Z}}_{th}\ddot{\Pi}_o, \qquad h = 1, \ldots, p, t = 1, \ldots, n,$$

where $\ddot{\Pi}_o$ is an $l \times k$ matrix of full column rank containing no zero rows, and for $\ddot{\mathbf{P}}_n = (\ddot{\mathbf{Z}}'\ddot{\mathbf{Z}}/n)^{-1}$. Define

$$\ddot{\beta}_n \equiv (\ddot{\mathbf{X}}'\ddot{\mathbf{Z}}(\ddot{\mathbf{Z}}'\ddot{\mathbf{Z}})^{-1}\ddot{\mathbf{Z}}'\ddot{\mathbf{X}})^{-1}\ddot{\mathbf{X}}'\ddot{\mathbf{Z}}(\ddot{\mathbf{Z}}'\ddot{\mathbf{Z}})^{-1}\ddot{\mathbf{Z}}'\ddot{\mathbf{y}}.$$

Then $\ddot{\mathbf{D}}_n^{-1/2}\sqrt{n}(\ddot{\beta}_n - \beta_o) \overset{A}{\sim} N(\mathbf{0}, \mathbf{I})$, where $\ddot{\mathbf{D}}_n \equiv (\ddot{\mathbf{Q}}_n'\ddot{\mathbf{L}}_n^{-1}\ddot{\mathbf{Q}}_n)^{-1}$, $\ddot{\mathbf{Q}}_n \equiv E(\ddot{\mathbf{Z}}'\ddot{\mathbf{X}}/n)$, and $\ddot{\mathbf{L}}_n \equiv E(\ddot{\mathbf{Z}}'\ddot{\mathbf{Z}}/n)$.

Now define $\mathbf{A}_n \equiv \mathbf{B}_n\mathbf{C}_n$ with $t\tau$th block $\mathbf{a}_{t\tau}$, each with elements $\mathbf{a}_{t\tau hg}$. Suppose that

$$\sigma(\ddot{\mathbf{W}}_{th}) = \bigwedge_{\{1\le\tau\le n, 1\le g\le p: \mathbf{a}_{t\tau hg}\neq 0, \text{a.s.}\}} \sigma(\mathbf{W}_{\tau g}),$$

$$h = 1, \ldots, p,\ t = 1, \ldots, n,$$

and that $\mathbf{a}_{t\tau hg}$ is measurable with respect to $\sigma(\ddot{\mathbf{W}}_{th})$. Suppose that $\mathbf{A}_n^{-1}$ has $t\tau$th block $\mathbf{a}^{t\tau}$, each with elements $\mathbf{a}^{t\tau hg}$. If

$$\sigma(\mathbf{W}_{th}) = \bigwedge_{\{1\le\tau\le n, 1\le g\le p; \mathbf{a}^{t\tau hg}\neq 0, \text{a.s.}\}} \sigma(\ddot{\mathbf{W}}_{\tau g}),$$

$$h = 1, \ldots, p,\ t = 1, \ldots, n,$$

and if $\mathbf{a}^{t\tau hg}$ is measurable with respect to $\sigma(\mathbf{W}_{th})$, then avar $\ddot{\beta}_n -$ avar $\beta_n^* \to \mathbf{0}$.

Proof: See White [1983, Theorem 3.7].

The simplest situation in which to verify the conditions of this theorem is when one has only contemporaneous correlation or heteroskedasticity and the instrumental variable candidates are identical for all equations of the system. In time-series contexts, the measurability requirements on $\mathbf{a}_{t\tau hg}$ and $\mathbf{a}^{t\tau hg}$ will be satisfied if $\mathbf{A}_n$ has elements that are functions only of instrumental variables strictly exogeneous with respect to $\boldsymbol{\epsilon}_t$ (e.g., if $\mathbf{A}_n$ is a matrix of constants). Note also that the requirements on $\sigma(\ddot{\mathbf{W}}_{th})$ and $\sigma(\mathbf{W}_{th})$ imply $\sigma(\ddot{\mathbf{W}}_{th}) = \sigma(\mathbf{W}_{th})$.

Just as in the classical development of the GLS estimator, we have assumed that $\boldsymbol{\Omega}_n$ or $\mathbf{C}_n$ is known. This is too unrealistic. If $\boldsymbol{\Omega}_n$ is completely unknown, then the estimator of Proposition 4.45 is still available. Often it is assumed that $\boldsymbol{\Omega}_n$ is known up to a finite number of parameters. These are estimated (e.g., in a first-stage using OLS or 2SLS residuals) and used to form an estimate $\hat{\boldsymbol{\Omega}}_n$, which replaces $\boldsymbol{\Omega}_n$ in computations. The consequences of doing this are considered in Chapter VII. There we see that for several important special cases, replacing $\boldsymbol{\Omega}_n$ by $\hat{\boldsymbol{\Omega}}_n$ has no effect on the asymptotic properties of the estimators.

So far, we have seen that additional instrumental variables can increase asymptotic efficiency and that appropriate transformations of a nonspherical model can also improve efficiency. Another way of increasing the efficiency of our estimators is through the imposition of prior knowledge embodied in linear or nonlinear constraints on the parameters. Because the case of linear restrictions is a special case of nonlinear restrictions, we formally consider only the latter, and leave derivation of the results for linear restrictions as an exercise.

Given constraints $\mathbf{s}(\boldsymbol{\beta}_o) = \mathbf{0}$, where $s\colon \mathbb{R}^k \to \mathbb{R}^q$ is a known continuously differentiable function, such that rank $\nabla\mathbf{s}(\boldsymbol{\beta}_o) = q$ and $\nabla\mathbf{s}(\boldsymbol{\beta}_o) < \infty$, the constrained instrumental variables estimator can be found as the solution to the problem

$$\min_{\beta}\, (\mathbf{y} - \mathbf{X}\boldsymbol{\beta})'\mathbf{Z}\hat{\mathbf{P}}_n\mathbf{Z}'(\mathbf{y} - \mathbf{X}\boldsymbol{\beta}) \qquad \text{s.t.} \quad \mathbf{s}(\boldsymbol{\beta}) = \mathbf{0},$$

which is equivalent to finding the saddle point of the Lagrangean

$$\mathcal{L} = (\mathbf{y} - \mathbf{X}\boldsymbol{\beta})'\mathbf{Z}\hat{\mathbf{P}}_n\mathbf{Z}'(\mathbf{y} - \mathbf{X}\boldsymbol{\beta}) + \mathbf{s}(\boldsymbol{\beta})'\boldsymbol{\lambda}.$$

The first-order conditions are

$$\frac{\partial \mathcal{L}}{\partial \boldsymbol{\beta}} = 2(\mathbf{X}'\mathbf{Z}\hat{\mathbf{P}}_n\mathbf{Z}'\mathbf{X})\boldsymbol{\beta} - 2\mathbf{X}'\mathbf{Z}\hat{\mathbf{P}}_n\mathbf{Z}'\mathbf{y} + \nabla\mathbf{s}(\boldsymbol{\beta})'\boldsymbol{\lambda} = \mathbf{0}$$

$$\frac{\partial \mathcal{L}}{\partial \lambda} = \mathbf{s}(\boldsymbol{\beta}) = \mathbf{0}.$$

Setting $\tilde{\boldsymbol{\beta}}_n = (\mathbf{X}'\mathbf{Z}\hat{\mathbf{P}}_n\mathbf{Z}'\mathbf{X})^{-1}\mathbf{X}'\mathbf{Z}\hat{\mathbf{P}}_n\mathbf{Z}'\mathbf{y}$ and taking a mean value expansion of $\mathbf{s}(\boldsymbol{\beta})$ around $\mathbf{s}(\tilde{\boldsymbol{\beta}}_n)$ yields the equations

$$\frac{\partial \mathcal{L}}{\partial \boldsymbol{\beta}} = 2(\mathbf{X}'\mathbf{Z}\hat{\mathbf{P}}_n\mathbf{Z}'\mathbf{X})(\boldsymbol{\beta} - \tilde{\boldsymbol{\beta}}_n) + \nabla\mathbf{s}(\boldsymbol{\beta})'\boldsymbol{\lambda} = \mathbf{0},$$

$$\frac{\partial \mathcal{L}}{\partial \boldsymbol{\lambda}} = \mathbf{s}(\tilde{\boldsymbol{\beta}}_n) + \nabla\bar{\mathbf{s}}(\boldsymbol{\beta} - \tilde{\boldsymbol{\beta}}_n) = \mathbf{0},$$

where $\nabla\bar{s}$ is the $q \times k$ Jacobian matrix with i^{th} row evaluated at a mean value $\bar{\boldsymbol{\beta}}_n^{(i)}$. To solve for $\boldsymbol{\lambda}$ in the first equation premultiply by $\nabla\bar{s}(\mathbf{X}'\mathbf{Z}\hat{\mathbf{P}}_n\mathbf{Z}'\mathbf{X})^{-1}$ to get

$$2\nabla\bar{\mathbf{s}}(\boldsymbol{\beta} - \tilde{\boldsymbol{\beta}}_n) + \nabla\bar{\mathbf{s}}(\mathbf{X}'\mathbf{Z}\hat{\mathbf{P}}_n\mathbf{Z}'\mathbf{X})^{-1}\nabla\mathbf{s}(\boldsymbol{\beta})'\boldsymbol{\lambda} = \mathbf{0},$$

substitute $-\mathbf{s}(\tilde{\boldsymbol{\beta}}_n) = \nabla\bar{\mathbf{s}}(\boldsymbol{\beta} - \tilde{\boldsymbol{\beta}}_n)$, and invert $\nabla\bar{\mathbf{s}}(\mathbf{X}'\mathbf{Z}\hat{\mathbf{P}}_n\mathbf{Z}'\mathbf{X})^{-1}\nabla\mathbf{s}(\boldsymbol{\beta})$ to obtain

$$\boldsymbol{\lambda} = 2[\nabla\bar{\mathbf{s}}(\mathbf{X}'\mathbf{Z}\hat{\mathbf{P}}_n\mathbf{Z}'\mathbf{X})^{-1}\nabla\mathbf{s}(\boldsymbol{\beta})]^{-1}\mathbf{s}(\tilde{\boldsymbol{\beta}}_n).$$

The expression for $\partial\mathcal{L}/\partial\boldsymbol{\beta}$ above yields

$$\boldsymbol{\beta}-\tilde{\boldsymbol{\beta}}_n=\frac{-(\mathbf{X}'\mathbf{Z}\hat{\mathbf{P}}_n\mathbf{Z}'\mathbf{X})^{-1}\nabla\mathbf{s}(\boldsymbol{\beta})'\boldsymbol{\lambda}}{2},$$

so we obtain the solution for $\boldsymbol{\beta}$ by substituting for λ:

$$\boldsymbol{\beta}=\tilde{\boldsymbol{\beta}}_n-(\mathbf{X}'\mathbf{Z}\hat{\mathbf{P}}_n\mathbf{Z}'\mathbf{X})^{-1}\nabla\mathbf{s}(\boldsymbol{\beta})'[\nabla\bar{\mathbf{s}}(\mathbf{X}'\mathbf{Z}\hat{\mathbf{P}}_n\mathbf{Z}'\mathbf{X})^{-1}\nabla\mathbf{s}(\boldsymbol{\beta})]^{-1}\mathbf{s}(\tilde{\boldsymbol{\beta}}_n).$$

The difficulty with this solution is that it is not in closed form, because the unknown $\boldsymbol{\beta}$ appears on both sides of the equation. Further, appearing in this expression is $\nabla\bar{\mathbf{s}}$, which has rows each of which depend on a mean value lying between $\boldsymbol{\beta}$ and $\tilde{\boldsymbol{\beta}}_n$.

Nevertheless, a computationally practical and asymptotically equivalent result can be obtained by replacing $\nabla\bar{\mathbf{s}}$ and $\nabla\mathbf{s}(\boldsymbol{\beta})$ by $\nabla\mathbf{s}(\tilde{\boldsymbol{\beta}}_n)$ on the right-hand side of the expression above, which yields

$$\begin{aligned}\boldsymbol{\beta}_n^*=\tilde{\boldsymbol{\beta}}_n&-(\mathbf{X}'\mathbf{Z}\hat{\mathbf{P}}_n\mathbf{Z}'\mathbf{X})^{-1}\nabla\mathbf{s}(\tilde{\boldsymbol{\beta}}_n)'[\nabla\mathbf{s}(\tilde{\boldsymbol{\beta}}_n)\\&\times(\mathbf{X}'\mathbf{Z}\hat{\mathbf{P}}_n\mathbf{Z}'\mathbf{X})^{-1}\nabla\mathbf{s}(\tilde{\boldsymbol{\beta}}_n)']^{-1}\mathbf{s}(\tilde{\boldsymbol{\beta}}_n).\end{aligned}$$

This gives us a convenient way of computing a constrained IV estimator. First we compute the unconstrained estimator, and then we "impose" the constraints by subtracting a "correction factor"

$$(\mathbf{X}'\mathbf{Z}\hat{\mathbf{P}}_n\mathbf{Z}'\mathbf{X})^{-1}\nabla\mathbf{s}(\tilde{\boldsymbol{\beta}}_n)'[\nabla\mathbf{s}(\tilde{\boldsymbol{\beta}}_n)(\mathbf{X}'\mathbf{Z}\hat{\mathbf{P}}_n\mathbf{Z}'\mathbf{X})^{-1}\nabla\mathbf{s}(\tilde{\boldsymbol{\beta}}_n)']^{-1}\mathbf{s}(\tilde{\boldsymbol{\beta}}_n)$$

from the unconstrained estimator. We say "impose" because $\boldsymbol{\beta}_n^*$ will not satisfy the constraints exactly for any finite n. However, an estimator which does satisfy the constraints to any desired degree of accuracy can be obtained by iterating the procedure just described, that is, by replacing $\tilde{\boldsymbol{\beta}}_n$ by $\boldsymbol{\beta}_n^*$ in the formula above to get a second round estimator, say, $\boldsymbol{\beta}_n^{**}$. This process could continue until the change in the resulting estimator was sufficiently small. Nevertheless, this iteration process does not improve the asymptotic efficiency beyond that of $\boldsymbol{\beta}_n^*$.

EXERCISE 4.59: Define

$$\begin{aligned}\boldsymbol{\beta}_n^{**}=\boldsymbol{\beta}_n^*&-(\mathbf{X}'\mathbf{Z}\hat{\mathbf{P}}_n\mathbf{Z}'\mathbf{X})^{-1}\nabla\mathbf{s}(\boldsymbol{\beta}_n^*)'[\nabla\mathbf{s}(\boldsymbol{\beta}_n^*)\\&\times(\mathbf{X}'\mathbf{Z}\hat{\mathbf{P}}_n\mathbf{Z}'\mathbf{X})^{-1}\nabla\mathbf{s}(\boldsymbol{\beta}_n^*)']^{-1}\mathbf{s}(\boldsymbol{\beta}_n^*).\end{aligned}$$

Show that under the conditions of Exercise 4.26 and the conditions on s that $\sqrt{n}(\boldsymbol{\beta}_n^{**}-\boldsymbol{\beta}_n^*)\xrightarrow{p}\mathbf{0}$, so that $\sqrt{n}(\boldsymbol{\beta}_n^*-\boldsymbol{\beta}_o)$ has the same asymptotic distribution as $\sqrt{n}(\boldsymbol{\beta}_n^{**}-\boldsymbol{\beta}_o)$. (*Hint:* Show that $\sqrt{n}s(\boldsymbol{\beta}_n^*)\xrightarrow{p}\mathbf{0}$.)

In establishing the asymptotic efficiency result, we only consider the improvement that can be achieved over the best IV estimator for given instrumental variables that does not embody the constraints, that is, $\tilde{\boldsymbol{\beta}}_n = (\mathbf{X}'\mathbf{Z}\hat{\mathbf{V}}_n^{-1}\mathbf{Z}'\mathbf{X})^{-1}\mathbf{X}'\mathbf{Z}\hat{\mathbf{V}}_n^{-1}\mathbf{Z}'\mathbf{y}$.

THEOREM 4.60: Suppose the conditions of Exercise 4.26 hold for $\hat{\mathbf{P}}_n = \hat{\mathbf{V}}_n^{-1}$ and that $\mathbf{s}: \mathbb{R}^k \to \mathbb{R}^q$ is a continuously differentiable function such that $\mathbf{s}(\boldsymbol{\beta}_o) = 0$, $\nabla\mathbf{s}(\boldsymbol{\beta}_o) < \infty$ and rank $\nabla\mathbf{s}(\boldsymbol{\beta}_o) = q$. Define $\tilde{\boldsymbol{\beta}}_n = (\mathbf{X}'\mathbf{Z}\hat{\mathbf{V}}_n^{-1}\mathbf{Z}'\mathbf{X})^{-1}\mathbf{X}'\mathbf{Z}\hat{\mathbf{V}}_n^{-1}\mathbf{Z}'\mathbf{y}$ and define $\boldsymbol{\beta}_n^*$ as above with $\hat{\mathbf{P}}_n = \hat{\mathbf{V}}_n^{-1}$. Then

$$\begin{aligned}&\operatorname{avar} \tilde{\boldsymbol{\beta}}_n - \operatorname{avar} \boldsymbol{\beta}_n^* \\ &\qquad = \operatorname{avar} \tilde{\boldsymbol{\beta}}_n \nabla\mathbf{s}(\boldsymbol{\beta}_o)'[\nabla\mathbf{s}(\boldsymbol{\beta}_o) \operatorname{avar} \tilde{\boldsymbol{\beta}}_n \nabla\mathbf{s}(\boldsymbol{\beta}_o)']^{-1}\nabla\mathbf{s}(\boldsymbol{\beta}_o) \operatorname{avar} \tilde{\boldsymbol{\beta}}_n,\end{aligned}$$

which is a positive semidefinite matrix.

Proof: From Exercise 4.26 it follows that

$$\operatorname{avar} \tilde{\boldsymbol{\beta}}_n = (\mathbf{Q}_n'\mathbf{V}_n^{-1}\mathbf{Q}_n)^{-1}.$$

Taking a mean value expansion of $\mathbf{s}(\tilde{\boldsymbol{\beta}}_n)$ around $\boldsymbol{\beta}_o$ gives $\mathbf{s}(\tilde{\boldsymbol{\beta}}_n) = \mathbf{s}(\boldsymbol{\beta}_o) + \nabla\bar{\mathbf{s}}(\tilde{\boldsymbol{\beta}}_n - \boldsymbol{\beta}_o)$, and because $\mathbf{s}(\boldsymbol{\beta}_o) = \mathbf{0}$, we have $\mathbf{s}(\tilde{\boldsymbol{\beta}}_n) = \nabla\bar{\mathbf{s}}(\tilde{\boldsymbol{\beta}}_n - \boldsymbol{\beta}_o)$. Substituting this in the formula for $\boldsymbol{\beta}_n^*$ allows us to write

$$\sqrt{n}(\boldsymbol{\beta}_n^* - \boldsymbol{\beta}_o) = \tilde{\mathbf{A}}_n\sqrt{n}(\tilde{\boldsymbol{\beta}}_n - \boldsymbol{\beta}_o),$$

where

$$\begin{aligned}\tilde{\mathbf{A}}_n = \mathbf{I} - (\mathbf{X}'\mathbf{Z}\hat{\mathbf{V}}_n^{-1}\mathbf{Z}'\mathbf{X})^{-1}\nabla\mathbf{s}(\tilde{\boldsymbol{\beta}}_n)'[\nabla\mathbf{s}(\tilde{\boldsymbol{\beta}}_n) \\ \cdot (\mathbf{X}'\mathbf{Z}\hat{\mathbf{V}}_n^{-1}\mathbf{Z}'\mathbf{X})^{-1}\nabla\mathbf{s}(\tilde{\boldsymbol{\beta}}_n)]^{-1}\nabla\bar{\mathbf{s}}.\end{aligned}$$

Under the conditions of Exercise 4.26, $\tilde{\boldsymbol{\beta}}_n \xrightarrow{p} \boldsymbol{\beta}_o$ and Proposition 2.30 applies to ensure that $\tilde{\mathbf{A}}_n - \mathbf{A}_n \xrightarrow{p} \mathbf{0}$, where

$$\mathbf{A}_n = \mathbf{I} - \operatorname{avar} \tilde{\boldsymbol{\beta}}_n \nabla\mathbf{s}(\boldsymbol{\beta}_o)'[\nabla\mathbf{s}(\boldsymbol{\beta}_o) \operatorname{avar} \tilde{\boldsymbol{\beta}}_n \nabla\mathbf{s}(\boldsymbol{\beta}_o)']^{-1}\nabla\mathbf{s}(\boldsymbol{\beta}_o).$$

Hence, by Lemma 4.6,

$$\begin{aligned}&\sqrt{n}(\boldsymbol{\beta}_n^* - \boldsymbol{\beta}_o) - \mathbf{A}_n\sqrt{n}(\tilde{\boldsymbol{\beta}}_n - \boldsymbol{\beta}_o) \\ &\qquad = (\tilde{\mathbf{A}}_n - \mathbf{A}_n)\sqrt{n}(\tilde{\boldsymbol{\beta}}_n - \boldsymbol{\beta}_o) \xrightarrow{p} \mathbf{0},\end{aligned}$$

because $\sqrt{n}(\tilde{\boldsymbol{\beta}}_n - \boldsymbol{\beta}_o)$ is $O_p(1)$ as a consequence of Exercise 4.26. From the Asymptotic equivalence lemma 4.7 it follows that $\sqrt{n}(\boldsymbol{\beta}_n^* - \boldsymbol{\beta}_o)$ has the same asymptotic distribution as $\mathbf{A}_n\sqrt{n}(\tilde{\boldsymbol{\beta}}_n - \boldsymbol{\beta}_o)$. If follows from Corollary 4.24 that $\boldsymbol{\Gamma}_n^{-1/2}\mathbf{A}_n\sqrt{n}(\tilde{\boldsymbol{\beta}}_n - \boldsymbol{\beta}_o)$ (hence $\boldsymbol{\Gamma}_n^{-1/2}\sqrt{n}(\boldsymbol{\beta}_n^* - \boldsymbol{\beta}_o)$) is asymptotically $N(\mathbf{0}, \mathbf{I})$, so that

$$\text{avar}\,\boldsymbol{\beta}_n^* = \Gamma_n = \mathbf{A}_n\,\text{avar}\,\tilde{\boldsymbol{\beta}}_n\mathbf{A}_n'.$$

Straightforward algebra yields

$$\begin{aligned}\text{avar}\,\boldsymbol{\beta}_n^* = {} & \text{avar}\,\tilde{\boldsymbol{\beta}}_n - \text{avar}\,\tilde{\boldsymbol{\beta}}_n\nabla\mathbf{s}(\boldsymbol{\beta}_o)' \\ & \times [\nabla\mathbf{s}(\boldsymbol{\beta}_o)\,\text{avar}\,\tilde{\boldsymbol{\beta}}_n\nabla\mathbf{s}(\boldsymbol{\beta}_o)']^{-1}\nabla\mathbf{s}(\boldsymbol{\beta}_o)\,\text{avar}\,\tilde{\boldsymbol{\beta}}_n,\end{aligned}$$

and the result follows immediately.

This result guarantees that imposing correct a priori restrictions leads to an efficiency improvement over the efficient IV estimator that does not impose these restrictions. Interestingly, imposing the restrictions using the formula for $\boldsymbol{\beta}_n^*$ with an inefficient estimator $\tilde{\boldsymbol{\beta}}_n$ for given instrumental variables may or may not lead to efficiency gains relative to $\tilde{\boldsymbol{\beta}}_n$.

The result of Theorem 4.60 does not allow us to compare the efficiency of estimators obtained from different transformations of the underlying model $\mathbf{y} = \mathbf{X}\boldsymbol{\beta}_o + \boldsymbol{\epsilon}$. Nevertheless, it is reasonable to expect that when the restrictions are imposed on a relatively efficient estimator, the resulting estimator is more efficient than the estimator obtained by imposing the constraints on a relatively inefficient estimator (although one efficient within its class). The next result formalizes this notion, which is helpful in guaranteeing the efficiency of some estimators considered in Chapter VII.

THEOREM 4.61: Consider the models

$$\mathbf{y} = \mathbf{X}\boldsymbol{\beta}_o + \boldsymbol{\epsilon},$$
$$\tilde{\mathbf{y}} = \tilde{\mathbf{X}}\boldsymbol{\beta}_o + \tilde{\boldsymbol{\epsilon}},$$

and associated instrumental variables $\mathbf{Z}$ and $\tilde{\mathbf{Z}}$, and suppose that the conditions of Exercise 4.26 hold for both. Define the unconstrained estimators

$$\tilde{\boldsymbol{\beta}}_n = (\tilde{\mathbf{X}}'\tilde{\mathbf{Z}}\tilde{\mathbf{V}}_n^{-1}\tilde{\mathbf{Z}}'\tilde{\mathbf{X}})^{-1}\tilde{\mathbf{X}}'\tilde{\mathbf{Z}}\tilde{\mathbf{V}}_n^{-1}\tilde{\mathbf{Z}}'\tilde{\mathbf{y}},$$
$$\boldsymbol{\beta}_n^* = (\mathbf{X}'\mathbf{Z}\hat{\mathbf{V}}_n^{-1}\mathbf{Z}'\mathbf{X})^{-1}\mathbf{X}'\mathbf{Z}\hat{\mathbf{V}}_n^{-1}\mathbf{Z}'\mathbf{y},$$

and suppose that $\boldsymbol{\beta}_n^*$ is asymptotically efficient relative to $\tilde{\boldsymbol{\beta}}_n$ so that avar $\tilde{\boldsymbol{\beta}}_n$ − avar $\boldsymbol{\beta}_n^*$ is positive semidefinite for all n sufficiently large. Define the constrained estimators

$$\bar{\boldsymbol{\beta}}_n = \tilde{\boldsymbol{\beta}}_n - (\tilde{\mathbf{X}}'\tilde{\mathbf{Z}}\tilde{\mathbf{V}}_n^{-1}\tilde{\mathbf{Z}}'\tilde{\mathbf{X}})^{-1}\nabla\mathbf{s}(\tilde{\boldsymbol{\beta}}_n)' \cdot [\nabla\mathbf{s}(\tilde{\boldsymbol{\beta}}_n)(\tilde{\mathbf{X}}'\tilde{\mathbf{Z}}\tilde{\mathbf{V}}_n^{-1}\tilde{\mathbf{Z}}'\tilde{\mathbf{X}})^{-1}\nabla\mathbf{s}(\tilde{\boldsymbol{\beta}}_n)']^{-1}\mathbf{s}(\tilde{\boldsymbol{\beta}}_n)$$

and

$$\ddot{\boldsymbol{\beta}}_n = \boldsymbol{\beta}_n^* - (\mathbf{X}'\mathbf{Z}\hat{\mathbf{V}}_n^{-1}\mathbf{Z}'\mathbf{X})^{-1}\nabla\mathbf{s}(\boldsymbol{\beta}_n^*)'[\nabla\mathbf{s}(\boldsymbol{\beta}_n^*)(\mathbf{X}'\mathbf{Z}\hat{\mathbf{V}}_n^{-1}\mathbf{Z}'\mathbf{X})^{-1} \cdot \nabla\mathbf{s}(\boldsymbol{\beta}_n^*)']^{-1}\mathbf{s}(\boldsymbol{\beta}_n^*).$$

Then avar $\bar{\boldsymbol{\beta}}_n$ − avar $\ddot{\boldsymbol{\beta}}_n$ is positive semidefinite for all n sufficiently large.

Proof: Following the proof of Theorem 4.60, we have

$$\text{avar}\,\ddot{\boldsymbol{\beta}}_n = \text{avar}\,\boldsymbol{\beta}_n^* - \text{avar}\,\boldsymbol{\beta}_n^*\nabla\mathbf{s}(\boldsymbol{\beta}_o)'[\nabla\mathbf{s}(\boldsymbol{\beta}_o) \cdot \text{avar}\,\boldsymbol{\beta}_n^*\nabla\mathbf{s}(\boldsymbol{\beta}_o)']^{-1}\nabla\mathbf{s}(\boldsymbol{\beta}_o)\,\text{avar}\,\boldsymbol{\beta}_n^*$$

$$\text{avar}\,\bar{\boldsymbol{\beta}}_n = \mathbf{A}_n\,(\text{avar}\,\tilde{\boldsymbol{\beta}}_n)\mathbf{A}_n',$$

where

$$\mathbf{A}_n = \mathbf{I} - (\tilde{\mathbf{Q}}_n'\tilde{\mathbf{V}}_n^{-1}\tilde{\mathbf{Q}}_n)^{-1}\nabla\mathbf{s}(\boldsymbol{\beta}_o)'[\nabla\mathbf{s}(\boldsymbol{\beta}_o)(\tilde{\mathbf{Q}}_n'\tilde{\mathbf{V}}_n^{-1}\tilde{\mathbf{Q}}_n)^{-1}\nabla\mathbf{s}(\boldsymbol{\beta}_o)']^{-1}\nabla\mathbf{s}(\boldsymbol{\beta}_o).$$

Hence,

$$\begin{aligned}
&\text{avar}\,\bar{\boldsymbol{\beta}}_n - \text{avar}\,\ddot{\boldsymbol{\beta}}_n \\
&\quad = \mathbf{A}_n\,\text{avar}\,\tilde{\boldsymbol{\beta}}_n\,\mathbf{A}_n' - \text{avar}\,\boldsymbol{\beta}_n^* \\
&\qquad + \text{avar}\,\boldsymbol{\beta}_n^*\nabla\mathbf{s}(\boldsymbol{\beta}_o)'[\nabla\mathbf{s}(\boldsymbol{\beta}_o)\,\text{avar}\,\boldsymbol{\beta}_n^*\nabla\mathbf{s}(\boldsymbol{\beta}_o)']^{-1}\nabla\mathbf{s}(\boldsymbol{\beta}_o)\,\text{avar}\,\boldsymbol{\beta}_n^* \\
&\quad = \mathbf{A}_n\,(\text{avar}\,\tilde{\boldsymbol{\beta}}_n)\mathbf{A}_n' - \mathbf{A}_n\,(\text{avar}\,\boldsymbol{\beta}_n^*)\mathbf{A}_n' \\
&\qquad + \mathbf{A}_n\,(\text{avar}\,\boldsymbol{\beta}_n^*)\mathbf{A}_n' - \text{avar}\,\boldsymbol{\beta}_n^* \\
&\qquad + \text{avar}\,\boldsymbol{\beta}_n^*\nabla\mathbf{s}(\boldsymbol{\beta}_o)'[\nabla\mathbf{s}(\boldsymbol{\beta}_o)\,\text{avar}\,\boldsymbol{\beta}_n^*\nabla\mathbf{s}(\boldsymbol{\beta}_o)']^{-1}\nabla\mathbf{s}(\boldsymbol{\beta}_o)\,\text{avar}\,\boldsymbol{\beta}_n^*.
\end{aligned}$$

The first term is positive semidefinite for all n sufficiently large because

$$\mathbf{A}_n\,(\text{avar}\,\tilde{\boldsymbol{\beta}}_n)\mathbf{A}_n' - \mathbf{A}_n\,(\text{avar}\,\boldsymbol{\beta}_n^*)\mathbf{A}_n' = \mathbf{A}_n\,(\text{avar}\,\tilde{\boldsymbol{\beta}}_n - \text{avar}\,\boldsymbol{\beta}_n^*)\mathbf{A}_n',$$

and avar $\tilde{\boldsymbol{\beta}}_n$ − avar $\boldsymbol{\beta}_n^*$ is positive semidefinite for all n sufficiently large by assumption. The result then follows, provided that

$$\mathbf{A}_n\,(\text{avar}\,\boldsymbol{\beta}_n^*)\mathbf{A}_n' - \text{avar}\,\boldsymbol{\beta}_n^* + \text{avar}\,\boldsymbol{\beta}_n^*\nabla\mathbf{s}(\boldsymbol{\beta}_o)'[\nabla\mathbf{s}(\boldsymbol{\beta}_o)\,\text{avar}\,\boldsymbol{\beta}_n^*\nabla\mathbf{s}(\boldsymbol{\beta}_o)']^{-1}\nabla\mathbf{s}(\boldsymbol{\beta}_o)\,\text{avar}\,\boldsymbol{\beta}_n^*$$

is positive semidefinite for all n sufficiently large.

Let

$$\mathbf{B}_n \equiv (\tilde{\mathbf{Q}}_n'\tilde{\mathbf{V}}_n^{-1}\tilde{\mathbf{Q}}_n)^{-1}\nabla\mathbf{s}(\boldsymbol{\beta}_o)'[\nabla\mathbf{s}(\boldsymbol{\beta}_o)(\tilde{\mathbf{Q}}_n'\tilde{\mathbf{V}}_n^{-1}\tilde{\mathbf{Q}}_n)^{-1}\nabla\mathbf{s}(\boldsymbol{\beta}_o)']^{-1},$$

so that

$$\mathbf{A}_n = \mathbf{I} - \mathbf{B}_n\nabla\mathbf{s}(\boldsymbol{\beta}_o).$$

Then, by definition of $\mathbf{A}_n$,

$$\begin{aligned}
&\mathbf{A}_n\,(\text{avar}\,\boldsymbol{\beta}_n^*)\mathbf{A}_n' - \text{avar}\,\boldsymbol{\beta}_n^* \\
&\quad = -\mathbf{B}_n\nabla\mathbf{s}(\boldsymbol{\beta}_o)\,\text{avar}\,\boldsymbol{\beta}_n^* - \text{avar}\,\boldsymbol{\beta}_n^*\nabla\mathbf{s}(\boldsymbol{\beta}_o)'\mathbf{B}_n' \\
&\qquad + \mathbf{B}_n\nabla\mathbf{s}(\boldsymbol{\beta}_o)\,\text{avar}\,\boldsymbol{\beta}_n^*\nabla\mathbf{s}(\boldsymbol{\beta}_o)'\mathbf{B}_n',
\end{aligned}$$

so that

$$\begin{aligned}
&\mathbf{A}_n\,(\text{avar}\,\boldsymbol{\beta}_n^*)\mathbf{A}_n' - \text{avar}\,\boldsymbol{\beta}_n^* \\
&\qquad + \text{avar}\,\boldsymbol{\beta}_n^*\nabla\mathbf{s}(\boldsymbol{\beta}_o)' \\
&\qquad \cdot [\nabla\mathbf{s}(\boldsymbol{\beta}_o)\,\text{avar}\,\boldsymbol{\beta}_n^*\nabla\mathbf{s}(\boldsymbol{\beta}_o)']^{-1}\nabla\mathbf{s}(\boldsymbol{\beta}_o)\,\text{avar}\,\boldsymbol{\beta}_n^* \\
&\quad = \mathbf{B}_n[\nabla\mathbf{s}(\boldsymbol{\beta}_o)\,\text{avar}\,\boldsymbol{\beta}_n^*\nabla\mathbf{s}(\boldsymbol{\beta}_o)']\mathbf{B}_n' \\
&\qquad - \mathbf{B}_n\nabla\mathbf{s}(\boldsymbol{\beta}_o)\,\text{avar}\,\boldsymbol{\beta}_n^* - \text{avar}\,\boldsymbol{\beta}_n^*\nabla\mathbf{s}(\boldsymbol{\beta}_o)'\mathbf{B}_n' \\
&\qquad + \text{avar}\,\boldsymbol{\beta}_n^*\nabla\mathbf{s}(\boldsymbol{\beta}_o)' \\
&\qquad \cdot [\nabla\mathbf{s}(\boldsymbol{\beta}_o)\,\text{avar}\,\boldsymbol{\beta}_n^*\nabla\mathbf{s}(\boldsymbol{\beta}_o)']^{-1}\nabla\mathbf{s}(\boldsymbol{\beta}_o)\,\text{avar}\,\boldsymbol{\beta}_n^*.
\end{aligned}$$

Now let

$$\mathbf{C}_n^{1/2} = [\nabla\mathbf{s}(\boldsymbol{\beta}_o)\,\text{avar}\,\boldsymbol{\beta}_n^*\nabla\mathbf{s}(\boldsymbol{\beta}_o)']^{1/2},$$

$$\mathbf{D}_n = \nabla\mathbf{s}(\boldsymbol{\beta}_o)\,\text{avar}\,\boldsymbol{\beta}_n^*.$$

Then

$$\begin{aligned}
&\mathbf{A}_n\,(\text{avar}\,\boldsymbol{\beta}_n^*)\mathbf{A}_n' - \text{avar}\,\boldsymbol{\beta}_n^* \\
&\qquad + \text{avar}\,\boldsymbol{\beta}_n^*\nabla\mathbf{s}(\boldsymbol{\beta}_o)'[\nabla\mathbf{s}(\boldsymbol{\beta}_o)\,\text{avar}\,\boldsymbol{\beta}_n^*\nabla\mathbf{s}(\boldsymbol{\beta}_o)']^{-1}\nabla\mathbf{s}(\boldsymbol{\beta}_o)\,\text{avar}\,\boldsymbol{\beta}_n^* \\
&\quad = \mathbf{B}_n\mathbf{C}_n^{1/2}\mathbf{C}_n^{1/2}\mathbf{B}_n' - \mathbf{B}_n\mathbf{D}_n - \mathbf{D}_n'\mathbf{B}_n' + \mathbf{D}_n'\mathbf{C}_n^{-1/2}\mathbf{C}_n^{-1/2}\mathbf{D}_n \\
&\quad = \mathbf{B}_n\mathbf{C}_n^{1/2}\mathbf{C}_n^{1/2}\mathbf{B}_n' - \mathbf{B}_n\mathbf{C}_n^{1/2}\mathbf{C}_n^{-1/2}\mathbf{D}_n - \mathbf{D}_n'\mathbf{C}_n^{-1/2}\mathbf{C}_n^{1/2}\mathbf{B}_n' \\
&\qquad + \mathbf{D}_n'\mathbf{C}_n^{-1/2}\mathbf{C}_n^{-1/2}\mathbf{D}_n \\
&\quad = (\mathbf{B}_n\mathbf{C}_n^{1/2} - \mathbf{D}_n'\mathbf{C}_n^{-1/2})(\mathbf{B}_n\mathbf{C}_n^{1/2} - \mathbf{D}_n'\mathbf{C}_n^{-1/2})',
\end{aligned}$$

which is positive semidefinite for all n, and the result follows.

References

Bartle, R. G. [1976]. "The Elements of Real Analysis." New York: Wiley.

Chamberlain, G. [1982]. Multivariate regression models for panel data, *J. Econometrics* **18**:5–46.

Cragg, J. [1983]. More efficient estimation in the presence of heteroskedasticity of unknown form, *Econometrica:* **51**:751–764.

Engle, R. F. [1981]. Wald, likelihood ratio, and Lagrange multiplier tests in econometrics, *in* "Handbook of Econometrics," Z. Griliches and M. Intrilligator, eds. Amsterdam: North Holland.

Engle, R. F. [1982]. Autoregressive conditional heteroskedasticity with estimates of the variance of United Kingdom inflations, *Econometrica* **50**:987–1008.

Goldberger, A. S. [1964]. "Econometric Theory." New York: Wiley.

Lukacs, E. [1970]. "Characteristic Functions." London: Griffin.

Lukacs, E. [1975]. "Stochastic Convergence." New York: Academic Press.

Rao, C. R. [1973]. "Linear Statistical Inference and Its Applications." New York: Wiley.

White, H. [1982]. Instrumental variables regression with independent observations, *Econometrica* **50**:483–500.

White, H. [1983]. Instrumental variables analogues of generalized least squares estimators, Discussion Paper, Department of Economics, University of California, San Diego, San Diego, California.

Zellner, A. [1962]. An efficient method of estimating seemingly unrelated regressions and tests for aggregation bias, *J. Amer. Statis. Assoc.* **58**:348–368.

Zellner, A. and H. Theil [1962]. Three-stage least squares: simultaneous estimation of simultaneous equations, *Econometrica* **30,** 54–78.

CHAPTER V

Central Limit Theory

In this chapter we study different versions of the central limit theorem that provide conditions guaranteeing the asymptotic normality of $n^{-1/2}\mathbf{X}'\boldsymbol{\epsilon}$ or $n^{-1/2}\mathbf{Z}'\boldsymbol{\epsilon}$ required for the results of the previous chapter. As with laws of large numbers, different conditions will apply to different kinds of economic data. Central limit results are generally available for each of the situations considered in Chapter III, and we shall pay particular attention to the parallels involved.

The central limit theorems we consider are all of the following form.

PROPOSITION 5.0: Given restrictions on the dependence, heterogeneity, and moments of a scalar sequence $\{Z_t\}$, $(\bar{Z}_n - \bar{\mu}_n)/(\bar{\sigma}_n/\sqrt{n}) = \sqrt{n}(\bar{Z}_n - \bar{\mu}_n)/\bar{\sigma}_n \overset{A}{\sim} N(0, 1)$, where $\bar{\mu}_n \equiv E(\bar{Z}_n)$ and $\bar{\sigma}_n^2/n \equiv \text{var } \bar{Z}_n$.

In other words, under general conditions the sample average of a sequence has a limiting unit normal distribution when appropriately standardized. The results that follow specify precisely the restrictions that are sufficient to imply asymptotic normality. As with the laws of large numbers, there are natural trade-offs among these restrictions. Typically, greater dependence or heterogeneity is allowed at the expense of imposing more stringent moment requirements.

Although the results of the preceding chapter imposed the asymptotic normality requirement on the joint distribution of vectors such as $n^{-1/2}\mathbf{X}'\boldsymbol{\epsilon}$ or $n^{-1/2}\mathbf{Z}'\boldsymbol{\epsilon}$, it is actually only necessary to study central limit theory for sequences of scalars. This simplicity is a consequence of the following result.

PROPOSITION 5.1 (*Cramêr–Wold device*): Let $\{b_n\}$ be a sequence of random $k \times 1$ vectors and suppose that for any real $k \times 1$ vector λ such that $\lambda'\lambda = 1$, $\lambda' b_n \overset{A}{\sim} \lambda' Z$, where Z is a $k \times 1$ vector with joint distribution function $F(z)$. Then the limiting distribution function of b_n exists and equals $F(z)$.

Proof: See Rao [1973, p. 123].

We shall apply this result by showing that under general conditions,

$$n^{-1/2} \sum_{t=1}^{n} \lambda' \mathbf{V}_n^{-1/2} \mathbf{X}_t' \boldsymbol{\epsilon}_t \overset{A}{\sim} \lambda' Z \qquad \text{or} \qquad n^{-1/2} \sum_{t=1}^{n} \lambda' \mathbf{V}_n^{-1/2} \mathbf{Z}_t' \boldsymbol{\epsilon}_t \overset{A}{\sim} \lambda' Z,$$

where $Z \sim N(\mathbf{0}, \mathbf{I})$, which, by Propositions 5.1, allows us to obtain the desired conclusion, i.e.,

$$\mathbf{V}_n^{-1/2} n^{-1/2} \mathbf{X}' \boldsymbol{\epsilon} \overset{A}{\sim} N(\mathbf{0}, \mathbf{I}) \qquad \text{or} \qquad \mathbf{V}_\mathbf{n}^{-1/2} n^{-1/2} \mathbf{Z}' \boldsymbol{\epsilon} \overset{A}{\sim} N(\mathbf{0}, \mathbf{I}).$$

When used in this context below, the vector λ will always be understood to have unit norm, i.e., $\lambda'\lambda = 1$.

V.1 Independent Identically Distributed Observations

As with laws of large numbers, the case of independent identically distributed observations is the simplest.

THEOREM 5.2 (*Lindeberg–Levy*): Let $\{Z_t\}$ be a sequence of i.i.d. random scalars. If var $Z_t \equiv \sigma^2 < \infty$, $\sigma^2 \neq 0$, then

$$\sqrt{n}(\bar{Z}_n - \bar{\mu}_n)/\bar{\sigma}_n = \sqrt{n}(\bar{Z}_n - \mu)/\sigma = n^{-1/2} \sum_{t=1}^{n} (Z_t - \mu)/\sigma \overset{A}{\sim} N(0, 1).$$

Proof: Let $f(\lambda)$ be the characteristic function of $Z_t - \mu$ and let $f_n(\lambda)$ be the characteristic function of $\sqrt{n}(\bar{Z}_n - \bar{\mu}_n)/\bar{\sigma}_n = n^{-1/2} \sum_{t=1}^{n} (Z_t - \mu)/\sigma$. From Propositions 4.13 and 4.14 we have

$$f_n(\lambda) = f(\lambda/(\sigma\sqrt{n}))^n$$

or

$$\log f_n(\lambda) = n \log f(\lambda/(\sigma\sqrt{n})).$$

Taking a Taylor expansion of $f(\lambda)$ around $\lambda = 0$ gives $f(\lambda) = 1 - \sigma^2\lambda^2/2 + o(\lambda^2)$, since $\sigma^2 < \infty$ by Proposition 4.15. Hence

$$\log f_n(\lambda) = n \log[1 - \lambda^2/2n + o(\lambda^2/n)] \to -\lambda^2/2 \quad \text{as} \quad n \to \infty$$

Hence $f_n(\lambda) \to \exp(-\lambda^2/2)$. Since this is continuous at zero, it follows from the continuity theorem 4.17, the uniqueness theorem 4.11 and Exercise 4.10(i) that $\sqrt{n}(\bar{Z}_n - \bar{\mu}_n)/\bar{\sigma}_n \overset{A}{\sim} N(0, 1)$.

Compared with the law of large numbers for i.i.d. observations, we impose a single additional requirement, i.e., that var $Z_t = \sigma^2 < \infty$. Note that this implies $E|Z_t| < \infty$. (Why?) Also note that without loss of generality, we can set $E(Z_t) = 0$.

We can apply Theorem 5.2 to give conditions which ensure that the conditions of Theorem 4.25 and Exercise 4.26 are satisfied.

THEOREM 5.3: Given

(i) $\mathbf{y} = \mathbf{X}\boldsymbol{\beta}_o + \boldsymbol{\epsilon}$;
(ii) $\{(\mathbf{X}_t, \boldsymbol{\epsilon}_t)'\}$ is an i.i.d. sequence;
(iii) (a) $E(\mathbf{X}_t'\boldsymbol{\epsilon}_t) = \mathbf{0}$;
(b) $E|\mathbf{X}_{thi}\boldsymbol{\epsilon}_{th}|^2 < \infty$, $h = 1, \ldots, p$, $i = 1, \ldots, k$;
(c) $\mathbf{V}_n \equiv \text{var}(n^{-1/2}\mathbf{X}'\boldsymbol{\epsilon}) = \mathbf{V}$ is positive definite;
(iv) (a) $E|\mathbf{X}_{thi}|^2 < \infty$, $h = 1, \ldots, p$, $i = 1, \ldots, k$;
(b) $\mathbf{M} \equiv E(\mathbf{X}_t'\mathbf{X}_t)$ is positive definite.

Then $\mathbf{D}^{-1/2}\sqrt{n}(\hat{\boldsymbol{\beta}}_n - \boldsymbol{\beta}_o) \overset{A}{\sim} N(\mathbf{0}, \mathbf{I})$, where $\mathbf{D} \equiv \mathbf{M}^{-1}\mathbf{V}\mathbf{M}^{-1}$. Suppose in addition that

(v) there exists $\hat{\mathbf{V}}_n$ symmetric and positive semidefinite such that $\hat{\mathbf{V}}_n - \mathbf{V} \xrightarrow{p} \mathbf{0}$.

Then $\hat{\mathbf{D}}_n - \mathbf{D} \xrightarrow{p} \mathbf{0}$, where $\hat{\mathbf{D}}_n = (\mathbf{X}'\mathbf{X}/n)^{-1}\hat{\mathbf{V}}_n(\mathbf{X}'\mathbf{X}/n)^{-1}$.

Proof: We verify the conditions of Theorem 4.25. We apply Theorem 5.2 and set $Z_t = \boldsymbol{\lambda}'\mathbf{V}^{-1/2}\mathbf{X}_t'\boldsymbol{\epsilon}_t$. The summands $\boldsymbol{\lambda}'\mathbf{V}^{-1/2}\mathbf{X}_t'\boldsymbol{\epsilon}_t$ are i.i.d. given (ii), with $E(Z_t) = 0$ given (iiia), and var $Z_t = 1$ given (iiib) and (iiic). Hence $n^{-1/2} \sum_{t=1}^n Z_t = n^{-1/2} \sum_{t=1}^n \boldsymbol{\lambda}'\mathbf{V}^{-1/2}\mathbf{X}_t'\boldsymbol{\epsilon}_t \overset{A}{\sim} N(0, 1)$ by the Lindeberg–Levy theorem 5.2. It follows from Proposition 5.1 that $\mathbf{V}^{-1/2}n^{-1/2}\mathbf{X}'\boldsymbol{\epsilon} \overset{A}{\sim} N(\mathbf{0}, \mathbf{I})$, where $\mathbf{V}$ is $O(1)$ given (iiib) and positive definite given (iiic). It follows from Komolgorov's strong law of large numbers, Theorem 3.1, and from Theorem 2.4, that $\mathbf{X}'\mathbf{X}/n - \mathbf{M} \xrightarrow{p} \mathbf{0}$ given (ii) and (iv). Since the rest of the conditions of Theorem 4.25 are satisfied by assumption, the result follows.

In many cases $\mathbf{V}$ may simplify. For example, it may be known that $E(\boldsymbol{\epsilon}_t^2|\mathbf{X}_t) = \sigma_o^2$, $(p = 1)$. If so, $\mathbf{V} \equiv E(\mathbf{X}_t'\boldsymbol{\epsilon}_t\boldsymbol{\epsilon}_t'\mathbf{X}_t) = E(\boldsymbol{\epsilon}_t^2\mathbf{X}_t'\mathbf{X}_t) = E(E(\boldsymbol{\epsilon}_t^2\mathbf{X}_t'\mathbf{X}_t|\mathbf{X}_t))E(E(\boldsymbol{\epsilon}_t^2|\mathbf{X}_t)\mathbf{X}_t'\mathbf{X}_t) = \sigma_o^2 E(\mathbf{X}_t'\mathbf{X}_t) = \sigma_o^2\mathbf{M}$. The obvious estimator for $\mathbf{V}$ is then $\hat{\mathbf{V}}_n = \hat{\sigma}_n^2(\mathbf{X}'\mathbf{X}/n)$, where $\hat{\sigma}_n^2$ is consistent for σ_o^2. A similar result holds for systems of equations in which it is known that $E(\boldsymbol{\epsilon}_t\boldsymbol{\epsilon}_t'|\mathbf{X}_t) = \mathbf{I}$ (after suitable transformation of an underlying model). Then $\mathbf{V} = \mathbf{M}$ and a consistent estimator is $\hat{\mathbf{V}}_n = (\mathbf{X}'\mathbf{X}/n)$. Consistency results for more general cases are studied in the next chapter.

In comparison with the consistency result for the OLS estimator, we have obtained the asymptotic normality result by imposing the additional second moment conditions of (iiib) and (iiic). Otherwise, the conditions are identical. A similar result holds for the IV estimator.

EXERCISE 5.4: Prove the following result. Given

(i) $\mathbf{y} = \mathbf{X}\boldsymbol{\beta}_o + \boldsymbol{\epsilon}$;
(ii) $\{(\mathbf{Z}_t, \mathbf{X}_t, \boldsymbol{\epsilon}_t)'\}$ is an i.i.d. sequence;
(iii) (a) $E(\mathbf{Z}_t'\boldsymbol{\epsilon}_t) = \mathbf{0}$;
(b) $E|\mathbf{Z}_{thi}\boldsymbol{\epsilon}_{th}|^2 < \infty$, $h = 1, \ldots, p$, $i = 1, \ldots, l$;
(c) $\mathbf{V}_n \equiv \text{var}(n^{-1/2}\mathbf{Z}'\boldsymbol{\epsilon}) = \mathbf{V}$ is positive definite;
(iv) (a) $E|\mathbf{Z}_{thi}\mathbf{X}_{thj}| < \infty$, $h = 1, \ldots, p$, $i = 1, \ldots, l$, and $j = 1, \ldots, k$;
(b) $\mathbf{Q} \equiv E(\mathbf{Z}_t'\mathbf{X}_t)$ has full column rank;
(c) $\hat{\mathbf{P}}_n \xrightarrow{p} \mathbf{P}$, finite and positive definite.

Then $\mathbf{D}^{-1/2}\sqrt{n}(\tilde{\boldsymbol{\beta}}_n - \boldsymbol{\beta}_0) \overset{A}{\sim} N(\mathbf{0}, \mathbf{I})$, where

$$\mathbf{D} \equiv (\mathbf{Q}'\mathbf{P}\mathbf{Q})^{-1}\mathbf{Q}'\mathbf{P}\mathbf{V}\mathbf{P}\mathbf{Q}(\mathbf{Q}'\mathbf{P}\mathbf{Q})^{-1}.$$

Suppose further that

(v) there exists $\hat{\mathbf{V}}_n$ symmetric and positive semidefinite such that $\hat{\mathbf{V}}_n - \mathbf{V} \xrightarrow{p} \mathbf{0}$.

Then $\hat{\mathbf{D}}_n - \mathbf{D} \xrightarrow{p} \mathbf{0}$, where

$$\hat{\mathbf{D}}_n \equiv (\mathbf{X}'\mathbf{Z}\hat{\mathbf{P}}_n\mathbf{Z}'\mathbf{X}/n^2)^{-1}(\mathbf{X}'\mathbf{Z}/n)\hat{\mathbf{P}}_n\hat{\mathbf{V}}_n\hat{\mathbf{P}}_n(\mathbf{Z}'\mathbf{X}/n)(\mathbf{X}'\mathbf{Z}\hat{\mathbf{P}}_n\mathbf{Z}'\mathbf{X}/n^2)^{-1}.$$

EXERCISE 5.5: If $p = 1$ and $E(\epsilon_t^2|\mathbf{Z}_t) = \sigma_o^2$, what is the efficient IV estimator? What is the natural estimator for $\mathbf{V}$? What additional conditions ensure that $\hat{\mathbf{P}}_n - \mathbf{P} \xrightarrow{p} \mathbf{0}$ and $\hat{\mathbf{V}}_n - \mathbf{V} \xrightarrow{p} \mathbf{0}$?

These results apply to observations from a random sample. However, they do not apply to situations such as the standard regression model with fixed regressors, or to stratified cross sections, because in these situations the elements of the sum $n^{-1/2}\sum_{t=1}^n \mathbf{X}_t'\boldsymbol{\epsilon}_t$ are no longer identically distributed. For example, with $\mathbf{X}_t$ fixed and $E(\epsilon_t^2) = \sigma_o^2$, var $\mathbf{X}_t'\boldsymbol{\epsilon}_t = \sigma_o^2\mathbf{X}_t'\mathbf{X}_t$, which depends on $\mathbf{X}_t'\mathbf{X}_t$ and hence differs from observation to observation. For these cases we need to relax the identical distribution assumption.

V.2 Independent Heterogeneously Distributed Observations

Several different central limit theorems are available for the case in which our observations are not identically distributed. The most general result is in fact the centerpiece of all asymptotic distribution theory.

THEOREM 5.6 (*Lindeberg–Feller*): Let $\{Z_t\}$ be a sequence of independent random scalars with $E(Z_t) \equiv \mu_t$, var $Z_t \equiv \sigma_t^2 < \infty$, $\sigma_t^2 \neq 0$, and distribution functions $F_t(z)$. Then

$$\sqrt{n}(\bar{Z}_n - \bar{\mu}_n)/\bar{\sigma}_n \overset{A}{\sim} N(0, 1)$$

and

$$\lim_{n\to\infty} \max_{1\le t\le n} n^{-1}(\sigma_t^2/\bar{\sigma}_n^2) = 0$$

if and only if for every $\epsilon > 0$,

$$\lim_{n\to\infty} \bar{\sigma}_n^{-2} n^{-1} \sum_{t=1}^{n} \int_{(z-\mu_t)^2 > \epsilon n \bar{\sigma}_n^2} (z-\mu_t)^2 \, dF_t(z) = 0.$$

Proof: See Loeve [1977, pp. 292–294].

The last condition of this result is called the Lindeberg condition. It essentially requires the average contribution of the extreme tails to the variance of Z_t to be zero in the limit. When the Lindeberg condition holds, not only does asymptotic normality follow, but the "uniform asymptotic negligibility" condition $\max_{1\le t\le n} n^{-1}(\sigma_t^2/\bar{\sigma}_n^2) \to 0$ as $n \to \infty$ also holds. This condition says that none of the Z_t has a variance so great that it dominates the variance of $\bar{Z}_n$. Further, since $\sigma_t^2 \neq 0$, it must be true that $n\bar{\sigma}_n^2 \to \infty$, so $n\bar{\sigma}_n^2 = \sum_{t=1}^n \sigma_t^2$ is prevented from converging to some finite value. Together, asymptotic normality and uniform asymptotic negligibility imply the Lindeberg condition.

EXAMPLE 5.7: Let $\sigma_t^2 = \rho^t$, $0 < \rho < 1$. Then $n\bar{\sigma}_n^2 = \sum_{t=1}^n \rho^t \to \rho/(1-\rho)$ as $n \to \infty$, and $\max_{1\le t\le n} n^{-1}(\sigma_t^2/\bar{\sigma}_n^2) = \rho/[\rho/(1-\rho)] = 1-\rho \neq 0$.

Hence $\{Z_t\}$ is not uniformly asymptotically negligible. It follows that the Lindeberg condition is not satisfied, so asymptotic normality may or may not hold for such a sequence.

EXAMPLE 5.8: Let $\{Z_t\}$ be i.i.d. with var $Z_t = \sigma^2 < \infty$. By Theorem 5.2, $\sqrt{n}(\bar{Z}_n - \bar{\mu}_n)/\bar{\sigma}_n \overset{A}{\sim} N(0, 1)$. Further, $\bar{\sigma}_n^2 = \sigma^2$, so $\max_{1<t<n} n^{-1}(\sigma_t^2/\bar{\sigma}_n^2) = n^{-1}(\sigma^2/\sigma^2) \to 0$. It follows that the Lindeberg condition is satisfied.

EXERCISE 5.9: Give a direct demonstration that the Lindeberg condition is satisfied for identically distributed $\{Z_t\}$ with var $Z_t = \sigma^2 < \infty$, so that Theorem 5.2 follows as a corollary to Theorem 5.6. Hint: apply the Monotone Convergence Theorem (Rao [1973, p. 135]).

In general, the Lindeberg condition can be somewhat difficult to verify, so it is convenient to have a simpler condition that implies the Lindeberg condition. This is provided by the following result.

THEOREM 5.10 (*Liapounov*†): Let $\{Z_t\}$ be a sequence of independent random scalars with $E(Z_t) = \mu_t$, var $Z_t = \sigma_t^2$, $\sigma_t^2 \neq 0$, and $E|Z_t - \mu_t|^{2+\delta} < \Delta < \infty$ for some $\delta > 0$ and all t. If $\bar{\sigma}_n^2 > \delta' > 0$ for all n sufficiently large, then $\sqrt{n}(\bar{Z}_n - \bar{\mu}_n)/\bar{\sigma}_n \overset{A}{\sim} N(0, 1)$.

Proof: We verify that the Lindeberg condition is satisfied.

$$\int_{(z-\mu_t)^2 > \epsilon n \bar{\sigma}_n^2} (z - \mu_t)^2 \, dF_t(z)$$
$$= \int_{(z-\mu_t)^2 > \epsilon n \bar{\sigma}_n^2} |z - \mu_t|^{\delta} |z - \mu_t|^{-\delta} (z - \mu_t)^2 \, dF_t(z).$$

Whenever $(z - \mu_t)^2 > \epsilon n \bar{\sigma}_n^2$, it follows that $|z - \mu_t|^{-\delta} < (\epsilon n \bar{\sigma}_n^2)^{-\delta/2}$, so

$$\int_{(z-\mu_t)^2 > \epsilon n \bar{\sigma}_n^2} (z - \mu_t)^2 \, dF_t(z) < (\epsilon n \bar{\sigma}_n^2)^{-\delta/2} \int_{(z-\mu_t)^2 > \epsilon n \bar{\sigma}_n^2} |z - \mu_t|^{2+\delta} \, dF_t(z)$$
$$\leq (\epsilon n \bar{\sigma}_n^2)^{-\delta/2} E|Z_t - \mu_t|^{2+\delta}$$
$$< (\epsilon n \bar{\sigma}_n^2)^{-\delta/2} \Delta.$$

† As stated, this result is actually a corollary to Liapounov's original theorem. See Loeve [1977, p. 287].

Hence for any $\epsilon > 0$,

$$\bar{\sigma}_n^{-2} n^{-1} \sum_{t=1}^{n} \int_{(z-\mu_t)^2 > \epsilon n \bar{\sigma}_n^2} (z - \mu_t)^2 \, dF_t(z) < \bar{\sigma}_n^{-2} (\epsilon n \bar{\sigma}_n^2)^{-\delta/2} \Delta = n^{-\delta/2} \bar{\sigma}_n^{-2-\delta} \epsilon^{-\delta/2} \Delta.$$

Since $\bar{\sigma}_n^2 > \delta'$, $\bar{\sigma}_n^{-2-\delta} < (\delta')^{-1-\delta/2}$ for all n sufficiently large. It follows that

$$\bar{\sigma}_n^{-2} n^{-1} \sum_{t=1}^{n} \int_{(z-\mu_t)^2 > \epsilon n \bar{\sigma}_n^2} (z - \mu_t)^2 \, dF_t(z) < n^{-\delta/2} (\delta')^{-1-\delta/2} \epsilon^{-\delta/2} \Delta \rightarrow 0 \quad \text{as} \quad n \rightarrow \infty.$$

This result allows us to substitute the requirement that some moment of order slightly greater than two is uniformly bounded in place of the more complicated Lindeberg condition. Note that $E|Z_t|^{2+\delta} < \Delta$ would also imply that $E|Z_t - \mu_t|^{2+\delta}$ is also uniformly bounded. Also note the analogy with Corollary 3.9. There we obtained a law of large numbers for independent random variables by imposing a uniform bound on $E|Z_t|^{1+\delta}$. Now we obtain a central limit theorem imposing a uniform bound on $E|Z_t|^{2+\delta}$.

We seek an asymptotic normality result analogous to Theorem 5.3 for independent heterogeneous random variables. If we apply Theorem 5.10 instead of Theorem 5.2, we run into a small difficulty. Recall that we applied the Cramér–Wold device to the sums $n^{-1/2} \sum_{t=1}^{n} \lambda' \mathbf{V}^{-1/2} \mathbf{X}_t' \boldsymbol{\epsilon}_t$, where $\mathbf{V} = \text{var}(n^{-1/2} \mathbf{X}' \boldsymbol{\epsilon})$. In the present case the random variables $\mathbf{X}_t' \boldsymbol{\epsilon}_t$ are no longer identically distributed, and there is now no reason to suppose that $\mathbf{V}_n$ is a constant or has a constant limit, in general. By analogy, we would like to apply the Cramér–Wold device to $n^{-1/2} \sum_{t=1}^{n} \lambda' \mathbf{V}_n^{-1/2} \mathbf{X}_t' \boldsymbol{\epsilon}_t$. But the summands $\lambda' \mathbf{V}_n^{-1/2} \mathbf{X}_t' \boldsymbol{\epsilon}_t$ now depend explicitly on n, a possibility not covered by Theorem 5.10. Nevertheless, the needed generalization is readily available.

THEOREM 5.11: Let $\{Z_{nt}\}$ be a sequence of independent random scalars with $E(Z_{nt}) = \mu_{nt}$, var $Z_{nt} = \sigma_{nt}^2$, $\sigma_{nt}^2 \neq 0$, and $E|Z_{nt}|^{2+\delta} < \Delta < \infty$ for some $\delta > 0$ and all t. Define $\bar{Z}_n \equiv n^{-1} \sum_{t=1}^{n} Z_{nt}$, $\bar{\mu}_n \equiv n^{-1} \sum_{t=1}^{n} \mu_{nt}$ and $\bar{\sigma}_n^2 \equiv \text{var} \sqrt{n} \bar{Z}_n = n^{-1} \sum_{t=1}^{n} \sigma_{nt}^2$. If $\bar{\sigma}_n^2 > \delta' > 0$ for all n sufficiently large, then $\sqrt{n}(\bar{Z}_n - \bar{\mu}_n)/\bar{\sigma}_n \overset{A}{\sim} N(0, 1)$.

Proof: See Loeve [1977, pp. 287–290].

EXERCISE 5.12: Prove the following result. Given

(i) $\mathbf{y} = \mathbf{X}\boldsymbol{\beta}_o + \boldsymbol{\epsilon}$;
(ii) $\{(\mathbf{X}_t, \boldsymbol{\epsilon}_t)'\}$ is an independent sequence;
(iii) (a) $E(\mathbf{X}_t'\boldsymbol{\epsilon}_t) = \mathbf{0}$;
(b) $E|\mathbf{X}_{thi}\boldsymbol{\epsilon}_{th}|^{2+\delta} < \Delta < \infty$ for some $\delta > 0$ and all $h = 1, \ldots, p$, $i = 1, \ldots, k$, and t;
(c) $\mathbf{V}_n \equiv \text{var}(n^{-1/2}\mathbf{X}'\boldsymbol{\epsilon})$ is uniformly positive definite;
(iv) (a) $E|\mathbf{X}_{thi}^2|^{1+\delta} < \Delta < \infty$ for some $\delta > 0$ and all $h = 1, \ldots, p$, $i = 1, \ldots, k$, and t;
(b) $\mathbf{M}_n \equiv E(\mathbf{X}'\mathbf{X}/n)$ is uniformly positive definite.

Then $\mathbf{D}_n^{-1/2}\sqrt{n}(\hat{\boldsymbol{\beta}}_n - \boldsymbol{\beta}_o) \overset{A}{\sim} N(\mathbf{0}, \mathbf{I})$, where $\mathbf{D}_n \equiv \mathbf{M}_n^{-1}\mathbf{V}_n\mathbf{M}_n^{-1}$. Suppose in addition that

(v) there exists $\hat{\mathbf{V}}_n$ symmetric and positive semidefinite such that $\hat{\mathbf{V}}_n - \mathbf{V}_n \xrightarrow{p} \mathbf{0}$.

Then $\hat{\mathbf{D}}_n - \mathbf{D}_n \xrightarrow{p} \mathbf{0}$, where $\hat{\mathbf{D}}_n \equiv (\mathbf{X}'\mathbf{X}/n)^{-1}\hat{\mathbf{V}}_n(\mathbf{X}'\mathbf{X}/n)^{-1}$.

Note the general applicability of this result. We can let $\mathbf{X}_t$ be fixed or stochastic (although independence is required), and the errors may be homoscedastic or heteroscedastic. A similarly general result holds for instrumental variables estimators.

PROPOSITION 5.13: Given

(i) $\mathbf{y} = \mathbf{X}\boldsymbol{\beta}_o + \boldsymbol{\epsilon}$;
(ii) $\{(\mathbf{Z}_t, \mathbf{X}_t, \boldsymbol{\epsilon}_t)'\}$ is an independent sequence;
(iii) (a) $E(\mathbf{Z}_t'\boldsymbol{\epsilon}_t) = \mathbf{0}$;
(b) $E|\mathbf{Z}_{thi}\boldsymbol{\epsilon}_{th}|^{2+\delta} < \Delta < \infty$ for some $\delta > 0$ and all $h = 1, \ldots, p$, $i = 1, \ldots, l$, and t;
(c) $\mathbf{V}_n \equiv \text{var}(n^{-1/2}\mathbf{Z}'\boldsymbol{\epsilon})$ is uniformly positive definite;
(iv) (a) $E|\mathbf{Z}_{thi}\mathbf{X}_{thj}|^{1+\delta} < \Delta < \infty$ for some $\delta > 0$ and all $h = 1, \ldots, p$, $i = 1, \ldots, l$, $j = 1, \ldots, k$, and t;
(b) $\mathbf{Q}_n \equiv E(\mathbf{Z}'\mathbf{X}/n)$ has uniformly full column rank;
(c) $\hat{\mathbf{P}}_n - \mathbf{P}_n \xrightarrow{p} \mathbf{0}$, where $\{\mathbf{P}_n\}$ is $O(1)$ and uniformly positive definite.

Then $\mathbf{D}_n^{-1/2}\sqrt{n}(\tilde{\boldsymbol{\beta}}_n - \boldsymbol{\beta}_o) \overset{A}{\sim} N(\mathbf{0}, \mathbf{I})$, where

$$\mathbf{D}_n \equiv (\mathbf{Q}_n'\mathbf{P}_n\mathbf{Q}_n)^{-1}\mathbf{Q}_n'\mathbf{P}_n\mathbf{V}_n\mathbf{P}_n\mathbf{Q}_n(\mathbf{Q}_n'\mathbf{P}_n\mathbf{Q}_n)^{-1}.$$

Suppose in addition that

(v) there exists $\hat{\mathbf{V}}_n$ symmetric and positive semidefinite such that $\hat{\mathbf{V}}_n - \mathbf{V}_n \xrightarrow{p} \mathbf{0}$.

Then $\hat{\mathbf{D}}_n - \mathbf{D}_n \xrightarrow{p} \mathbf{0}$, where

$$\hat{\mathbf{D}}_n \equiv (\mathbf{X}'\mathbf{Z}\hat{\mathbf{P}}_n\mathbf{Z}'\mathbf{X}/n^2)^{-1}(\mathbf{X}'\mathbf{Z}/n)\hat{\mathbf{P}}_n\hat{\mathbf{V}}_n\hat{\mathbf{P}}_n(\mathbf{Z}'\mathbf{X}/n)(\mathbf{X}'\mathbf{Z}\hat{\mathbf{P}}_n\mathbf{Z}'\mathbf{X}/n^2)^{-1}.$$

Proof: We verify the conditions of Exercise 4.26. To apply Theorem 5.11, let $Z_{nt} \equiv \lambda'\mathbf{V}_n^{-1/2}\mathbf{Z}_t'\boldsymbol{\epsilon}_t$ and consider $n^{-1/2} \sum_{t=1}^n \lambda'\mathbf{V}_n^{-1/2}\mathbf{Z}_t'\boldsymbol{\epsilon}_t$. The summands Z_{nt} are independent given (ii) with $E(Z_{nt}) = 0$ given (iiia), $\bar{\sigma}_n^2 = 1$ given (iiic), and $E|Z_{nt}|^{2+\delta}$ uniformly bounded (apply Minkowski's inequality) given (iiib). Hence $n^{-1/2} \sum_{t=1}^n Z_{nt} = n^{-1/2} \sum_{t=1}^n \lambda'\mathbf{V}_n^{-1/2}\mathbf{Z}_t'\boldsymbol{\epsilon}_t \overset{A}{\sim} N(0, 1)$ by Theorem 5.11 and $\mathbf{V}_n^{-1/2}n^{-1/2}\mathbf{Z}'\boldsymbol{\epsilon} \overset{A}{\sim} N(\mathbf{0}, \mathbf{I})$ by the Cramér–Wold device, Proposition 5.1.

Assumptions (ii), (iva), and (ivb) ensure that $\mathbf{Z}'\mathbf{X}/n - \mathbf{Q}_n \xrightarrow{p} \mathbf{0}$ by Corollary 3.9 and Theorem 2.24. Since the remaining conditions of Exercise 4.26 are satisfied by assumption, the result follows.

Note the close similarity of the present result to that of Exercise 5.4. We have dropped the identical distribution assumption made there at the expense of imposing just slightly more in the way of moment requirements in (iiib) and (iva). Otherwise, the conditions are identical. This relatively minor trade-off has greatly increased the applicability of the results. Not only do the present results apply to situations with fixed regressors and either homoscedastic or heteroscedastic disturbances, but they also apply to cross-sectional data with either homoscedastic or heteroscedastic disturbances. Further, by setting $1 < p < \infty$, the present results apply to panel data (i.e., time-series cross-sectional data) when p observations are available for each individual.

As previously discussed, the independence assumption is not as appropriate in time-series applications, so we now turn to central limit results applicable to time-series data.

V.3 Dependent Identically Distributed Observations

In the last two sections we saw that obtaining central limit theorems for independent processes typically required strengthening the moment restrictions beyond what was sufficient for obtaining laws of large numbers. In the case of stationary ergodic processes, not only will we strengthen the moment requirements, but we will also impose stronger conditions on the memory of the process.

A very general statement of the central limit theorem for stationary ergodic processes was given by Gordin [1969]. However, Gordin's conditions are not particularly easy to interpret. Here we adopt an approach suggested by Hannan [1973] that has somewhat greater intuitive appeal and is still quite general.

To motivate the memory conditions that we add, consider a random scalar Z_t, and let $\mathfrak{F}_t$ be a σ-algebra such that $\{Z_t, \mathfrak{F}_t\}$ is an adapted stochastic sequence, (Z_t is measurable with respect to $\mathfrak{F}_t$ and $\mathfrak{F}_{t-1} \subset \mathfrak{F}_t \subset \mathfrak{F}$.) We can think of $\mathfrak{F}_t$ as being the σ-algebra generated by the entire current and past history of Z_t or, more generally, as the σ-algebra generated by the entire current and past history of Z_t as well as other random variables, say $\mathcal{Y}_t$. Given $E|Z_t| < \infty$, we can write

$$Z_t = Z_t - E(Z_t|\mathfrak{F}_{t-1}) + E(Z_t|\mathfrak{F}_{t-1}).$$

Similarly,

$$Z_t = Z_t - E(Z_t|\mathfrak{F}_{t-1}) + E(Z_t|\mathfrak{F}_{t-1}) - E(Z_t|\mathfrak{F}_{t-2}) + E(Z_t|\mathfrak{F}_{t-2}).$$

Proceeding in this way we can write

$$Z_t = \sum_{j=0}^{m-1} \mathcal{R}_{tj} + E(Z_t|\mathfrak{F}_{t-m}), \qquad m = 1, 2, \ldots,$$

where $\mathcal{R}_{tj}$ is the revision made in forecasting Z_t when information becomes available at time $t-j$:

$$\mathcal{R}_{tj} \equiv E(Z_t|\mathfrak{F}_{t-j}) - E(Z_t|\mathfrak{F}_{t-j-1}).$$

Note that for fixed j, $\{\mathcal{R}_{tj}, \mathfrak{F}_{t-j}\}$ is a martingale difference sequence, because it is an adapted stochastic sequence and

$$\begin{aligned} E(\mathcal{R}_{tj}|\mathfrak{F}_{t-j-1}) &= E[E(Z_t|\mathfrak{F}_{t-j}) - E(Z_t|\mathfrak{F}_{t-j-1})|\mathfrak{F}_{t-j-1}] \\ &= E[E(Z_t|\mathfrak{F}_{t-j})|\mathfrak{F}_{t-j-1}] - E[E(Z_t|\mathfrak{F}_{t-j-1})|\mathfrak{F}_{t-j-1}] \\ &= E(Z_t|\mathfrak{F}_{t-j-1}) - E(Z_t|\mathfrak{F}_{t-j-1}) = 0, \end{aligned}$$

where we have applied the limearity property and the law of iterated expectations, Proposition 3.72.

Thus we have written Z_t as a sum of martingale differences plus a remainder. The validity of the central limit theorem we discuss rests on being able to write

$$Z_t = \sum_{j=0}^{\infty} \mathcal{R}_{tj}.$$

In this form, Z_t is expressed as a "telescoping sum," because adjacent elements of $\mathcal{R}_{tj}$ cancel out. Among other things, the validity of this expression requires that $E(Z_t|\mathfrak{F}_{t-m})$ tend appropriately to zero as $m \to \infty$. Remember that $E(Z_t|\mathfrak{F}_{t-m})$ is a random variable, so the convergence to zero must be stochastic. In fact, the condition we impose is that

$$E([E(Z_t|\mathfrak{F}_{t-m})]^2) \to 0 \quad \text{as} \quad m \to \infty,$$

which can be stated in terms of convergence in quadratic mean as defined in Chapter 2, i.e.,

$$E(Z_t|\mathfrak{F}_{t-m}) \xrightarrow{\text{q. m.}} 0 \quad \text{as} \quad m \to \infty.$$

One way of interpreting this condition is that as we forecast Z_t based only on the information available at more and more distant points in the past, our forecast approaches zero (in a mean squared error sense). Further, this condition actually implies that $E(Z_t) = 0$ as we prove below, so that as our forecast becomes based on less and less information, it approaches the forecast we would make with no information, i.e., the unconditional expectation $E(Z_t)$.

LEMMA 5.14: Let $\{Z_t, \mathfrak{F}_t\}$ be an adapted stochastic sequence and suppose $E(Z_t|\mathfrak{F}_{t-m}) \xrightarrow{\text{q. m.}} 0$ as $m \to \infty$. Then $E(Z_t) = 0$.

Proof: By Theorem 2.40 $E(Z_t|\mathfrak{F}_{t-m}) \xrightarrow{\text{q. m.}} 0$ as $m \to \infty$ implies that $E(|E(Z_t|\mathfrak{F}_{t-m})|) \to 0$ as $m \to \infty$. Hence, for every $\epsilon > 0$ there exists $M(\epsilon)$ such that $0 \leq E(|E(Z_t|\mathfrak{F}_{t-m})|) < \epsilon$ for all $m > M(\epsilon)$. By Jensen's inequality, $|E[E(Z_t|\mathfrak{F}_{t-m})]| \leq E(|E(Z_t|\mathfrak{F}_{t-m})|)$, so $0 \leq |E[E(Z_t|\mathfrak{F}_{t-m})]| < \epsilon$ for all $m > M(\epsilon)$. But by the law of iterated expectations, $E(Z_t) = E[E(Z_t|\mathfrak{F}_{t-m})]$, so $0 \leq |E(Z_t)| < \epsilon$. Since ϵ is arbitrary, it follows that $E(Z_t) = 0$.

Next, consider var Z_t. Given that we can write

$$Z_t = \sum_{j=0}^{\infty} \mathcal{R}_{tj},$$

it follows that if var $Z_t = \sigma^2 < \infty$, then

$$\text{var } Z_t = \text{var}\left(\sum_{j=0}^{\infty} \mathcal{R}_{tj}\right) < \infty.$$

Now for $i < j$, $\text{cov}(\mathcal{R}_{ti}, \mathcal{R}_{tj}) = 0$ since

$$\text{cov}(\mathcal{R}_{ti}, \mathcal{R}_{tj}) = E(\mathcal{R}_{ti}\mathcal{R}_{tj}) = E[E(\mathcal{R}_{ti}\mathcal{R}_{tj}|\mathfrak{F}_{t-j-1})]$$
$$= E[\mathcal{R}_{ti}E(\mathcal{R}_{tj}|\mathfrak{F}_{t-j-1})] = 0.$$

Hence $\text{var}(\Sigma_{j=0}^{\infty} \mathcal{R}_{tj}) = \Sigma_{j=0}^{\infty} \text{var } \mathcal{R}_{tj}$, implying that

$$\text{var } Z_t = \sum_{j=0}^{\infty} \text{var } \mathcal{R}_{tj} < \infty.$$

In establishing the central limit result, it is necessary to have $\bar{\sigma}_n^2 = \text{var } \sqrt{n}\bar{Z}_n$ finite. However, for this it does not suffice simply to have $\text{var } Z_t$ finite. Inspecting $\bar{\sigma}_n^2$, we see that

$$\begin{aligned}\bar{\sigma}_n^2 &= n \text{ var } \bar{Z}_n \\ &= nE\left(\left(n^{-1}\sum_{t=1}^{n} Z_t\right)^2\right) \\ &= n^{-1}\sum_{t=1}^{n} E(Z_t^2) + 2n^{-1}\sum_{\tau=1}^{n-1}\sum_{t=\tau+1}^{n} E(Z_t Z_{t-\tau}).\end{aligned}$$

When Z_t is stationary, $\rho_\tau \equiv E(Z_t Z_{t-\tau})/\sigma^2$ does not depend on t. Hence,

$$\begin{aligned}\bar{\sigma}_n^2 &= \sigma^2 + 2\sigma^2 n^{-1}\sum_{\tau=1}^{n-1}(n-\tau)\rho_\tau \\ &= \sigma^2 + 2\sigma^2\sum_{\tau=1}^{n-1}\rho_\tau(1-\tau/n).\end{aligned}$$

This last term contains a growing number of terms as $n \to \infty$, and without further conditions is not guaranteed to converge. It turns out that the condition

$$\sum_{j=0}^{\infty} (\text{var } \mathcal{R}_{0j})^{1/2} < \infty$$

is sufficient to ensure that ρ_τ declines fast enough to ensure that $\bar{\sigma}_n^2$ converges to a finite limit, say, $\bar{\sigma}^2$, as $n \to \infty$ and that this, together with stationarity and ergodicity, provides enough structure to obtain a central limit result.

THEOREM 5.15: Let $\{Z_t, \mathfrak{F}_t\}$ be an adapted stochastic sequence such that $\{Z_t\}$ is stationary and ergodic with $E(Z_t^2) = \sigma^2 < \infty$. Suppose that $E(Z_0|\mathfrak{F}_{-m}) \xrightarrow{\text{q. m.}} 0$ as $m \to \infty$ and $\Sigma_{j=0}^{\infty} (\text{var } \mathcal{R}_{0j})^{1/2} < \infty$. Then $\bar{\sigma}_n^2 \to \bar{\sigma}^2 < \infty$ as $n \to \infty$, and if $\bar{\sigma}^2 > 0$, then $\sqrt{n}\bar{Z}_n/\bar{\sigma} \overset{A}{\sim} N(0, 1)$.

Proof: This follows as a corollary to Theorem 2 of Gordin [1969] with Gordin's $\delta = 0$.

Note that the stationarity property has been exploited to impose conditions on $E(Z_0|\mathfrak{F}_{-m})$ alone rather than on $E(Z_t|\mathfrak{F}_{t-m})$ for all t and on $\Sigma_{j=0}^{\infty} (\text{var } \mathcal{R}_{0j})^{1/2}$ alone rather than on $\Sigma_{j=0}^{\infty} (\text{var } \mathcal{R}_{tj})^{1/2}$ for all t.
Applying Theorem 5.15 and Proposition 5.1 we obtain the following result for the OLS estimator.

THEOREM 5.16: Given

(i) $\mathbf{y} = \mathbf{X}\boldsymbol{\beta}_o + \boldsymbol{\epsilon}$;
(ii) $\{(\mathbf{X}_t, \boldsymbol{\epsilon}_t)'\}$ is a stationary ergodic sequence;
(iii) (a) $E(\mathbf{X}_{0hi}\boldsymbol{\epsilon}_{0h}|\mathfrak{F}_{-m}) \xrightarrow{\text{q. m.}} 0$ as $m \to \infty$, where $\{\mathfrak{F}_t\}$ is adapted to $\{\mathbf{X}_{thi}\boldsymbol{\epsilon}_{th}\}$, $h = 1, \ldots, p$, $i = 1, \ldots, k$;
(b) $E|\mathbf{X}_{thi}\boldsymbol{\epsilon}_{th}|^2 < \infty$, $h = 1, \ldots, p$, $i = 1, \ldots, k$;
(c) $\mathbf{V}_n \equiv \text{var}(n^{-1/2}\mathbf{X}'\boldsymbol{\epsilon})$ is uniformly positive definite;
(d) Define $\mathcal{R}_{0hij} \equiv E(\mathbf{X}_{0hi}\boldsymbol{\epsilon}_{0h}|\mathfrak{F}_{-j}) - E(\mathbf{X}_{0hi}\boldsymbol{\epsilon}_{0h}|\mathfrak{F}_{-j-1})$, $h = 1, \ldots, p$, $i = 1, \ldots, k$. For $h = 1, \ldots, p$, $i = 1, \ldots, k$, assume that $\Sigma_{j=0}^{\infty} (\text{var } \mathcal{R}_{0hij})^{1/2} < \infty$.
(iv) (a) $E|\mathbf{X}_{thi}|^2 < \infty$, $h = 1, \ldots, p$, $i = 1, \ldots, k$;
(b) $\mathbf{M} \equiv E(\mathbf{X}_t'\mathbf{X}_t)$ is positive definite;

Then $\mathbf{V}_n \to \mathbf{V}$ finite and positive definite as $n \to \infty$, and $\mathbf{D}^{-1/2}\sqrt{n}(\hat{\boldsymbol{\beta}}_n - \boldsymbol{\beta}_o) \overset{A}{\sim} N(\mathbf{0}, \mathbf{I})$, where $\mathbf{D} = \mathbf{M}^{-1}\mathbf{V}\mathbf{M}^{-1}$.
Suppose in addition that

(v) There exists $\hat{\mathbf{V}}_n$ symmetric and positive semidefinite such that $\hat{\mathbf{V}}_n - \mathbf{V}_n \xrightarrow{p} \mathbf{0}$.

Then $\hat{\mathbf{D}}_n - \mathbf{D} \xrightarrow{p} \mathbf{0}$, where $\hat{\mathbf{D}}_n = (\mathbf{X}'\mathbf{X}/n)^{-1}\hat{\mathbf{V}}_n(\mathbf{X}'\mathbf{X}/n)^{-1}$.

Proof: We verify the conditions of Theorem 4.25. First we apply Theorem 5.15 and Proposition 5.1 to show that $\mathbf{V}_n^{-1/2}n^{-1/2}\mathbf{X}'\boldsymbol{\epsilon} \overset{A}{\sim} N(\mathbf{0}, \mathbf{I})$. Consider $n^{-1/2}\Sigma_{t=1}^{n} \lambda'\mathbf{V}^{-1/2}\mathbf{X}_t'\boldsymbol{\epsilon}_t$, where $\mathbf{V}$ is any finite positive definite matrix. By Theorem 3.35, $\{Z_t \equiv \lambda'\mathbf{V}^{-1/2}\mathbf{X}_t'\boldsymbol{\epsilon}_t\}$ is a stationary ergodic sequence given (ii), and $\{Z_t, \mathfrak{F}_t\}$ is an adapted stochastic sequence because Z_t is measurable with respect to $\mathfrak{F}_t$ by Proposition 3.23, and $\mathfrak{F}_{t-1} \subset \mathfrak{F}_t \subset \mathfrak{F}$. To see that $E(Z_t^2) < \infty$, note that we can write

$$
\begin{aligned}
Z_t &= \lambda' \mathbf{V}^{-1/2} \mathbf{X}_t' \boldsymbol{\epsilon}_t \\
&= \sum_{h=1}^{p} \lambda' \mathbf{V}^{-1/2} \mathbf{X}_{th}' \boldsymbol{\epsilon}_{th} \\
&= \sum_{h=1}^{p} \sum_{i=1}^{k} \tilde{\lambda}_i \mathbf{X}_{thi} \boldsymbol{\epsilon}_{th},
\end{aligned}
$$

where $\tilde{\lambda}_i$ is the ith element of the $k \times 1$ vector $\tilde{\lambda} \equiv \mathbf{V}^{-1/2}\lambda$. By definition of λ and $\mathbf{V}$, there exists $\Delta < \infty$ such that $|\tilde{\lambda}_i| < \Delta$ for all i. It follows from Minkowski's inequality that

$$
\begin{aligned}
E(Z_t^2) &\leq \left[\sum_{h=1}^{p} \sum_{i=1}^{k} (E|\tilde{\lambda}_i \mathbf{X}_{thi} \boldsymbol{\epsilon}_{th}|^2)^{1/2} \right]^2 \\
&\leq \left[\Delta \sum_{h=1}^{p} \sum_{i=1}^{k} (E|\mathbf{X}_{thi} \boldsymbol{\epsilon}_{th}|^2)^{1/2} \right]^2 \\
&\leq [\Delta pk\, \Delta^{1/2}]^2 < \infty,
\end{aligned}
$$

since for Δ sufficiently large, $E|\mathbf{X}_{thi}\boldsymbol{\epsilon}_{th}| < \Delta < \infty$ given (iii.b) and the stationarity assumption.

Next, we verify that $E(Z_0|\mathfrak{F}_{-m}) \xrightarrow{\text{q. m.}} 0$. Using the expression for Z_t just given, we can write

$$
\begin{aligned}
E([E(Z_0|\mathfrak{F}_{-m})]^2) &= E\left(\left[E\left(\sum_{h=1}^{p} \sum_{i=1}^{k} \tilde{\lambda}_i \mathbf{X}_{0hi} \boldsymbol{\epsilon}_{0h} | \mathfrak{F}_{-m}\right)\right]^2\right) \\
&= E\left[\left\{\sum_{h=1}^{p} \sum_{i=1}^{k} E(\tilde{\lambda}_i \mathbf{X}_{0hi} \boldsymbol{\epsilon}_{0h} | \mathfrak{F}_{-m})\right\}^2\right].
\end{aligned}
$$

Applying Minkowski's inequality it follows that

$$
\begin{aligned}
E([E(Z_0|\mathfrak{F}_{-m})]^2) &\leq \left\{ \sum_{h=1}^{p} \sum_{i=1}^{k} (E[E(\tilde{\lambda}_i \mathbf{X}_{0hi} \boldsymbol{\epsilon}_{0h} | \mathfrak{F}_{-m})^2])^{1/2} \right\}^2 \\
&\leq \left\{ \Delta \sum_{h=1}^{p} \sum_{i=1}^{k} (E[E(\mathbf{X}_{0hi} \boldsymbol{\epsilon}_{0h} | \mathfrak{F}_{-m})^2])^{1/2} \right\}^2.
\end{aligned}
$$

Given assumption (iiia), it follows from Definition 2.3 (continuity) that the right-hand side of the expression above converges to zero as $m \to \infty$. Since $E([E(Z_0|\mathfrak{F}_{-m})]^2)$ is nonnegative, it follows that $E([E(Z_0|\mathfrak{F}_{-m})]^2) \to 0$ as $m \to \infty$, or $E(Z_0|\mathfrak{F}_{-m}) \xrightarrow{\text{q.m.}} 0$.

Now define

$$\mathcal{R}_{0j} \equiv E(Z_0|\mathfrak{F}_{-j}) - E(Z_0|\mathfrak{F}_{-j-1}).$$

We need to show that $\Sigma_{j=0}^{\infty}$ (var $\mathcal{R}_{0j})^{1/2} < \infty$. Since $Z_t = \Sigma_{h=1}^{p} \Sigma_{i=1}^{k} \tilde{\lambda}_i \mathbf{X}_{thi}\boldsymbol{\epsilon}_{th}$, we can write

$$\mathcal{R}_{0j} = \sum_{h=1}^{p} \sum_{i=1}^{k} \tilde{\lambda}_i \mathcal{R}_{0hij}.$$

Now (var $\mathcal{R}_{0j})^{1/2} = (E(\mathcal{R}_{0j}^2))^{1/2}$. It follows from Minkowski's inequality that

$$\begin{aligned}(\text{var } \mathcal{R}_{0j})^{1/2} &\leq \sum_{h=1}^{p} \sum_{i=1}^{k} (\tilde{\lambda}_i^2 E(\mathcal{R}_{0hij}^2))^{1/2} \\ &\leq \Delta \sum_{h=1}^{p} \sum_{i=1}^{k} (\text{var } \mathcal{R}_{0hij})^{1/2}.\end{aligned}$$

Hence

$$\begin{aligned}\sum_{j=0}^{\infty} (\text{var } \mathcal{R}_{0j})^{1/2} &\leq \sum_{j=0}^{\infty} \Delta \sum_{h=1}^{p} \sum_{i=1}^{k} (\text{var } \mathcal{R}_{0hij})^{1/2} \\ &= \Delta \sum_{h=1}^{p} \sum_{i=1}^{k} \sum_{j=0}^{\infty} (\text{var } \mathcal{R}_{0hij})^{1/2}.\end{aligned}$$

By assumption (iiid), $\Sigma_{j=0}^{\infty}$ (var $\mathcal{R}_{0hij})^{1/2} < \infty$ for all $h = 1, \ldots, p$ and $i = 1, \ldots, k$, so, for $\Delta < \infty$ sufficiently large, $\Sigma_{j=0}^{\infty}$ (var $\mathcal{R}_{0hij})^{1/2} < \Delta$ for $h = 1, \ldots, p$, and $i = 1, \ldots, k$. Thus

$$\sum_{j=0}^{\infty} (\text{var } \mathcal{R}_{0j})^{1/2} \leq \Delta^2 pk < \infty,$$

as we wished to show.

By Theorem 5.15, it follows that

$$\text{var } \sqrt{n}\,\bar{Z}_n = \text{var } (n^{-1/2} \sum_{t=1}^{n} \lambda' \mathbf{V}^{-1/2} \mathbf{X}_t' \boldsymbol{\epsilon}_t) = \lambda' \mathbf{V}^{-1/2} \mathbf{V}_n \mathbf{V}^{-1/2} \lambda \to \bar{\sigma} < \infty.$$

Hence $\mathbf{V}_n$ converges to a finite matrix. Set $\mathbf{V} = \lim_{n\to\infty} \mathbf{V}_n$, which is positive definite given (iiic). Then $\bar{\sigma} = \lambda' \mathbf{V}^{-1/2} \mathbf{V} \mathbf{V}^{-1/2} \lambda = 1$. It then follows from Theorem 5.15 that $n^{-1/2} \Sigma_{t=1}^{n} \lambda' \mathbf{V}^{-1/2} \mathbf{X}_t' \boldsymbol{\epsilon}_t \overset{A}{\sim} N(0, 1)$. Since this holds for every λ such that $\lambda'\lambda = 1$, it follows from Proposition 5.1 that $\mathbf{V}^{-1/2}n^{-1/2}\sum_{t=1}^{n}\mathbf{X}_t'\boldsymbol{\epsilon}_t \overset{A}{\sim} N(\mathbf{0}, \mathbf{I})$. Now

$$\mathbf{V}_n^{-1/2}n^{-1/2}\sum_{t=1}^{n}\mathbf{X}_t'\boldsymbol{\epsilon}_t - \mathbf{V}^{-1/2}n^{-1/2}\sum_{t=1}^{n}\mathbf{X}_t'\boldsymbol{\epsilon}_t$$

$$= (\mathbf{V}_n^{-1/2}\mathbf{V}^{1/2} - \mathbf{I})\mathbf{V}^{-1/2}n^{-1/2}\sum_{t=1}^{n}\mathbf{X}_t'\boldsymbol{\epsilon}_t \xrightarrow{p} \mathbf{0},$$

since $\mathbf{V}_n^{-1/2}\mathbf{V}^{1/2} - \mathbf{I}$ is $o(1)$ by Definition 2.3 and $\mathbf{V}^{-1/2}n^{-1/2}\sum_{t=1}^{n}\mathbf{X}_t'\boldsymbol{\epsilon}_t \overset{A}{\sim} N(\mathbf{0}, \mathbf{I})$, which allows application of Lemma 4.6. Hence by Lemma 4.7, $\mathbf{V}_n^{-1/2}n^{-1/2}\mathbf{X}'\boldsymbol{\epsilon} \overset{A}{\sim} N(\mathbf{0}, \mathbf{I})$.

Next $\mathbf{X}'\mathbf{X}/n - \mathbf{M} \xrightarrow{p} \mathbf{0}$ by the ergodic theorem 3.34 and Theorem 2.24 given (ii) and (iv), where $\mathbf{M}$ is finite and positive definite. Since the conditions of Theorem 4.25 are satisfied, it follows that $\mathbf{D}_n^{-1/2}\sqrt{n}(\hat{\boldsymbol{\beta}}_n - \boldsymbol{\beta}_o) \overset{A}{\sim} N(\mathbf{0}, \mathbf{I})$, where $\mathbf{D}_n \equiv \mathbf{M}^{-1}\mathbf{V}_n\mathbf{M}^{-1}$. Because $\mathbf{D}_n - \mathbf{D} \to \mathbf{0}$ as $n \to \infty$, it follows that

$$\mathbf{D}^{-1/2}\sqrt{n}(\hat{\boldsymbol{\beta}}_n - \boldsymbol{\beta}_o) - \mathbf{D}_n^{-1/2}\sqrt{n}(\hat{\boldsymbol{\beta}}_n - \boldsymbol{\beta}_o)$$

$$= (\mathbf{D}^{-1/2}\mathbf{D}_n^{1/2} - \mathbf{I})\mathbf{D}_n^{-1/2}\sqrt{n}(\hat{\boldsymbol{\beta}}_n - \boldsymbol{\beta}_o) \xrightarrow{p} \mathbf{0}$$

by Lemma 4.6. Hence, by Lemma 4.7, $\mathbf{D}^{-1/2}\sqrt{n}(\hat{\boldsymbol{\beta}}_n - \boldsymbol{\beta}_o) \overset{A}{\sim} N(\mathbf{0}, \mathbf{I})$.

Comparing this result with the OLS result in Theorem 5.3 for i.i.d. regressors, we have replaced the i.i.d. assumption with stationarity, ergodicity, and the memory requirements of (iii). Because these conditions are always satisfied for i.i.d. sequences, Theorem 5.3 is in fact a direct corollary of Theorem 5.16. Condition (iiia) is satisfied because for i.i.d. sequences $E(\mathbf{X}_{0hi}\boldsymbol{\epsilon}_{0h}|\mathfrak{F}_{-m}) = 0$ for all $m > 0$, and condition (iiid) is satisfied because $\mathcal{R}_{0hij} = 0$ for all $j > 0$ and $\mathcal{R}_{0hij} = \mathbf{X}_{0hi}\boldsymbol{\epsilon}_{0h}$ for $j = 0$. Note that these conditions impose the restrictions placed on Z_t in Theorem 5.15 for each regressor-error cross product $\mathbf{X}_{thi}\boldsymbol{\epsilon}_{th}$.

Although the present result now allows for the possibility that $\mathbf{X}_t$ contains lagged dependent variables $\mathbf{y}_{t-1}, \mathbf{y}_{t-2}, \ldots$, it does not allow $\boldsymbol{\epsilon}_t$ to be serially correlated at the same time. This is ruled out by (iiia) which implies $E(\mathbf{X}_t'\boldsymbol{\epsilon}_t) = \mathbf{0}$ by Lemma 5.14. This condition will be violated if lagged dependent variables are present when $\boldsymbol{\epsilon}_t$ is serially correlated. Also note that if lagged dependent variables are present in $\mathbf{X}_t$, condition (iva) requires that $E(\mathbf{y}_t^2)$ is finite. This in turn places restrictions on the possible values allowed for $\boldsymbol{\beta}_o$.

EXERCISE 5.17: Suppose that the model is $\mathbf{y}_t = \beta_1 \mathbf{y}_{t-1} + \beta_2 \mathbf{y}_{t-2} + \epsilon_t$. State general conditions on $\{\mathbf{y}_t\}$ and (β_1, β_2) which ensure the consistency and asymptotic normality of the OLS estimator for β_1 and β_2.

As just mentioned, OLS is inappropriate when the model contains lagged dependent variables in the presence of serially correlated errors. However, useful instrumental variables estimators are often available.

EXERCISE 5.18: Prove the following result. Given

(i) $\mathbf{y} = \mathbf{X}\beta_o + \epsilon$;
(ii) $\{(\mathbf{Z}_t, \mathbf{X}_t, \epsilon_t)'\}$ is a stationary ergodic sequence;
(iii) (a) $E(\mathbf{Z}_{0hi}\epsilon_{0h}|\mathfrak{F}_{-m}) \xrightarrow{\text{q. m.}} 0$ as $m \to \infty$, where $\{\mathfrak{F}_t\}$ is adapted to $\{\mathbf{Z}_{thi}\epsilon_{th}\}$, $h = 1, \ldots, p$, $i = 1, \ldots, l$;
(b) $E|\mathbf{Z}_{thi}\epsilon_{th}|^2 < \infty$, $h = 1, \ldots, p$, $i = 1, \ldots, l$;
(c) $\mathbf{V}_n \equiv \text{var}(n^{-1/2}\mathbf{Z}'\epsilon)$ is uniformly positive definite;
(d) $\sum_{j=0}^{\infty} (\text{var}\, \mathcal{R}_{0hij})^{1/2} < \infty$, $h = 1, \ldots, p$, $i = 1, \ldots, l$, where $\mathcal{R}_{0hij} \equiv E(\mathbf{Z}_{0hi}\epsilon_{0h}|\mathfrak{F}_{-j}) - E(\mathbf{Z}_{0hi}\epsilon_{0h}|\mathfrak{F}_{-j-1})$;
(iv) (a) $E|\mathbf{Z}_{thi}\mathbf{X}_{thj}| < \infty$, $h = 1, \ldots, p$, $i = 1, \ldots, l$, and $j = 1, \ldots, k$;
(b) $\mathbf{Q} \equiv E(\mathbf{Z}_t'\mathbf{X}_t)$ has full column rank;
(c) $\hat{\mathbf{P}}_n \xrightarrow{p} \mathbf{P}$ finite and positive definite.

Then $\mathbf{V}_n \to \mathbf{V}$ finite and positive definite as $n \to \infty$, and $\mathbf{D}^{1/2}\sqrt{n}(\tilde{\beta}_n - \beta_o) \overset{A}{\sim} N(\mathbf{0}, \mathbf{I})$, where

$$\mathbf{D} \equiv (\mathbf{Q}'\mathbf{P}\mathbf{Q})^{-1}\mathbf{Q}'\mathbf{P}\mathbf{V}\mathbf{P}\mathbf{Q}(\mathbf{Q}'\mathbf{P}\mathbf{Q})^{-1}.$$

Suppose further that

(v) there exists $\hat{\mathbf{V}}_n$ symmetric and positive semidefinite such that $\hat{\mathbf{V}}_n - \mathbf{V} \xrightarrow{p} \mathbf{0}$.

Then $\hat{\mathbf{D}}_n - \mathbf{D} \xrightarrow{p} \mathbf{0}$, where

$$\hat{\mathbf{D}}_n \equiv (\mathbf{X}'\mathbf{Z}\hat{\mathbf{P}}_n\mathbf{Z}'\mathbf{X}/n^2)^{-1}(\mathbf{X}'\mathbf{Z}/n)\hat{\mathbf{P}}_n\hat{\mathbf{V}}_n\hat{\mathbf{P}}_n(\mathbf{Z}'\mathbf{X}/n)(\mathbf{X}'\mathbf{Z}\hat{\mathbf{P}}_n\mathbf{Z}'\mathbf{X}/n^2)^{-1}.$$

This result follows as a corollary to a more general theorem for nonlinear equations given by Hansen [1982]. However, all the essential features of his assumptions are illustrated in the present result.

Since the results of this section are based on a stationarity assumption, unconditional heteroscedasticity is explicitly ruled out. However, conditional heteroscedasticity is nevertheless a possibility, so efficiency improvements along the lines of Theorem 4.57 may be obtained by eliminating conditional heteroscedasticity or serial correlation.

V.4 Dependent Heterogeneously Distributed Observations

To allow for situations in which the errors exhibit unconditional heteroscedasticity, or the explanatory variables contain fixed as well as lagged dependent variables, we apply central limit results for sequences of mixing random variables. A convenient version of the Liapounov theorem for mixing processes is the following.

THEOREM 5.19 (*Serfling; White and Domowitz*): Let $\{Z_t\}$ be a sequence of mixing random scalars such that either $\phi(m)$ or $\alpha(m)$ is of size $r/(r-1)$, $r > 1$, with $E(Z_t) \equiv \mu_t$, var $Z_t \equiv \sigma_t^2$, $\sigma_t^2 \neq 0$, and $E|Z_t|^{2r} < \Delta < \infty$ for all t. Define $\bar{\sigma}_{a,n}^2 \equiv \text{var}(n^{-1/2} \sum_{t=a+1}^{a+n} Z_t)$. If there exists $\bar{\sigma}^2$, $0 < \bar{\sigma}^2 < \infty$, such that $\bar{\sigma}_{a,n}^2 \to \bar{\sigma}^2$ as $n \to \infty$ uniformly in a, then $\sqrt{n}(\bar{Z}_n - \bar{\mu}_n)/\bar{\sigma}_n \overset{A}{\sim} N(0, 1)$, where $\bar{\sigma}_n^2 \equiv \bar{\sigma}_{0,n}^2$.

Proof: The result for ϕ-mixing is proved by Serfling [1968]. The result for α-mixing is proved by White and Domowitz [1984].

Compared with the Liapounov central limit theorem 5.11, the moment requirements are now potentially stronger to allow for considerably more dependence in Z_t. Note, however, that if $\phi(m)$ or $\alpha(m)$ decrease exponentially in m, we can set r arbitrarily close to one, implying essentially the same moment restrictions as in the independent case.

The other major difference between Theorem 5.11 and the present result is the requirement that $\bar{\sigma}_{a,n}^2 \to \bar{\sigma}^2$ uniformly in a. Before, we only required $\bar{\sigma}_n^2$ to eventually be bounded away from zero. Now, we are requiring $\bar{\sigma}_{a,n}^2$ to converge to a nonzero *constant* as $n \to \infty$ regardless of when we start the summation, i.e., regardless of the date of our first observation. Moreover, the speed of convergence cannot depend on the date of the first observation, since it must be uniform in a.

That the $\bar{\sigma}_n^2$ approach a constant is a much stronger restriction on the heterogeneity of Z_t than we needed to impose to obtain a law of large numbers. Essentially, we are imposing the requirement that Z_t

be covariance stationary asymptotically. This still allows a good deal more heterogeneity than a covariance stationary process; however, there is much less potential for heterogeneity than if $\bar{\sigma}_n^2$ were only required to be bounded away from zero.

The analog to Exercise 5.12 is as follows.

EXERCISE 5.20: Prove the following result. Given

(i) $\mathbf{y} = \mathbf{X}\boldsymbol{\beta}_o + \boldsymbol{\epsilon}$;
(ii) $\{(\mathbf{X}_t, \boldsymbol{\epsilon}_t)'\}$ is a mixing sequence with either $\phi(m)$ of size $r'/(r'-1)$, $r' > 1$ or $\alpha(m)$ of size $(r'/r'-1)$, $r' > 1$, where $r' = r + \delta$ for some $r \geq 1$ and $\delta > 0$;
(iii) (a) $E(\mathbf{X}_t'\boldsymbol{\epsilon}_t) = \mathbf{0}$;
(b) $E|X_{thi}\epsilon_{th}|^{2r'} < \Delta < \infty$ for $r' > 1$, $h = 1, \ldots, p$, $i = 1, \ldots, k$, and all t;
(c) $\mathbf{V}_{an} \equiv \text{var}(n^{-1/2} \sum_{t=a+1}^{a+n} \mathbf{X}_t'\boldsymbol{\epsilon}_t)$, $\mathbf{V}_n \equiv \mathbf{V}_{0n}$, and there exists $\mathbf{V}$ positive definite such that $\mathbf{V}_{an} - \mathbf{V} \to \mathbf{0}$ as $n \to \infty$ uniformly in a;
(iv) (a) $E|X_{thi}^2|^{r'} < \Delta < \infty$ for $r'1$ and all $h = 1, \ldots, p$, $i = 1, \ldots, k$, and t;
(b) $\mathbf{M}_n \equiv E(\mathbf{X}'\mathbf{X}/n)$ is uniformly positive definite.

Then $\mathbf{D}_n^{-1/2}\sqrt{n}(\hat{\boldsymbol{\beta}}_n - \boldsymbol{\beta}_o) \overset{A}{\sim} N(\mathbf{0}, \mathbf{I})$, where $\mathbf{D}_n = \mathbf{M}_n^{-1}\mathbf{V}_n\mathbf{M}_n^{-1}$. Suppose in addition that

(v) there exists $\hat{\mathbf{V}}_n$ symmetric and positive semidefinite such that $\hat{\mathbf{V}}_n - \mathbf{V}_n \xrightarrow{p} \mathbf{0}$.

Then $\hat{\mathbf{D}}_n - \mathbf{D}_n \xrightarrow{p} \mathbf{0}$, where $\hat{\mathbf{D}}_n \equiv (\mathbf{X}'\mathbf{X}/n)^{-1}\hat{\mathbf{V}}_n(\mathbf{X}'\mathbf{X}/n)^{-1}$.

Compared with Exercise 5.12, we have relaxed the memory requirement from independence to mixing (asymptotic independence). Depending on the amount of dependence the observations exhibit, the moment conditions may or may not be stronger than those of Exercise 5.12. We have also imposed the requirement that $\mathbf{V}_{an} - \mathbf{V} \to \mathbf{0}$ as $n \to \infty$, which is not needed in Exercise 5.12. If this condition were not imposed, Exercise 5.12 would be a direct corollary of the present result.

The flexibility gained by dispensing with the stationarity assumption of Theorem 5.16 is that the present result can accommodate the inclusion of fixed regressors as well as lagged dependent variables in the explanatory variables of the model. The price paid is an increase in the moment restrictions, as well as an increase in the strength of the memory conditions.

EXERCISE 5.21: Suppose the model is $\mathbf{y}_t = \beta_1 \mathbf{y}_{t-1} + \beta_2 \mathbf{x}_t + \epsilon_t$, where $\mathbf{x}_t$ is a fixed scalar. Let $\mathbf{X}_t = (\mathbf{y}_{t-1}, \mathbf{x}_t)$ and provide conditions on $\{(\mathbf{X}_t, \epsilon_t)'\}$ and (β_1, β_2) that ensure that the OLS estimator of β_1 and β_2 is consistent and asymptotically normal.

The result for the instrumental variables estimator is the following.

THEOREM 5.22: Given

(i) $\mathbf{y} = \mathbf{X}\beta_o + \epsilon$;
(ii) $\{(\mathbf{Z}_t, \mathbf{X}_t, \epsilon_t)'\}$ is a mixing sequence with either $\phi(m)$ of size $r'/(r'-1)$, $r' > 1$ or $\alpha(m)$ of size $r'/(r'-1)$, $r' > 1$, where $r' = r + \delta$ for some $r \geq 1$ and $0 < \delta \leq r$;
(iii) (a) $E(\mathbf{Z}_t' \epsilon_t) = \mathbf{0}$;
(b) $E|\mathbf{Z}_{thi} \epsilon_{th}|^{2r'} < \Delta < \infty$ for $r' > 1$, $h = 1, \ldots, p$, $i = 1, \ldots, l$, and all t;
(c) $\mathbf{V}_{an} \equiv \text{var}(n^{-1/2} \sum_{t=a+1}^{a+n} \mathbf{Z}_t' \epsilon_t)$, $\mathbf{V}_n \equiv \mathbf{V}_{0n}$, and there exists $\mathbf{V}$ finite and positive definite such that $\mathbf{V}_{an} - \mathbf{V} \to \mathbf{0}$ as $n \to \infty$ uniformly in a;
(iv) (a) $E|\mathbf{Z}_{thi} \mathbf{X}_{thj}|^{r'} < \Delta < \infty$ for $r'1$ and all $h = 1, \ldots, p$, $i = 1, \ldots, l$, $j = 1, \ldots, k$, and t;
(b) $\mathbf{Q}_n \equiv E(\mathbf{Z}'\mathbf{X}/n)$ has uniformly full column rank;
(c) $\hat{\mathbf{P}}_n - \mathbf{P}_n \xrightarrow{p} \mathbf{0}$, where $\{\mathbf{P}_n\}$ is $O(1)$ and uniformly positive definite.

Then $\mathbf{D}_n^{-1/2} \sqrt{n}(\tilde{\beta}_n - \beta_o) \stackrel{A}{\sim} N(\mathbf{0}, \mathbf{I})$, where

$$\mathbf{D}_n \equiv (\mathbf{Q}_n' \mathbf{P}_n \mathbf{Q}_n)^{-1} \mathbf{Q}_n' \mathbf{P}_n \mathbf{V}_n \mathbf{P}_n \mathbf{Q}_n (\mathbf{Q}_n' \mathbf{P}_n \mathbf{Q}_n)^{-1}.$$

Suppose further that

(v) there exists $\hat{\mathbf{V}}_n$ symmetric and positive semidefinite such that $\hat{\mathbf{V}}_n - \mathbf{V}_n \xrightarrow{p} \mathbf{0}$.

Then $\hat{\mathbf{D}}_n - \mathbf{D}_n \xrightarrow{p} \mathbf{0}$, where

$$\hat{\mathbf{D}}_n \equiv (\mathbf{X}'\mathbf{Z}\hat{\mathbf{P}}_n \mathbf{Z}'\mathbf{X}/n^2)^{-1} (\mathbf{X}'\mathbf{Z}/n) \hat{\mathbf{P}}_n \hat{\mathbf{V}}_n \hat{\mathbf{P}}_n (\mathbf{Z}'\mathbf{X}/n) (\mathbf{X}'\mathbf{Z}\hat{\mathbf{P}}_n \mathbf{Z}'\mathbf{X}/n^2)^{-1}.$$

Proof: We verify that the conditions of Exercise 4.26 hold. First we apply Proposition 5.1 to show $\mathbf{V}_n^{-1/2} n^{-1/2} \mathbf{Z}'\epsilon \stackrel{A}{\sim} N(\mathbf{0}, \mathbf{I})$. Consider $n^{-1/2} \sum_{t=1}^{n} \lambda' \mathbf{V}^{-1/2} \mathbf{Z}_t' \epsilon_t$. By Theorem 3.49, $\lambda' \mathbf{V}^{-1/2} \mathbf{Z}_t' \epsilon_t$ is a sequence of mixing random variables with either $\phi(m)$ of size $r'/(r'-1)$, $r' > 1$

or $\alpha(m)$ of size $r'/(r'-1)$, $r'>1$, given (ii). Further, $E(\lambda'\mathbf{V}^{-1/2}\mathbf{Z}_t'\boldsymbol{\epsilon}_t)=0$ given (iiia), $E|\lambda'\mathbf{V}^{-1/2}\mathbf{Z}_t'\boldsymbol{\epsilon}_t|^{2r'}<\Delta<\infty$ for all t given (iiib), and if $\bar{\sigma}_{an}^2\equiv \text{var}(n^{-1/2}\sum_{t=a+1}^{a+n}\lambda'\mathbf{V}^{-1/2}\mathbf{Z}_t'\boldsymbol{\epsilon}_t)=\lambda'\mathbf{V}^{-1/2}\mathbf{V}_{an}\mathbf{V}^{-1/2}\lambda$, we have $\bar{\sigma}_{an}^2\rightarrow 1$ uniformly in a by (iiic). It follows from Theorem 5.19 that $n^{-1/2}\sum_{t=1}^n\lambda'\mathbf{V}^{-1/2}\mathbf{Z}_t'\boldsymbol{\epsilon}_t\overset{A}{\sim}N(0,1)$. Since this holds for every λ, $\lambda'\lambda=1$, it follows from Proposition 5.1 that $\mathbf{V}^{-1/2}n^{-1/2}\sum_{t=1}^n\mathbf{Z}_t'\boldsymbol{\epsilon}_t\overset{A}{\sim}N(\mathbf{0},\mathbf{I})$. Now

$$\mathbf{V}_n^{-1/2}n^{-1/2}\sum_{t=1}^n\mathbf{Z}_t'\boldsymbol{\epsilon}_t-\mathbf{V}^{-1/2}n^{-1/2}\sum_{t=1}^n\mathbf{Z}_t'\boldsymbol{\epsilon}_t$$
$$=(\mathbf{V}_n^{-1/2}\mathbf{V}^{1/2}-\mathbf{I})\mathbf{V}^{-1/2}n^{-1/2}\sum_{t=1}^n\mathbf{Z}_t'\boldsymbol{\epsilon}_t\xrightarrow{p}\mathbf{0},$$

because $\mathbf{V}_n^{-1/2}\mathbf{V}^{1/2}-\mathbf{I}$ is $o(1)$ by Definition 2.3 and $\mathbf{V}^{-1/2}n^{-1/2}\sum_{t=1}^n\mathbf{Z}_t'\boldsymbol{\epsilon}_t\overset{A}{\sim}\mathrm{N}(\mathbf{0},\mathbf{I})$, which allows application of Lemma 4.6. Hence by Lemma 4.7, $\mathbf{V}_n^{-1/2}n^{-1/2}\mathbf{Z}_t'\boldsymbol{\epsilon}\overset{A}{\sim}N(\mathbf{0},\mathbf{I})$.

Next, $\mathbf{Z}'\mathbf{X}/n-\mathbf{Q}_n\xrightarrow{p}\mathbf{0}$ by Corollary 3.48 given (iva), where $\{\mathbf{Q}_n\}$ is $O(1)$ and has uniformly full column rank by (iva) and (ivb). Since (ivc) also holds, the desired result now follows from Exercise 4.26.

This result is in a sense the most general of all the results that we have obtained, because it contains so many special cases. Specifically, it covers every situation previously considered (i.i.d., i.h.d., and d.i.d. observations), although at the explicit cost of imposing slightly stronger conditions in various respects. Note, too, this result applies to systems of equations or panel data since we can choose $p>1$.

Finally, we remark that condition (ii) of Theorem 5.22 is actually stronger than necessary. Instead of requiring that $\mathbf{Z}_t$, $\mathbf{X}_t$, and $\boldsymbol{\epsilon}_t$ be jointly mixing of the specified size, it would be sufficient to require only that $\{(\mathbf{Z}_t,\mathbf{X}_t)'\}$ have $\phi(m)$ of size $r/(2r-1)$, $r\geq 1$ or $\alpha(m)$ of size $r/(r-1)$, $r>1$ and $\{(\mathbf{Z}_t,\boldsymbol{\epsilon}_t)'\}$ have $\phi(m)$ or $\alpha(m)$ of size $r'/(r'-1)$, $r'>1$. The condition imposed by (ii) becomes useful later in estimating covariance matrices.

V.5 Martingale Difference Sequences

In Chapter 3 we discussed laws of large numbers for martingale difference sequences and mentioned that economic theory is often used to justify the martingale difference assumption. If the martingale difference assumption is valid, then it often allows us to simplify or weaken some of the other conditions imposed in establishing the asymptotic normality of our estimators.

There are a variety of central limit theorems available for martingale difference sequences. One version that is relatively convenient is an extension of the Lindeberg–Feller theorem 5.6. In stating it, we consider sequences of random variables $\{Z_{nt}\}$ and associated σ-algebras $\{\mathfrak{F}_{nt}, 1 \leq t \leq n\}$, where $\mathfrak{F}_{nt-1} \subset \mathfrak{F}_{nt}$ and Z_{nt} is measurable with respect to $\mathfrak{F}_{nt}$. We can think of $\mathfrak{F}_{nt}$ as being the σ-field generated by the current and past of Z_{nt} as well as any other relevant random variables.

THEOREM 5.23: Let $\{Z_{nt}, \mathfrak{F}_{nt}\}$ be a martingale difference sequence such that $\sigma_{nt}^2 \equiv E(Z_{nt}^2) < \infty$, $\sigma_{nt}^2 \neq 0$, and let F_{nt} be the distribution function of Z_{nt}. Define $\bar{Z}_n \equiv n^{-1} \sum_{t=1}^n Z_{nt}$ and $\bar{\sigma}_n^2 \equiv \text{var } \sqrt{n}\,\bar{Z}_n = n^{-1} \sum_{t=1}^n \sigma_{nt}^2$. If for every $\epsilon > 0$

$$\lim_{n\to\infty} \bar{\sigma}_n^{-2} n^{-1} \sum_{t=1}^n \int_{z^2 > \epsilon n \bar{\sigma}_n^2} z^2 \, dF_{nt}(z) = 0,$$

and

$$n^{-1} \sum_{t=1}^n Z_{nt}^2 / \bar{\sigma}_n^2 - 1 \xrightarrow{p} 0,$$

then $\sqrt{n}\,\bar{Z}_n / \bar{\sigma}_n \overset{A}{\sim} N(0, 1)$.

Proof: This follows immediately as a corollary to Theorem 2.3 of McLeish [1974].

Comparing this result with the Lindeberg–Feller theorem, we see that both impose the Lindeberg condition, whereas the independence assumption has here been weakened to the martingale difference assumption. The present result also imposes a condition not explicit in the Lindeberg–Feller theorem, i.e., essentially that the sample variance $n^{-1} \sum_{t=1}^n Z_{nt}^2$ is a consistent estimator for $\bar{\sigma}_n^2$. This condition is unnecessary in the independent case because it is implied there by the Lindeberg condition. Without independence, we make use of additional conditions, e.g., stationarity and ergodicity or mixing, to ensure that the sample variance is indeed consistent for $\bar{\sigma}_n^2$.

To illustrate how use of the martingale difference assumption allows us to simplify our results, consider the IV estimator in the case of stationary observations. We have the following result.

THEOREM 5.24: Suppose conditions (i), (ii), (iv) and (v) of Exercise 5.18 hold, and replace condition (iii) with

(iii′) (a) $E(\mathbf{Z}_{thi}\epsilon_{th}|\mathfrak{F}_{t-1})=0$ for all t, where $\{\mathfrak{F}_t\}$ is adapted to $\{\mathbf{Z}_{thi}\epsilon_{th}\}$, $h=1, \ldots, p$, $i=1, \ldots, l$;
(b) $E|\mathbf{Z}_{thi}\epsilon_{th}|^2<\infty$, $h=1, \ldots, p$, $i=1, \ldots, l$;
(c) $\mathbf{V}_n \equiv \text{var}(n^{-1/2}\mathbf{Z}'\epsilon)=\text{var}(\mathbf{Z}_t'\epsilon_t)\equiv \mathbf{V}$ is nonsingular.

Then the conclusions of Exercise 5.18 hold.

Proof: One way to prove this is to show that (iii′) implies (iii). This is direct, and it is left to the reader to verify.

Alternatively, we can apply Proposition 5.1 and Theorem 5.23 to verify that $\mathbf{V}_n^{-1/2}n^{-1/2}\mathbf{Z}'\epsilon \overset{A}{\sim} N(\mathbf{0}, \mathbf{I})$. Since $\{\mathbf{Z}_t'\epsilon_t\}$ is a stationary martingale difference sequence, $\text{var}(n^{-1/2}\mathbf{Z}'\epsilon)= n^{-1} \Sigma_{t=1}^n E(\mathbf{Z}_t'\epsilon_t\epsilon_t'\mathbf{Z}_t)=\mathbf{V}$, finite by (iiib) and positive definite by (iiic). Hence, consider $n^{-1/2}\Sigma_{t=1}^n \lambda'\mathbf{V}^{-1/2}\mathbf{Z}_t'\epsilon_t$. By Proposition 3.23, $\lambda'\mathbf{V}^{-1/2}\mathbf{Z}_t'\epsilon_t$ is measurable with respect to $\mathfrak{F}_t$ given (iii′a). Writing $\lambda'\mathbf{V}^{-1/2}\mathbf{Z}_t'\epsilon_t = \Sigma_{h=1}^p \Sigma_{i=1}^k \tilde{\lambda}_i \mathbf{Z}_{thi}\epsilon_{th}$, it follows from the linearity of condition expectations that $E(\lambda'\mathbf{V}^{-1/2}\mathbf{Z}_t'\epsilon_t|\mathfrak{F}_{t-1})= \Sigma_{h=1}^p \Sigma_{i=1}^k \tilde{\lambda}_i E(\mathbf{Z}_{thi}\epsilon_{thi}|\mathfrak{F}_{t-1})=0$ given (iii′a). Hence $\{\lambda'\mathbf{V}^{-1/2}\mathbf{Z}_t'\epsilon_t, \mathfrak{F}_t\}$ is a martingale difference sequence. As a consequence of stationarity, $\text{var}(\lambda'\mathbf{V}^{-1/2}\mathbf{Z}_t'\epsilon_t)= \lambda'\mathbf{V}^{-1/2}\mathbf{V}\mathbf{V}^{-1/2}\lambda=1$ for all t, and for all t, $F_{nt}=F$, the distribution function of $\lambda'\mathbf{V}^{-1/2}\mathbf{Z}_t'\epsilon_t$. It follows from Exercise 5.9 that the Lindeberg condition is satisfied. Since $\{\lambda'\mathbf{V}^{-1/2}\mathbf{Z}_t'\epsilon_t\epsilon_t'\mathbf{Z}_t\mathbf{V}^{-1/2}\lambda\}$ is a stationary and ergodic sequence by Proposition 3.30 with finite expected absolute values given (iii′b) and (iii′c) the ergodic theorem 3.34 and Theorem 2.24 imply

$$n^{-1}\sum_{t=1}^{n} \lambda'\mathbf{V}^{-1/2}\mathbf{Z}_t'\epsilon_t\epsilon_t'\mathbf{Z}_t\mathbf{V}^{-1/2}\lambda - \lambda'\mathbf{V}^{-1/2}\mathbf{V}\mathbf{V}^{-1/2}\lambda$$

$$=n^{-1}\sum_{t=1}^{n} \lambda'\mathbf{V}^{-1/2}\mathbf{Z}_t'\epsilon_t\epsilon_t'\mathbf{Z}_t\mathbf{V}^{-1/2}\lambda - 1 \xrightarrow{p} 0.$$

Hence, by Theorem 5.23 $n^{-1/2}\Sigma_{t=1}^n \lambda'\mathbf{V}^{-1/2}\mathbf{Z}_t'\epsilon_t \overset{A}{\sim} N(0, 1)$. It follows from Proposition 5.1 that $\mathbf{V}^{-1/2}n^{-1/2}\mathbf{Z}'\epsilon \overset{A}{\sim} N(\mathbf{0}, \mathbf{I})$, and since $\mathbf{V}=\mathbf{V}_n$, $\mathbf{V}_n^{-1/2}n^{-1/2}\mathbf{Z}'\epsilon \overset{A}{\sim} N(\mathbf{0}, \mathbf{I})$. The rest of the results follow as before.

Whereas use of the martingale difference assumption allows us to state simpler conditions for stationary ergodic processes, it also allows us to state weaker conditions on certain aspects of the behavior of mixing processes. To do this conveniently, we apply a Liapounov-like corollary to the central limit theorem just given.

COROLLARY 5.25: Let $\{Z_{nt}, \mathfrak{F}_{nt}\}$ be a martingale difference sequence such that $E(Z_{nt}^2) \equiv \sigma_{nt}^2 \neq 0$ and $E|Z_{nt}|^{2+\delta} < \Delta < \infty$ for some $\delta > 0$ and all t. If $\bar{\sigma}_n^2 > \delta' > 0$ for all n sufficiently large and $n^{-1} \Sigma_{t=1}^n Z_{nt}^2 - \bar{\sigma}_n^2 \xrightarrow{p} 0$, then $\sqrt{n}\,\bar{Z}_n/\bar{\sigma} \overset{A}{\sim} N(0, 1)$.

Proof: Given $E|Z_{nt}|^{2+\delta} < \Delta < \infty$, the Lindeberg condition holds as shown in the proof of Theorem 5.10. Since $\bar{\sigma}_n^2 > \delta' > 0$, $\bar{\sigma}_n^{-2}$ is O(1), so $n^{-1} \Sigma_{t=1}^n Z_{nt}^2/\bar{\sigma}_n^2 - 1 = \bar{\sigma}_n^{-2}(n^{-1} \Sigma_{t=1}^n Z_{nt}^2 - \bar{\sigma}_n^2) \xrightarrow{p} 0$ by Exercise 2.35. The conditions of Theorem 5.24 hold and the result follows.

We use this result to obtain an analog to Theorem 5.24.

EXERCISE 5.26: Prove the following. Suppose conditions (i), (iv), and (v) of Theorem 5.22 hold, and replace (ii) and (iii) with

(ii′) $\{(\mathbf{Z}_t, \mathbf{X}_t, \boldsymbol{\epsilon}_t)'\}$ is a mixing sequence with either $\phi(m)$ of size $r/(2r - 1)$, $r \geq 1$, or $\alpha(m)$ of size $r/(r - 1)$, $r > 1$;

(iii′) (a) $E(\mathbf{Z}_{thi}\boldsymbol{\epsilon}_{th}|\mathfrak{F}_{t-1}) = 0$ for all t, where $\{\mathfrak{F}_t\}$ is adapted to $\{\mathbf{Z}_{thi}\boldsymbol{\epsilon}_{th}\}$, $h = 1, \ldots, p$, $i = 1, \ldots, l$;

(b) $E|\mathbf{Z}_{thi}\boldsymbol{\epsilon}_{th}|^{2(r+\delta)} < \Delta < \infty$ for some $\delta > 0$ and all $h = 1, \ldots, p$, $i = 1, \ldots, l$ and all t;

(c) $\mathbf{V}_n \equiv \text{var}(n^{-1/2}\mathbf{Z}'\boldsymbol{\epsilon})$ is uniformly positive definite.

Then the conclusions of Theorem 5.22 hold.

Note that although the assumption (iiia) has been strengthened from $E(\mathbf{Z}_t'\boldsymbol{\epsilon}_t) = 0$ to the martingale difference assumption, we have weakened the memory requirements from (ii) to (ii′), maintained the moment requirements of (iiib), and weakened the homogeneity condition (iiic) to the requirement that $\mathbf{V}_n$ be O(1) and uniformly positive definite. No longer is $\mathbf{V}_n$ required to converge to some limit.

References

Gordin, M. I. [1969]. The central limit theorem for stationary processes, *Soviet Math. Dokl.* **10**:1174–1176.

Hannan, E. J. [1973]. Central limit theorems for time series regression, *Z. Wahrsch. Verw. Gebiete* **26**:157–170.

Hansen, L. P. [1982]. Large sample properties of generalized method of moments estimators, *Econometrica* **50**:1029–1054.

Loeve, M. [1977]. "Probability Theory." Vol. 1 New York: Springer-Verlag.

McLeish, D. L. [1974]. Dependent central limit theorems and invariance principles, *Ann. Probab.* **2**:620–628.

Rao, C. R. [1973]. "Linear Statistical Inference and Its Applications." New York: Wiley.

Serfling, R. J. [1968]. Contributions to central limit theory for dependent variables, *Annals of Mathematical Statistics* **39**:1158–1175.

White, H. and I. Domowitz [1984]. Nonlinear regression with dependent observations, *Econometrica*, forthcoming.

CHAPTER VI

Estimating Asymptotic Covariance Matrices

In all the preceding chapters, we defined $\mathbf{V}_n \equiv \text{var}(n^{-1/2}\mathbf{X}'\boldsymbol{\epsilon})$ or $\mathbf{V}_n \equiv \text{var}(n^{-1/2}\mathbf{Z}'\boldsymbol{\epsilon})$ and assumed that a consistent estimator $\hat{\mathbf{V}}_n$ for $\mathbf{V}_n$ is available. In this chapter we obtain conditions that allow us to find convenient consistent estimators $\hat{\mathbf{V}}_n$. Because the theory of estimating $\text{var}(n^{-1/2}\mathbf{X}'\boldsymbol{\epsilon})$ is identical to that of estimating $\text{var}(n^{-1/2}\mathbf{Z}'\boldsymbol{\epsilon})$, we consider only the latter. Further, because the optimal choice for $\mathbf{P}_n$ is $\mathbf{V}_n^{-1}$, as we saw in Chapter IV, conditions that permit consistent estimation of $\mathbf{V}_n$ will also permit consistent estimation of $\mathbf{P}_n = \mathbf{V}_n^{-1}$ by $\hat{\mathbf{P}}_n = \hat{\mathbf{V}}_n^{-1}$.

VI.1 General Structure of $\mathbf{V}_n$

Before proceeding to look at special cases, it is helpful to examine the general form of $\mathbf{V}_n$.

$$\mathbf{V}_n \equiv \text{var}(n^{-1/2}\mathbf{Z}'\boldsymbol{\epsilon}) = E(\mathbf{Z}'\boldsymbol{\epsilon}\boldsymbol{\epsilon}'\mathbf{Z}/n),$$

because we assume that $E(n^{-1/2}\mathbf{Z}'\boldsymbol{\epsilon}) = \mathbf{0}$. In terms of individual observations, this can be expressed as

$$\mathbf{V}_n = E\left(n^{-1}\sum_{t=1}^{n}\sum_{\tau=1}^{n}\mathbf{Z}_t'\epsilon_t\epsilon_\tau'\mathbf{Z}_\tau\right).$$

An equivalent way of writing the summation on the right is helpful in obtaining further insight. We can also write

$$\begin{aligned}\mathbf{V}_n &= n^{-1}\sum_{t=1}^{n} E(\mathbf{Z}_t'\boldsymbol{\epsilon}_t\boldsymbol{\epsilon}_t'\mathbf{Z}_t) \\ &\quad + n^{-1}\sum_{\tau=1}^{n-1}\sum_{t=\tau+1}^{n} E(\mathbf{Z}_t'\boldsymbol{\epsilon}_t\boldsymbol{\epsilon}_{t-\tau}'\mathbf{Z}_{t-\tau} + \mathbf{Z}_{t-\tau}'\boldsymbol{\epsilon}_{t-\tau}\boldsymbol{\epsilon}_t'\mathbf{Z}_t) \\ &= n^{-1}\sum_{t=1}^{n} \operatorname{var}(\mathbf{Z}_t'\boldsymbol{\epsilon}_t) \\ &\quad + n^{-1}\sum_{\tau=1}^{n-1}\sum_{t=\tau+1}^{n} \operatorname{cov}(\mathbf{Z}_t'\boldsymbol{\epsilon}_t, \mathbf{Z}_{t-\tau}'\boldsymbol{\epsilon}_{t-\tau}) + \operatorname{cov}(\mathbf{Z}_{t-\tau}'\boldsymbol{\epsilon}_{t-\tau}, \mathbf{Z}_t'\boldsymbol{\epsilon}_t).\end{aligned}$$

The last expression reveals that $\mathbf{V}_n$ is the average of the variances of $Z_t'\boldsymbol{\epsilon}_t$ plus a term that takes into account the covariances between $\mathbf{Z}_t'\boldsymbol{\epsilon}_t$ and $\mathbf{Z}_{t-\tau}'\boldsymbol{\epsilon}_{t-\tau}$ for all t and τ.

As we saw in Chapter IV, it is sometimes possible to express variances or covariances of $\boldsymbol{\epsilon}_{th}$ as functions of the instrumental variable candidates $\mathbf{W}_{th}$. Under the conditions given by Exercise 4.55, we saw that we can express $\mathbf{V}_n$ as

$$\mathbf{V}_n = E(\mathbf{Z}'\boldsymbol{\Omega}_n\mathbf{Z}/n).$$

We consider three important special cases.

Case 1. The first case considered is when $\operatorname{cov}(\mathbf{Z}_t'\boldsymbol{\epsilon}_t, \mathbf{Z}_{t-\tau}'\boldsymbol{\epsilon}_{t-\tau}) = \operatorname{cov}(\mathbf{Z}_{t-\tau}'\boldsymbol{\epsilon}_{t-\tau}, \mathbf{Z}_t'\boldsymbol{\epsilon}_t)' = 0$ for all $t \neq \tau$, so $\boldsymbol{\Omega}_n$ is (block) diagonal and

$$\mathbf{V}_n = n^{-1}\sum_{t=1}^{n} E(\mathbf{Z}_t'\boldsymbol{\epsilon}_t\boldsymbol{\epsilon}_t'\mathbf{Z}_t).$$

This occurs when $\{(\mathbf{Z}_t, \boldsymbol{\epsilon}_t)'\}$ is an independent sequence or when $\{\mathbf{Z}_t'\boldsymbol{\epsilon}_t, \mathfrak{F}_t\}$ is a martingale difference sequence for some adapted σ-fields $\mathfrak{F}_t$.

Case 2. The next case arises when $\operatorname{cov}(\mathbf{Z}_t'\boldsymbol{\epsilon}_t, \mathbf{Z}_{t-\tau}'\boldsymbol{\epsilon}_{t-\tau}) = \operatorname{cov}(\mathbf{Z}_{t-\tau}'\boldsymbol{\epsilon}_{t-\tau}, \mathbf{Z}_t'\boldsymbol{\epsilon}_t)' = \mathbf{0}$ for all $\tau \geq m$, $1 < m < \infty$, so $\boldsymbol{\Omega}_n$ is a (block) band diagonal matrix and

$$\begin{aligned}\mathbf{V}_n &= n^{-1}\sum_{t=1}^{n} E(\mathbf{Z}_t'\boldsymbol{\epsilon}_t\boldsymbol{\epsilon}_t'\mathbf{Z}_t) \\ &\quad + n^{-1}\sum_{\tau=1}^{m-1}\sum_{t=\tau+1}^{n} E(\mathbf{Z}_t'\boldsymbol{\epsilon}_t\boldsymbol{\epsilon}_{t-\tau}'\mathbf{Z}_{t-\tau}) + E(\mathbf{Z}_{t-\tau}'\boldsymbol{\epsilon}_{t-\tau}\boldsymbol{\epsilon}_t'\mathbf{Z}_t).\end{aligned}$$

This case arises when $E(\mathbf{Z}_t'\boldsymbol{\epsilon}_t|\mathfrak{F}_{t-m}) = \mathbf{0}$ for $1 < m < \infty$ and adapted σ-fields $\mathfrak{F}_t$. A simple example of this case arises when Z_t is nonstochastic and $\boldsymbol{\epsilon}_t$ is an MA(1) process, i.e.,

$$\boldsymbol{\epsilon}_t = \alpha \boldsymbol{\nu}_t + \boldsymbol{\nu}_{t-1},$$

where $\{\boldsymbol{\nu}_t\}$ is an i.i.d. sequence with $E(\boldsymbol{\nu}_t) = \mathbf{0}$. Setting $\mathfrak{F}_t = \sigma(\ldots, \boldsymbol{\epsilon}_t)$ it is readily verified that $E(\mathbf{Z}_t'\boldsymbol{\epsilon}_t|\mathfrak{F}_{t-m}) = \mathbf{Z}_t'E(\boldsymbol{\epsilon}_t|\mathfrak{F}_{t-m}) = 0$ for $m \geq 2$, implying that

$$\mathbf{V}_n = n^{-1}\sum_{t=1}^{n} E(\mathbf{Z}_t'\boldsymbol{\epsilon}_t\boldsymbol{\epsilon}_t'\mathbf{Z}_t)$$

$$+ n^{-1}\sum_{t=2}^{n} E(\mathbf{Z}_t'\boldsymbol{\epsilon}_t\boldsymbol{\epsilon}_{t-1}'\mathbf{Z}_{t-1}) + E(\mathbf{Z}_{t-1}'\boldsymbol{\epsilon}_{t-1}\boldsymbol{\epsilon}_t'\mathbf{Z}_t).$$

Case 3. The last case that we consider occurs when $\{\mathbf{Z}_t'\boldsymbol{\epsilon}_t\}$ is an asymptotically uncorrelated sequence so that $\text{cov}(\mathbf{Z}_t'\boldsymbol{\epsilon}_t, \mathbf{Z}_{t-\tau}'\boldsymbol{\epsilon}_{t-\tau}) = \text{cov}(\mathbf{Z}_{t-\tau}'\boldsymbol{\epsilon}_{t-\tau}, \mathbf{Z}_t'\boldsymbol{\epsilon}_t)' \to 0$ as $\tau \to \infty$. Rather than making direct use of the assumption that $\{(\mathbf{Z}_t, \boldsymbol{\epsilon}_t)'\}$ is asymptotically uncorrelated, we shall assume that $\{(\mathbf{Z}_t, \boldsymbol{\epsilon}_t)'\}$ is a mixing sequence, which will suffice for asymptotic uncorrelatedness.

In this chapter we generally assume that the transformation $\mathbf{C}_n$ and therefore the elements of $\boldsymbol{\Omega}_n$ are unknown beyond the information specified in the three cases just discussed. If $\boldsymbol{\Omega}_n$ were known, then it could be used directly in estimating $\mathbf{V}_n$. But more importantly, efficient estimation would be possible, as discussed in Section 3 of Chapter IV. The linear transformation involved in obtaining the efficient estimator then allows the covariance matrix to be obtained as a special instance of Case 1. In the following chapter we shall consider some situations in which the elements of $\mathbf{C}_n$ can be consistently estimated.

VI.2 Case 1: $\boldsymbol{\Omega}_n$ (Block) Diagonal

In this section, we treat the case in which

$$\mathbf{V}_n = n^{-1}\sum_{t=1}^{n} E(\mathbf{Z}_t'\boldsymbol{\epsilon}_t\boldsymbol{\epsilon}_t'\mathbf{Z}_t).$$

A special case of major importance arises when

$$E(\epsilon_{th}^2|\mathbf{W}_{th}) = \sigma_o^2,$$

$$E(\epsilon_{th}\epsilon_{\tau g}|\mathbf{W}_{th}, \mathbf{W}_{\tau g}) = 0, \qquad t \neq \tau, h \neq g,$$

so that

$$\mathbf{V}_n = n^{-1} \sum_{t=1}^{n} \sigma_o^2 E(\mathbf{Z}_t'\mathbf{Z}_t) = \sigma_o^2 \mathbf{L}_n.$$

Our first result applies to this case.

THEOREM 6.1: Suppose $\mathbf{V}_n = \sigma_o^2 \mathbf{L}_n$, where $\sigma_o^2 < \infty$ and $\mathbf{L}_n$ is $O(1)$. If there exists $\tilde{\sigma}_n^2$ such that $\tilde{\sigma}_n^2 \xrightarrow{p} \sigma_o^2$ and if $\mathbf{Z}'\mathbf{Z}/n - \mathbf{L}_n \xrightarrow{p} \mathbf{0}$, then $\hat{\mathbf{V}}_n \equiv \tilde{\sigma}_n^2 \mathbf{Z}'\mathbf{Z}/n$ is such that $\hat{\mathbf{V}}_n - \mathbf{V}_n \xrightarrow{p} \mathbf{0}$.

Proof: Immediate from Proposition 2.30.

EXERCISE 6.2: Using Exercise 3.80, find conditions that ensure that $\tilde{\sigma}_n^2 \xrightarrow{p} \sigma_o^2$ and $\mathbf{Z}'\mathbf{Z}/n - \mathbf{L}_n \xrightarrow{p} \mathbf{0}$, where $\tilde{\sigma}_n^2 = (\mathbf{y} - \mathbf{X}\tilde{\boldsymbol{\beta}}_n)'(\mathbf{y} - \mathbf{X}\tilde{\boldsymbol{\beta}}_n)/(np)$.

Conditions under which $\tilde{\sigma}_n^2 \to \sigma_o^2$ and $\mathbf{Z}'\mathbf{Z}/n - \mathbf{L}_n \xrightarrow{p} \mathbf{0}$ are easily found from the results of Chapter III.

In the remainder of this section we consider the cases in which $\{(\mathbf{Z}_t, \mathbf{X}_t, \boldsymbol{\epsilon}_t)'\}$ is a stationary sequence and $\{(\mathbf{Z}_t, \mathbf{X}_t, \boldsymbol{\epsilon}_t)'\}$ a heterogeneous sequence. We invoke the martingale difference assumption in each case, which allows results for independent observations to follow as direct corrollaries.

The results that we obtain below are motivated by the following considerations. We are interested in estimating

$$\mathbf{V}_n = n^{-1} \sum_{t=1}^{n} E(\mathbf{Z}_t'\boldsymbol{\epsilon}_t\boldsymbol{\epsilon}_t'\mathbf{Z}_t).$$

If both $\mathbf{Z}_t$ and $\boldsymbol{\epsilon}_t$ were observable, a consistent estimator is easily available from the results of Chapter III, say,

$$\tilde{\mathbf{V}}_n \equiv n^{-1} \sum_{t=1}^{n} \mathbf{Z}_t'\boldsymbol{\epsilon}_t\boldsymbol{\epsilon}_t'\mathbf{Z}_t.$$

For example, if $\{(\mathbf{Z}_t, \boldsymbol{\epsilon}_t)'\}$ were a stationary ergodic sequence, then as long as the elements of $\mathbf{Z}_t'\boldsymbol{\epsilon}_t\boldsymbol{\epsilon}_t'\mathbf{Z}_t$ have finite expected absolute value, it follows from the ergodic theorem that $\tilde{\mathbf{V}}_n - \mathbf{V}_n \xrightarrow{a.s.} \mathbf{0}$. Of course, $\boldsymbol{\epsilon}_t$ is not observable. However, it can be estimated by

$$\tilde{\boldsymbol{\epsilon}}_t = \mathbf{y}_t - \mathbf{X}_t\tilde{\boldsymbol{\beta}}_n,$$

where $\tilde{\boldsymbol{\beta}}_n$ is consistent for $\boldsymbol{\beta}_o$. This leads us to consider estimators of the form

$$\hat{\mathbf{V}}_n \equiv n^{-1} \sum_{t=1}^{n} \mathbf{Z}_t \tilde{\boldsymbol{\epsilon}}_t \tilde{\boldsymbol{\epsilon}}_t' \mathbf{Z}_t.$$

As we prove below, replacing $\boldsymbol{\epsilon}_t$ with $\tilde{\boldsymbol{\epsilon}}_t$ makes no difference asymptotically under general conditions, so $\hat{\mathbf{V}}_n - \mathbf{V}_n \xrightarrow{\text{a. s.}} \mathbf{0}$. These conditions are precisely specified for stationary sequences by the next result.

THEOREM 6.3: Suppose that

(i) $\mathbf{y} = \mathbf{X}\boldsymbol{\beta}_o + \boldsymbol{\epsilon}$;
(ii) $\{(\mathbf{Z}_t, \mathbf{X}_t, \boldsymbol{\epsilon}_t)'\}$ is a stationary ergodic sequence;
(iii) (a) $\{\mathbf{Z}_t'\boldsymbol{\epsilon}_t, \mathfrak{F}_t\}$ is a martingale difference sequence;
(b) $E|\mathbf{Z}_{thi}\boldsymbol{\epsilon}_{th}|^2 < \infty$, $h = 1, \ldots, p$, $i = 1, \ldots, l$;
(c) $\mathbf{V}_n \equiv \text{var}(n^{-1/2}\mathbf{Z}'\boldsymbol{\epsilon}) = \text{var}(\mathbf{Z}_t'\boldsymbol{\epsilon}_t) \equiv \mathbf{V}$ is positive definite;
(iv) (a) $E|\mathbf{Z}_{thi}\mathbf{X}_{thj}|^2 < \infty$, $h = 1, \ldots, p$, $i = 1, \ldots, l$, $j = 1, \ldots, k$;
(b) $\mathbf{Q}_n \equiv E(\mathbf{Z}'\mathbf{X}/n) = E(\mathbf{Z}_t'\mathbf{X}_t) \equiv \mathbf{Q}$ has full column rank;
(c) $\hat{\mathbf{P}}_n \xrightarrow{p} \mathbf{P}$, finite and positive definite.

Then $\hat{\mathbf{V}}_n - \mathbf{V} \xrightarrow{p} \mathbf{0}$, and $\hat{\mathbf{V}}_n^{-1} - \mathbf{V}^{-1} \xrightarrow{p} \mathbf{0}$.

Proof: By definition and assumption (iiia),

$$\hat{\mathbf{V}}_n - \mathbf{V} = n^{-1} \sum_{t=1}^{n} \mathbf{Z}_t' \tilde{\boldsymbol{\epsilon}}_t \tilde{\boldsymbol{\epsilon}}_t' \mathbf{Z}_t - E(\mathbf{Z}_t'\boldsymbol{\epsilon}_t\boldsymbol{\epsilon}_t'\mathbf{Z}_t).$$

We consider explicitly the case where $p = 1$; the extension to $p > 1$ is straight-forward but notationally cumbersome. Accordingly, we drop the h subscript in what follows. With $p = 1$,

$$\begin{aligned}
\hat{\mathbf{V}}_n - \mathbf{V} &= n^{-1} \sum_{t=1}^{n} \tilde{\boldsymbol{\epsilon}}_t^2 \mathbf{Z}_t'\mathbf{Z}_t - E(\boldsymbol{\epsilon}_t^2 \mathbf{Z}_t'\mathbf{Z}_t) \\
&= n^{-1} \sum_{t=1}^{n} (\mathbf{y}_t - \mathbf{X}_t\tilde{\boldsymbol{\beta}}_n)^2 \mathbf{Z}_t'\mathbf{Z}_t - E(\boldsymbol{\epsilon}_t^2 \mathbf{Z}_t'\mathbf{Z}_t) \\
&= n^{-1} \sum_{t=1}^{n} (\boldsymbol{\epsilon}_t - \mathbf{X}_t(\tilde{\boldsymbol{\beta}}_n - \boldsymbol{\beta}_o))^2 \mathbf{Z}_t'\mathbf{Z}_t - E(\boldsymbol{\epsilon}_t^2 \mathbf{Z}_t'\mathbf{Z}_t) \\
&= n^{-1} \sum_{t=1}^{n} \boldsymbol{\epsilon}_t^2 \mathbf{Z}_t'\mathbf{Z}_t - E(\boldsymbol{\epsilon}_t^2 \mathbf{Z}_t'\mathbf{Z}_t) \\
&\quad - 2n^{-1} \sum_{t=1}^{n} (\tilde{\boldsymbol{\beta}}_n - \boldsymbol{\beta}_o)' \mathbf{X}_t' \boldsymbol{\epsilon}_t \mathbf{Z}_t'\mathbf{Z}_t \\
&\quad + n^{-1} \sum_{t=1}^{n} (\tilde{\boldsymbol{\beta}}_n - \boldsymbol{\beta}_o)' \mathbf{X}_t'\mathbf{X}_t (\tilde{\boldsymbol{\beta}}_n - \boldsymbol{\beta}_o) \mathbf{Z}_t'\mathbf{Z}_t.
\end{aligned}$$

The result follows from Exercise 2.35 if each of the three terms in the last equation converges in probability to zero.

Because the elements of $\mathbf{Z}_t'\boldsymbol{\epsilon}_t\boldsymbol{\epsilon}_t'\mathbf{Z}_t$ have finite expected absolute value by assumption (iiib), it follows from the ergodic theorem 3.34 that

$$n^{-1}\sum_{t=1}^{n}\epsilon_t^2\mathbf{Z}_t'\mathbf{Z}_t - E(\epsilon_t^2\mathbf{Z}_t'\mathbf{Z}_t) \xrightarrow{\text{a. s.}} \mathbf{0}.$$

Convergence in probability then follows from Theorem 2.24.

Next consider

$$2n^{-1}\sum_{t=1}^{n}(\tilde{\beta}_n - \beta_o)'\mathbf{X}_t'\boldsymbol{\epsilon}_t\mathbf{Z}_t'\mathbf{Z}_t.$$

This can be written as the sum of k matrices. The i, j element of the κth term ($\kappa = 1, \ldots, k$) in this sum can be written

$$(\tilde{\beta}_{n\kappa} - \beta_{o\kappa})2n^{-1}\sum_{t=1}^{n}\mathbf{X}_{t\kappa}\mathbf{Z}_{ti}\mathbf{Z}_{tj}\boldsymbol{\epsilon}_t$$

under the conditions given $(\tilde{\beta}_{n\kappa} - \beta_{o\kappa}) \xrightarrow{p} 0$; further,

$$E|\mathbf{X}_{t\kappa}\mathbf{Z}_{ti}\mathbf{Z}_{tj}\boldsymbol{\epsilon}_t| \le E(|\mathbf{X}_{t\kappa}\mathbf{Z}_{ti}|^2)^{1/2}E(|\mathbf{Z}_{tj}\boldsymbol{\epsilon}_t|^2)^{1/2}$$

by the Cauchy–Schwartz inequality. Since assumption (iva) guarantees that

$$E(|\mathbf{X}_{t\kappa}\mathbf{Z}_{ti}|^2) < \infty$$

and, by (iiib),

$$E(|\mathbf{Z}_{tj}\boldsymbol{\epsilon}_t|^2) < \infty,$$

it follows that

$$E|\mathbf{X}_{t\kappa}\mathbf{Z}_{ti}\mathbf{Z}_{tj}\boldsymbol{\epsilon}_t| < \infty,$$

so, by the ergodic theorem,

$$n^{-1}\sum_{t=1}^{n}\mathbf{X}_{t\kappa}\mathbf{Z}_{ti}\mathbf{Z}_{tj}\boldsymbol{\epsilon}_t - E(\mathbf{X}_{t\kappa}\mathbf{Z}_{ti}\mathbf{Z}_{tj}\boldsymbol{\epsilon}_t) \xrightarrow{\text{a. s.}} 0.$$

This implies that $2n^{-1}\sum_{t=1}^{n}\mathbf{X}_{t\kappa}\mathbf{Z}_{ti}\mathbf{Z}_{tj}\boldsymbol{\epsilon}_t$ is $O_p(1)$, so that

$$(\tilde{\beta}_{n\kappa} - \beta_{o\kappa})2n^{-1}\sum_{t=1}^{n}\mathbf{X}_{t\kappa}\mathbf{Z}_{ti}\mathbf{Z}_{tj}\boldsymbol{\epsilon}_t \xrightarrow{p} 0$$

by Corollary 2.36. It follows from Exercise 2.35 that

$$2n^{-1}\sum_{t=1}^{1}(\tilde{\beta}_n - \beta_o)'\mathbf{X}_t'\boldsymbol{\epsilon}_t\mathbf{Z}_t'\mathbf{Z}_t \xrightarrow{p} \mathbf{0}.$$

Finally, consider

$$n^{-1}\sum_{t=1}^{n}(\tilde{\beta}_n-\beta_o)'X_t'X_t(\tilde{\beta}_n-\beta_o)Z_t'Z_t.$$

This can be written as the sum of k^2 matrices, where the i, j element of the κ, λth ($\kappa, \lambda = 1, \ldots, k$) term has the form

$$(\tilde{\beta}_{n\kappa}-\beta_{o\kappa})(\tilde{\beta}_{n\lambda}-\beta_{o\lambda})n^{-1}\sum_{t=1}^{n}X_{t\kappa}X_{t\lambda}Z_{ti}Z_{tj}.$$

Under the conditions given, $(\tilde{\beta}_{n\lambda}-\beta_{o\lambda})\xrightarrow{p}0$, $\lambda = 1, \ldots, k$; further, the Cauchy–Schwartz inequality applies to yield

$$E|X_{t\kappa}X_{t\lambda}Z_{ti}Z_{tj}| < \infty,$$

given assumption (ivb), so, by the ergodic theorem,

$$n^{-1}\sum_{t=1}^{n}X_{t\kappa}X_{t\lambda}Z_{ti}Z_{tj}-E(X_{t\kappa}X_{t\lambda}Z_{ti}Z_{tj})\xrightarrow{a.s.}0.$$

This implies that $n^{-1}\sum_{t=1}^{n}X_{t\kappa}X_{t\lambda}Z_{ti}Z_{tj}$ is $O_p(1)$, so that

$$(\tilde{\beta}_{n\kappa}-\beta_{o\kappa})(\tilde{\beta}_{n\lambda}-\beta_{o\lambda})n^{-1}\sum_{t=1}^{n}X_{t\kappa}X_{t\lambda}Z_{ti}Z_{tj}\xrightarrow{p}0$$

by Corollary 2.36. It follows from Exercise 2.35 that

$$n^{-1}\sum_{t=1}^{n}(\tilde{\beta}_n-\beta_o)'X_t'X_t(\tilde{\beta}_n-\beta_o)Z_t'Z_t\xrightarrow{p}\mathbf{0}.$$

It follows that $\hat{V}_n - V \xrightarrow{p} \mathbf{0}$ by Exercise 2.35. Since V is positive definite given (iiic), it follows from Proposition 2.30 that $\hat{V}_n^{-1} - V^{-1} \xrightarrow{p} \mathbf{0}$.

Comparing the conditions of this result with those of Theorem 5.24, we see that we have strengthened moment condition (iva) and that this, together with the other assumptions, implies assumption (v) of Theorem 5.24. An immediate corollary of this fact is that the conclusions of Theorem 5.24 hold under the conditions of Theorem 6.3.

COROLLARY 6.4: Suppose conditions (i)–(iv) of Theorem 6.3 hold. Then $D^{-1}\sqrt{n}(\tilde{\beta}_n-\beta_o)\overset{A}{\sim}N(\mathbf{0}, \mathbf{I})$ where

$$D \equiv (Q'PQ)^{-1}Q'PVPQ(Q'PQ)^{-1}.$$

Further, $\hat{D}_n - D \xrightarrow{p} \mathbf{0}$, where

$$\hat{\mathbf{D}}_n = (\mathbf{X}'\mathbf{Z}\hat{\mathbf{P}}_n\mathbf{Z}'\mathbf{X}/n^2)^{-1}(\mathbf{X}'\mathbf{Z}/n)\hat{\mathbf{P}}_n\hat{\mathbf{V}}_n\hat{\mathbf{P}}_n(\mathbf{Z}'\mathbf{X}/n)(\mathbf{X}'\mathbf{Z}\hat{\mathbf{P}}_n\mathbf{Z}'\mathbf{X}/n^2)^{-1}.$$

Proof: Immediate from Theorem 5.24 and Theorem 6.3.

The usefulness of this result arises in situations in which it is inappropriate to assume that

$$E(\epsilon_{thl}^2|\mathbf{W}_{th}) = \sigma_o^2,$$

for example, when the errors obey an ARCH model (Engle [1982]), e.g., for $p = 1$, it is known that

$$E(\epsilon_t^2|\mathbf{W}_t) = \rho_1\epsilon_{t-1}^2 + \rho_2\epsilon_{t-2}^2 + \cdots + \rho_\tau\epsilon_{t-\tau}^2, \qquad \tau < \infty.$$

Note that $\mathbf{W}_t$ must contain current and lagged values of $\mathbf{X}_t$ and $\mathbf{y}_{t-1}$ in this instance.

The results of Theorem 6.3 and Corollary 6.4 suggest a simple two-step procedure for obtaining the efficient estimator of Proposition 4.45, i.e.,

$$\boldsymbol{\beta}_n^* = (\mathbf{X}'\mathbf{Z}\hat{\mathbf{V}}_n^{-1}\mathbf{Z}'\mathbf{X})^{-1}\mathbf{X}'\mathbf{Z}\hat{\mathbf{V}}_n^{-1}\mathbf{Z}'\mathbf{y}.$$

First, one obtains a consistent estimator for $\boldsymbol{\beta}_o$, for example, the 2SLS estimator,

$$\tilde{\boldsymbol{\beta}}_n = (\mathbf{X}'\mathbf{Z}(\mathbf{Z}'\mathbf{Z})^{-1}\mathbf{Z}'\mathbf{X})^{-1}\mathbf{X}'\mathbf{Z}(\mathbf{Z}'\mathbf{Z})^{-1}\mathbf{Z}'\mathbf{y},$$

and forms

$$\hat{\mathbf{V}}_n = n^{-1}\sum_{t=1}^{n}\mathbf{Z}_t'\tilde{\boldsymbol{\epsilon}}_t\tilde{\boldsymbol{\epsilon}}_t'\mathbf{Z}_t,$$

where $\tilde{\boldsymbol{\epsilon}}_t \equiv \mathbf{y}_t - \mathbf{X}_t\tilde{\boldsymbol{\beta}}_n$. Second, this estimator is then used to compute the efficient estimator $\boldsymbol{\beta}_n^*$. Because $\boldsymbol{\beta}_n^*$ can be computed in this way, it is called the *two-stage instrumental variables* (2SIV) estimator, introduced by White [1982]. Formally, we have the following result.

COROLLARY 6.5: Suppose that

(i) $\mathbf{y} = \mathbf{X}\boldsymbol{\beta}_o + \boldsymbol{\epsilon}$;
(ii) $\{(\mathbf{Z}_t, \mathbf{X}_t, \boldsymbol{\epsilon}_t)'\}$ is a stationary ergodic sequence;
(iii) (a) $\{\mathbf{Z}_t'\boldsymbol{\epsilon}_t, \mathfrak{F}_t\}$ is a martingale difference sequence;
(b) $E|Z_{thi}\epsilon_{th}|^2 < \infty$, $h = 1, \ldots, p$, $i = 1, \ldots, l$;
(c) $\mathbf{V}_n \equiv \text{var}(n^{-1/2}\mathbf{Z}'\boldsymbol{\epsilon}) = \text{var}(\mathbf{Z}_t'\boldsymbol{\epsilon}_t) \equiv \mathbf{V}$ is positive definite;

(iv) (a) $E|\mathbf{Z}_{thi}\mathbf{X}_{thj}|^2 < \infty$, $h = 1, \ldots, p$, $i = 1, \ldots, l$, $j = 1, \ldots, k$, and $E|\mathbf{Z}_{thi}|^2 < \infty$, $h = 1, \ldots, p$, $i = 1, \ldots, l$;
(b) $\mathbf{Q}_n \equiv E(\mathbf{Z}'\mathbf{X}/n) = E(\mathbf{Z}_t'\mathbf{X}_t) \equiv \mathbf{Q}$ has full column rank;
(c) $\mathbf{L}_n \equiv E(\mathbf{Z}'\mathbf{Z}/n) = E(\mathbf{Z}_t'\mathbf{Z}_t) \equiv \mathbf{L}$ is positive definite.

Define

$$\hat{\mathbf{V}}_n \equiv n^{-1} \sum_{t=1}^{n} \mathbf{Z}_t'\tilde{\boldsymbol{\epsilon}}_t\tilde{\boldsymbol{\epsilon}}_t'\mathbf{Z}_t,$$

where $\tilde{\boldsymbol{\epsilon}}_t \equiv \mathbf{y}_t - \mathbf{X}_t\tilde{\boldsymbol{\beta}}_n$, $\tilde{\boldsymbol{\beta}}_n \equiv (\mathbf{X}'\mathbf{Z}(\mathbf{Z}'\mathbf{Z})^{-1}\mathbf{Z}'\mathbf{X})^{-1}\mathbf{X}'\mathbf{Z}(\mathbf{Z}'\mathbf{Z})^{-1}\mathbf{Z}'\mathbf{y}$, and define

$$\boldsymbol{\beta}_n^* \equiv (\mathbf{X}'\mathbf{Z}\hat{\mathbf{V}}_n^{-1}\mathbf{Z}'\mathbf{X})^{-1}\mathbf{X}'\mathbf{Z}\hat{\mathbf{V}}_n^{-1}\mathbf{Z}'\mathbf{y}.$$

Then $\mathbf{D}^{-1/2}\sqrt{n}(\boldsymbol{\beta}_n^* - \boldsymbol{\beta}_o) \overset{A}{\sim} N(\mathbf{0}, \mathbf{I})$, where

$$\mathbf{D} = (\mathbf{Q}'\mathbf{V}^{-1}\mathbf{Q})^{-1}.$$

Further, $\hat{\mathbf{D}}_n - \mathbf{D} \xrightarrow{p} \mathbf{0}$, where

$$\hat{\mathbf{D}}_n = (\mathbf{X}'\mathbf{Z}\hat{\mathbf{V}}_n^{-1}\mathbf{Z}'\mathbf{X}/n^2)^{-1}.$$

Proof: Conditions (i)–(iv) ensure that Theorem 6.3 holds for $\tilde{\boldsymbol{\beta}}_n$. (Note that the second part of (iva) is redundant if $\mathbf{X}_t$ contains a constant.) Next set $\hat{\mathbf{P}}_n = \hat{\mathbf{V}}_n^{-1}$ in Corollary 6.4. Then $\mathbf{P} = \mathbf{V}^{-1}$, and the result follows.

This result is the most explicit asymptotic normality result obtained so far, because all of the conditions are stated directly in terms of the stochastic properties of the instrumental variables, regressors, and errors. The remainder of the asymptotic normality results stated in this chapter will also share this convenient feature.

We note that results for the OLS estimator follow at a special case upon setting $\mathbf{Z}_t = \mathbf{X}_t$ and that results for the i.i.d. case follow as immediate corollaries, since an i.i.d. sequence is a stationary ergodic martingale difference sequence when $E(\mathbf{Z}_t'\boldsymbol{\epsilon}_t) = \mathbf{0}$.

Analogous results hold for heterogeneous sequences. Because the proofs are completely parallel to those just given, they are left as an exercise for the reader.

EXERCISE 6.6: Prove the following result. Suppose

(i) $\mathbf{y} = \mathbf{X}\boldsymbol{\beta}_o + \boldsymbol{\epsilon}$;
(ii) $\{(\mathbf{Z}_t, \mathbf{X}_t, \boldsymbol{\epsilon}_t)'\}$ is a mixing sequence with either $\phi(m)$ of size $r/(2r-1)$, $r \geq 1$, or $\alpha(m)$ of size $r/(r-1)$, $r > 1$;
(iii) (a) $\{\mathbf{Z}_t'\boldsymbol{\epsilon}_t, \mathfrak{F}_t\}$ is a martingale difference sequence;
(b) $E|\mathbf{Z}_{thi}\boldsymbol{\epsilon}_{th}|^{2(r+\delta)} < \Delta < \infty$ for some $\delta > 0$ and all $h = 1, \ldots, p$, $i = 1, \ldots, l$, and t;
(c) $\mathbf{V}_n \equiv \text{var}(n^{-1/2}\mathbf{Z}'\boldsymbol{\epsilon})$ is uniformly positive definite;
(iv) (a) $E|\mathbf{Z}_{thi}\mathbf{X}_{thj}|^{2(r+\delta)} < \Delta < \infty$ for some $\delta > 0$ and all $h = 1, \ldots, p$, $i = 1, \ldots, l$, $j = 1, \ldots, k$, and t;
(b) $\mathbf{Q}_n \equiv E(\mathbf{Z}'\mathbf{X}/n)$ has uniformly full column rank;
(c) $\hat{\mathbf{P}}_n - \mathbf{P}_n \xrightarrow{p} \mathbf{0}$, where $\{\mathbf{P}_n\}$ is $O(1)$ and uniformly positive definite.

Then $\hat{\mathbf{V}}_n - \mathbf{V}_n \xrightarrow{p} \mathbf{0}$ and $\hat{\mathbf{V}}_n^{-1} - \mathbf{V}_n^{-1} \xrightarrow{p} \mathbf{0}$.

EXERCISE 6.7: Prove the following result. Suppose conditions (i)–(iv) of Exercise 6.6 hold. Then $\mathbf{D}_n^{-1/2}\sqrt{n}(\tilde{\boldsymbol{\beta}}_n - \boldsymbol{\beta}_o) \overset{A}{\sim} N(\mathbf{0}, \mathbf{I})$ where

$$\mathbf{D}_n \equiv (\mathbf{Q}_n'\mathbf{P}_n\mathbf{Q}_n)^{-1}\mathbf{Q}_n'\mathbf{P}_n\mathbf{V}_n\mathbf{P}_n\mathbf{Q}_n(\mathbf{Q}_n'\mathbf{P}_n\mathbf{Q}_n)^{-1}.$$

Further, $\hat{\mathbf{D}}_n - \mathbf{D}_n \xrightarrow{p} \mathbf{0}$, where

$$\hat{\mathbf{D}}_n = (\mathbf{X}'\mathbf{Z}\hat{\mathbf{P}}_n\mathbf{Z}'\mathbf{X}/n^2)^{-1}(\mathbf{X}'\mathbf{Z}/n)\hat{\mathbf{P}}_n\hat{\mathbf{V}}_n\hat{\mathbf{P}}_n(\mathbf{Z}'\mathbf{X}/n)(\mathbf{X}'\mathbf{Z}\hat{\mathbf{P}}_n\mathbf{Z}'\mathbf{X}/n^2)^{-1}.$$

EXERCISE 6.8: Prove the following result. Suppose

(i) $\mathbf{y} = \mathbf{X}\boldsymbol{\beta}_o + \boldsymbol{\epsilon}$;
(ii) $\{(\mathbf{Z}_t, \mathbf{X}_t, \boldsymbol{\epsilon}_t)'\}$ is a mixing sequence with either $\phi(m)$ of size $r(2r-1)$, $r \geq 1$, or $\alpha(m)$ of size $r/(r-1)$, $r > 1$;
(iii) (a) $\{\mathbf{Z}_t'\boldsymbol{\epsilon}_t, \mathfrak{F}_t\}$ is a martingale difference sequence;
(b) $E|\mathbf{Z}_{thi}\boldsymbol{\epsilon}_{th}|^{2(r+\delta)} < \Delta < \infty$ for some $\delta > 0$ and all $h = 1, \ldots, p$, $i = 1, \ldots, l$, and t;
(c) $\mathbf{V}_n \equiv \text{var}(n^{-1/2}\mathbf{Z}'\boldsymbol{\epsilon})$ is uniformly positive definite;
(iv) (a) $E|\mathbf{Z}_{thi}\mathbf{X}_{thj}|^{2(r+\delta)} < \Delta < \infty$ and $E|\mathbf{Z}_{thi}|^{2(r+\delta)} < \Delta < \infty$, for some $\delta > 0$ and all $h = 1, \ldots, p$, $i = 1, \ldots, l$, $j = 1, \ldots, k$, and t;
(b) $\mathbf{Q}_n \equiv E(\mathbf{Z}'\mathbf{X}/n)$ has uniformly full column rank;
(c) $\mathbf{L}_n \equiv E(\mathbf{Z}'\mathbf{Z}/n)$ is uniformly positive definite.

Define

$$\hat{\mathbf{V}}_n \equiv n^{-1} \sum_{t=1}^{n} \mathbf{Z}_t'\tilde{\boldsymbol{\epsilon}}_t\tilde{\boldsymbol{\epsilon}}_t'\mathbf{Z}_t,$$

where $\tilde{\boldsymbol{\epsilon}}_t = \mathbf{y}_t - \mathbf{X}_t\tilde{\boldsymbol{\beta}}_n$, $\tilde{\boldsymbol{\beta}}_n \equiv (\mathbf{X}'\mathbf{Z}(\mathbf{Z}'\mathbf{Z})^{-1}\mathbf{Z}'\mathbf{X})^{-1}\mathbf{X}'\mathbf{Z}(\mathbf{Z}'\mathbf{Z})^{-1}\mathbf{Z}'\mathbf{y}$, and

$$\boldsymbol{\beta}_n^* \equiv (\mathbf{X}'\mathbf{Z}\hat{\mathbf{V}}_n^{-1}\mathbf{Z}'\mathbf{X})^{-1}\mathbf{X}'\mathbf{Z}\hat{\mathbf{V}}_n^{-1}\mathbf{Z}'\mathbf{y}.$$

Then $\mathbf{D}_n^{-1/2}\sqrt{n}(\boldsymbol{\beta}_n^* - \boldsymbol{\beta}_o) \overset{A}{\sim} N(\mathbf{0}, \mathbf{I})$, where

$$\mathbf{D}_n = (\mathbf{Q}_n'\mathbf{V}_n^{-1}\mathbf{Q}_n)^{-1}.$$

Further, $\hat{\mathbf{D}}_n - \mathbf{D}_n \xrightarrow{p} \mathbf{0}$, where

$$\hat{\mathbf{D}}_n = (\mathbf{X}'\mathbf{Z}\hat{\mathbf{V}}_n^{-1}\mathbf{Z}'\mathbf{X}/n^2)^{-1}.$$

This result allows for unconditional heterogeneity not allowed by Corollary 6.5, at the expense of imposing somewhat stronger memory and moment conditions. Results for the independent case follow as corollaries because independent sequences are ϕ-mixing sequences for which we can set $r = 1$. Thus the present result contains the result of White [1982] as a special case but also allows for the presence of dynamic effects not permitted there, as well as applying explicitly to systems of equations or panel data.

VI.3 Case 2: $\boldsymbol{\Omega}_n$ (Block) Band Diagonal

Here we treat the case in which, for $m < \infty$,

$$\begin{aligned}
\mathbf{V}_n &= n^{-1}\sum_{t=1}^{n} E(\mathbf{Z}_t'\boldsymbol{\epsilon}_t\boldsymbol{\epsilon}_t'\mathbf{Z}_t) \\
&\quad + n^{-1}\sum_{t=2}^{n} E(\mathbf{Z}_t'\boldsymbol{\epsilon}_t\boldsymbol{\epsilon}_{t-1}'\mathbf{Z}_{t-1}) + E(\mathbf{Z}_{t-1}'\boldsymbol{\epsilon}_{t-1}\boldsymbol{\epsilon}_t'\mathbf{Z}_t) \\
&\quad + \cdots \\
&\quad + n^{-1}\sum_{t=m}^{n} E(\mathbf{Z}_t'\boldsymbol{\epsilon}_t\boldsymbol{\epsilon}_{t-m+1}'\mathbf{Z}_{t-m+1}) + E(\mathbf{Z}_{t-m+1}'\boldsymbol{\epsilon}_{t-m+1}\boldsymbol{\epsilon}_t'\mathbf{Z}_t) \\
&= n^{-1}\sum_{t=1}^{n} E(\mathbf{Z}_t'\boldsymbol{\epsilon}_t\boldsymbol{\epsilon}_t'\mathbf{Z}_t) \\
&\quad + n^{-1}\sum_{\tau=1}^{m-1}\sum_{t=\tau+1}^{n} E(\mathbf{Z}_t'\boldsymbol{\epsilon}_t\boldsymbol{\epsilon}_{t-\tau}'\mathbf{Z}_{t-\tau}) + E(\mathbf{Z}_{t-\tau}'\boldsymbol{\epsilon}_{t-\tau}\boldsymbol{\epsilon}_t'\mathbf{Z}_t).
\end{aligned}$$

Throughout, we shall assume that this structure is generated by a knowledge that $E(\mathbf{Z}_t'\boldsymbol{\epsilon}_t|\mathfrak{F}_{t-\mathrm{m}}) = 0$ for $1 \le m < \infty$ and adapted σ-fields

$\mathfrak{F}_t$. The other conditions imposed and methods of proof will be nearly identical to those of the preceding section. We consider estimators $\hat{\mathbf{V}}_n$ of the form

$$\hat{\mathbf{V}}_n = n^{-1} \sum_{t=1}^{n} \mathbf{Z}_t'\tilde{\boldsymbol{\epsilon}}_t\tilde{\boldsymbol{\epsilon}}_t'\mathbf{Z}_t$$

$$+ n^{-1} \sum_{\tau=1}^{m-1} \sum_{t=\tau+1}^{n} \mathbf{Z}_t'\tilde{\boldsymbol{\epsilon}}_t\tilde{\boldsymbol{\epsilon}}_{t-\tau}'\mathbf{Z}_{t-\tau} + \mathbf{Z}_{t-\tau}'\tilde{\boldsymbol{\epsilon}}_{t-\tau}\tilde{\boldsymbol{\epsilon}}_t'\mathbf{Z}_t.$$

It turns out that $\hat{\mathbf{V}}_n - \mathbf{V}_n \xrightarrow{p} \mathbf{0}$ under general conditions, as we now demonstrate.

THEOREM 6.9: Suppose that

(i) $\mathbf{y} = \mathbf{X}\boldsymbol{\beta}_o + \boldsymbol{\epsilon}$;
(ii) $\{(\mathbf{Z}_t, \mathbf{X}_t, \boldsymbol{\epsilon}_t)'\}$ is a stationary ergodic sequence;
(iii) (a) $E(\mathbf{Z}_t'\boldsymbol{\epsilon}_t|\mathfrak{F}_{t-m}) = \mathbf{0}$ for $1 \leq m < \infty$ and adapted σ-fields $\mathfrak{F}_t$;
(b) $E|\mathbf{Z}_{thi}\boldsymbol{\epsilon}_{th}|^2 < \infty$, $h = 1, \ldots, p$, $i = 1, \ldots, l$;
(c) $\mathbf{V}_n \equiv \text{var}(n^{-1/2}\mathbf{Z}'\boldsymbol{\epsilon}) = \mathbf{V}$ is positive definite;
(iv) (a) $E|\mathbf{Z}_{thi}\mathbf{X}_{thj}|^2 < \infty$, $h = 1, \ldots, p$, $i = 1, \ldots, l$, $j = 1, \ldots, k$;
(b) $\mathbf{Q}_n \equiv E(\mathbf{Z}'\mathbf{X}/n) = E(\mathbf{Z}_t'\mathbf{X}_t) \equiv \mathbf{Q}$ has full column rank;
(c) $\hat{\mathbf{P}}_n \xrightarrow{p} \mathbf{P}$, finite and positive definite.

Then $\hat{\mathbf{V}}_n - \mathbf{V} \xrightarrow{p} 0$ and $\hat{\mathbf{V}}_n^{-1} - \mathbf{V}^{-1} \xrightarrow{p} 0$.

Proof: By definition and assumption (iiia),

$$\hat{\mathbf{V}}_n - \mathbf{V} = n^{-1} \sum_{t=1}^{n} \mathbf{Z}_t'\tilde{\boldsymbol{\epsilon}}_t\tilde{\boldsymbol{\epsilon}}_t'\mathbf{Z}_t - E(\mathbf{Z}_t'\boldsymbol{\epsilon}_t\boldsymbol{\epsilon}_t'\mathbf{Z}_t)$$

$$+ n^{-1} \sum_{\tau=1}^{m-1} \sum_{t=\tau+1}^{n} [\mathbf{Z}_t'\tilde{\boldsymbol{\epsilon}}_t\tilde{\boldsymbol{\epsilon}}_{t-\tau}'\mathbf{Z}_{t-\tau} - E(\mathbf{Z}_t'\boldsymbol{\epsilon}_t\boldsymbol{\epsilon}_{t-\tau}'\mathbf{Z}_{t-\tau})$$

$$+ \mathbf{Z}_{t-\tau}'\tilde{\boldsymbol{\epsilon}}_{t-\tau}\tilde{\boldsymbol{\epsilon}}_t'\mathbf{Z}_t - E(\mathbf{Z}_{t-\tau}\boldsymbol{\epsilon}_{t-\tau}\boldsymbol{\epsilon}_t'\mathbf{Z}_t)].$$

If we can show that

$$n^{-1} \sum_{t=\tau+1}^{n} \mathbf{Z}_t'\tilde{\boldsymbol{\epsilon}}_t\tilde{\boldsymbol{\epsilon}}_{t-\tau}'\mathbf{Z}_{t-\tau}$$

$$- E(\mathbf{Z}_t'\boldsymbol{\epsilon}_t\boldsymbol{\epsilon}_{t-\tau}'\mathbf{Z}_{t-\tau}) \xrightarrow{p} \mathbf{0}, \qquad \tau = 0, \ldots, m-1,$$

then the desired result follows by Exercise 2.35. As before, we consider explicitly the case $p = 1$ and drop the h subscript. With $p = 1$, we have

$$n^{-1} \sum_{t=\tau+1}^{n} \mathbf{Z}_t' \tilde{\boldsymbol{\epsilon}}_t \tilde{\boldsymbol{\epsilon}}_{t-\tau} \mathbf{Z}_{t-\tau} - E(\mathbf{Z}_t' \boldsymbol{\epsilon}_t \boldsymbol{\epsilon}_{t-\tau} \mathbf{Z}_{t-\tau})$$

$$= ((n-\tau)/n)(n-\tau)^{-1} \sum_{t=\tau+1}^{n} \tilde{\boldsymbol{\epsilon}}_t \tilde{\boldsymbol{\epsilon}}_{t-\tau} \mathbf{Z}_t' \mathbf{Z}_{t-\tau} - E(\boldsymbol{\epsilon}_t \boldsymbol{\epsilon}_{t-\tau} \mathbf{Z}_t' \mathbf{Z}_{t-\tau}).$$

For $\tau = 0, \ldots, m-1$, we have $((n-\tau)/n) \rightarrow 1$ as $n \rightarrow \infty$, so it suffices to show that for $\tau = 0, \ldots, m-1$,

$$(n-\tau)^{-1} \sum_{t=\tau+1}^{n} \tilde{\boldsymbol{\epsilon}}_t \tilde{\boldsymbol{\epsilon}}_{t-\tau} \mathbf{Z}_t' \mathbf{Z}_{t-\tau} - E(\boldsymbol{\epsilon}_t \boldsymbol{\epsilon}_{t-\tau} \mathbf{Z}_t' \mathbf{Z}_{t-\tau}) \xrightarrow{p} \mathbf{0}.$$

Because $\tilde{\boldsymbol{\epsilon}}_t = \mathbf{y}_t - \mathbf{X}_t \tilde{\boldsymbol{\beta}}_n$, we have

$$(n-\tau)^{-1} \sum_{t=\tau+1}^{n} \tilde{\boldsymbol{\epsilon}}_t \tilde{\boldsymbol{\epsilon}}_{t-\tau} \mathbf{Z}_t' \mathbf{Z}_{t-\tau} - E(\boldsymbol{\epsilon}_t \boldsymbol{\epsilon}_{t-\tau} \mathbf{Z}_t' \mathbf{Z}_{t-\tau})$$

$$= (n-\tau)^{-1} \sum_{t=\tau+1}^{n} \boldsymbol{\epsilon}_t \boldsymbol{\epsilon}_{t-\tau} \mathbf{Z}_t' \mathbf{Z}_{t-\tau} - E(\boldsymbol{\epsilon}_t \boldsymbol{\epsilon}_{t-\tau} \mathbf{Z}_t' \mathbf{Z}_{t-\tau})$$

$$- (n-\tau)^{-1} \sum_{t=\tau+1}^{n} (\tilde{\boldsymbol{\beta}}_n - \boldsymbol{\beta}_o)' \mathbf{X}_t' \boldsymbol{\epsilon}_{t-\tau} \mathbf{Z}_t' \mathbf{Z}_{t-\tau}$$

$$- (n-\tau)^{-1} \sum_{t=\tau+1}^{n} (\tilde{\boldsymbol{\beta}}_n - \boldsymbol{\beta}_o)' \mathbf{X}_{t-\tau}' \boldsymbol{\epsilon}_t \mathbf{Z}_t' \mathbf{Z}_{t-\tau}$$

$$+ (n-\tau)^{-1} \sum_{t=\tau+1}^{n} (\tilde{\boldsymbol{\beta}}_n - \boldsymbol{\beta}_o) \mathbf{X}_t' \mathbf{X}_{t-\tau} (\tilde{\boldsymbol{\beta}}_n - \boldsymbol{\beta}_o) \mathbf{Z}_t' \mathbf{Z}_{t-\tau}.$$

The proof now proceeds identically to that of Theorem 6.3, and the result follows by showing that each term above converges in probability to zero. Note that Theorem 3.35 is invoked to guarantee that the summands involved are stationary and ergodic and that the Cauchy–Schwartz inequality is applied exactly as in the proof of Theorem 6.3 to guarantee the finiteness of the relevant expectations.

Results analogous to Corollaries 6.4 and 6.5 also follow similarly.

COROLLARY 6.10: Suppose conditions (i)–(iv) of Theorem 6.9 hold. Then $\mathbf{D}^{-1/2}\sqrt{n}(\tilde{\boldsymbol{\beta}}_n - \boldsymbol{\beta}_o) \overset{A}{\sim} N(\mathbf{0}, \mathbf{I})$, where

$$\mathbf{D} \equiv (\mathbf{Q}'\mathbf{P}\mathbf{Q})^{-1}\mathbf{Q}'\mathbf{P}\mathbf{V}\mathbf{P}\mathbf{Q}(\mathbf{Q}'\mathbf{P}\mathbf{Q})^{-1}.$$

Further, $\hat{\mathbf{D}}_n - \mathbf{D} \xrightarrow{p} \mathbf{0}$, where

$$\hat{\mathbf{D}}_n = (\mathbf{X}'\mathbf{Z}\hat{\mathbf{P}}_n\mathbf{Z}'\mathbf{X}/n^2)^{-1}(\mathbf{X}'\mathbf{Z}/n)\hat{\mathbf{P}}_n\hat{\mathbf{V}}_n\hat{\mathbf{P}}_n(\mathbf{Z}'\mathbf{X}/n)(\mathbf{X}'\mathbf{Z}\hat{\mathbf{P}}_n\mathbf{Z}'\mathbf{X}/n^2)^{-1}.$$

Proof: Immediate from Exercise 5.18 and Theorem 6.9.

COROLLARY 6.11: Suppose that

(i) $\mathbf{y} = \mathbf{X}\boldsymbol{\beta}_o + \boldsymbol{\epsilon}$;
(ii) $\{(\mathbf{Z}_t, \mathbf{X}_t, \boldsymbol{\epsilon}_t)'\}$ is a stationary ergodic sequence;
(iii) (a) $E(\mathbf{Z}_t'\boldsymbol{\epsilon}_t|\mathfrak{F}_{t-m}) = \mathbf{0}$ for $1 \le m < \infty$ and adapted σ-fields $\mathfrak{F}_t$;
(b) $E|\mathbf{Z}_{thi}\boldsymbol{\epsilon}_{th}|^2 < \infty$, $h = 1, \ldots, p$, $i = 1, \ldots, l$;
(c) $\mathbf{V}_n \equiv \text{var}(n^{-1/2}\mathbf{Z}'\boldsymbol{\epsilon}) = \mathbf{V}$ is positive definite;
(iv) (a) $E|\mathbf{Z}_{thi}\mathbf{X}_{thj}|^2 < \infty$, $h = 1, \ldots, p$, $i = 1, \ldots, l$, $j = 1, \ldots, k$, and $E|\mathbf{Z}_{thi}|^2 < \infty$, $h = 1, \ldots, p$, $i = 1, \ldots, l$;
(b) $\mathbf{Q}_n \equiv E(\mathbf{Z}'\mathbf{X}/n) = E(\mathbf{Z}_t'\mathbf{X}_t) \equiv \mathbf{Q}$ has full column rank;
(c) $\mathbf{L}_n \equiv E(\mathbf{Z}'\mathbf{Z}/n) = E(\mathbf{Z}_t'\mathbf{Z}_t) \equiv \mathbf{L}$ is positive definite.

Define

$$\hat{\mathbf{V}}_n \equiv n^{-1}\sum_{t=1}^{n} \mathbf{Z}_t'\tilde{\boldsymbol{\epsilon}}_t\tilde{\boldsymbol{\epsilon}}_t'\mathbf{Z}_t + n^{-1}\sum_{\tau=1}^{m-1}\sum_{t=\tau+1}^{n} \mathbf{Z}_t'\tilde{\boldsymbol{\epsilon}}_t\tilde{\boldsymbol{\epsilon}}_{t-\tau}'\mathbf{Z}_{t-\tau} + \mathbf{Z}_{t-\tau}'\tilde{\boldsymbol{\epsilon}}_{t-\tau}\tilde{\boldsymbol{\epsilon}}_t'\mathbf{Z}_t,$$

where $\tilde{\boldsymbol{\epsilon}}_t \equiv \mathbf{y}_t - \mathbf{X}_t\tilde{\boldsymbol{\beta}}_n$, $\tilde{\boldsymbol{\beta}}_n \equiv (\mathbf{X}'\mathbf{Z}(\mathbf{Z}'\mathbf{Z})^{-1}\mathbf{Z}'\mathbf{X})^{-1}\mathbf{X}'\mathbf{Z}(\mathbf{Z}'\mathbf{Z})^{-1}\mathbf{Z}'\mathbf{y}$, and define

$$\boldsymbol{\beta}_n^* \equiv (\mathbf{X}'\mathbf{Z}\hat{\mathbf{V}}_n^{-1}\mathbf{Z}'\mathbf{X})^{-1}\mathbf{X}'\mathbf{Z}\hat{\mathbf{V}}_n^{-1}\mathbf{Z}'\mathbf{y}.$$

Then $\mathbf{D}^{-1/2}\sqrt{n}(\boldsymbol{\beta}_n^* - \boldsymbol{\beta}_o) \overset{A}{\sim} N(\mathbf{0}, \mathbf{I})$, where

$$\mathbf{D} = (\mathbf{Q}'\mathbf{V}^{-1}\mathbf{Q})^{-1}.$$

Further, $\hat{\mathbf{D}}_n - \mathbf{D} \xrightarrow{p} \mathbf{0}$, where

$$\hat{\mathbf{D}}_n = (\mathbf{X}'\mathbf{Z}\hat{\mathbf{V}}_n^{-1}\mathbf{Z}'\mathbf{X}/n^2)^{-1}.$$

Proof: Conditions (i)–(iv) ensure that Theorem 6.9 holds for $\tilde{\boldsymbol{\beta}}_n$. Set $\hat{\mathbf{P}}_n = \hat{\mathbf{V}}_n^{-1}$ in Corollary 6.10. Then $\mathbf{P} = \mathbf{V}^{-1}$ and the result follows.

Results for mixing sequences parallel those of Exercises 6.6–6.8.

EXERCISE 6.12: Prove the following result. Suppose

(i) $\mathbf{y} = \mathbf{X}\boldsymbol{\beta}_o + \boldsymbol{\epsilon}$;
(ii) $\{(\mathbf{Z}_t, \mathbf{X}_t, \boldsymbol{\epsilon}_t)'\}$ is a mixing sequence with either $\phi(m)$ of size $r'/(r'-1), r' > 1$, or $\alpha(m)$ of size $r'/(r'-1), r' > 1$, where $r' = r + \delta$ for some $r \geq 1$ and $\delta > 0$;
(iii) (a) $E(\mathbf{Z}_t'\boldsymbol{\epsilon}_t|\mathfrak{F}_{t-m}) = \mathbf{0}$ for $1 \leq m < \infty$ and adapted σ-fields $\mathfrak{F}_t$;
(b) $E|\mathbf{Z}_{thi}\boldsymbol{\epsilon}_{th}|^{2r'} < \Delta < \infty$ for $r' > 1$ and all $h = 1, \ldots, p, i = 1, \ldots, l$, and t;
(c) $\mathbf{V}_{an} \equiv \text{var}(n^{-1/2} \sum_{t=a+1}^{a+n} \mathbf{Z}_t'\boldsymbol{\epsilon}_t)$, $\mathbf{V}_n \equiv \mathbf{V}_{0n}$, and there exists $\mathbf{V}$ finite and positive definite such that $\mathbf{V}_{an} - \mathbf{V} \to \mathbf{0}$ as $n \to \infty$ uniformly in a;
(iv) (a) $E|\mathbf{Z}_{thi}\mathbf{X}_{thj}|^{2r'} < \Delta < \infty$ for $r' > 1$ and all $h = 1, \ldots, p$, $i = 1, \ldots, l, j = 1, \ldots, k$, and t;
(b) $\mathbf{Q}_n \equiv E(\mathbf{Z}'\mathbf{X}/n)$ has uniformly full column rank;
(c) $\hat{\mathbf{P}}_n - \mathbf{P}_n \xrightarrow{p} \mathbf{0}$, where $\{\mathbf{P}_n\}$ is $O(1)$ and uniformly positive definite.

Then $\hat{\mathbf{V}}_n - \mathbf{V}_n \xrightarrow{p} \mathbf{0}$ and $\hat{\mathbf{V}}_n^{-1} - \mathbf{V}_n^{-1} \xrightarrow{p} \mathbf{0}$.

EXERCISE 6.13: Prove the following result. Suppose conditions (i)–(iv) of Exercise 6.12 hold. Then $\mathbf{D}_n^{-1/2}\sqrt{n}(\tilde{\boldsymbol{\beta}}_n - \boldsymbol{\beta}_o) \overset{A}{\sim} N(\mathbf{0}, \mathbf{I})$, where

$$\mathbf{D}_n \equiv (\mathbf{Q}_n'\mathbf{P}_n\mathbf{Q}_n)^{-1}\mathbf{Q}_n'\mathbf{P}_n\mathbf{V}_n\mathbf{P}_n\mathbf{Q}_n(\mathbf{Q}_n'\mathbf{P}_n\mathbf{Q}_n)^{-1}.$$

Further, $\hat{\mathbf{D}}_n - \mathbf{D}_n \xrightarrow{p} \mathbf{0}$, where

$$\hat{\mathbf{D}}_n = (\mathbf{X}'\mathbf{Z}\hat{\mathbf{P}}_n\mathbf{Z}'\mathbf{X}/n^2)^{-1}(\mathbf{X}'\mathbf{Z}/n)\hat{\mathbf{P}}_n\hat{\mathbf{V}}_n\hat{\mathbf{P}}_n(\mathbf{Z}'\mathbf{X}/n)(\mathbf{X}'\mathbf{Z}\hat{\mathbf{P}}_n\mathbf{Z}'\mathbf{X}/n^2)^{-1}.$$

(*Hint:* apply Theorem 5.22.)

EXERCISE 6.14: Prove the following result. Suppose

(i) $\mathbf{y} = \mathbf{X}\boldsymbol{\beta}_o + \boldsymbol{\epsilon}$;
(ii) $\{(\mathbf{Z}_t, \mathbf{X}_t, \boldsymbol{\epsilon}_t)'\}$ is a mixing sequence with either $\phi(m)$ of size $r'/(r'-1), r' > 1$, or $\alpha(m)$ of size $r'/(r'-1), r' > 1$, where $r' = r + \delta$ for some $r \geq 1$ and $\delta > 0$;
(iii) (a) $E(\mathbf{Z}_t'\boldsymbol{\epsilon}_t|\mathfrak{F}_{t-\mathrm{m}}) = \mathbf{0}$ for $1 \leq m < \infty$ and adapted σ-fields $\mathfrak{F}_t$;
(b) $E|\mathbf{Z}_{thi}\boldsymbol{\epsilon}_{th}|^{2r'} < \Delta < \infty$ for $r' > 1$ and all $h = 1, \ldots, p, i = 1, \ldots, l$, and t;
(c) $\mathbf{V}_{an} \equiv \text{var}(n^{-1/2} \sum_{t=a+1}^{a+n} \mathbf{Z}_t'\boldsymbol{\epsilon}_t)$, $\mathbf{V}_n \equiv \mathbf{V}_{0n}$, and there exists $\mathbf{V}$ finite and positive definite such that $\mathbf{V}_{an} - \mathbf{V} \to \mathbf{0}$ as $n \to \infty$ uniformly in a;

(iv) (a) $E|\mathbf{Z}_{thi}\mathbf{X}_{thj}|^{2r'} < \Delta < \infty$ and $E|\mathbf{Z}_{thi}|^{2r'} < \Delta < \infty$ for $r' > 1$, and all $h = 1, \ldots, p$, $i = 1, \ldots, l$, $j = 1, \ldots, k$, and t;

(b) $\mathbf{Q}_n \equiv E(\mathbf{Z}'\mathbf{X}/n)$ has uniformly full column rank;

(c) $\mathbf{L}_n \equiv E(\mathbf{Z}'\mathbf{Z}/n)$ is uniformly positive definite.

Define

$$\hat{\mathbf{V}}_n \equiv n^{-1} \sum_{t=1}^{n} \mathbf{Z}_t'\tilde{\boldsymbol{\epsilon}}_t\tilde{\boldsymbol{\epsilon}}_t'\mathbf{Z}_t + n^{-1} \sum_{\tau=1}^{m-1} \sum_{t=\tau+1}^{n} \mathbf{Z}_t'\tilde{\boldsymbol{\epsilon}}_t\tilde{\boldsymbol{\epsilon}}_{t-\tau}'\mathbf{Z}_{t-\tau} + \mathbf{Z}_{t-\tau}'\tilde{\boldsymbol{\epsilon}}_{t-\tau}\tilde{\boldsymbol{\epsilon}}_t'\mathbf{Z}_t,$$

where $\tilde{\boldsymbol{\epsilon}}_t \equiv \mathbf{y}_t - \mathbf{X}_t\tilde{\boldsymbol{\beta}}_n$, $\tilde{\boldsymbol{\beta}}_n \equiv (\mathbf{X}'\mathbf{Z}(\mathbf{Z}'\mathbf{Z})^{-1}\mathbf{Z}'\mathbf{X})^{-1}\mathbf{X}'\mathbf{Z}(\mathbf{Z}'\mathbf{Z})^{-1}\mathbf{Z}'y$, and define

$$\boldsymbol{\beta}_n^* \equiv (\mathbf{X}'\mathbf{Z}\hat{\mathbf{V}}_n\mathbf{Z}'\mathbf{X})^{-1}\mathbf{X}'\mathbf{Z}\hat{\mathbf{V}}_n^{-1}\mathbf{Z}'\mathbf{y}.$$

Then $\mathbf{D}_n^{-1/2}\sqrt{n}(\boldsymbol{\beta}_n^* - \boldsymbol{\beta}_o) \overset{A}{\sim} N(\mathbf{0}, \mathbf{I})$, where

$$\mathbf{D}_n = (\mathbf{Q}_n'\mathbf{V}_n^{-1}\mathbf{Q}_n)^{-1}.$$

Further, $\hat{\mathbf{D}}_n - \mathbf{D}_n \xrightarrow{p} \mathbf{0}$, where

$$\hat{\mathbf{D}}_n = (\mathbf{X}'\mathbf{Z}\hat{\mathbf{V}}_n^{-1}\mathbf{Z}'\mathbf{X}/n^2)^{-1}.$$

VI.4 Case 3: General Case

In this section we consider the general case in which

$$\mathbf{V}_n = n^{-1} \sum_{t=1}^{n} E(\mathbf{Z}_t'\boldsymbol{\epsilon}_t\boldsymbol{\epsilon}_t'\mathbf{Z}_t) + n^{-1} \sum_{\tau=1}^{n-1} \sum_{t=\tau+1}^{n} E(\mathbf{Z}_t'\boldsymbol{\epsilon}_t\boldsymbol{\epsilon}_{t-\tau}'\mathbf{Z}_t) + E(\mathbf{Z}_{t-\tau}'\boldsymbol{\epsilon}_{t-\tau}\boldsymbol{\epsilon}_t'\mathbf{Z}_t).$$

The essential restriction we impose is that as $\tau \to \infty$ the covariance between $\mathbf{Z}_t'\boldsymbol{\epsilon}_t$ and $\mathbf{Z}_{t-\tau}'\boldsymbol{\epsilon}_{t-\tau}$ goes to zero. This behavior is ensured by assuming that $\{(\mathbf{Z}_t, \mathbf{X}_t, \boldsymbol{\epsilon}_t)'\}$ is a mixing sequence. In the stationary case then, we replace ergodicity with mixing, which, as we saw in Chapter III, implies ergodicity.

The fact that mixing sequences are asymptotically uncorrelated is a consequence of the following lemma.

LEMMA 6.15: Let Z be a random variable measurable with respect to $\mathcal{B}_{n+m}^{\infty}$, such that $\|Z\|_q \equiv [E|Z|^q]^{1/q} < \infty$ for some $q > 1$, and let $1 \le r \le q$. Then

$$\|E(Z|\mathcal{B}_{-\infty}^{n}) - E(Z)\|_r \le 2[\phi(m)]^{1-1/q}\|Z\|_q$$

and

$$\|E(Z|\mathcal{B}_{-\infty}^{n}) - E(Z)\|_r \le 2(2^{1/r} + 1)[\alpha(m)]^{1/r-1/q}\|Z\|_q.$$

Proof: This follows immediately from Lemma 2.1 of McLeish [1975].

For mixing sequences, $\phi(m)$ or $\alpha(m)$ goes to zero as $m \to \infty$, so this result imposes bounds on the rate that the conditional expectation of Z, given the past up to period n, converges to the unconditional expectation as the time separation m gets larger and larger.

By setting $q = r = 2$ for ϕ-mixing sequences and $r = 2$, $q > 2$ for α-mixing sequences, we obtain the following result.

COROLLARY 6.16: Let $E(Z_n) = E(Z_{n+m}) = 0$ and suppose var $Z_n < \infty$, and for some $\delta > 0$, $E|Z_{n+m}|^{2+2\delta} < \infty$. Then

$$|E(Z_n Z_{n+m})| \le 2\phi(m)^{1/2}(\text{var } Z_n)^{1/2}(\text{var } Z_{n+m})^{1/2}$$

and

$$|E(Z_n Z_{n+m})| \le 2(2^{1/2} + 1)\alpha(m)^{\delta/(2+2\delta)}(\text{var } Z_n)^{1/2} \times (E|Z_{n+m}|^{2+2\delta})^{1/(2+2\delta)}.$$

Proof: By the law of iterated expectations,

$$\begin{aligned} E(Z_n Z_{n+m}) &= E(E(Z_n Z_{n+m}|\mathcal{B}_{-\infty}^{n})) \\ &= E(Z_n E(Z_{n+m}|\mathcal{B}_{-\infty}^{n})) \end{aligned}$$

by Proposition 3.65. It follows from the Cauchy–Schwartz inequality that

$$|E(Z_n Z_{n+m})| \le E(Z_n^2)^{1/2} E(E(Z_{n+m}|\mathcal{B}_{-\infty}^{n})^2)^{1/2}.$$

By Lemma 6.15, we have

$$E(E(Z_{n+m}|\mathcal{B}_{-\infty}^{n})^2)^{1/2} \le 2\phi(m)^{1/2}(\text{var } Z_{n+m})^{1/2}$$

and

$$E(E(Z_{n+m}|\mathcal{B}_{-\infty}^{n})^2)^{1/2} \le 2(2^{1/2} + 1)\alpha(m)^{\delta/(2+2\delta)}(E|Z_{n+m}|^{2+2\delta})^{1/(2+2\delta)},$$

where we set $q=r=2$ to obtain the first inequality and $r=2$, $q=2+2\delta$, $\delta>0$, to obtain the second inequality. Combining these inequalities yields the final result.

$$|E(Z_n Z_{n+m})| \leq 2\phi(m)^{1/2}(\text{var } Z_n)^{1/2}(\text{var } Z_{n+m})^{1/2}$$

and

$$|E(Z_n Z_{n+m})| \leq 2(2^{1/2}+1)\alpha(m)^{\delta/(2+2\delta)}(\text{var } Z_n)^{1/2} \times (E|Z_{n+m}|^{2+2\delta})^{1/(2+2\delta)}.$$

The direct implication of this result is that mixing sequences are asymptotically uncorrelated, because $\phi(m)\to 0$ or $\alpha(m)\to 0$ implies $|E(Z_n Z_{n+m})|\to 0$ as $m\to\infty$. For mixing sequences, it follows that $\mathbf{V}_n$ might be well approximated by

$$\tilde{\mathbf{V}}_n \equiv n^{-1}\sum_{t=1}^{n} E(\mathbf{Z}_t'\boldsymbol{\epsilon}_t\boldsymbol{\epsilon}_t'\mathbf{Z}_t) + n^{-1}\sum_{\tau=1}^{l}\sum_{t=\tau+1}^{n} E(\mathbf{Z}_t'\boldsymbol{\epsilon}_t\boldsymbol{\epsilon}_{t-\tau}'\mathbf{Z}_{t-\tau}) + E(\mathbf{Z}_{t-\tau}\boldsymbol{\epsilon}_{t-\tau}\boldsymbol{\epsilon}_t'\mathbf{Z}_t)$$

for some value l, because the neglected terms (those with $l<\tau\leq n$) will be small in absolute value if l is sufficiently large. Note, however, that if l is simply kept fixed as n grows, the number of neglected terms grows, and may grow in such a way that the sum of the neglected terms does not remain negligible.

This suggests that l will have to grow with n, so that the terms in $\mathbf{V}_n$ ignored by $\tilde{\mathbf{V}}_n$ remain negligible. Actually, we require that $\mathbf{V}_n - \tilde{\mathbf{V}}_n \to \mathbf{0}$ as $n\to\infty$, and this turns out to require additional restrictions on the size of $\phi(m)$ or $\alpha(m)$, as the next lemma demonstrates.

LEMMA 6.17: Let $\{Z_t\}$ be a scalar sequence such that $E(Z_t)=0$ and $E|Z_t|^{2+2\eta}<\Delta<\infty$ for some $\eta>0$, and all t. Define

$$\bar{\sigma}_n^2 \equiv \text{var}\left(n^{-1/2}\sum_{t=1}^{n} Z_t\right) = n^{-1}\sum_{t=1}^{n} E(Z_t^2) + n^{-1}\sum_{\tau=1}^{n-1}\sum_{t=\tau+1}^{n} E(Z_t Z_{t-\tau}) + E(Z_{t-\tau}Z_t),$$

and consider the approximation

$$\tilde{\sigma}_n^2 \equiv n^{-1} \sum_{t=1}^{n} E(Z_t^2) + n^{-1} \sum_{\tau=1}^{l} \sum_{t=\tau+1}^{n} E(Z_t Z_{t-\tau}) + E(Z_{t-\tau} Z_t).$$

If $l \to \infty$ as $n \to \infty$ and if either $\phi(m)$ is of size 2 or $\alpha(m)$ is of size $(2 + 2\eta)/\eta$, then $\bar{\sigma}_n^2 - \tilde{\sigma}_n^2 \to 0$ as $n \to \infty$.

Proof: By definition,

$$\bar{\sigma}_n^2 - \tilde{\sigma}_n^2 = n^{-1} \sum_{\tau=l+1}^{n-1} \sum_{t=\tau+1}^{n} E(Z_t Z_{t-\tau}) + E(Z_{t-\tau} Z_t).$$

Because

$$|\bar{\sigma}_n^2 - \tilde{\sigma}_n^2| \leq n^{-1} \sum_{\tau=l+1}^{n-1} \sum_{t=\tau+1}^{n} |E(Z_t Z_{t-\tau})| + |E(Z_{t-\tau} Z_t)|$$

by the triangle inequality, it suffices to show that

$$n^{-1} \sum_{\tau=l+1}^{n-1} \sum_{t=\tau+1}^{n} |E(Z_t Z_{t-\tau})| \to 0 \qquad \text{as} \quad n \to \infty.$$

By Corollary 6.16, we have

$$|E(Z_t Z_{t-\tau})| \leq 2\phi(\tau)^{1/2} (\text{var } Z_t)^{1/2} (\text{var } Z_{t-\tau})^{1/2}$$

and

$$|E(Z_t Z_{t-\tau})| \leq 2(2^{1/2} + 1)\alpha(\tau)^{\eta/(2+2\eta)} (\text{var } Z_{t-\tau})^{1/2} (E|Z_t|^{2+2\eta})^{1/(2+2\eta)}.$$

Because $E|Z_t|^{2+2\eta} < \Delta$ for all t by assumption, it follows that

$$\text{var } Z_t \leq [E|Z_t|^{2+2\eta}]^{2/(2+2\eta)} < \Delta^{1/1+\eta}$$

for all t by Jensen's inequality. Hence

$$|E(Z_t Z_{t-\tau})| \leq 2\phi(\tau)^{1/2} \Delta^{1/(1+\eta)}$$

and

$$|E(Z_t Z_{t-\tau}) \leq 2(2^{1/2} + 1)\alpha(\tau)^{\eta/(2+2\eta)} \Delta^{1/(1+\eta)}.$$

Set $\Delta' = 2\Delta^{1/(1+\eta)}$ and $\Delta^* = (2^{1/2} + 1)\Delta'$. Then

$$n^{-1}\sum_{\tau=l+1}^{n-1}\sum_{t=\tau+1}^{n}|E(Z_tZ_{t-\tau})| \leq n^{-1}\sum_{\tau=l+1}^{n-1}\sum_{t=\tau+1}^{n}\Delta'\phi(\tau)^{1/2}$$

and

$$n^{-1}\sum_{\tau=l+1}^{n-1}\sum_{t=\tau+1}^{n}|E(Z_tZ_{t-\tau})| \leq n^{-1}\sum_{\tau=l+1}^{n-1}\sum_{t=\tau+1}^{n}\Delta^*\alpha(\tau)^{\eta/(2+2\eta)}.$$

Now

$$\begin{aligned} n^{-1}\sum_{\tau=l+1}^{n-1}\sum_{t=\tau+1}^{n}\Delta'\phi(\tau)^{1/2} &= \Delta'\sum_{\tau=l+1}^{n-1}\phi(\tau)^{1/2}(n-\tau)/n \\ &< \Delta'\sum_{\tau=l+1}^{n-1}\phi(\tau)^{1/2} \end{aligned}$$

and

$$\begin{aligned} n^{-1}\sum_{\tau=l+1}^{n-1}\sum_{t=\tau+1}^{n}\Delta^*\alpha(\tau)^{\eta/(2+2\eta)} &= \Delta^*\sum_{\tau=l+1}^{n-1}\alpha(\tau)^{\eta/(2+2\eta)}(n-\tau)/n \\ &< \Delta^*\sum_{\tau=l+1}^{n-1}\alpha(\tau)^{\eta/(2+2\eta)}, \end{aligned}$$

so that

$$n^{-1}\sum_{\tau=l+1}^{n-1}\sum_{t=\tau+1}^{n}|E(Z_tZ_{t-\tau})| \leq \Delta'\sum_{\tau=l+1}^{n-1}\phi(\tau)^{1/2}$$

and

$$n^{-1}\sum_{\tau=l+1}^{n-1}\sum_{t=\tau+1}^{n}|E(Z_tZ_{t-\tau})| \leq \Delta^*\sum_{\tau=l+1}^{n-1}\alpha(\tau)^{\eta/(2+2\eta)}.$$

If $\phi(\tau)$ is of size 2, there exists $\Delta < \infty$ sufficiently large such that $\phi(\tau) < \Delta\tau^{-2-2\delta}$ for some $\delta > 0$. Hence

$$\sum_{\tau=0}^{n}\phi(\tau)^{1/2} < \Delta\sum_{\tau=0}^{n}\tau^{-1-\delta},$$

so that

$$\lim_{n\to\infty}\sum_{\tau=0}^{n}\phi(\tau)^{1/2} < \lim_{n\to\infty}\Delta\sum_{\tau=0}^{n}\tau^{-1-\delta} < \infty.$$

Because

$$\sum_{\tau=l+1}^{n-1} \phi(\tau)^{1/2} = \sum_{\tau=0}^{n-1} \phi(\tau)^{1/2} - \sum_{\tau=0}^{l} \phi(\tau)^{1/2},$$

it follows that if $\phi(\tau)$ is of size 2, then

$$\lim_{n\to\infty} \sum_{\tau=l+1}^{n-1} \phi(\tau)^{1/2} = \lim_{n\to\infty} \sum_{\tau=0}^{n-1} \phi(\tau)^{1/2} - \lim_{n\to\infty} \sum_{\tau=0}^{l} \phi(\tau)^{1/2}$$
$$= 0,$$

provided $l \to \infty$ as $n \to \infty$. A similar argument establishes that, if $\alpha(\tau)$ is of size $(2 + 2\eta)/\eta$, then

$$\lim_{n\to\infty} \sum_{\tau=l+1}^{n-1} \alpha(\tau)^{\eta/(2+2\eta)} = 0.$$

Hence

$$n^{-1} \sum_{\tau=l+1}^{n-1} \sum_{t=\tau+1}^{n} |E(Z_t Z_{t-\tau})| \to 0 \qquad \text{as} \quad n \to \infty,$$

so $|\bar{\sigma}_n^2 - \tilde{\sigma}_{nl}^2| \to 0$ as $n \to \infty$.

The implication of this result is that, if $l \to \infty$ as $n \to \infty$ and either $\phi(m)$ or $\alpha(m)$ decreases sufficiently fast, then finding a consistent estimator for $\mathbf{V}_n$ amounts to finding a consistent estimator for $\tilde{\mathbf{V}}_n$. The form of $\tilde{\mathbf{V}}_n$ is nearly the same as the form of $\mathbf{V}_n$ in the preceding section. The essential difference is that here l increases with n, whereas in the previous section, m is fixed. This means that the method of proof used in establishing the consistency of $\hat{\mathbf{V}}_n$ in the previous section no longer applies, because the result of Exercise 2.35 does not apply to sums with a growing number of terms. Nevertheless, the estimator

$$\hat{\mathbf{V}}_n = n^{-1} \sum_{t=1}^{n} \mathbf{Z}_t' \tilde{\boldsymbol{\epsilon}}_t \tilde{\boldsymbol{\epsilon}}_t' \mathbf{Z}_t$$
$$+ n^{-1} \sum_{\tau=1}^{l} \sum_{t=\tau+1}^{n} \mathbf{Z}_t' \tilde{\boldsymbol{\epsilon}}_t \tilde{\boldsymbol{\epsilon}}_{t-\tau}' \mathbf{Z}_t + \mathbf{Z}_{t-\tau}' \tilde{\boldsymbol{\epsilon}}_{t-\tau} \tilde{\boldsymbol{\epsilon}}_t' \mathbf{Z}_t$$

is consistent for $\tilde{\mathbf{V}}_n$ (hence $\mathbf{V}_n$) provided that l does not grow too fast.

The proof of the consistency of $\hat{\mathbf{V}}_n$ relies heavily on Lemma 6.19

below, which in turn requires a lemma closely related to Theorem 3.49.

LEMMA 6.18: Let $g_{t\tau}$ be a measurable function onto $\mathbb{R}^k$ for each t and τ and define $Z_{t\tau} \equiv g_{t\tau}(\mathcal{X}_t, \mathcal{X}_{t-1}, \ldots, \mathcal{X}_{t-\tau})$, $t = \tau + 1, \ldots$. If the sequence of $1 \times q$ vectors $\{\mathcal{X}_t\}$ has mixing coefficients $\phi(m)$ and $\alpha(m)$, then $\{Z_{t\tau}\}$ has mixing coefficients $\phi_\tau(m) \le \phi(m - \tau)$ and $\alpha_\tau(m) \le \alpha(m - \tau)$ for $m > \tau$ and $\phi_\tau(m) \le 1$, $\alpha_\tau(m) \le 1$ for $m \le \tau$.

Proof: Let $\mathcal{B}_a^b \equiv \sigma(\mathcal{X}_a, \ldots, \mathcal{X}_b)$ and let $\mathcal{G}_a^b \equiv \sigma(Z_{a\tau}, \ldots, Z_{b\tau})$. Define $\phi_\tau(m) \equiv \sup_n \phi(\mathcal{G}_{-\infty}^n, \mathcal{G}_{n+m}^\infty)$. Since g is measurable, $\mathcal{G}_a^b \subset \mathfrak{F}_{a-\tau}^b$. It follows that $\phi_\tau(m) \le \sup_n \phi(\mathfrak{F}_{-\infty}^n, \mathfrak{F}_{n+m-\tau}^\infty)$, so

$$\phi_\tau(m) \le \begin{cases} 1 & \text{for} \quad m \le \tau, \\ \phi(m - \tau) & \text{for} \quad m > \tau. \end{cases}$$

The result for the α coefficients follows by replacing ϕ with α.

In fact, Theorem 3.49 follows as a corollary to this result.

The next lemma establishes an inequality which allows application of Chebyshev's inequality. It provides the key to proving the consistency of $\hat{\mathbf{V}}_n$.

LEMMA 6.19: Let $g_{t\tau}$ be a measurable function onto $\mathbb{R}^k$ for each t and τ, and define $Z_{t\tau} \equiv g_{t\tau}(\mathcal{X}_t, \ldots, \mathcal{X}_{t-\tau})$, $t = \tau + 1, \ldots$. Suppose $\{\mathcal{X}_t\}$ is a mixing sequence of $1 \times q$ vectors with either $\phi(m)$ of size 2 or $\alpha(m)$ of size $(2 + 2\eta)/\eta$, $\eta > 0$. If $E|Z_{t\tau}|^{2+2\eta} \le \Delta < \infty$ and $E(Z_{t\tau}) = 0$ for all t and τ, then there exists $\Delta^* < \infty$ independent of τ such that

$$E\left(\left[\sum_{t=\tau+1}^{n} Z_{t\tau}\right]^2\right) \le (n - \tau)\Delta^*.$$

Proof: By the triangle inequality

$$E\left(\left[\sum_{t=\tau+1}^{n} Z_{t\tau}\right]^2\right) = \sum_{t=\tau+1}^{n} E(Z_{t\tau}^2) + \sum_{m=\tau+1}^{n-1} \sum_{t=m+1}^{n} E(Z_{t\tau} Z_{t-m\tau})$$

$$\le \sum_{t=\tau+1}^{n} E(Z_{t\tau}^2) + \sum_{m=\tau+1}^{n-1} \sum_{t=m+1}^{n} |E(Z_{t\tau} Z_{t-m\tau})|.$$

By Corollary 6.16

$$|E(Z_{t\tau} Z_{t-m\tau})| \le 2\phi_\tau(m)^{1/2} (\text{var } Z_{t\tau})^{1/2} (\text{var } Z_{t-m\tau})^{1/2}$$

or

$$|E(Z_{t\tau}Z_{t-m\tau})| \leq 2(2^{1/2}+1)\alpha_\tau(m)^{\eta/(2+2\eta)}(\text{var } Z_{t-m\tau})^{1/2} \\ \times (E|Z_{t\tau}|^{2+2\eta})^{1/(2+2\eta)},$$

where $\phi_\tau(m)$ and $\alpha_\tau(m)$ are the mixing coefficients associated with $\{Z_{t\tau}\}$. Since $E|Z_{t\tau}|^{2+2\eta} \leq \Delta$ by assumption, $E|Z_{t\tau}|^2 \leq \Delta'$ by Jensen's inequality, where $\Delta' = \Delta^{1/(1+\eta)}$. It follows that

$$E\left(\left[\sum_{t=\tau+1}^{n} Z_{t\tau}\right]^2\right) \leq (n-\tau)\Delta' + 2\Delta' \sum_{m=\tau+1}^{n-1} \phi_\tau(m)^{1/2}(n-m)$$

or

$$E\left(\left[\sum_{t=\tau+1}^{n} Z_{t\tau}\right]^2\right) \leq (n-\tau)\Delta' + 2\Delta'' \sum_{m=\tau+1}^{n-1} \alpha_\tau(m)^{\eta/(2+2\eta)}(n-m),$$

where $\Delta'' = (2^{1/2}+1)\Delta'$. Because $Z_{t\tau} = g_{t\tau}(\mathcal{X}_t, \ldots, \mathcal{X}_{t-\tau})$ it follows from Lemma 6.18 that $\phi_\tau(m) \leq \phi(m-\tau)$ and $\alpha_\tau(m) \leq \alpha(m-\tau)$. Substituting this into the expressions above and reindexing the summation gives

$$E\left(\left[\sum_{t=\tau+1}^{n} Z_{t\tau}\right]^2\right) \leq (n-\tau)\Delta' + 2\Delta' \sum_{m=1}^{n-\tau-1} \phi(m)^{1/2}(n-m-\tau)$$

or

$$E\left(\left[\sum_{t=\tau+1}^{n} Z_{t-\tau}\right]^2\right) \\ \leq (n-\tau)\Delta' + 2\Delta'' \sum_{m=1}^{n-\tau-1} \alpha(m)^{\eta/(2+2\eta)}(n-m-\tau).$$

Because $n-m-\tau < n-\tau$ and because $\sum_{m=0}^{\infty} \phi(m)^{1/2} < \infty$ when $\phi(m)$ is of size 2 or $\sum_{m=0}^{\infty} \alpha(m)^{\eta/(2+2\eta)} < \infty$ when $\alpha(m)$ is of size $(2+2\eta)/\eta$, it follows that

$$E\left(\left[\sum_{t=\tau+1}^{n} Z_{t\tau}\right]^2\right) \leq (n-\tau)\Delta^*,$$

where either $\Delta^* = \Delta' + 2\Delta' \sum_{m=0}^{\infty} \phi(m)^{1/2}$ or $\Delta^* = \Delta' + 2\Delta'' \sum_{m=0}^{\infty} \alpha(m)^{\eta/(2+2\eta)}$.

The results for stationary mixing sequences follow as corollaries to the results for general mixing sequences, so we state only the results for general mixing sequences.

THEOREM 6.20: Suppose

(i) $\mathbf{y} = \mathbf{X}\beta_o + \epsilon$;
(ii) $\{(\mathbf{Z}_t, \mathbf{X}_t, \epsilon_t)'\}$ is a mixing sequence with either $\phi(m)$ of size 2 or $\alpha(m)$ of size $2(r+\delta)/(r+\delta-1)$, $r > 1$;
(iii) (a) $E(\mathbf{Z}_t'\epsilon_t) = 0$;
(b) $E|\mathbf{Z}_{thi}\epsilon_{th}|^{4(r+\delta)} < \Delta < \infty$ for some $\delta > 0$, $h = 1, \ldots, p$, $i = 1, \ldots, l$, and all t;
(c) $\mathbf{V}_{an} \equiv \text{var}(n^{-1/2} \sum_{t=a+1}^{a+n} \mathbf{Z}_t'\epsilon_t)$, $\mathbf{V}_n \equiv \mathbf{V}_{0n}$, and there exists $\mathbf{V}$ finite and nonsingular such that $\mathbf{V}_{an} - \mathbf{V} \to \mathbf{0}$ as $n \to \infty$ uniformly in a;
(iv) (a) $E|\mathbf{Z}_{thi}\mathbf{X}_{thj}|^{4(r+\delta)} < \Delta < \infty$ for some $\delta > 0$ and all $h = 1, \ldots, p$, $i = 1, \ldots, l$, $j = 1, \ldots, k$, and t;
(b) $\mathbf{Q}_n \equiv E(\mathbf{Z}'\mathbf{X}/n)$ has uniformly full column rank;
(c) $\hat{\mathbf{P}}_n - \mathbf{P}_n \xrightarrow{p} \mathbf{0}$, where $\{\mathbf{P}_n\}$ is $O(1)$ and uniformly positive definite.

Define $\hat{\mathbf{V}}_n$ as above. If $l \to \infty$ as $n \to \infty$ such that $l = o(n^{1/3})$, then $\hat{\mathbf{V}}_n - \mathbf{V} \xrightarrow{p} \mathbf{0}$ and $\hat{\mathbf{V}}_n^{-1} - \mathbf{V}^{-1} \xrightarrow{p} \mathbf{0}$.

Proof: First we show that $\hat{\mathbf{V}}_n - \tilde{\mathbf{V}}_n \xrightarrow{p} \mathbf{0}$ and then invoke Lemma 6.17 to show that $\tilde{\mathbf{V}}_n - \mathbf{V} \to \mathbf{0}$, so that $\hat{\mathbf{V}}_n - \mathbf{V} \xrightarrow{p} \mathbf{0}$ by Exercise 2.35.

By definition,

$$\hat{\mathbf{V}}_n - \tilde{\mathbf{V}}_n = n^{-1} \sum_{t=1}^{n} \mathbf{Z}_t'\tilde{\epsilon}_t\tilde{\epsilon}_t'\mathbf{Z}_t - E(\mathbf{Z}_t'\epsilon_t\epsilon_t'\mathbf{Z}_t)$$
$$+ n^{-1} \sum_{\tau=1}^{l} \sum_{t=\tau+1}^{n} \{\mathbf{Z}_t'\tilde{\epsilon}_t\tilde{\epsilon}_{t-\tau}'\mathbf{Z}_{t-\tau} - E(\mathbf{Z}_t'\epsilon_t\epsilon_{t-\tau}'\mathbf{Z}_{t-\tau})$$
$$+ \mathbf{Z}_{t-\tau}'\tilde{\epsilon}_{t-\tau}\tilde{\epsilon}_t'\mathbf{Z}_t - E(\mathbf{Z}_{t-\tau}'\epsilon_{t-\tau}\epsilon_t'\mathbf{Z}_t)\}.$$

The first term, $n^{-1} \sum_{t=1}^{n} \mathbf{Z}_t'\tilde{\epsilon}_t\tilde{\epsilon}_t'\mathbf{Z}_t - E(\mathbf{Z}_t'\epsilon_t\epsilon_t'\mathbf{Z}_t)$, converges to zero in probability by an argument identical to that of Theorem 6.3, except that Corollary 3.48 is applied instead of the ergodic theorem 3.34. We note that because $2 > r/(2r-1)$ for all $r \geq 1$, it follows that $\phi(m)$ is of size $r/(2r-1)$ if $\phi(m)$ is of size 2 and because $2(r+\delta)/(r+\delta-1) > r/(r-1)$ for all $r > 1$, it follows that $\alpha(m)$ is of size $r/(r-1)$ if $\alpha(m)$ is of size $2(r+\delta)/(r+\delta-1)$.

The desired result then follows if we can show that

$$n^{-1} \sum_{\tau=1}^{l} \sum_{t=\tau+1}^{n} \mathbf{Z}_t'\tilde{\epsilon}_t\tilde{\epsilon}_{t-\tau}'\mathbf{Z}_{t-\tau} - E(\mathbf{Z}_t'\epsilon_t\epsilon_{t-\tau}'\mathbf{Z}_{t-\tau}) \xrightarrow{p} 0.$$

Again we consider only the case where $p = 1$, and ignore the h subscript in what follows. Because $\tilde{\boldsymbol{\epsilon}}_t = \mathbf{y}_t - \mathbf{X}_t\tilde{\boldsymbol{\beta}}_n$, it follows that, with $p = 1$,

$$\begin{aligned}
n^{-1} \sum_{\tau=1}^{l} \sum_{t=\tau+1}^{n} & \tilde{\boldsymbol{\epsilon}}_t \tilde{\boldsymbol{\epsilon}}_{t-\tau} \mathbf{Z}_t' \mathbf{Z}_{t-\tau} - E(\boldsymbol{\epsilon}_t \boldsymbol{\epsilon}_{t-\tau} \mathbf{Z}_t' \mathbf{Z}_{t-\tau}) \\
&= n^{-1} \sum_{\tau=1}^{l} \sum_{t=\tau+1}^{n} \boldsymbol{\epsilon}_t \boldsymbol{\epsilon}_{t-\tau} \mathbf{Z}_t' \mathbf{Z}_{t-\tau} - E(\boldsymbol{\epsilon}_t \boldsymbol{\epsilon}_{t-\tau} \mathbf{Z}_t' \mathbf{Z}_{t-\tau}) \\
&\quad - n^{-1} \sum_{\tau=1}^{l} \sum_{t=\tau+1}^{n} (\tilde{\boldsymbol{\beta}}_n - \boldsymbol{\beta}_o)' \mathbf{X}_t' \boldsymbol{\epsilon}_{t-\tau} \mathbf{Z}_t' \mathbf{Z}_{t-\tau} \\
&\quad - n^{-1} \sum_{\tau=1}^{l} \sum_{t=\tau+1}^{n} (\tilde{\boldsymbol{\beta}}_n - \boldsymbol{\beta}_o)' \mathbf{X}_{t-\tau}' \boldsymbol{\epsilon}_t \mathbf{Z}_t' \mathbf{Z}_{t-\tau} \\
&\quad + n^{-1} \sum_{\tau=1}^{l} \sum_{t=\tau+1}^{n} (\tilde{\boldsymbol{\beta}}_n - \boldsymbol{\beta}_o)' \mathbf{X}_t' \mathbf{X}_{t-\tau} (\tilde{\boldsymbol{\beta}}_n - \boldsymbol{\beta}_o) \mathbf{Z}_t' \mathbf{Z}_{t-\tau}.
\end{aligned}$$

We show that each term on the right above converges to zero in probability by making repeated use of Lemma 6.19.

Consider the first term and set $Z_{t\tau} = \boldsymbol{\epsilon}_t \boldsymbol{\epsilon}_{t-\tau} \mathbf{Z}_t' \mathbf{Z}_{t-\tau} - E(\boldsymbol{\epsilon}_t \boldsymbol{\epsilon}_{t-\tau} \mathbf{Z}_t' \mathbf{Z}_{t-\tau})$. Letting $\mathcal{X}_t$ correspond to $(\mathbf{Z}_t, \boldsymbol{\epsilon}_t)$ it is straightforward to verify that the conditions of Lemma 6.19 hold, where $\eta = \mathrm{r} + \delta - 1$. Hence

$$\begin{aligned}
P\left[\left| n^{-1} \sum_{\tau=1}^{l} \sum_{t=\tau+1}^{n} Z_{t\tau} \right| \geq \epsilon \right] &\leq P\left[\sum_{\tau=1}^{l} \left| n^{-1} \sum_{t=\tau+1}^{n} Z_{t\tau} \right| \geq \epsilon \right] \\
&\leq \sum_{\tau=1}^{l} P\left[\left| n^{-1} \sum_{t=\tau+1}^{n} Z_{t\tau} \right| \geq \epsilon/l \right]
\end{aligned}$$

by the implication rule (Proposition 2.26). By Chebyshev's inequality, we have

$$P\left[\left| n^{-1} \sum_{t=\tau+1}^{n} Z_{t\tau} \right| \geq \epsilon/l \right] \leq E\left(\left[\sum_{t=\tau+1}^{n} Z_{t\tau} \right]^2 \right) l^2/\epsilon^2 n^2.$$

From Lemma 6.19, $E([\Sigma_{t=\tau+1}^{n} Z_{t\tau}]^2) \leq (n - \tau)\Delta^* < n\Delta^*$, so

$$P\left[\left| n^{-1} \sum_{t=\tau+1}^{n} Z_{t\tau} \right| \geq \epsilon/l \right] \leq \Delta^* l^2/\epsilon^2 n,$$

which implies

$$P\left[\left|n^{-1}\sum_{\tau=1}^{l}\sum_{t=\tau+1}^{n} \mathcal{Z}_{t\tau}\right| \geq \epsilon\right] \leq \Delta^* l^3/\epsilon^2 n.$$

Since $l = o(n^{1/3})$, it follows that $\Delta l^3/\epsilon^2 n \longrightarrow 0$, which implies that

$$n^{-1}\sum_{\tau=1}^{l}\sum_{t=\tau+1}^{n} \boldsymbol{\epsilon}_t\boldsymbol{\epsilon}_{t-\tau}\mathbf{Z}_t'\mathbf{Z}_{t-\tau} - E(\boldsymbol{\epsilon}_t\boldsymbol{\epsilon}_{t-\tau}\mathbf{Z}_t'\mathbf{Z}_{t-\tau}) \xrightarrow{p} 0,$$

since ϵ is arbitrary.

Next consider

$$n^{-1}\sum_{\tau=1}^{l}\sum_{t=\tau+1}^{n} (\tilde{\beta}_n - \beta_o)'\mathbf{X}_t'\boldsymbol{\epsilon}_{t-\tau}\mathbf{Z}_t'\mathbf{Z}_{t-\tau}.$$

This can be written as the sum of k matrices. The i,jth element of the κth term ($\kappa = 1, \ldots, k$) in this sum can be written as

$$\begin{aligned}
&(\tilde{\beta}_{n\kappa} - \beta_{o\kappa})n^{-1}\sum_{\tau=1}^{l}\sum_{t=\tau+1}^{n} \mathbf{X}_{t\kappa}\mathbf{Z}_{ti}\mathbf{Z}_{t-\tau j}\boldsymbol{\epsilon}_{t-\tau}\\
&\quad = (\tilde{\beta}_{n\kappa} - \beta_{o\kappa})n^{-1}\sum_{\tau=1}^{l}\sum_{t=\tau+1}^{n} \mathbf{X}_{t\kappa}\mathbf{Z}_{ti}\mathbf{Z}_{t-\tau j}\boldsymbol{\epsilon}_{t-\tau}\\
&\qquad - E(\mathbf{X}_{t\kappa}\mathbf{Z}_{ti}\mathbf{Z}_{t-\tau j}\boldsymbol{\epsilon}_{t-\tau})\\
&\qquad + (\tilde{\beta}_{n\kappa} - \beta_{o\kappa})n^{-1}\sum_{\tau=1}^{l}\sum_{t=\tau+1}^{n} E(\mathbf{X}_{t\kappa}\mathbf{Z}_{ti}\mathbf{Z}_{t-\tau j}\boldsymbol{\epsilon}_{t-\tau}).
\end{aligned}$$

By argument analogous to that above, it follows from Lemma 6.19 that

$$n^{-1}\sum_{\tau=1}^{l}\sum_{t=\tau+1}^{n} \mathbf{X}_{t\kappa}\mathbf{Z}_{ti}\mathbf{Z}_{t-\tau j}\boldsymbol{\epsilon}_{t-\tau} - E(\mathbf{X}_{t\kappa}\mathbf{Z}_{ti}\mathbf{Z}_{t-\tau j}\boldsymbol{\epsilon}_{t-\tau}) \xrightarrow{p} 0,$$

setting $\mathcal{Z}_{t\tau} = \mathbf{X}_{t\kappa}\mathbf{Z}_{ti}\mathbf{Z}_{t-\tau j}\boldsymbol{\epsilon}_{t-\tau} - E(\mathbf{X}_{t\kappa}\mathbf{Z}_{ti}\mathbf{Z}_{t-\tau j}\boldsymbol{\epsilon}_{t-\tau})$ and letting $\mathcal{X}_t$ correspond to $(\mathbf{Z}_t, \mathbf{X}_t, \boldsymbol{\epsilon}_t)$. Since $(\tilde{\beta}_{n\kappa} - \beta_{o\kappa}) \xrightarrow{p} 0$ under the conditions of the theorem, it follows from Exercise 2.35(ii) that

$$(\tilde{\beta}_{n\kappa} - \beta_{o\kappa})n^{-1}\sum_{\tau=1}^{l}\sum_{t=\tau+1}^{n} \mathbf{X}_{t\kappa}\mathbf{Z}_{ti}\mathbf{Z}_{t-\tau j}\boldsymbol{\epsilon}_{t-\tau} \xrightarrow{p} 0$$

provided that

$$(\tilde{\beta}_{n\kappa}-\beta_{o\kappa})n^{-1}\sum_{\tau=1}^{l}\sum_{t=\tau+1}^{n}E(\mathbf{X}_{t\kappa}\mathbf{Z}_{ti}\mathbf{Z}_{t-\tau j}\boldsymbol{\epsilon}_{t-\tau})\xrightarrow{p}0.$$

Multiplying and dividing by $n^{1/2}$ gives

$$(\tilde{\beta}_{n\kappa}-\beta_{o\kappa})n^{-1}\sum_{\tau=1}^{l}\sum_{t=\tau+1}^{n}E(\mathbf{X}_{t\kappa}\mathbf{Z}_{ti}\mathbf{Z}_{t-\tau j}\boldsymbol{\epsilon}_{t-\tau})$$

$$=n^{1/2}(\tilde{\beta}_{n\kappa}-\beta_{o\kappa})n^{-3/2}\sum_{\tau=1}^{l}\sum_{t=\tau+1}^{n}E(\mathbf{X}_{t\kappa}\mathbf{Z}_{ti}\mathbf{Z}_{t-\tau j}\boldsymbol{\epsilon}_{t-\tau}).$$

Now the triangle inequality implies

$$\left|n^{-3/2}\sum_{\tau=1}^{l}\sum_{t=\tau+1}^{n}E(\mathbf{X}_{t\kappa}\mathbf{Z}_{ti}\mathbf{Z}_{t-\tau j}\boldsymbol{\epsilon}_{t-\tau})\right|$$

$$<n^{-3/2}\sum_{\tau=1}^{l}\sum_{t=\tau+1}^{n}|E(\mathbf{X}_{t\kappa}\mathbf{Z}_{ti}\mathbf{Z}_{t-\tau j}\boldsymbol{\epsilon}_{t-\tau})|.$$

Given (iii.b) and (iv.b), Jensen's inequality and the Cauchy–Schwartz inequality ensure that there exists $\Delta'<\infty$ such that $|E(\mathbf{X}_t\mathbf{Z}_{ti}\mathbf{Z}_{t-\tau j}\boldsymbol{\epsilon}_{t-\tau})|<\Delta'$. Hence

$$\left|n^{-3/2}\sum_{\tau=1}^{l}\sum_{t=\tau+1}^{n}E(\mathbf{X}_{t\kappa}\mathbf{Z}_{ti}\mathbf{Z}_{t-\tau j}\boldsymbol{\epsilon}_{t-\tau})\right|<l\Delta' n^{-1/2}$$

Since $l=o(n^{1/3})$, the term above is $o(1)$. Since $n^{1/2}(\tilde{\beta}_{n\kappa}-\beta_{o\kappa})$ is $\mathbf{O}_p(1)$, it follows from Exercise 2.35(iii) that

$$(\tilde{\beta}_{n\kappa}-\beta_{o\kappa})n^{-1}\sum_{\tau=1}^{l}\sum_{t=\tau+1}^{n}E(\mathbf{X}_{t\kappa}\mathbf{Z}_{ti}\mathbf{Z}_{t-\tau j}\boldsymbol{\epsilon}_{t-\tau})\xrightarrow{p}0;$$

so that

$$n^{-1}\sum_{\tau=1}^{l}\sum_{t=\tau+1}^{n}(\tilde{\beta}_n-\beta_o)'\mathbf{X}_t'\boldsymbol{\epsilon}_{t-\tau}\mathbf{Z}_t'\mathbf{Z}_{t-\tau}\xrightarrow{p}0$$

by Exercise 2.35(ii).

Now consider

$$n^{-1}\sum_{\tau=1}^{l}\sum_{t=\tau+1}^{n}(\tilde{\beta}_n-\beta_o)'\mathbf{X}_t'\mathbf{X}_{t-\tau}(\tilde{\beta}_n-\beta_o)\mathbf{Z}_t'\mathbf{Z}_{t-\tau}.$$

This can be written as the sum of k^2 matrices where the i,jth element of the κ, λ term ($\kappa,\lambda = 1, \ldots, k$) has the form

$$(\tilde{\beta}_{n\kappa} - \beta_{o\kappa})(\tilde{\beta}_{n\lambda} - \beta_{o\lambda})n^{-1} \sum_{\tau=1}^{l} \sum_{t=\tau+1}^{n} \mathbf{X}_{t\kappa}\mathbf{X}_{t-\tau\lambda}\mathbf{Z}_{ti}\mathbf{Z}_{t-\tau j}.$$

Argument analogous to that above shows that

$$(\tilde{\beta}_{n\kappa} - \beta_{o\kappa})n^{-1} \sum_{\tau=1}^{l} \sum_{t=\tau+1}^{n} \mathbf{X}_{t\kappa}\mathbf{X}_{t-\tau\lambda}\mathbf{Z}_{ti}\mathbf{Z}_{t-\tau j} \xrightarrow{p} 0$$

and since $\tilde{\beta}_n \xrightarrow{p} \beta_o$,

$$(\tilde{\beta}_{n\kappa} - \beta_{o\kappa})(\tilde{\beta}_{n\lambda} - \beta_o)n^{-1} \sum_{\tau=1}^{l} \sum_{t=\tau+1}^{n} \mathbf{X}_{t\kappa}\mathbf{X}_{t-\tau\lambda}\mathbf{Z}_{ti}\mathbf{Z}_{t-\tau j} \xrightarrow{p} 0$$

by Exercise 2.35(ii). It follows that

$$n^{-1} \sum_{\tau=1}^{l} \sum_{t=\tau+1}^{n} (\tilde{\beta}_n - \beta_o)'\mathbf{X}_t'\mathbf{X}_{t-\tau}(\tilde{\beta}_n - \beta_o)\mathbf{Z}_t'\mathbf{Z}_{t-\tau}$$

by Exercise 2.35(ii). Exercise 2.35(ii) now implies that $\hat{\mathbf{V}}_n - \tilde{\mathbf{V}}_n \xrightarrow{p} 0$.

By Lemma 6.17, $\tilde{\mathbf{V}}_n - \mathbf{V} \to 0$ under the conditions given, so that $\hat{\mathbf{V}}_n - \mathbf{V} \xrightarrow{p} 0$ by Exercise 2.35(ii), and $\hat{\mathbf{V}}_n^{-1} - \mathbf{V}^{-1} \xrightarrow{p} 0$ from Proposition 2.27.

This result says that $\hat{\mathbf{V}}_n$ is consistent for $\mathbf{V}$ as long as l grows with n, but more slowly than $n^{1/3}$. Beyond this, the present result offers little guidance as to how to choose l, and the question of what the optimal growth rate for l might be is an interesting open question. White and Domowitz [1984] discuss an heuristically appealing way of choosing l; however, there is no evidence as yet to demonstrate that any way of choosing l yields an estimator of $\mathbf{V}$ which is a useful approximation in samples of the size typically available to economists. The present result is a "possibility theorem," since it shows that $\mathbf{V}$ can be consistently estimated with very little structure imposed on the covariance structure of the regressors and errors. The practical usefulness of these results in applications has yet to be demonstrated.

COROLLARY 6.21: Suppose the conditions of Theorem 6.20 hold. Then $\mathbf{D}_n^{-1/2}\sqrt{n}(\tilde{\beta}_n - \beta_o) \overset{A}{\sim} N(\mathbf{0}, \mathbf{I})$, where

$$\mathbf{D}_n \equiv (\mathbf{Q}_n'\mathbf{P}_n\mathbf{Q}_n)^{-1}\mathbf{Q}_n'\mathbf{P}_n\mathbf{V}\mathbf{P}_n\mathbf{Q}_n(\mathbf{Q}_n'\mathbf{P}_n\mathbf{Q}_n)^{-1}.$$

Further, $\hat{\mathbf{D}}_n - \mathbf{D}_n \xrightarrow{p} \mathbf{0}$, where

$$\hat{\mathbf{D}}_n = (\mathbf{X}'\mathbf{Z}\hat{\mathbf{P}}_n\mathbf{Z}'\mathbf{X}/n^2)^{-1}(\mathbf{X}'\mathbf{Z}/n)\hat{\mathbf{P}}_n\hat{\mathbf{V}}_n\hat{\mathbf{P}}_n(\mathbf{Z}'\mathbf{Z}/n)(\mathbf{X}'\mathbf{Z}\hat{\mathbf{P}}_n\mathbf{Z}'\mathbf{X}/n^2)^{-1}.$$

Proof: Immediate from Theorem 5.22 (set $r' = r + \delta$) and Theorem 6.20.

This result is extremely general because it contains versions of all preceding asymptotic normality results as special cases while making very minimal assumptions on the error covariance structure.

Finally, we state the general result for the 2SIV estimator.

COROLLARY 6.22: Suppose

(i) $\mathbf{y} = \mathbf{X}\boldsymbol{\beta}_o + \boldsymbol{\epsilon}$;

(ii) $\{(\mathbf{Z}_t, \mathbf{X}_t, \boldsymbol{\epsilon}_t)'\}$ is a mixing sequence with either $\phi(m)$ of size 2 or $\alpha(m)$ of size $2(r+\delta)/(r+\delta-1)$, $r > 1$;

(iii) (a) $E(\mathbf{Z}_t'\boldsymbol{\epsilon}_t) = 0$;

(b) $E|\mathbf{Z}_{thi}\boldsymbol{\epsilon}_{th}|^{4(r+\delta)} < \Delta < \infty$ for some $\delta > 0$ and all $h = 1, \ldots, p$, $i = 1, \ldots, l$, and t;

(c) $\mathbf{V}_{an} \equiv \text{var}(n^{-1/2} \sum_{t=a+1}^{a+n} \mathbf{Z}_t'\boldsymbol{\epsilon}_t)$, $\mathbf{V}_n \equiv \mathbf{V}_{0n}$, and there exists $\mathbf{V}$ finite and positive definite such that $\mathbf{V}_{an} - \mathbf{V} \to \mathbf{0}$ as $n \to \infty$, uniformly in a;

(iv) (a) $E|\mathbf{Z}_{thi}\mathbf{X}_{thj}|^{4(r+\delta)} < \Delta < \infty$ and $E|Z_{thi}|^{2(r+\delta)} < \Delta < \infty$ for some $\delta > 0$ and all $h = 1, \ldots, p$, $i = 1, \ldots, l$, and $j = 1, \ldots, k$ for t;

(b) $\mathbf{Q}_n \equiv E(\mathbf{Z}'\mathbf{X}/n)$ has uniformly full column rank;

(c) $\mathbf{L}_n \equiv E(\mathbf{Z}'\mathbf{Z}/n)$ is uniformly positive definite.

Define

$$\hat{\mathbf{V}}_n \equiv n^{-1} \sum_{t=1}^{n} \mathbf{Z}_t'\tilde{\boldsymbol{\epsilon}}_t\tilde{\boldsymbol{\epsilon}}_t'\mathbf{Z}_t + n^{-1} \sum_{\tau=1}^{l} \sum_{t=\tau+1}^{n} \mathbf{Z}_t'\tilde{\boldsymbol{\epsilon}}_t\tilde{\boldsymbol{\epsilon}}_{t-\tau}'\mathbf{Z}_{t-\tau} + \mathbf{Z}_{t-\tau}'\tilde{\boldsymbol{\epsilon}}_{t-\tau}\tilde{\boldsymbol{\epsilon}}_t'\mathbf{Z}_t,$$

where $\tilde{\boldsymbol{\epsilon}}_t \equiv \mathbf{y}_t - \mathbf{X}_t\tilde{\boldsymbol{\beta}}_n$, $\tilde{\boldsymbol{\beta}}_n \equiv (\mathbf{X}'\mathbf{Z}(\mathbf{Z}'\mathbf{Z})^{-1}\mathbf{Z}'\mathbf{X})^{-1}\mathbf{X}'\mathbf{Z}(\mathbf{Z}'\mathbf{Z})^{-1}\mathbf{Z}'\mathbf{y}$, and define

$$\boldsymbol{\beta}_n^* \equiv (\mathbf{X}'\mathbf{Z}\hat{\mathbf{V}}_n^{-1}\mathbf{Z}'\mathbf{X})^{-1}\mathbf{X}'\mathbf{Z}\hat{\mathbf{V}}_n^{-1}\mathbf{Z}'\mathbf{y}.$$

If $l \to \infty$ as $n \to \infty$ such that $l = o(n^{1/2})$, then $\mathbf{D}_n^{-1/2}\sqrt{n}(\boldsymbol{\beta}_n^* - \boldsymbol{\beta}_o) \overset{A}{\sim} N(\mathbf{0}, \mathbf{I})$, where

$$\mathbf{D}_n = (\mathbf{Q}_n'\mathbf{V}_n^{-1}\mathbf{Q}_n)^{-1}.$$

Further, $\hat{\mathbf{D}}_n - \mathbf{D}_n \xrightarrow{p} \mathbf{0}$, where

$$\hat{\mathbf{D}}_n = (\mathbf{X}'\mathbf{Z}\hat{\mathbf{V}}_n^{-1}\mathbf{Z}'\mathbf{X}/n^2)^{-1}.$$

Proof: Conditions (i)–(iv) ensure that Theorem 6.20 holds for $\tilde{\boldsymbol{\beta}}_n$. Set $\hat{\mathbf{P}}_n = \hat{\mathbf{V}}_n^{-1}$ in Corollary 6.21. Then $\mathbf{P} = \mathbf{V}^{-1}$ and the result follows.

References

Bartle, R. G. [1966]. "The Elements of Integration." New York: Wiley.

Engle, R. [1982]. Autoregressive conditional heteroskedasticity with estimates of the variance of United Kingdom inflations, *Econometrica* **50**:987–1008.

McLeish, D. L. [1975]. A maximal inequality and dependent strong laws, *Ann. Probab.* **3**:826–836.

White, H. [1982]. Instrumental variables regression with independent observations, *Econometrica* **50**:483–500.

White, H., and Domowitz, I. [1984]. Nonlinear regression with dependent observations, *Econometrica,* forthcoming.

CHAPTER VII

Efficient Estimation with Estimated Error Covariance Matrices

In Chapter IV we saw that if $\mathbf{C}_n$ or the error covariance matrix $\mathbf{\Omega}_n = \mathbf{C}_n\mathbf{C}_n'$ is known, then efficient instrumental variables estimators analogous to GLS may be available. In most practical circumstances, $\mathbf{\Omega}_n$ is unknown so the results of Theorem 4.57 are not immediately available. However, it is often assumed that the form of $\mathbf{\Omega}_n$ is known up to a finite number of unknown parameters. Typically, sufficient information is available to estimate these parameters consistently, and estimators analogous to the GLS estimator can be formed by replacing $\mathbf{\Omega}_n$ with an estimator, say, $\hat{\mathbf{\Omega}}_n$. The purpose of this chapter is to examine some important special cases in which an asymptotically efficient estimator can be obtained by replacing $\mathbf{\Omega}_n$ by $\hat{\mathbf{\Omega}}_n$. Because the cases we consider are covered by Theorem 4.58, we do not need to know $\mathbf{C}_n$. A general treatment in which the elements of $\mathbf{C}_n$ or $\mathbf{\Omega}_n$ can be arbitrary known parametric functions of the data is beyond the scope of this book.

Because results for OLS estimators follow as special cases from results for IV estimators, we consider only the latter. Results for independent observations will follow as corollaries to results for martingale difference sequences, and results for stationary processes will follow as corollaries to results for mixing processes. We treat only the mixing processes for economy of exposition and also because these allow inclusion of fixed (nonstochastic) instrumental variables and regressors whereas the stationarity assumption rules these out.

VII.1 General Results

The estimators which are the focus of this chapter are the estimators

$$\beta_n^* = (\mathbf{X}'\mathbf{Z}(\mathbf{Z}'\mathbf{Z})^{-1}\mathbf{Z}'\mathbf{X})^{-1}\mathbf{X}'\mathbf{Z}(\mathbf{Z}'\mathbf{Z})^{-1}\mathbf{Z}'\mathbf{y},$$

where $\mathbf{X} = \mathbf{C}_n^{-1}\tilde{\mathbf{X}}$ and $\mathbf{y} = \mathbf{C}_n^{-1}\tilde{\mathbf{y}}$, as in Section 3 of Chapter IV. To obtain easily stated results, we shall assume that the instrumental variables are given by $\mathbf{Z} = \mathbf{C}_n^{-1}\tilde{\mathbf{Z}}$ for suitable choice of $\tilde{\mathbf{Z}}$. For the cases we consider, this entails no real loss of generality. Thus we can write

$$\beta_n^* = (\tilde{\mathbf{X}}'\mathbf{\Omega}_n^{-1}\tilde{\mathbf{Z}}(\tilde{\mathbf{Z}}'\mathbf{\Omega}_n^{-1}\tilde{\mathbf{Z}})^{-1}\tilde{\mathbf{Z}}'\mathbf{\Omega}_n^{-1}\tilde{\mathbf{X}})^{-1}\tilde{\mathbf{X}}'\mathbf{\Omega}_n^{-1}\tilde{\mathbf{Z}}(\tilde{\mathbf{Z}}'\mathbf{\Omega}_n^{-1}\tilde{\mathbf{Z}})^{-1}\tilde{\mathbf{Z}}'\mathbf{\Omega}_n^{-1}\tilde{\mathbf{y}}.$$

We are concerned with the properties of the EGIV (estimated GIV) estimator

$$\hat{\beta}_n^* = (\tilde{\mathbf{X}}'\hat{\mathbf{\Omega}}_n^{-1}\tilde{\mathbf{Z}}(\tilde{\mathbf{Z}}'\hat{\mathbf{\Omega}}_n^{-1}\tilde{\mathbf{Z}})^{-1}\tilde{\mathbf{Z}}'\hat{\mathbf{\Omega}}_n^{-1}\tilde{\mathbf{X}})^{-1}\tilde{\mathbf{X}}'\hat{\mathbf{\Omega}}_n^{-1}\tilde{\mathbf{Z}}(\tilde{\mathbf{Z}}'\hat{\mathbf{\Omega}}_n^{-1}\tilde{\mathbf{Z}})^{-1}\tilde{\mathbf{Z}}'\hat{\mathbf{\Omega}}_n^{-1}\tilde{\mathbf{y}}.$$

The fundamental result from which subsequent results follow is a simple extension of a result given by Theil [1971, p. 399].

THEOREM 7.1: Suppose that the conditions of Theorem 4.57 hold with $\tilde{\mathbf{Z}} = \mathbf{C}_n\mathbf{Z}$. If there exists $\hat{\mathbf{\Omega}}_n$ such that

(i) $\tilde{\mathbf{Z}}'(\mathbf{\Omega}_n^{-1} - \hat{\mathbf{\Omega}}_n^{-1})\tilde{\boldsymbol{\epsilon}}/\sqrt{n} \xrightarrow{p} \mathbf{0}$;
(ii) $\tilde{\mathbf{Z}}'(\mathbf{\Omega}_n^{-1} - \hat{\mathbf{\Omega}}_n^{-1})\tilde{\mathbf{X}}/n \xrightarrow{p} \mathbf{0}$; and
(iii) $\tilde{\mathbf{Z}}'(\mathbf{\Omega}_n^{-1} - \hat{\mathbf{\Omega}}_n^{-1})\tilde{\mathbf{Z}}/n \xrightarrow{p} \mathbf{0}$,

then $\sqrt{n}(\beta_n^* - \hat{\beta}_n^*) \xrightarrow{p} \mathbf{0}$. Further, $\hat{\mathbf{D}}_n - \mathbf{D}_n \xrightarrow{p} \mathbf{0}$, where

$$\hat{\mathbf{D}}_n \equiv (\tilde{\mathbf{X}}'\hat{\mathbf{\Omega}}_n^{-1}\tilde{\mathbf{Z}}(\tilde{\mathbf{Z}}'\hat{\mathbf{\Omega}}_n^{-1}\tilde{\mathbf{Z}}/n)^{-1}\tilde{\mathbf{Z}}'\hat{\mathbf{\Omega}}_n^{-1}\tilde{\mathbf{X}}/n^2)^{-1},$$

and the conclusions of Theorem 4.57 hold for $\hat{\beta}_n^*$.

Proof: The result follows immediately from Lemma 4.29, where $\mathbf{b}_n$ contains the elements of $\tilde{\mathbf{Z}}'\mathbf{\Omega}_n^{-1}\tilde{\boldsymbol{\epsilon}}/\sqrt{n}$, $\tilde{\mathbf{Z}}'\mathbf{\Omega}_n^{-1}\tilde{\mathbf{X}}/n$ and $\tilde{\mathbf{Z}}'\mathbf{\Omega}_n^{-1}\tilde{\mathbf{Z}}/n$ and $\mathbf{a}_n$ contains the elements of $\tilde{\mathbf{Z}}'\hat{\mathbf{\Omega}}_n^{-1}\tilde{\boldsymbol{\epsilon}}/\sqrt{n}$, $\tilde{\mathbf{Z}}'\hat{\mathbf{\Omega}}_n^{-1}\tilde{\mathbf{X}}/n$ and $\tilde{\mathbf{Z}}'\hat{\mathbf{\Omega}}_n^{-1}\tilde{\mathbf{Z}}/n$.

We consider three special cases. The first case is that of contemporaneously correlated errors and we obtain results for the standard 3SLS estimator as well as a useful estimator for panel data. In the second case, we consider a form of heteroskedasticity in which $E(\tilde{\boldsymbol{\epsilon}}_t\tilde{\boldsymbol{\epsilon}}_t')$ can take on a finite number of different values. In the third case, we consider serial correlation arising from a finite order vector autoregressive structure for the error terms.

VII.2 Case 1: Contemporaneous Covariance

For simplicity, we assume that the instrumental variable candidates are identical for all equations. Accordingly, let $\{\mathbf{W}_t\}$ be the sequence of instrumental variable candidates, so $E(\boldsymbol{\epsilon}_t|\mathbf{W}_t)=0$. Because $\boldsymbol{\epsilon}_t$ exhibits no heteroskedasticity or serial correlation, we have

$$E(\boldsymbol{\epsilon}_t\boldsymbol{\epsilon}_t'|\mathbf{W}_t)=\mathbf{I}, \quad t=1,\ldots,n,$$

$$E(\boldsymbol{\epsilon}_t\boldsymbol{\epsilon}_\tau'|\mathbf{W}_t,\mathbf{W}_\tau)=\mathbf{0}, \quad t\neq\tau=1,\ldots,n.$$

Contemporaneous correlation is induced by a transformation

$$\tilde{\boldsymbol{\epsilon}}_t=\mathbf{c}\boldsymbol{\epsilon}_t$$

where $\mathbf{c}$ is a constant $p\times p$ matrix such that $\mathbf{cc}'=\boldsymbol{\Sigma}$. In this case we have $E(\tilde{\boldsymbol{\epsilon}}_t|\mathbf{W}_t)=\mathbf{0}$ because

$$E(\tilde{\boldsymbol{\epsilon}}_t|\mathbf{W}_t)=E(\mathbf{c}\boldsymbol{\epsilon}_t|\mathbf{W}_t)=\mathbf{c}E(\boldsymbol{\epsilon}_t|\mathbf{W}_t)=\mathbf{0}.$$

This implies that $\sigma(\mathbf{W}_t)\subset\sigma(\tilde{\mathbf{W}}_t)$, where $\sigma(\tilde{\mathbf{W}}_t)$ is the σ-field generated by row vectors $\{\tilde{\mathbf{W}}_t\}$ such that $E(\tilde{\boldsymbol{\epsilon}}_t|\tilde{\mathbf{W}}_t)=\mathbf{0}$, $t=1,\ldots,n$. But because $\mathbf{c}$ is nonsingular,

$$E(\boldsymbol{\epsilon}_t|\tilde{\mathbf{W}}_t)=E(\mathbf{c}^{-1}\tilde{\boldsymbol{\epsilon}}_t|\tilde{\mathbf{W}}_t)=\mathbf{c}^{-1}E(\tilde{\boldsymbol{\epsilon}}_t|\tilde{\mathbf{W}}_t)=\mathbf{0},$$

so $\sigma(\tilde{\mathbf{W}}_t)\subset\sigma(\mathbf{W}_t)$. It follows that $\sigma(\tilde{\mathbf{W}}_t)=\sigma(\mathbf{W}_t)$, that is, precisely the same instrumental variables are available for the nonspherical model as for the spherical model.

Further, contemporaneous correlation only is induced because

$$\begin{aligned}E(\tilde{\boldsymbol{\epsilon}}_t\tilde{\boldsymbol{\epsilon}}_t'|\mathbf{W}_t)&=E(\mathbf{c}\boldsymbol{\epsilon}_t\boldsymbol{\epsilon}_t'\mathbf{c}'|\mathbf{W}_t)\\&=\mathbf{c}E(\boldsymbol{\epsilon}_t\boldsymbol{\epsilon}_t'|\mathbf{W}_t)\mathbf{c}'=\mathbf{cc}'=\boldsymbol{\Sigma}\end{aligned}$$

and

$$\begin{aligned}E(\tilde{\boldsymbol{\epsilon}}_t\tilde{\boldsymbol{\epsilon}}_\tau'|\mathbf{W}_t,\mathbf{W}_\tau)&=E(\mathbf{c}\boldsymbol{\epsilon}_t\boldsymbol{\epsilon}_\tau'\mathbf{c}'|\mathbf{W}_t,\mathbf{W}_\tau)\\&=\mathbf{c}E(\boldsymbol{\epsilon}_t\boldsymbol{\epsilon}_\tau'|\mathbf{W}_t,\mathbf{W}_\tau)\mathbf{c}'=\mathbf{0}.\end{aligned}$$

In this case $\mathbf{C}_n=\mathbf{I}_n\otimes\mathbf{c}$ and $\boldsymbol{\Omega}_n=\mathbf{C}_n\mathbf{C}_n'=(\mathbf{I}_n\otimes\mathbf{c})(\mathbf{I}_n\otimes\mathbf{c}')=\mathbf{I}_n\otimes\mathbf{cc}'=\mathbf{I}\otimes\boldsymbol{\Sigma}$.

Observe that in this case the instrumental variables candidates for the nonspherical model do not depend on the form of $\mathbf{c}$. For this reason, a knowledge of $\boldsymbol{\Sigma}$ is all that is needed to construct the efficient estimator.

Generally, however, $\boldsymbol{\Sigma}$ is unknown, so we must estimate it. If $\tilde{\boldsymbol{\epsilon}}_t$

were observable, a natural estimator would be

$$\tilde{\Sigma}_n \equiv n^{-1} \sum_{t=1}^{n} \tilde{\epsilon}_t \tilde{\epsilon}_t'.$$

Of course, $\tilde{\epsilon}_t$ is not observable, but it can be consistently estimated by $\hat{\epsilon}_t = \tilde{y}_t - \tilde{X}_t \tilde{\beta}_n$ for some IV estimator $\tilde{\beta}_n$. Replacing $\tilde{\epsilon}_t$ with $\hat{\epsilon}_t$ gives the estimator

$$\hat{\Sigma}_n \equiv n^{-1} \sum_{t=1}^{n} \hat{\epsilon}_t \hat{\epsilon}_t'.$$

The next result specifies general conditions under which $\hat{\Sigma}_n$ is strongly consistent for Σ.

PROPOSITION 7.2: Suppose that the conditions of Exercise 3.80 are satisfied for the model $\tilde{y} = \tilde{X}\beta_o + \tilde{\epsilon}$, instrumental variables $\tilde{Z}$ and norming matrix $\tilde{P}_n$ and suppose in addition that $E|\tilde{\epsilon}_{th}|^{2(r+\delta)} < \Delta < \infty$ and $E|\tilde{X}_{thj}|^{2(r+\delta)} < \Delta < \infty$ for some $\delta > 0$ and all $h = 1, \ldots, p$, $j = 1, \ldots, k$ and t. If

$$E(\tilde{\epsilon}_t \tilde{\epsilon}_t') = \Sigma, \quad t = 1, \ldots, n,$$

then $\hat{\Sigma}_n \xrightarrow{\text{a. s.}} \Sigma$, where

$$\hat{\Sigma}_n \equiv n^{-1} \sum_{t=1}^{n} \hat{\epsilon}_t \hat{\epsilon}_t'$$

and $\hat{\epsilon}_t = \tilde{y}_t - \tilde{X}_t \tilde{\beta}_n$, $\tilde{\beta}_n = (\tilde{X}'\tilde{Z}\tilde{P}_n\tilde{Z}'\tilde{X})^{-1}\tilde{X}'\tilde{Z}\tilde{P}_n\tilde{Z}'\tilde{y}$.

Proof: A typical element of $\hat{\Sigma}_n$ is given by $n^{-1} \sum_{t=1}^{n} \hat{\epsilon}_{th}\hat{\epsilon}_{tg}$. Now

$$n^{-1} \sum_{t=1}^{n} \hat{\epsilon}_{th}\hat{\epsilon}_{tg} = n^{-1} \sum_{t=1}^{n} (\tilde{\epsilon}_{th} - \tilde{X}_{th}(\tilde{\beta}_n - \beta_o))(\tilde{\epsilon}_{tg} - \tilde{X}_{tg}(\tilde{\beta}_n - \beta_o))'$$

$$= n^{-1} \sum_{t=1}^{n} \tilde{\epsilon}_{th}\tilde{\epsilon}_{tg} - n^{-1} \sum_{t=1}^{n} \tilde{\epsilon}_{tg}\tilde{X}_{th}(\tilde{\beta}_n - \beta_o)$$

$$- n^{-1} \sum_{t=1}^{n} (\tilde{\beta}_n - \beta_o)'\tilde{X}_{tg}'\tilde{\epsilon}_{th} + n^{-1} \sum_{t=1}^{n} (\tilde{\beta}_n - \beta_o)'\tilde{X}_{tg}'\tilde{X}_{th}(\tilde{\beta}_n - \beta_o)$$

$$= n^{-1} \sum_{t=1}^{n} \tilde{\epsilon}_{th}\tilde{\epsilon}_{tg} - \left(n^{-1} \sum_{t=1}^{n} \tilde{\epsilon}_{tg}\tilde{X}_{th}\right)(\tilde{\beta}_n - \beta_o)$$

$$- (\tilde{\beta}_n - \beta_o)' n^{-1} \sum_{t=1}^{n} \tilde{X}_{tg}'\tilde{\epsilon}_{th}$$

$$+ (\tilde{\beta}_n - \beta_o)'\left(n^{-1} \sum_{t=1}^{n} \tilde{X}_{tg}'\tilde{X}_{th}\right)(\tilde{\beta}_n - \beta_o).$$

We can apply Proposition 2.16 to this expression, so we consider each component in turn.

By assumption (ii) of Exercise 3.80 and Theorem 3.49, $\tilde{\boldsymbol{\epsilon}}_{th}\tilde{\boldsymbol{\epsilon}}_{tg}$ is a mixing sequence with $\phi(m)$ of size $r/(2r-1)$ or $\alpha(m)$ of size $r/(r-1)$, $r > 1$. By assumption, $E(\tilde{\boldsymbol{\epsilon}}_{th}\tilde{\boldsymbol{\epsilon}}_{tg}) = \sigma_{hg}$, where $\boldsymbol{\Sigma} \equiv [\sigma_{hg}]$. Because $E|\tilde{\boldsymbol{\epsilon}}_{th}|^{2(r+\delta)}$ is uniformly bounded, it follows from the Cauchy–Schwartz inequality that $E|\tilde{\boldsymbol{\epsilon}}_{th}\tilde{\boldsymbol{\epsilon}}_{tg}|^{r+\delta}$ is uniformly bounded, so that the conditions of Corollary 3.48 are satisfied and

$$n^{-1}\sum_{t=1}^{n}\tilde{\boldsymbol{\epsilon}}_{th}\tilde{\boldsymbol{\epsilon}}_{tg} \xrightarrow{\text{a. s.}} \sigma_{hg}.$$

An identical argument establishes that

$$n^{-1}\sum_{t=1}^{n}\tilde{\mathbf{X}}_{tg}'\tilde{\boldsymbol{\epsilon}}_{th} \quad \text{is} \quad \mathrm{O}_{\text{a.s.}}(1) \qquad \text{and}$$

$$n^{-1}\sum_{t=1}^{n}\tilde{\mathbf{X}}_{th}'\tilde{\mathbf{X}}_{tg} \quad \text{is} \quad \mathrm{O}_{\text{a.s.}}(1).$$

Because $\tilde{\boldsymbol{\beta}}_n - \boldsymbol{\beta}_o \xrightarrow{\text{a. s.}} \mathbf{0}$ under the conditions of Exercise 3.80, it follows from Proposition 2.16 that

$$n^{-1}\sum_{t=1}^{n}\hat{\boldsymbol{\epsilon}}_{th}\hat{\boldsymbol{\epsilon}}_{tg} \xrightarrow{\text{a. s.}} \sigma_{hg} - 0 - 0 + 0 = \sigma_{hg}.$$

Hence, $\hat{\boldsymbol{\Sigma}}_n \xrightarrow{\text{a. s.}} \boldsymbol{\Sigma}$.

Note that $\boldsymbol{\Sigma}$ is consistently estimated using any choice of $\tilde{\mathbf{Z}}$ and $\tilde{\mathbf{P}}_n$ that satisfy the conditions of Exercise 3.80. It is not essential to choose $\tilde{\mathbf{Z}} = \mathbf{C}_n\mathbf{Z}$. Having a consistent estimator $\boldsymbol{\Sigma}_n$ available for $\boldsymbol{\Sigma}$ lets us estimate $\boldsymbol{\Omega}_n$ by

$$\hat{\boldsymbol{\Omega}}_n = \mathbf{I} \otimes \hat{\boldsymbol{\Sigma}}_n.$$

With this choice for $\hat{\boldsymbol{\Omega}}_n$, we have the following result.

THEOREM 7.3: Suppose that

(i) $\mathbf{y} = \mathbf{X}\boldsymbol{\beta}_o + \boldsymbol{\epsilon}$

and suppose there exists a unique σ-field generated by row vectors $\{\mathbf{W}_t\}$ such that

$$E(\boldsymbol{\epsilon}_t|\mathbf{W}_t) = \mathbf{0} \qquad \text{and}$$

$$E(\boldsymbol{\epsilon}_t|\mathcal{G}_t) \neq \mathbf{0} \qquad \text{for all} \quad \mathcal{G}_t \supset \sigma(\mathbf{W}_t), \quad t = 1, \ldots, n;$$

$$E(\boldsymbol{\epsilon}_t \boldsymbol{\epsilon}_t' | \mathbf{W}_t) = \mathbf{I},\ t = 1, \ldots, n;$$

$$E(\boldsymbol{\epsilon}_t \boldsymbol{\epsilon}_\tau' | \mathbf{W}_t, \mathbf{W}_\tau) = \mathbf{0},\ t \neq \tau = 1, \ldots, n;$$

and define instrumental variables $\mathbf{Z}$ satisfying

$$E(\mathbf{X}_t | \mathbf{W}_t) = \mathbf{Z}_t \Pi_o,\ t = 1, \ldots, n,$$

where Π_o is an $l \times k$ matrix of full column rank containing no zero rows.

Let $\mathbf{c}$ be any finite nonsingular nonstochastic $p \times p$ matrix such that $\mathbf{cc}' = \boldsymbol{\Sigma}$. Define

$$\tilde{\mathbf{y}}_t = \mathbf{c}\mathbf{y}_t, \qquad \tilde{\mathbf{X}}_t = \mathbf{c}\mathbf{X}_t, \qquad \tilde{\boldsymbol{\epsilon}} = \mathbf{c}\boldsymbol{\epsilon}_t,$$

and let $\tilde{\mathbf{Z}}_t = \mathbf{c}\mathbf{Z}_t$.

In addition, suppose that

(ii) $\{(\tilde{\mathbf{Z}}_t, \tilde{\mathbf{X}}_t, \tilde{\boldsymbol{\epsilon}}_t)'\}$ is a mixing sequence with either $\phi(m)$ of size $r/(2r-1)$, $r \geq 1$ or $\alpha(m)$ of size $r/(r-1)$, $r > 1$;

(iii) (a) for all t, $E(\tilde{\mathbf{Z}}_{tgi} \tilde{\boldsymbol{\epsilon}}_{th} | \mathfrak{F}_{t-1}) = 0$, where $\{\mathfrak{F}_t\}$ is adapted to $\{\tilde{\mathbf{Z}}_{tgi} \tilde{\boldsymbol{\epsilon}}_{th}\}$, $g, h = 1, \ldots, p$, $i = 1, \ldots, l$;

(b) for some $\delta > 0$ and all $g, h = 1, \ldots, p$, $i = 1, \ldots, l$, and t, $E|\tilde{\mathbf{Z}}_{tgi} \tilde{\boldsymbol{\epsilon}}_{th}|^{2(r+\delta)} < \Delta < \infty$ and $E|\tilde{\boldsymbol{\epsilon}}_{th}|^{2(r+\delta)} < \Delta < \infty$;

(c) $\mathbf{V}_n \equiv \operatorname{var}(n^{-1/2} \mathbf{Z}' \boldsymbol{\epsilon}) = \operatorname{var}(n^{-1/2} \tilde{\mathbf{Z}}' \boldsymbol{\Omega}_n^{-1} \tilde{\boldsymbol{\epsilon}})$ is uniformly positive definite;

(iv) (a) $E|\tilde{\mathbf{Z}}_{thi}|^{2(r+\delta)} < \Delta < \infty$ and $E|\tilde{\mathbf{X}}_{thj}|^{2(r+\delta)} < \Delta < \infty$ for some $\delta > 0$ and all $h = 1, \ldots, p$, $i = 1, \ldots, l$, $j = 1, \ldots, k$, and t;

(b) $\tilde{\mathbf{Q}}_n \equiv E(\tilde{\mathbf{Z}}' \tilde{\mathbf{X}}/n)$ and $\mathbf{Q}_n \equiv E(\mathbf{Z}'\mathbf{X}/n) = E(\tilde{\mathbf{Z}}' \boldsymbol{\Omega}_n^{-1} \tilde{\mathbf{X}}/n)$ have uniformly full column rank;

(c) $\tilde{\mathbf{L}}_n \equiv E(\tilde{\mathbf{Z}}' \tilde{\mathbf{Z}}/n)$ is uniformly positive definite.

Define

$$\hat{\boldsymbol{\Sigma}}_n \equiv n^{-1} \sum_{t=1}^{n} \hat{\boldsymbol{\epsilon}}_t \hat{\boldsymbol{\epsilon}}_t',$$

where

$$\hat{\boldsymbol{\epsilon}}_t = \tilde{\mathbf{y}}_t - \tilde{\mathbf{X}}_t \tilde{\boldsymbol{\beta}}_n, \qquad \tilde{\boldsymbol{\beta}}_n = (\tilde{\mathbf{X}}' \tilde{\mathbf{Z}} (\tilde{\mathbf{Z}}' \tilde{\mathbf{Z}})^{-1} \tilde{\mathbf{Z}}' \tilde{\mathbf{X}})^{-1} \tilde{\mathbf{X}}' \tilde{\mathbf{Z}} (\tilde{\mathbf{Z}}' \tilde{\mathbf{Z}})^{-1} \tilde{\mathbf{Z}}' \tilde{\mathbf{y}}.$$

Let

$$\hat{\boldsymbol{\Omega}}_n = \mathbf{I} \otimes \hat{\boldsymbol{\Sigma}}_n$$

and define

$$\hat{\boldsymbol{\beta}}_n^* = (\tilde{\mathbf{X}}'\hat{\boldsymbol{\Omega}}_n^{-1}\tilde{\mathbf{Z}}(\tilde{\mathbf{Z}}'\hat{\boldsymbol{\Omega}}_n^{-1}\tilde{\mathbf{Z}})^{-1}\tilde{\mathbf{Z}}'\hat{\boldsymbol{\Omega}}_n^{-1}\tilde{\mathbf{X}})^{-1}\tilde{\mathbf{X}}'\hat{\boldsymbol{\Omega}}_n^{-1}\tilde{\mathbf{Z}}(\tilde{\mathbf{Z}}'\hat{\boldsymbol{\Omega}}_n^{-1}\tilde{\mathbf{Z}})^{-1}\tilde{\mathbf{Z}}'\hat{\boldsymbol{\Omega}}_n^{-1}\tilde{\mathbf{y}},$$

and

$$\boldsymbol{\beta}_n^* = (\mathbf{X}'\mathbf{Z}(\mathbf{Z}'\mathbf{Z})^{-1}\mathbf{Z}'\mathbf{X})^{-1}\mathbf{X}'\mathbf{Z}(\mathbf{Z}'\mathbf{Z})^{-1}\mathbf{Z}'\mathbf{y}.$$

Then $\sqrt{n}(\hat{\boldsymbol{\beta}}_n^* - \boldsymbol{\beta}_n^*) \xrightarrow{p} 0$, $\mathbf{D}_n^{-1/2}n^{-1/2}(\hat{\boldsymbol{\beta}}_n^* - \boldsymbol{\beta}_o) \overset{A}{\sim} N(\mathbf{0}, \mathbf{I})$, where $\mathbf{D}_n = (\mathbf{Q}_n'\mathbf{V}_n^{-1}\mathbf{Q}_n)^{-1}$, and the conclusions of Theorem 4.57 hold for $\hat{\boldsymbol{\beta}}_n^*$. Further, $\hat{\mathbf{D}}_n - \mathbf{D}_n \xrightarrow{p} 0$, where

$$\hat{\mathbf{D}}_n \equiv (\tilde{\mathbf{X}}'\hat{\boldsymbol{\Omega}}_n^{-1}\mathbf{Z}(\tilde{\mathbf{Z}}'\hat{\boldsymbol{\Omega}}_n^{-1}\tilde{\mathbf{Z}})^{-1}\tilde{\mathbf{Z}}'\hat{\boldsymbol{\Omega}}_n^{-1}\tilde{\mathbf{X}}/n)^{-1}.$$

Proof: We verify the conditions of Theorem 7.1. First consider $\mathbf{Z}'(\boldsymbol{\Omega}_n^{-1} - \hat{\boldsymbol{\Omega}}_n^{-1})\tilde{\boldsymbol{\epsilon}}/\sqrt{n}$. When $\boldsymbol{\Omega}_n = \mathbf{I} \otimes \boldsymbol{\Sigma}$ and $\hat{\boldsymbol{\Omega}}_n = \mathbf{I} \otimes \hat{\boldsymbol{\Sigma}}_n$ we have

$$n^{-1/2}\tilde{\mathbf{Z}}'(\boldsymbol{\Omega}_n^{-1} - \hat{\boldsymbol{\Omega}}_n^{-1})\tilde{\boldsymbol{\epsilon}} = n^{-1/2}\sum_{t=1}^{n}\tilde{\mathbf{Z}}_t'(\boldsymbol{\Sigma}^{-1} - \hat{\boldsymbol{\Sigma}}_n^{-1})\tilde{\boldsymbol{\epsilon}}_t.$$

Let $\boldsymbol{\Sigma}^{-1} = [\sigma^{gh}]$ and $\hat{\boldsymbol{\Sigma}}_n^{-1} = [\hat{\sigma}_n^{gh}]$. The ith element of $n^{-1/2}\tilde{\mathbf{Z}}'(\boldsymbol{\Omega}_n^{-1} - \hat{\boldsymbol{\Omega}}_n^{-1})\tilde{\boldsymbol{\epsilon}}$ can then be written as

$$\begin{aligned} n^{-1/2}\sum_{t=1}^{n}\sum_{g=1}^{p}\sum_{h=1}^{p}\tilde{\mathbf{Z}}_{tgi}(\sigma^{gh} - \hat{\sigma}_n^{gh})\tilde{\boldsymbol{\epsilon}}_{th} \\ = \sum_{g=1}^{p}\sum_{h=1}^{p}(\sigma^{gh} - \hat{\sigma}_n^{gh})n^{-1/2}\sum_{t=1}^{n}\tilde{\mathbf{Z}}_{tgi}\tilde{\boldsymbol{\epsilon}}_{th}. \end{aligned}$$

We show that this converges in probability to zero by applying the result of Exercise 2.35(c) for products to each term in the double summation over g and h and then use the addition rule of Exercise 2.35(b).

First, we note that the conditions of Exercise 3.80 are satisfied for $\tilde{\boldsymbol{\beta}}_n$ (choosing $\tilde{\mathbf{P}}_n = \tilde{\mathbf{L}}_n^{-1}$) so that $\hat{\boldsymbol{\Sigma}}_n - \boldsymbol{\Sigma} \xrightarrow{a.s.} \mathbf{0}$ by Proposition 7.2. Hence, $\hat{\boldsymbol{\Sigma}}_n - \boldsymbol{\Sigma} \xrightarrow{p} \mathbf{0}$ by Theorem 2.24, so that $\boldsymbol{\Sigma}^{-1} - \hat{\boldsymbol{\Sigma}}^{-1} \xrightarrow{p} \mathbf{0}$ by Proposition 2.27, that is, $\sigma^{gh} - \hat{\sigma}^{gh} \xrightarrow{p} 0$, $g, h = 1, \ldots, p$.

Next consider $n^{-1/2}\sum_{t=1}^{n}\tilde{\mathbf{Z}}_{tgi}\tilde{\boldsymbol{\epsilon}}_{th}$. Given (iii.a), $\{\tilde{\mathbf{Z}}_{tgi}\tilde{\boldsymbol{\epsilon}}_{th}, \mathfrak{F}_t\}$ is a martingale difference sequence, so $\text{var}(n^{-1/2}\sum_{t=1}^{n}\tilde{\mathbf{Z}}_{tgi}\tilde{\boldsymbol{\epsilon}}_{th}) = n^{-1}\sum_{t=1}^{n}E(\tilde{\mathbf{Z}}_{tgi}^2\tilde{\boldsymbol{\epsilon}}_{th}^2)$. By Chebyshev's inequality,

$$\begin{aligned} P\left[\left|n^{-1/2}\sum_{t=1}^{n}\tilde{\mathbf{Z}}_{tgi}\tilde{\boldsymbol{\epsilon}}_{th}\right| \geq \Delta\right] &\leq \text{var}\left(n^{-1/2}\sum_{t=1}^{n}\tilde{\mathbf{Z}}_{tgi}\tilde{\boldsymbol{\epsilon}}_{th}\right)/\Delta^2 \\ &= n^{-1}\sum_{t=1}^{n}E(\tilde{\mathbf{Z}}_{tgi}^2\tilde{\boldsymbol{\epsilon}}_{th}^2)/\Delta^2. \end{aligned}$$

It follows from (iii.b) and Jensen's inequality that there exists $\Delta' < \infty$ such that

$$n^{-1} \sum_{t=1}^{n} E(\tilde{\mathbf{Z}}_{tgi}^2 \tilde{\boldsymbol{\epsilon}}_{th}^2) < \Delta',$$

so that

$$P\left[\left| n^{-1/2} \sum_{t=1}^{n} \tilde{\mathbf{Z}}_{tgi} \tilde{\boldsymbol{\epsilon}}_{th} \right| \geq \Delta\right] < \Delta'/\Delta^2.$$

Because Δ can be chosen arbitrarily, it follows from Definition 2.33 that $n^{-1/2} \sum_{t=1}^{n} \tilde{\mathbf{Z}}_{tgi} \tilde{\boldsymbol{\epsilon}}_{th}$ is $O_p(1)$.

Exercise 2.35(c) then guarantees that $(\sigma^{gh} - \hat{\sigma}^{gh}) n^{-1/2} \sum_{t=1}^{n} \tilde{\mathbf{Z}}_{tgi} \tilde{\boldsymbol{\epsilon}}_{th}$ is $o_p(1)$, so that

$$\sum_{g=1}^{p} \sum_{h=1}^{p} (\sigma^{gh} - \hat{\sigma}_n^{gh}) n^{-1/2} \sum_{t=1}^{n} \tilde{\mathbf{Z}}_{tgi} \tilde{\boldsymbol{\epsilon}}_{th} \xrightarrow{p} 0$$

by Exercise 2.35(b). Hence, $n^{-1/2} \tilde{\mathbf{Z}}'(\boldsymbol{\Omega}_n^{-1} - \hat{\boldsymbol{\Omega}}_n^{-1}) \tilde{\boldsymbol{\epsilon}} \xrightarrow{p} 0$.

Next consider $\mathbf{Z}'(\boldsymbol{\Omega}_n^{-1} - \hat{\boldsymbol{\Omega}}_n^{-1})\mathbf{X}/n$. When $\boldsymbol{\Omega}_n = \mathbf{I} \otimes \boldsymbol{\Sigma}$ and $\boldsymbol{\Omega}_n = \mathbf{I} \otimes \hat{\boldsymbol{\Sigma}}_n$, we have

$$\tilde{\mathbf{Z}}'(\boldsymbol{\Omega}_n^{-1} - \hat{\boldsymbol{\Omega}}_n^{-1}) \tilde{\mathbf{X}}/n = n^{-1} \sum_{t=1}^{n} \tilde{\mathbf{Z}}_t'(\boldsymbol{\Sigma}^{-1} - \hat{\boldsymbol{\Sigma}}_n^{-1}) \tilde{\mathbf{X}}_t.$$

The i, jth element of this matrix can be written as

$$\begin{aligned} n^{-1} \sum_{t=1}^{n} \sum_{g=1}^{p} \sum_{h=1}^{p} & \tilde{\mathbf{Z}}_{tgi} (\sigma^{gh} - \hat{\sigma}_n^{gh}) \tilde{\mathbf{X}}_{thj} \\ &= \sum_{g=1}^{p} \sum_{h=1}^{p} (\sigma^{gh} - \hat{\sigma}_n^{gh}) n^{-1} \sum_{t=1}^{n} \tilde{\mathbf{Z}}_{tgi} \tilde{\mathbf{X}}_{thj}. \end{aligned}$$

As before, $\sigma^{gh} - \hat{\sigma}^{gh} \xrightarrow{p} 0$. Further, given (ii) and (iv.a) it follows from Corollary 3.48 that

$$n^{-1} \sum_{t=1}^{n} \tilde{\mathbf{Z}}_{tgi} \tilde{\mathbf{X}}_{thj} - E\left(n^{-1} \sum_{t=1}^{n} \tilde{\mathbf{Z}}_{tgi} \tilde{\mathbf{X}}_{thj}\right) \xrightarrow{\text{a. s.}} 0,$$

and because $E(n^{-1} \sum_{t=1}^{n} \tilde{\mathbf{Z}}_{tgi} \tilde{\mathbf{X}}_{thj})$ is $O(1)$ by (iv.a) and Jensen's inequality, it follows that $n^{-1} \sum_{t=1}^{n} \tilde{\mathbf{Z}}_{tgi} \tilde{\mathbf{X}}_{thj}$ is $O_p(1)$. As before, it follows from Exercise 2.35 that

$$\sum_{g=1}^{p} \sum_{h=1}^{p} (\sigma^{gh} - \hat{\sigma}_n^{gh}) n^{-1} \sum_{t=1}^{n} \tilde{\mathbf{Z}}_{tgi} \tilde{\mathbf{X}}_{thj} \xrightarrow{p} 0,$$

so that $\tilde{\mathbf{Z}}'(\boldsymbol{\Omega}_n^{-1} - \hat{\boldsymbol{\Omega}}_n^{-1}) \tilde{\mathbf{X}}/n \xrightarrow{p} \mathbf{0}$.

The proof that $\tilde{\mathbf{Z}}'(\mathbf{\Omega}_n^{-1} - \hat{\mathbf{\Omega}}_n^{-1})\tilde{\mathbf{Z}}/n \xrightarrow{p} \mathbf{0}$ is exactly parallel to the proof just given, except that $\tilde{\mathbf{Z}}_{thj}$ replaces $\tilde{\mathbf{X}}_{thj}$ and the Cauchy–Schwartz inequality ensures that $E|\tilde{\mathbf{Z}}_{tgi}\tilde{\mathbf{Z}}_{thj}|^{r+\delta} < \Delta$, given (iva).

The desired result follows, provided that the conditions of Exercise 4.26 hold for $\mathbf{Z}$, $\mathbf{X}$, and $\boldsymbol{\epsilon}$. For this, it suffices to show that the conditions of Exercise 5.27 hold for $\mathbf{Z}_t \equiv \mathbf{c}^{-1}\tilde{\mathbf{Z}}_t$, $\mathbf{X}_t \equiv \mathbf{c}^{-1}\tilde{\mathbf{X}}_t$, and $\boldsymbol{\epsilon}_t = \mathbf{c}^{-1}\tilde{\boldsymbol{\epsilon}}_t$. This is tedious but straightforward and the details are left to the reader.

To ensure the greatest comparability of results, the sufficient conditions are stated in terms of the nonspherical model rather than the spherical model, with the exception of condition (i). There we could equally well have specified that the model is

$$\tilde{\mathbf{y}} = \tilde{\mathbf{X}}\boldsymbol{\beta}_o + \tilde{\boldsymbol{\epsilon}},$$

where

$$E(\tilde{\boldsymbol{\epsilon}}_t|\tilde{\mathbf{W}}_t) = \mathbf{0}$$

and

$$E(\tilde{\boldsymbol{\epsilon}}_t\tilde{\boldsymbol{\epsilon}}_t'|\tilde{\mathbf{W}}_t) = \boldsymbol{\Sigma}, \qquad t = 1, \ldots, n$$

$$E(\tilde{\boldsymbol{\epsilon}}_t\tilde{\boldsymbol{\epsilon}}_\tau'|\tilde{\mathbf{W}}_t, \tilde{\mathbf{W}}_\tau) = \mathbf{0}, \qquad t \neq \tau = 1, \ldots, n$$

for suitable instrumental variable candidates $\tilde{\mathbf{W}}_t$, and $\boldsymbol{\Sigma}$ nonsingular. Then (i) follows for any nonsingular transformation $\mathbf{c}$ such that $\mathbf{cc}' = \boldsymbol{\Sigma}$. We state (i) in terms of the spherical model so that the optimal instrumental variables are easily characterized.

Comparing the conditions of the present result with the analogous result of Exercise 6.8, we find two noticeable differences. The first is that, unlike assumption (iii) of Exercise 6.8, assumption (iii) of Theorem 7.2 imposes conditions on the relationship between the errors of equation h and the instrumental variables for equation g. Of course, this leads to no loss of generality in the present context, because we have assumed the same instrumental variable candidates are available for each equation. A second difference is that in (iv.a), $E|\tilde{\mathbf{Z}}_{thi}\tilde{\mathbf{X}}_{thj}|^{2(r+\delta)}$ is no longer restricted but only $E|\tilde{\mathbf{Z}}_{thi}|^{2(r+\delta)}$ and $E|\tilde{\mathbf{X}}_{thj}|^{2(r+\delta)}$. The former restriction was needed in estimating the robust covariance matrix of Chapter VI, but is not needed here. The latter restriction helps ensure that $\hat{\boldsymbol{\Sigma}}_n$ is consistent for $\boldsymbol{\Sigma}$.

To keep the statement of this result relatively simple, we assumed that $\tilde{\mathbf{Z}} = \mathbf{C}_n\mathbf{Z}$ was used to construct $\tilde{\boldsymbol{\beta}}_n$. However, it is easily seen from the proof that any choice of $\tilde{\mathbf{Z}}$ satisfying assumptions (ii), (iii.a,b), and (iv) will suffice in constructing $\tilde{\boldsymbol{\beta}}_n$. The choice $\tilde{\mathbf{Z}} = \mathbf{C}_n\mathbf{Z}$ is crucial only in constructing $\hat{\boldsymbol{\beta}}_n^*$.

Theorem 7.3 contains results for a variety of useful estimators, in particular, general asymptotic normality results for Zellner's [1962] seemingly unrelated regressions estimator (SURE) (set $\tilde{\mathbf{Z}} = \tilde{\mathbf{X}}$) as well as the three-stage least squares (3SLS) estimator (Zellner and Theil [1962]). The present result allows for the presence of both lagged dependent variables and nonstochastic variables in both the explanatory and instrumental variables.

At the same time, the theorem also contains results for panel data sets in which one has a cross section of individuals and each individual occurs p times. In such cases, the matrix $\boldsymbol{\Sigma}$ often is assumed to have a more specific form as a result of an assumed variance components structure, that is, $\tilde{\boldsymbol{\epsilon}}_{th} = \boldsymbol{\eta}_{th} + \boldsymbol{\nu}_t$, where $\boldsymbol{\nu}_t$ is an individual specific effect uncorrelated with $\boldsymbol{\eta}_{th}$ and the specific effects for other individuals. It is typically assumed that $E(\eta_{th}^2) = \sigma_\eta^2$, $E(\nu_t^2) = \sigma_\nu^2$, $E(\eta_{th}\nu_t) = 0$, for all τ and t, $h = 1, \ldots, p$, $E(\eta_{th}\eta_{\tau g}) = 0$, $t \neq \tau$, for all h and g, and $E(\nu_t\nu_\tau) = 0$, $t \neq \tau$. This implies that

$$E(\tilde{\epsilon}_{th}^2) = \sigma_\eta^2 + \sigma_\nu^2$$
$$E(\tilde{\epsilon}_{th}\tilde{\epsilon}_{tg}) = \sigma_\nu^2,$$

so that

$$\boldsymbol{\Sigma} = \sigma_\eta^2\mathbf{I} + \sigma_\nu^2\boldsymbol{\iota}\boldsymbol{\iota}',$$

where $\boldsymbol{\iota}$ is the $p \times 1$ vector $\boldsymbol{\iota}' = (1, 1, \ldots, 1)$.

When such a structure has been assumed, estimators besides $\hat{\boldsymbol{\Sigma}}_n = n^{-1}\sum_{t=1}^n \hat{\boldsymbol{\epsilon}}_t\hat{\boldsymbol{\epsilon}}_t'$ are available, and if such an estimator is consistent, it can replace $\hat{\boldsymbol{\Sigma}}_n$ in the preceding result without affecting the validity of the conclusion. However, such estimators have no advantage asymptotically over $\hat{\boldsymbol{\Sigma}}_n$, and because they impose additional restrictions that could be incorrect (e.g., η_{th} might have $E(\eta_{tg}\eta_{th}) \neq 0$), they can fail to be consistent for $\boldsymbol{\Sigma}$, which leads to an inefficient estimator.

VII.3 Case 2: Heteroskedasticity

Often it may be unrealistic to assume that $\boldsymbol{\Sigma}$ is identical for all t. A somewhat more general assumption is that there is a finite number, say, $\mathbf{G}$, of different groups, and that the variance within each group is constant, say, $\mathbf{\Sigma}_\gamma$, $\gamma = 1, \ldots, G$. For example, in time-series, the errors may have different covariance matrices depending on whether the Democrats or the Republicans are in office, or whether the Federal Reserve is headed by a Keynesian or a monetarist. In panels, individual error covariance matrices may differ according to observable demographic characteristics (region, union membership, race, etc.). In either case, the heterogeneity can be viewed as arising from a transformation of an underlying spherical model such as

$$\tilde{\boldsymbol{\epsilon}}_t = (\mathbf{c}_1 \mathbf{d}_{1t} + \mathbf{c}_2 \mathbf{d}_{2t} + \cdots + \mathbf{c}_G \mathbf{d}_{Gt}) \boldsymbol{\epsilon}_t,$$

where $\mathbf{d}_{\gamma t}$ is one if observation t falls in group γ and is zero otherwise, and $\mathbf{c}_\gamma$, $\gamma = 1, \ldots, G$ are unknown finite nonsingular nonstochastic $p \times p$ matrices. If $\mathbf{d}_t' = (\mathbf{d}_{1t}, \mathbf{d}_{2t}, \ldots, \mathbf{d}_{Gt})$ is included among the instrumental variable candidates $\mathbf{W}_t$, then

$$\begin{aligned} E(\tilde{\boldsymbol{\epsilon}}_t | \mathbf{W}_t) &= E\left(\left[\sum_{\gamma=1}^{G} \mathbf{c}_\gamma \mathbf{d}_{\gamma t}\right] \boldsymbol{\epsilon}_t | \mathbf{W}_t\right) \\ &= \left[\sum_{\gamma=1}^{G} \mathbf{c}_\gamma \mathbf{d}_{\gamma t}\right] E(\boldsymbol{\epsilon}_t | \mathbf{W}_t) = \mathbf{0}, \end{aligned}$$

so $\sigma(\mathbf{W}_t) \subset \sigma(\tilde{\mathbf{W}}_t)$, where $\sigma(\tilde{\mathbf{W}}_t)$ is generated by $\{\tilde{\mathbf{W}}_t\}$ such that $E(\tilde{\boldsymbol{\epsilon}}_t | \tilde{\mathbf{W}}_t) = \mathbf{0}$. Because the $\mathbf{c}_\gamma$, $\gamma = 1, \ldots, G$, are nonsingular, and because $[\Sigma_{\gamma=1}^{G} \mathbf{c}_\gamma \mathbf{d}_{\gamma t}]^{-1} = [\Sigma_{\gamma=1}^{G} \mathbf{c}_\gamma^{-1} \mathbf{d}_{\gamma t}]$, we have

$$\begin{aligned} E(\boldsymbol{\epsilon}_t | \tilde{\mathbf{W}}_t) &= E\left(\left[\sum_{\gamma=1}^{G} \mathbf{c}_\gamma^{-1} \mathbf{d}_{\gamma t}\right] \tilde{\boldsymbol{\epsilon}}_t | \tilde{\mathbf{W}}_t\right) \\ &= \left[\sum_{\gamma=1}^{G} \mathbf{c}_\gamma^{-1} \mathbf{d}_{\gamma t}\right] E(\tilde{\boldsymbol{\epsilon}}_t | \tilde{\mathbf{W}}_t) = \mathbf{0}, \end{aligned}$$

so $\sigma(\tilde{\mathbf{W}}_t) \subset \sigma(\mathbf{W}_t)$. Hence, $\sigma(\tilde{\mathbf{W}}_t) = \sigma(\mathbf{W}_t)$, that is, the same instrumental variables are available for both the spherical and the nonspherical model, provided that $\mathbf{d}_t'$ is included in $\mathbf{W}_t$. Note that in the second equality above, use is made of the fact that $\mathbf{d}_{\gamma t}$ is measurable with respect to $\sigma(\tilde{\mathbf{W}}_t)$ because $\mathbf{d}_t'$ is in $\sigma(\mathbf{W}_t)$ and $\sigma(\mathbf{W}_t) \subset \sigma(\tilde{\mathbf{W}}_t)$.

The covariance structure of $\tilde{\boldsymbol{\epsilon}}_t$ is given by

$$E(\tilde{\boldsymbol{\epsilon}}_t \tilde{\boldsymbol{\epsilon}}_t' | \mathbf{W}_t) = \mathbf{\Sigma}_1 \mathbf{d}_{1t} + \cdots + \mathbf{\Sigma}_G \mathbf{d}_{Gt}$$

and

$$E(\tilde{\boldsymbol{\epsilon}}_t \tilde{\boldsymbol{\epsilon}}_\tau' | \mathbf{W}_t, \mathbf{W}_\tau) = \mathbf{0}, \; t \neq \tau,$$

where $\boldsymbol{\Sigma}_\gamma = \mathbf{c}_\gamma \mathbf{c}_\gamma'$, $\gamma = 1, \ldots, G$. As in the previous case, the instrumental variable candidates do not depend on the form of $\mathbf{c}_\gamma$ and Theorem 4.58 applies, so a knowledge of $\boldsymbol{\Sigma}_\gamma$ will suffice for constructing the efficient estimator.

When $\boldsymbol{\Sigma}_\gamma$ is unknown we can proceed by finding a consistent estimator. A natural way to construct an estimator for $\boldsymbol{\Sigma}_\gamma$ is to average $\hat{\boldsymbol{\epsilon}}_t \hat{\boldsymbol{\epsilon}}_t'$ over only the observations in group γ, that is, those observations for which $\mathbf{d}_{\gamma t} = 1$, which gives

$$\hat{\boldsymbol{\Sigma}}_{\gamma n} = n_\gamma^{-1} \sum_{t=1}^{n} \mathbf{d}_{\gamma t} \hat{\boldsymbol{\epsilon}}_t \hat{\boldsymbol{\epsilon}}_t', \qquad \gamma = 1, \ldots, G,$$

where $\hat{\boldsymbol{\epsilon}}_t = \tilde{\mathbf{y}}_t - \tilde{\mathbf{X}}_t \tilde{\boldsymbol{\beta}}_n$ and $n_\gamma = \Sigma_{t=1}^n \mathbf{d}_{\gamma t}$ is the number of observations falling in group γ. Note that if the data have not been sampled in such a way as to ensure that a fixed number of observations belong to group γ, then n_γ must be treated as a random variable, and it is helpful to write $\hat{\boldsymbol{\Sigma}}_{\gamma n}$ as

$$\hat{\boldsymbol{\Sigma}}_{\gamma n} = \left(n^{-1} \sum_{t=1}^{n} \mathbf{d}_{\gamma t}^2 \right)^{-1} n^{-1} \sum_{t=1}^{n} \mathbf{d}_{\gamma t} \hat{\boldsymbol{\epsilon}}_t \hat{\boldsymbol{\epsilon}}_t', \ \gamma = 1, \ldots, G,$$

where we use the fact that $\mathbf{d}_{\gamma t} = \mathbf{d}_{\gamma t}^2$. In this form, $\hat{\boldsymbol{\Sigma}}_{\gamma n}$ can be interpreted as the OLS regression of $\hat{\boldsymbol{\epsilon}}_t \hat{\boldsymbol{\epsilon}}_t'$ on $\mathbf{d}_{\gamma t}$.

Given appropriate regularity conditions, it is straightforward to show that $\hat{\boldsymbol{\Sigma}}_{\gamma n}$ is consistent for $\boldsymbol{\Sigma}_\gamma$, as the following exercise asks you to verify.

EXERCISE 7.4: Prove the following result. Define $\hat{\boldsymbol{\Sigma}}_{\gamma n}$ as above, and let $\tilde{\boldsymbol{\beta}}_n \xrightarrow{p} \boldsymbol{\beta}_o$. Suppose that for $\gamma = 1, \ldots, G$,

(i) $n_\gamma/n - E(n_\gamma/n) \xrightarrow{p} 0$ and for all n sufficiently large $E(n_\gamma/n) > \delta > 0$;
(ii) $n^{-1} \Sigma_{t=1}^n \mathbf{d}_{\gamma t} \tilde{\boldsymbol{\epsilon}}_t \tilde{\boldsymbol{\epsilon}}_t' - E(\mathbf{d}_{\gamma t} \tilde{\boldsymbol{\epsilon}}_t \tilde{\boldsymbol{\epsilon}}_t') \xrightarrow{p} 0$;
(iii) $\{n^{-1} \Sigma_{t=1}^n \mathbf{d}_{\gamma t} \tilde{\mathbf{X}}_{tgi} \boldsymbol{\epsilon}_{th}\}$ is $O_p(1)$ for $g, h = 1, \ldots, p$, $i = 1, \ldots, k$;
(iv) $\{n^{-1} \Sigma_{t=1}^n \mathbf{d}_{\gamma t} \tilde{\mathbf{X}}_{tgi} \tilde{\mathbf{X}}_{thj}\}$ is $O_p(1)$ for $g, h = 1, \ldots, p$, $i, j = 1, \ldots, k$;

Then $\hat{\boldsymbol{\Sigma}}_{\gamma n} - \boldsymbol{\Sigma}_\gamma \xrightarrow{p} 0$, $\gamma = 1, \ldots, G$.

With this estimator for $\boldsymbol{\Sigma}_\gamma$ available, a natural estimator for $\boldsymbol{\Omega}_n$ is

$$\hat{\boldsymbol{\Omega}}_n = \text{diag}[\hat{\omega}_{11}, \hat{\omega}_{22}, \ldots, \hat{\omega}_{nn}],$$

where

$$\hat{\omega}_{tt} \equiv \hat{\boldsymbol{\Sigma}}_{1n}\mathbf{d}_{1t} + \hat{\boldsymbol{\Sigma}}_{2n}\mathbf{d}_{2t} + \cdots + \hat{\boldsymbol{\Sigma}}_{Gn}\mathbf{d}_{Gt},$$

that is, $\hat{\omega}_{tt} = \hat{\boldsymbol{\Sigma}}_{\gamma n}$ if observation t belongs to group γ.

This estimator is consistent and leads to efficient parameter estimates under the conditions of the following result. Note, however, that in obtaining this result, it must be assumed not just that $\{\tilde{\mathbf{Z}}_{tgi}\tilde{\boldsymbol{\epsilon}}_{th}, \mathfrak{F}_t\}$ is a martingale difference sequence, but also that $\{\mathbf{d}_{\gamma t}\tilde{\mathbf{Z}}_{tgi}\tilde{\boldsymbol{\epsilon}}_{th}, \mathfrak{F}_t\}$ is a martingale difference sequence. This means that the grouping does not occur in such a way as to affect the orthogonality between the instrumental variables and errors for observations within a given group. The following result does not hold (and should not be expected to hold) in situations in which $E(\tilde{\mathbf{Z}}_{tgi}\tilde{\boldsymbol{\epsilon}}_{th})$ depends on which group the observation belongs to. Further, because

$$\tilde{\mathbf{Z}}_{tgi}\tilde{\boldsymbol{\epsilon}}_{th} = \sum_{\gamma=1}^{G} \mathbf{d}_{\gamma t}\tilde{\mathbf{Z}}_{tgi}\tilde{\boldsymbol{\epsilon}}_{th},$$

the assumption that $\{\mathbf{d}_{\gamma t}\tilde{\mathbf{Z}}_{tgi}\tilde{\boldsymbol{\epsilon}}_{th}, \mathfrak{F}_t\}$ is a martingale difference sequence implies that $\{\tilde{\mathbf{Z}}_{tgi}\tilde{\boldsymbol{\epsilon}}_{th}, \mathfrak{F}_t\}$ is a martingale difference sequence.

THEOREM 7.5: Suppose

(i) $\mathbf{y} = \mathbf{X}\boldsymbol{\beta}_o + \boldsymbol{\epsilon}$;

and suppose there exists a unique σ-field generated by row vectors $\{\mathbf{W}_t\}$ such that

$$E(\boldsymbol{\epsilon}_t|\mathbf{W}_t) = \mathbf{0} \quad \text{and}$$
$$E(\boldsymbol{\epsilon}_t|\mathcal{G}_t) \neq \mathbf{0} \quad \text{for all} \quad \mathcal{G}_t \supset \sigma(W_t), \quad t = 1, \ldots, n;$$
$$E(\boldsymbol{\epsilon}_t\boldsymbol{\epsilon}_t'|\mathbf{W}_t) = \mathbf{I}, \; t = 1, \ldots, n;$$
$$E(\boldsymbol{\epsilon}_t\boldsymbol{\epsilon}_\tau'|\mathbf{W}_t, \mathbf{W}_\tau) = \mathbf{0}, \; t \neq \tau = 1, \ldots, n;$$

and define instrumental variables $\mathbf{Z}$ satisfying

$$E(\mathbf{X}_t|\mathbf{W}_t) = \mathbf{Z}_t\Pi_o, \; t = 1, \ldots, n,$$

where Π_o is an $l \times k$ matrix of full column rank containing no zero rows.

Let $\mathbf{W}_t$ include $\mathbf{d}_t'$ as defined above and let $\mathbf{c}_\gamma$, $\gamma = 1, \ldots, G$ be finite nonsingular nonstochastic $p \times p$ matrices such that $\mathbf{c}_\gamma\mathbf{c}_\gamma' = \boldsymbol{\Sigma}_\gamma$,

$$\tilde{\mathbf{y}}_t = \sum_{\gamma=1}^{G} \mathbf{d}_{\gamma t}\mathbf{c}_\gamma y_t,\ \tilde{\mathbf{X}}_t = \sum_{\gamma=1}^{G} \mathbf{d}_{\gamma t}\mathbf{c}_\gamma \mathbf{X}_t,\ \tilde{\boldsymbol{\epsilon}}_t = \sum_{\gamma=1}^{G} \mathbf{d}_{\gamma t}\mathbf{c}_\gamma \boldsymbol{\epsilon}_t,$$

and let $\tilde{\mathbf{Z}}_t = \Sigma_{\gamma=1}^{G} \mathbf{d}_{\gamma t}\mathbf{c}_\gamma \mathbf{Z}_t$.

In addition, suppose that

(ii) $\{(\mathbf{d}_t, \tilde{\mathbf{Z}}_t, \tilde{\mathbf{X}}_t, \tilde{\boldsymbol{\epsilon}}_t)'\}$ is a mixing sequence with either $\phi(m)$ of size $r/(2r-1)$, $r \geq 1$, or $\alpha(m)$ of size $r/(r-1)$, $r > 1$;

(iii) (a) for all t $E(\mathbf{d}_{\gamma t}\tilde{\mathbf{Z}}_{tgi}\tilde{\boldsymbol{\epsilon}}_{th}|\mathfrak{F}_{t-1}) = \mathbf{0}$, where $\{\mathfrak{F}_t\}$ is adapted to $\{\mathbf{d}_{\gamma t}\tilde{\mathbf{Z}}_{tgi}\tilde{\boldsymbol{\epsilon}}_{th}\}$, $\gamma = 1, \ldots, G$; $g, h = 1, \ldots, p$, $i = 1, \ldots, l$;

(b) $E|\tilde{\mathbf{Z}}_{tgi}\tilde{\boldsymbol{\epsilon}}_{th}|^{2(r+\delta)} < \Delta < \infty$ and $E|\tilde{\boldsymbol{\epsilon}}_{th}|^{2(r+\delta)} < \Delta < \infty$ for some $\delta > 0$, and all $g, h = 1, \ldots, p$, $i = 1, \ldots, l$, and t;

(c) $\mathbf{V}_n \equiv \text{var}(n^{-1/2}\mathbf{Z}'\boldsymbol{\epsilon}) = \text{var}(n^{-1/2}\tilde{\mathbf{Z}}'\boldsymbol{\Omega}_\mathbf{n}^{-1}\tilde{\boldsymbol{\epsilon}})$ is uniformly positive definite;

(iv) (a) $E|\tilde{\mathbf{Z}}_{thi}|^{2(r+\delta)} < \Delta < \infty$ and $E|\tilde{\mathbf{X}}_{thj}|^{2(r+\delta)} < \Delta < \infty$ for some $\delta > 0$, and all $g, h = 1, \ldots, p$, $i = 1, \ldots, l, j = 1, \ldots, k$, and t;

(b) $\tilde{\mathbf{Q}}_n \equiv E(\tilde{\mathbf{Z}}'\tilde{\mathbf{X}}/n)$ and $\mathbf{Q}_n \equiv E(\mathbf{Z}'\mathbf{X}/n) = E(\tilde{\mathbf{Z}}'\boldsymbol{\Omega}_n^{-1}\tilde{\mathbf{X}}/n)$ have uniformly full column rank;

(c) $\tilde{\mathbf{L}}_n \equiv E(\tilde{\mathbf{Z}}'\tilde{\mathbf{Z}}/n)$ is uniformly positive definite.

Define

$$\hat{\boldsymbol{\Sigma}}_{\gamma n} \equiv n_\gamma^{-1} \sum_{t=1}^{n} \mathbf{d}_{\gamma t}\hat{\boldsymbol{\epsilon}}_t\hat{\boldsymbol{\epsilon}}_t',\ \gamma = 1, \ldots, G,$$

where $n_\gamma = \Sigma_{t=1}^{n} \mathbf{d}_{\gamma t}$, $\hat{\boldsymbol{\epsilon}}_t = \tilde{\mathbf{y}}_t - \tilde{\mathbf{X}}_t\tilde{\beta}_n$ and

$$\tilde{\beta}_n = (\tilde{\mathbf{X}}'\tilde{\mathbf{Z}}(\tilde{\mathbf{Z}}'\tilde{\mathbf{Z}})^{-1}\tilde{\mathbf{Z}}'\tilde{\mathbf{X}})^{-1}\tilde{\mathbf{X}}'\tilde{\mathbf{Z}}(\tilde{\mathbf{Z}}'\tilde{\mathbf{Z}})^{-1}\tilde{\mathbf{Z}}'\tilde{\mathbf{y}}.$$

Let

$$\boldsymbol{\Omega}_n \equiv \text{diag}[\omega_{11}, \omega_{22}, \ldots, \omega_{nn}],$$
$$\omega_{tt} \equiv \boldsymbol{\Sigma}_1\mathbf{d}_{1t} + \cdots + \boldsymbol{\Sigma}_G\mathbf{d}_{Gt},$$

and define

$$\hat{\boldsymbol{\Omega}}_n \equiv \text{diag}[\hat{\omega}_{11}, \hat{\omega}_{22}, \ldots, \hat{\omega}_{nn}]$$
$$\hat{\omega}_{tt} \equiv \hat{\boldsymbol{\Sigma}}_{1n}\mathbf{d}_{1t} + \hat{\boldsymbol{\Sigma}}_{2n}\mathbf{d}_{2t} + \cdots + \hat{\boldsymbol{\Sigma}}_{\mathbf{G}n}\mathbf{d}_{\mathbf{G}t},\ t = 1, \ldots, n,$$

so that

$$\hat{\beta}_n^* = (\tilde{\mathbf{X}}'\hat{\boldsymbol{\Omega}}_n^{-1}\tilde{\mathbf{Z}}(\tilde{\mathbf{Z}}'\hat{\boldsymbol{\Omega}}_n^{-1}\tilde{\mathbf{Z}})^{-1}\tilde{\mathbf{Z}}'\hat{\boldsymbol{\Omega}}_n^{-1}\tilde{\mathbf{X}})^{-1}\tilde{\mathbf{X}}'\hat{\boldsymbol{\Omega}}_n^{-1}\tilde{\mathbf{Z}}(\tilde{\mathbf{Z}}'\hat{\boldsymbol{\Omega}}_n^{-1}\tilde{\mathbf{Z}})^{-1}\tilde{\mathbf{Z}}'\hat{\boldsymbol{\Omega}}_n^{-1}\tilde{\mathbf{y}}.$$

Let

$$\beta_n^* = (\mathbf{X}'\mathbf{Z}(\mathbf{Z}'\mathbf{Z})^{-1}\mathbf{Z}'\mathbf{X})^{-1}\mathbf{X}'\mathbf{Z}(\mathbf{Z}'\mathbf{Z})^{-1}\mathbf{Z}'\mathbf{y}.$$

If $E(n_\gamma/n) > \delta > 0$ for all n sufficiently large, $\gamma = 1, \ldots, G$, then $\sqrt{n}(\hat{\beta}_n^* - \beta_n^*) \xrightarrow{p} 0$, $\mathbf{D}_n^{-1/2} n^{-1/2}(\hat{\beta}_n^* - \beta_o) \overset{A}{\sim} N(\mathbf{0}, \mathbf{I})$, where $\mathbf{D}_n \equiv (\mathbf{Q}_n'\mathbf{V}_n^{-1}\mathbf{Q}_n)^{-1}$, and the conclusions of Theorem 4.57 hold for $\hat{\beta}_n^*$. Further, $\hat{\mathbf{D}}_n - \mathbf{D}_n \xrightarrow{p} \mathbf{0}$, where

$$\hat{\mathbf{D}}_n \equiv (\tilde{\mathbf{X}}'\Omega_n^{-1}\tilde{\mathbf{Z}}(\tilde{\mathbf{Z}}'\Omega_n^{-1}\tilde{\mathbf{Z}})^{-1}\tilde{\mathbf{Z}}'\Omega_n^{-1}\tilde{\mathbf{X}}/n)^{-1}.$$

Proof: First, we verify the conditions of Exercise 7.4 and then we verify the conditions of Theorem 7.1.

Given (ii), $\{\mathbf{d}_{\gamma t}\}$ is a mixing sequence satisfying the conditions of Corollary 3.48, $\gamma = 1, \ldots, G$. (Note that because $\mathbf{d}_{\gamma t} = 0$ or $\mathbf{d}_{\gamma t} = 1$, $|\mathbf{d}_{\gamma t}|^{r+\delta} \leq 1$ and $E|\mathbf{d}_{\gamma t}|^{r+\gamma} \leq 1$ for any $r + \delta$.) It follows that $n_\gamma/n - E(n_\gamma/n) = n^{-1}\sum_{t=1}^n \mathbf{d}_{\gamma t} - E(\mathbf{d}_{\gamma t}) \xrightarrow{p} 0$ by Corollary 3.48 and Theorem 2.24. $E(n_\gamma/n) > \delta > 0$ for all n sufficiently large by assumption.

Given (ii), $\{\mathbf{d}_{\gamma t}\tilde{\boldsymbol{\epsilon}}_t\tilde{\boldsymbol{\epsilon}}_t'\}$ is a mixing sequence. By the Cauchy–Schwartz inequality, $E|\tilde{\boldsymbol{\epsilon}}_{th}\tilde{\boldsymbol{\epsilon}}_{tg}|^{r+\delta} \leq (E|\tilde{\boldsymbol{\epsilon}}_{th}|^{2(r+\delta)})^{1/2}(E|\tilde{\boldsymbol{\epsilon}}_{tg}|^{2(r+\delta)})^{1/2} < \Delta$ by (iii.b). Then $|\mathbf{d}_{\gamma t}\tilde{\boldsymbol{\epsilon}}_{th}\tilde{\boldsymbol{\epsilon}}_{tg}|^{r+\delta} = |\mathbf{d}_{\gamma t}|^{r+\delta}|\tilde{\boldsymbol{\epsilon}}_{th}\tilde{\boldsymbol{\epsilon}}_{tg}|^{r+\delta} \leq |\tilde{\boldsymbol{\epsilon}}_{th}\tilde{\boldsymbol{\epsilon}}_{tg}|^{r+\delta}$ because $|\mathbf{d}_{\gamma t}| \leq 1$, so that $E|\mathbf{d}_{\gamma t}\tilde{\boldsymbol{\epsilon}}_{tg}\tilde{\boldsymbol{\epsilon}}_{th}|^{r+\delta} < \Delta$. It follows from Corollary 3.48 and Theorem 2.24 that

$$n^{-1}\sum_{t=1}^{n} \mathbf{d}_{\gamma t}\tilde{\boldsymbol{\epsilon}}_t\tilde{\boldsymbol{\epsilon}}_t' - E(\mathbf{d}_{\gamma t}\tilde{\boldsymbol{\epsilon}}_t\tilde{\boldsymbol{\epsilon}}_t') \xrightarrow{p} \mathbf{0}.$$

Next, given (ii), $\{\mathbf{d}_{\gamma t}\tilde{\mathbf{X}}_{tgi}\tilde{\boldsymbol{\epsilon}}_{th}\}$ is a mixing sequence. By the Cauchy–Schwartz inequality,

$$E|\tilde{\mathbf{X}}_{tgi}\tilde{\boldsymbol{\epsilon}}_{th}|^{r+\delta} \leq (E|\tilde{\mathbf{X}}_{tgi}|^{2(r+\delta)})^{1/2}(E|\tilde{\boldsymbol{\epsilon}}_{th}|^{2(r+\delta)})^{1/2} < \Delta,$$

given (iii.b) and (iv.a), and because $|\mathbf{d}_{\gamma t}|^{r+\delta} \leq 1$, it follows that $E|\mathbf{d}_{\gamma t}\tilde{\mathbf{X}}_{tgi}\tilde{\boldsymbol{\epsilon}}_{th}|^{r+\delta} < \Delta$. It follows from Corollary 3.48 and Theorem 2.24 that

$$n^{-1}\sum_{t=1}^{n} \mathbf{d}_{\gamma t}\tilde{\mathbf{X}}_{tgi}\tilde{\boldsymbol{\epsilon}}_{th} - E(\mathbf{d}_{\gamma t}\tilde{\mathbf{X}}_{tgi}\tilde{\boldsymbol{\epsilon}}_{th}) \xrightarrow{p} 0$$

and from Jensen's inequality that $|n^{-1}\sum_{t=1}^n E(\mathbf{d}_{\gamma t}\tilde{\mathbf{X}}_{tgi}\tilde{\boldsymbol{\epsilon}}_{th})| < \Delta < \infty$; hence $\{n^{-1}\sum_{t=1}^n \mathbf{d}_{\gamma t}\tilde{\mathbf{X}}_{tgi}\tilde{\boldsymbol{\epsilon}}_{th}\}$ is $O_p(1)$ for $g, h = 1, \ldots, p$ and $i = 1, \ldots, k$.

Finally, $\{n^{-1}\sum_{t=1}^n \mathbf{d}_{\gamma t}\tilde{\mathbf{X}}_{tgi}\tilde{\mathbf{X}}_{thj}\}$ is $O_p(1)$ by argument identical to that above with $\tilde{\mathbf{X}}_{thj}$ replacing $\tilde{\boldsymbol{\epsilon}}_{th}$. It follows from Exercise 3.80

that $\tilde{\beta}_n \xrightarrow{p} \beta_o$ choosing $\tilde{\mathbf{P}}_n = \tilde{\mathbf{L}}_n^{-1}$, so the conditions of Exercise 7.4 hold and $\hat{\mathbf{\Sigma}}_{\gamma n} - \mathbf{\Sigma}_\gamma \xrightarrow{p} \mathbf{0}$.

We now verify the conditions of Theorem 7.1. Considering $\tilde{\mathbf{Z}}'(\mathbf{\Omega}_n^{-1} - \hat{\mathbf{\Omega}}_n^{-1})\tilde{\boldsymbol{\epsilon}}/\sqrt{n}$, for the form of $\mathbf{\Omega}_n$ and $\hat{\mathbf{\Omega}}_n$ considered here we have

$$\tilde{\mathbf{Z}}'(\mathbf{\Omega}_n^{-1} - \hat{\mathbf{\Omega}}_n^{-1})\tilde{\boldsymbol{\epsilon}}/\sqrt{n} = n^{-1/2} \sum_{t=1}^{n} \tilde{\mathbf{Z}}_t'(\omega_{tt}^{-1} - \hat{\omega}_{tt}^{-1})\tilde{\boldsymbol{\epsilon}}_t.$$

Let $\omega_{tt}^{-1} = [\omega_{tt}^{gh}]$ and $\hat{\omega}_{tt}^{-1} = [\hat{\omega}_{tt}^{gh}]$. The ith element of $\tilde{\mathbf{Z}}'(\mathbf{\Omega}_n^{-1} - \hat{\mathbf{\Omega}}_n^{-1})\tilde{\boldsymbol{\epsilon}}/\sqrt{n}$ can be written as

$$\begin{aligned} n^{-1/2} &\sum_{t=1}^{n} \sum_{g=1}^{p} \sum_{h=1}^{p} \tilde{\mathbf{Z}}_{tgi}(\omega_{tt}^{gh} - \hat{\omega}_{tt}^{gh})\tilde{\boldsymbol{\epsilon}}_{th} \\ &= n^{-1/2} \sum_{t=1}^{n} \sum_{g=1}^{p} \sum_{h=1}^{p} \tilde{\mathbf{Z}}_{tgi}\left(\sum_{\gamma=1}^{G} [\sigma_\gamma^{gh} - \hat{\sigma}_{\gamma n}^{gh}]\mathbf{d}_{\gamma t}\right)\tilde{\boldsymbol{\epsilon}}_{th}, \end{aligned}$$

because $\omega_{tt}^{gh} = \Sigma_{\gamma=1}^{G} \sigma_\gamma^{gh}\mathbf{d}_{\gamma t}$ and $\hat{\omega}_{tt}^{gh} = \Sigma_{\gamma=1}^{G} \hat{\sigma}_{\gamma n}^{gh}\mathbf{d}_{\gamma t}$, with $\mathbf{\Sigma}_\gamma^{-1} = [\sigma_\gamma^{gh}]$ and $\hat{\mathbf{\Sigma}}_{\gamma n}^{-1} = [\hat{\sigma}_{\gamma n}^{gh}]$. Interchanging the order of summation, we have the ith element of $\tilde{\mathbf{Z}}'(\mathbf{\Omega}_n^{-1} - \hat{\mathbf{\Omega}}_n^{-1})\tilde{\boldsymbol{\epsilon}}/\sqrt{n}$ given by

$$\begin{aligned} n^{-1/2} &\sum_{t=1}^{n} \sum_{g=1}^{p} \sum_{h=1}^{p} \tilde{\mathbf{Z}}_{tgi}(\omega_{tt}^{gh} - \hat{\omega}_{tt}^{gh})\tilde{\boldsymbol{\epsilon}}_{th} \\ &= \sum_{\gamma=1}^{G} \sum_{g=1}^{p} \sum_{h=1}^{p} (\sigma_\gamma^{gh} - \hat{\sigma}_{\gamma n}^{gh}) n^{-1/2} \sum_{t=1}^{n} \mathbf{d}_{\gamma t}\tilde{\mathbf{Z}}_{tgi}\tilde{\boldsymbol{\epsilon}}_{th}. \end{aligned}$$

The argument now proceeds identically to that of Theorem 7.3. Because $\hat{\mathbf{\Sigma}}_{n\gamma} - \mathbf{\Sigma}_\gamma \xrightarrow{p} 0$, it follows from Proposition 2.27 that $\sigma_\gamma^{gh} - \hat{\sigma}_{\gamma n}^{gh} \xrightarrow{p} 0$, $\gamma = 1, \ldots, G$, g, $h = 1, \ldots, p$. The Chebyshev inequality applies to show that $n^{-1/2} \Sigma_{t=1}^{n} \mathbf{d}_{\gamma t}\tilde{\mathbf{Z}}_{tgi}\boldsymbol{\epsilon}_{th}$ is $O_p(1)$. Application of Exercise 2.35(c) and (d) then yields that, element by element,

$$\tilde{\mathbf{Z}}'(\mathbf{\Omega}_n^{-1} - \hat{\mathbf{\Omega}}_n^{-1})\tilde{\boldsymbol{\epsilon}}/\sqrt{n} \xrightarrow{p} \mathbf{0}.$$

Similar arguments establish that $\tilde{\mathbf{Z}}'(\mathbf{\Omega}_n^{-1} - \hat{\mathbf{\Omega}}_n^{-1})\tilde{\mathbf{X}}/n \xrightarrow{p} 0$ and that $\tilde{\mathbf{Z}}'(\mathbf{\Omega}_n^{-1} - \hat{\mathbf{\Omega}}_n^{-1})\tilde{\mathbf{Z}}/n \xrightarrow{p} \mathbf{0}$.

It remains to verify that the conditions of Exercise 4.26 hold under the assumptions given. For this, it suffices to show that the conditions of Exercise 5.27 hold for $\mathbf{Z}_t$, $\mathbf{X}_t$, and $\boldsymbol{\epsilon}_t$. This is tedious but straightforward to show, and the details are left to the reader. Care must be taken to treat ω_{tt} as a random variable, as the definition of ω_{tt} implies. For example, the elements of $\tilde{\mathbf{Z}}'\mathbf{\Omega}_n^{-1}\tilde{\boldsymbol{\epsilon}}/\sqrt{n} = \mathbf{Z}'\boldsymbol{\epsilon}/\sqrt{n}$ have the form

$$n^{-1/2}\sum_{t=1}^{n}\left(\sum_{\gamma=1}^{G}\sum_{g=1}^{p}\sum_{h=1}^{p}\sigma_{\gamma}^{gh}\mathbf{d}_{\gamma t}\tilde{\mathbf{Z}}_{tgi}\tilde{\boldsymbol{\epsilon}}_{th}\right).$$

As before, the choice $\mathbf{Z} = \mathbf{C}_n\mathbf{Z}$ is not critical for constructing $\tilde{\boldsymbol{\beta}}_n$, but only for constructing $\hat{\boldsymbol{\beta}}_n^*$.

This result is similar to a result for nonlinear models with a finite number of different error variances given by White [1980]. Although the present result applies only to linear rather than nonlinear models, it applies to systems of simultaneous equations and panels rather than only single reduced form equations and allows dependent observations (e.g., lagged dependent variables) instead of only independent observations.

VII.4 Case 3: Serial Correlation

In this section we consider finding the efficient estimator when the error covariance matrix has the structure which arises when the nonspherical error term is generated by a finite order vector autoregressive model of the form

$$\tilde{\boldsymbol{\epsilon}}_t = \mathbf{R}_1\tilde{\boldsymbol{\epsilon}}_{t-1} + \mathbf{R}_2\tilde{\boldsymbol{\epsilon}}_{t-2} + \cdots + \mathbf{R}_m\tilde{\boldsymbol{\epsilon}}_{t-m} + \boldsymbol{\eta}_t,$$

where $\mathbf{R}_\tau$, $\tau = 1, \ldots, m$ are $p \times p$ matrices of unknown coefficients and $\boldsymbol{\eta}_t$ is a $p \times 1$ disturbance vector with $E(\boldsymbol{\eta}_t) = 0$, $E(\boldsymbol{\eta}_t\boldsymbol{\eta}_t') = \boldsymbol{\Sigma}$, and other properties to be precisely specified below. The number of lags m is assumed to be known.

The covariance matrix $\boldsymbol{\Omega}_n$ which arises in this case has an extremely complicated and rather uninsightful form, so we omit writing it down. Although it is in principle possible to obtain a consistent estimator for $\boldsymbol{\Omega}_n$ and proceed by analogy to the cases just given, such an approach is extremely tedious.

Instead, we consider finding an estimator for $\boldsymbol{\beta}_o$ using the "pseudo-differenced" version of the original model

$$\begin{aligned}\tilde{\mathbf{y}}_t - \mathbf{R}_1\tilde{\mathbf{y}}_{t-1} - \cdots - \mathbf{R}_m\tilde{\mathbf{y}}_{t-m} \\ = \tilde{\mathbf{X}}_t\boldsymbol{\beta}_o - \mathbf{R}_1\tilde{\mathbf{X}}_{t-1}\boldsymbol{\beta}_o - \cdots - \mathbf{R}_m\tilde{\mathbf{X}}_{t-m}\boldsymbol{\beta}_o \\ + \tilde{\boldsymbol{\epsilon}}_t - \mathbf{R}_1\tilde{\boldsymbol{\epsilon}}_{t-1} - \cdots - \mathbf{R}_m\tilde{\boldsymbol{\epsilon}}_{t-m},\ t = m+1, \ldots, n\end{aligned}$$

or

$$\begin{aligned}\tilde{\mathbf{y}}_t - \mathbf{R}_1\tilde{\mathbf{y}}_{t-1} - \cdots - \mathbf{R}_m\tilde{\mathbf{y}}_{t-m} \\ = (\tilde{\mathbf{X}}_t - \mathbf{R}_1\tilde{\mathbf{X}}_{t-1} - \cdots - \mathbf{R}_m\tilde{\mathbf{X}}_{t-m})\boldsymbol{\beta}_o \\ + \boldsymbol{\eta}_t, \; t = m+1, \ldots, n.\end{aligned}$$

If $\mathbf{R}_1, \ldots, \mathbf{R}_m$ were known, the results of Section 2 would apply immediately, provided that the explanatory variables, errors, and instrumental variables satisfy the appropriate conditions.

Because $\mathbf{R}_1, \ldots, \mathbf{R}_m$ are unknown, they must be estimated, so we take the lagged $\tilde{\mathbf{y}}$'s to the right-hand side of the equation and consider estimating the parameters of the equation

$$\begin{aligned}\tilde{\mathbf{y}}_t = \mathbf{R}_1\tilde{\mathbf{y}}_{t-1} + \cdots + \mathbf{R}_m\tilde{\mathbf{y}}_{t-m} \\ + \tilde{\mathbf{X}}_t\boldsymbol{\beta}_o - \mathbf{R}_1\tilde{\mathbf{X}}_{t-1}\boldsymbol{\beta}_o - \cdots - \mathbf{R}_m\tilde{\mathbf{X}}_{t-m}\boldsymbol{\beta}_o \\ + \boldsymbol{\eta}_t, \; t = m+1, \ldots, n.\end{aligned}$$

This model resembles models previously considered, but differs in form, because the parameters $\mathbf{R}_1, \ldots, \mathbf{R}_m$ appear as premultiplying the explanatory variables rather than postmultiplying them.

This difference is purely formal, however, because we can algebraically manipulate this equation into an equivalent version in the familiar form by using the vec operator. If $\mathbf{A}$ is an $n \times k$ matrix with columns $\mathbf{A}_1, \mathbf{A}_2, \ldots, \mathbf{A}_k$, then vec $\mathbf{A}$ is the $nk \times 1$ column vector such that

$$\text{vec } \mathbf{A} = \begin{bmatrix}\mathbf{A}_1 \\ \mathbf{A}_2 \\ \cdot \\ \cdot \\ \cdot \\ \mathbf{A}_k\end{bmatrix}.$$

It is straightforward to show that for conformable matrices $\mathbf{A}$, $\mathbf{B}$ and $\mathbf{C}$,

$$\text{vec}(\mathbf{ABC}) = (\mathbf{C}' \otimes \mathbf{A}) \text{ vec } \mathbf{B}.$$

Now consider

$$\mathbf{R}_1\tilde{\mathbf{y}}_{t-1} + \cdots + \mathbf{R}_m\tilde{\mathbf{y}}_{t-m} = \text{vec} \sum_{\tau=1}^{m} \tilde{\mathbf{y}}'_{t-\tau}\mathbf{R}'_\tau = \text{vec } \check{\mathbf{y}}_t\mathbf{R}',$$

where $\check{\mathbf{y}}_t \equiv (\tilde{\mathbf{y}}'_{t-1}, \ldots, \tilde{\mathbf{y}}'_{t-m})$ is a $1 \times pm$ vector and $\mathbf{R}$ is the $p \times pm$

matrix defined as

$$\mathbf{R} \equiv [\mathbf{R}_1, \mathbf{R}_2, \ldots, \mathbf{R}_m].$$

Hence

$$\mathbf{R}_1\tilde{\mathbf{y}}_{t-1} + \cdots + \mathbf{R}_m\tilde{\mathbf{y}}_{t-m} = \text{vec}\ \check{\mathbf{y}}_t\mathbf{R}' = \text{vec}\ \check{\mathbf{y}}_t\mathbf{R}'\mathbf{I}_p = (\mathbf{I}_p \otimes \check{\mathbf{y}}_t)\text{vec}\ \mathbf{R}'.$$

Letting $\check{\mathbf{Y}}_t \equiv (\mathbf{I}_p \otimes \check{\mathbf{y}}_t)$, a $p \times p^2m$ matrix, and $\boldsymbol{\rho}_o \equiv \text{vec}\ \mathbf{R}'$, a $p^2m \times 1$ vector, we have

$$\mathbf{R}_1\tilde{\mathbf{y}}_{t-1} + \cdots + \mathbf{R}_m\tilde{\mathbf{y}}_{t-m} = \check{\mathbf{Y}}_t\boldsymbol{\rho}_o.$$

Next, consider rewriting $\mathbf{R}_1\tilde{\mathbf{X}}_{t-1}\boldsymbol{\beta}_o + \cdots \mathbf{R}_m\tilde{\mathbf{X}}_{t-m}\boldsymbol{\beta}_o$. Denoting the ith column of $\tilde{\mathbf{X}}_{t-\tau}$ by $\tilde{\mathbf{X}}_{t-\tau i}$, $i = 1, \ldots, k$, then the ith column of $\mathbf{R}_1\tilde{\mathbf{X}}_{t-1} + \cdots + \mathbf{R}_m\tilde{\mathbf{X}}_{t-m}$ is given by

$$\mathbf{R}_1\tilde{\mathbf{X}}_{t-1i} + \cdots + \mathbf{R}_m\tilde{\mathbf{X}}_{t-mi} = \text{vec}\ \check{\mathbf{x}}_{ti}\mathbf{R}',$$

where $\check{\mathbf{x}}_{ti} \equiv (\tilde{\mathbf{X}}'_{t-1i}, \ldots, \tilde{\mathbf{X}}'_{t-mi})$, a $1 \times pm$ vector, so that we have

$$\text{vec}\ \check{\mathbf{x}}_{ti}\mathbf{R}' = (\mathbf{I}_p \otimes \check{\mathbf{x}}_{ti})\text{vec R}' = \check{\mathbf{X}}_{ti}\boldsymbol{\rho}_o,$$

where $\check{\mathbf{X}}_{ti} \equiv (\mathbf{I} \otimes \check{\mathbf{x}}_{ti})$, a $p \times p^2m$ matrix. Hence

$$\begin{aligned}\mathbf{R}_1\tilde{\mathbf{X}}_{t-1} + \mathbf{R}_2\tilde{\mathbf{X}}_{t-2} + \cdots + \mathbf{R}_m\tilde{\mathbf{X}}_{t-m} &= [\check{\mathbf{X}}_{t1}\boldsymbol{\rho}_o, \check{\mathbf{X}}_{t2}\boldsymbol{\rho}_o, \ldots, \check{\mathbf{X}}_{tk}\boldsymbol{\rho}_o] \\ &= \check{\mathbf{X}}_t(\mathbf{I}_k \otimes \boldsymbol{\rho}_o),\end{aligned}$$

where $\check{\mathbf{X}}_t$ is the $p \times p^2mk$ matrix.

$$\check{\mathbf{X}}_t = [\check{\mathbf{X}}_{t1}, \check{\mathbf{X}}_{t2}, \ldots, \check{\mathbf{X}}_{tk}].$$

This allows us to write

$$\mathbf{R}_1\tilde{\mathbf{X}}_{t-1}\boldsymbol{\beta}_o + \cdots + \mathbf{R}_m\tilde{\mathbf{X}}_{t-m}\boldsymbol{\beta}_o = \check{\mathbf{X}}_t(\mathbf{I}_k \otimes \boldsymbol{\rho}_o)\boldsymbol{\beta}_o,$$

so that our model now becomes

$$\tilde{\mathbf{y}}_t = \check{\mathbf{Y}}_t\boldsymbol{\rho}_o + \tilde{\mathbf{X}}_t\boldsymbol{\beta}_o + \check{\mathbf{X}}_t\boldsymbol{\gamma}_o + \boldsymbol{\eta}_t, \qquad t = m+1, \ldots, n,$$

where $\boldsymbol{\gamma}_o = -(\mathbf{I}_k \otimes \boldsymbol{\rho}_o)\boldsymbol{\beta}_o$.

This model is in precisely the form considered in Section 2, except that nonlinear constraints are imposed on the parameters by the relationship $\boldsymbol{\gamma}_o = -(\mathbf{I}_k \otimes \boldsymbol{\rho}_o)\boldsymbol{\beta}_o$. In Chapter IV, we saw that the efficient estimator that imposes these constraints can be determined by obtaining the efficient unconstrained estimator and then subtracting a correction factor that imposes the constraints. To obtain the efficient unconstrained estimator, we use the results of Theorem 7.3 for the three-stage least squares estimator with optimal instrumental variables.

One detail remains to be taken care of before we can proceed. This arises from the fact that if $\tilde{\mathbf{X}}_t$ contains any lagged values of either dependent or explanatory variables, then $\check{\mathbf{Y}}_t$ or $\check{\mathbf{X}}_t$ may contain these variables also, leading to redundancies in the explanatory variables of the model

$$\tilde{\mathbf{y}}_t = \check{\mathbf{Y}}_t \rho_o + \tilde{\mathbf{X}}_t \beta_o + \check{\mathbf{X}}_t \gamma_o + \eta_t.$$

For example, suppose the original model is

$$\tilde{\mathbf{y}}_t = \tilde{\mathbf{y}}_{t-1}\alpha_o + \tilde{\mathbf{W}}_t \psi_o + \tilde{\epsilon}_t,$$

so that $\tilde{\mathbf{X}}_t = (\tilde{\mathbf{y}}_{t-1}, \tilde{\mathbf{W}}_t)$, $\beta_o' = (\alpha_o, \psi_o)$ and $\tilde{\epsilon}_t$ is a scalar such that

$$\tilde{\epsilon}_t = \tilde{\epsilon}_{t-1}\rho_o + \eta_t.$$

The pseudo differenced model is

$$\begin{aligned}\tilde{\mathbf{y}}_t = {} & \tilde{\mathbf{y}}_{t-1}\rho_o + \tilde{\mathbf{y}}_{t-1}\alpha_o + \tilde{\mathbf{W}}_t\psi_o - \tilde{\mathbf{y}}_{t-2}\rho_o\alpha_o \\ & - \tilde{\mathbf{W}}_{t-1}\rho_o\psi_o + \eta_t.\end{aligned}$$

In this example, $\check{\mathbf{Y}}_t = \tilde{\mathbf{y}}_{t-1}$, $\check{\mathbf{X}}_t = (\tilde{\mathbf{y}}_{t-2}, \tilde{\mathbf{W}}_{t-1})$ and $\gamma_o = (-\alpha_o\rho_o, -\psi_o\rho_o)$. Note, however, that both $\check{\mathbf{Y}}_t$ and $\tilde{\mathbf{X}}_t$ contain $\tilde{\mathbf{y}}_{t-1}$, which is a redundancy. The obvious solution is to collect terms, so that the model is written without redundancies as

$$\begin{aligned}\tilde{\mathbf{y}}_t = {} & \tilde{\mathbf{y}}_{t-1}(\alpha_o + \rho_o) + \tilde{\mathbf{W}}_t\psi_o - \tilde{\mathbf{y}}_{t-2}\rho_o\alpha_o \\ & - \tilde{\mathbf{W}}_{t-1}\rho_o\psi_o + \nu_t.\end{aligned}$$

Now observe that the constraints among the parameters of this model are no longer given by $\gamma_o = -\rho_o\beta_o$. If we write the model as

$$\tilde{\mathbf{y}}_t = \tilde{\mathbf{y}}_{t-1}\mathbf{a} + \tilde{\mathbf{W}}_t\mathbf{b} + \tilde{\mathbf{y}}_{t-2}\mathbf{c} + \tilde{\mathbf{W}}_{t-1}\mathbf{d} + \nu_t,$$

we can find α_o and ρ_o as the solutions to the equations $\mathbf{a} = \alpha_o + \rho_o$, $\mathbf{c} = -\rho_o\alpha_o$, which implies in particular that ρ_o is the solution to the quadratic equation $\rho_o^2 - \mathbf{a}\rho_o - \mathbf{c} = 0$. Denote the appropriate solution as $\rho_o(\mathbf{a}, \mathbf{c})$. Then the constraints can be expressed as

$$\mathbf{d} = \rho_o(\mathbf{a}, \mathbf{c})\mathbf{b}.$$

In general, whenever redundancies arise in the model

$$\mathbf{y}_t = \check{\mathbf{Y}}_t\rho_o + \tilde{\mathbf{X}}_t\beta_o + \check{\mathbf{X}}_t\gamma_o + \eta_t,$$

we can eliminate them by collecting terms. Once this has been done, we can write the model compactly as

$$\tilde{\mathbf{y}}_t = \ddot{\mathbf{X}}_t \boldsymbol{\delta}_o + \boldsymbol{\eta}_t,$$

where $\ddot{\mathbf{X}}_t$ contains the nonredundant columns of $\check{\mathbf{Y}}_t$, $\tilde{\mathbf{X}}_t$, and $\check{\mathbf{X}}_t$, and $\boldsymbol{\delta}_o$ is a parameter vector that satisfies restrictions $\mathbf{s}(\boldsymbol{\delta}_o) = \mathbf{0}$. For example, when $\tilde{\mathbf{X}}_t$ contains no lagged variables, we have $\ddot{\mathbf{X}}_t = (\check{\mathbf{Y}}_t, \tilde{\mathbf{X}}_t, \check{\mathbf{X}}_t)$, $\boldsymbol{\delta}_o' = (\boldsymbol{\rho}_o', \boldsymbol{\beta}_o', \boldsymbol{\gamma}_o')$, and $\mathbf{s}(\boldsymbol{\delta}_o) = \boldsymbol{\gamma}_o + (\mathbf{I}_k \otimes \boldsymbol{\rho}_o)\boldsymbol{\beta}_o = \mathbf{0}$.

The estimation problem now amounts to efficiently estimating the parameters of a linear model with contemporaneous covariance in $\boldsymbol{\eta}_t$ and nonlinear constraints on the parameters. This can be accomplished by the following three-step procedure.

First obtain consistent estimates of $\boldsymbol{\delta}_o$, for example, by 2SLS using appropriate instrumental variables $\ddot{\mathbf{Z}}_t$. Letting $\ddot{\mathbf{X}}$ be the matrix with tth block $\ddot{\mathbf{X}}_t$ and letting $\ddot{\mathbf{Z}}$ be the matrix with tth block $\ddot{\mathbf{Z}}_t$, the 2SLS estimator is

$$\tilde{\boldsymbol{\delta}}_n = (\ddot{\mathbf{X}}'\ddot{\mathbf{Z}}(\ddot{\mathbf{Z}}'\ddot{\mathbf{Z}})^{-1}\ddot{\mathbf{Z}}'\ddot{\mathbf{X}})^{-1}\ddot{\mathbf{X}}'\ddot{\mathbf{Z}}(\ddot{\mathbf{Z}}'\ddot{\mathbf{Z}})^{-1}\ddot{\mathbf{Z}}'\tilde{\mathbf{y}}.$$

Next, obtain a consistent estimator of $\boldsymbol{\Sigma}$ as

$$\hat{\boldsymbol{\Sigma}}_n = (n-m)^{-1} \sum_{t=m+1}^{n} \hat{\boldsymbol{\eta}}_t \hat{\boldsymbol{\eta}}_t',$$

where $\hat{\boldsymbol{\eta}}_t = \tilde{\mathbf{y}}_t - \ddot{\mathbf{X}}_t \tilde{\boldsymbol{\delta}}_n$, and form the 3SLS estimator

$$\hat{\boldsymbol{\delta}}_n = (\ddot{\mathbf{X}}'\hat{\boldsymbol{\Omega}}_n^{-1}\ddot{\mathbf{Z}}(\ddot{\mathbf{Z}}'\hat{\boldsymbol{\Omega}}_n^{-1}\ddot{\mathbf{Z}})^{-1}\ddot{\mathbf{Z}}'\hat{\boldsymbol{\Omega}}_n^{-1}\ddot{\mathbf{X}})^{-1}\ddot{\mathbf{X}}'\hat{\boldsymbol{\Omega}}_n^{-1}\ddot{\mathbf{Z}}(\ddot{\mathbf{Z}}'\hat{\boldsymbol{\Omega}}_n^{-1}\ddot{\mathbf{Z}})^{-1}\ddot{\mathbf{Z}}'\hat{\boldsymbol{\Omega}}_n^{-1}\tilde{\mathbf{y}},$$

where $\hat{\boldsymbol{\Omega}}_n = \mathbf{I}_{n-m} \otimes \hat{\boldsymbol{\Sigma}}_n$.

Finally, obtain the efficient estimator as

$$\begin{aligned} \hat{\boldsymbol{\delta}}_n^* = \hat{\boldsymbol{\delta}}_n &- (\ddot{\mathbf{X}}'\hat{\boldsymbol{\Omega}}_n^{-1}\ddot{\mathbf{Z}}(\ddot{\mathbf{Z}}'\hat{\boldsymbol{\Omega}}_n^{-1}\ddot{\mathbf{Z}})^{-1}\ddot{\mathbf{Z}}'\hat{\boldsymbol{\Omega}}_n^{-1}\ddot{\mathbf{X}})^{-1}\nabla\mathbf{s}(\hat{\boldsymbol{\delta}}_n) \\ &\cdot [\nabla\mathbf{s}(\hat{\boldsymbol{\delta}}_n)(\ddot{\mathbf{X}}'\hat{\boldsymbol{\Omega}}_n^{-1}\ddot{\mathbf{Z}}(\ddot{\mathbf{Z}}'\hat{\boldsymbol{\Omega}}_n^{-1}\ddot{\mathbf{Z}})^{-1}\ddot{\mathbf{Z}}'\hat{\boldsymbol{\Omega}}_n^{-1}\ddot{\mathbf{X}})^{-1}\nabla\mathbf{s}(\hat{\boldsymbol{\delta}}_n)']^{-1}\mathbf{s}(\hat{\boldsymbol{\delta}}_n), \end{aligned}$$

where $\mathbf{s}(\boldsymbol{\delta}_o) = \mathbf{0}$ expresses the parameter constraints. As mentioned in Chapter IV, further iterations of the equation above can be undertaken (replace $\hat{\boldsymbol{\delta}}_n$ with $\hat{\boldsymbol{\delta}}_n^*$, etc.), although no further gain in asymptotic efficiency is achieved.

Also note that the validity of the constraints (hence the validity of the autoregressive model for $\tilde{\boldsymbol{\epsilon}}_t$) can be tested using the Wald test of Exercise 4.42. If the hypothesis that the restrictions are true is rejected, one may want to consider reformulating the model before proceeding.

Applying Theorems 7.3, 4.60 and 4.61, we obtain the following result.

THEOREM 7.6: Suppose

(i) $\tilde{\mathbf{y}}_t = \tilde{\mathbf{X}}_t \beta_o + \tilde{\boldsymbol{\epsilon}}_t$ and $\tilde{\boldsymbol{\epsilon}}_t = \mathbf{R}_1 \tilde{\boldsymbol{\epsilon}}_{t-1} + \cdots + \mathbf{R}_m \tilde{\boldsymbol{\epsilon}}_{t-m} + \eta_t$, $t = 1, \ldots, n$, so that $\tilde{\mathbf{y}}_t = \ddot{\mathbf{X}}_t \delta_o + \eta_t$ as above, where $\mathbf{s}(\delta_o) = \mathbf{0}$, $t = m+1, \ldots, n$, and that $\eta_t = \mathbf{c}\boldsymbol{\epsilon}_t$ for some finite nonsingular nonstochastic $p \times p$ matrix such that $\mathbf{cc}' = \boldsymbol{\Sigma}$. Suppose there exists a unique σ-field generated by row vectors $\{\mathbf{W}_t\}$ such that

$$E(\boldsymbol{\epsilon}_t | \mathbf{W}_t) = \mathbf{0} \qquad \text{and}$$

$$E(\boldsymbol{\epsilon}_t | \mathcal{G}_t) \neq \mathbf{0} \qquad \text{for all } \mathcal{G}_t \supset \sigma(\mathbf{W}_t), \quad t = 1, \ldots, n;$$

$$E(\boldsymbol{\epsilon}_t \boldsymbol{\epsilon}_t' | \mathbf{W}_t) = \mathbf{I}, \ t = 1, \ldots, n;$$

$$E(\boldsymbol{\epsilon}_t \boldsymbol{\epsilon}_\tau' | \mathbf{W}_t, \mathbf{W}_\tau) = \mathbf{0}, \ t \neq \tau = 1, \ldots, n;$$

and define instrumental variables $\mathbf{Z}$ satisfying

$$E(\mathbf{X}_t | \mathbf{W}_t) = \mathbf{Z}_t \Pi_o, \ t = 1, \ldots, n,$$

where $\mathbf{X}_t = \mathbf{c}^{-1} \ddot{\mathbf{X}}_t$ and Π_o is an $l \times k$ matrix of full column rank containing no zero rows. Let $\ddot{\mathbf{Z}}_t = \mathbf{c}\mathbf{Z}_t$.

In addition, suppose that

(ii) $\{(\ddot{\mathbf{Z}}_t, \ddot{\mathbf{X}}_t, \eta_t)\}$ is a mixing sequence with either $\phi(m)$ of size $r/(2r-1)$, $r \geq 1$ or $\alpha(m)$ of size $r/(r-1)$, $r > 1$;

(iii) (a) $E(\ddot{Z}_{tgi} \eta_{th} | \mathfrak{F}_{t-1}) = 0$ for all t, where $\{\mathfrak{F}_t\}$ is adapted to $\{\ddot{Z}_{tgi} \eta_{th}\}$, $g, h = 1, \ldots, p$, $i = 1, \ldots, l$;
(b) $E|\ddot{Z}_{tgi} \eta_{th}|^{2(r+\delta)} < \Delta < \infty$ and $E|\eta_{th}|^{2(r+\delta)} < \Delta < \infty$ for some $\delta > 0$ and all t;
(c) $\mathbf{V}_n \equiv \text{var}(n^{-1/2} \mathbf{Z}' \boldsymbol{\epsilon})$ is uniformly positive definite;

(iv) (a) $E|\ddot{Z}_{thi}|^{2(r+\delta)} < \Delta < \infty$ and $E|\ddot{X}_{thj}|^{2(r+\delta)} < \Delta < \infty$ for some $0 < \delta \leq r$, g, $h = 1, \ldots, p$, $i = 1, \ldots, l$, $j = 1, \ldots, k$, and all t;
(b) $\ddot{\mathbf{Q}}_n \equiv E(\ddot{\mathbf{Z}}' \ddot{\mathbf{X}}/n)$ and $\mathbf{Q}_n \equiv E(\mathbf{Z}' \mathbf{X}/n)$ have uniformly full column rank;
(c) $\ddot{\mathbf{L}}_n \equiv E(\ddot{\mathbf{Z}}' \ddot{\mathbf{Z}}/n)$ is uniformly positive definite.

Define

$$\hat{\boldsymbol{\Sigma}}_n \equiv n^{-1} \sum_{t=1}^{n} \hat{\eta}_t \hat{\eta}_t',$$

where

$$\hat{\eta}_t = \tilde{\mathbf{y}}_t - \ddot{\mathbf{X}}_t \tilde{\boldsymbol{\beta}}_n, \; \tilde{\boldsymbol{\beta}}_n = (\ddot{\mathbf{X}}'\ddot{\mathbf{Z}}(\ddot{\mathbf{Z}}'\ddot{\mathbf{Z}})^{-1}\ddot{\mathbf{Z}}'\ddot{\mathbf{X}})^{-1}\ddot{\mathbf{X}}'\ddot{\mathbf{Z}}(\ddot{\mathbf{Z}}'\ddot{\mathbf{Z}})^{-1}\ddot{\mathbf{Z}}'\tilde{\mathbf{y}}.$$

Let

$$\hat{\boldsymbol{\Omega}}_n = \mathbf{I} \otimes \hat{\boldsymbol{\Sigma}}_n$$

and

$$\hat{\boldsymbol{\delta}}_n = (\ddot{\mathbf{X}}'\hat{\boldsymbol{\Omega}}_n^{-1}\ddot{\mathbf{Z}}(\ddot{\mathbf{Z}}'\hat{\boldsymbol{\Omega}}_n^{-1}\ddot{\mathbf{Z}})^{-1}\ddot{\mathbf{Z}}'\hat{\boldsymbol{\Omega}}_n^{-1}\ddot{\mathbf{X}})^{-1}\ddot{\mathbf{X}}'\hat{\boldsymbol{\Omega}}_n^{-1}\ddot{\mathbf{Z}}(\ddot{\mathbf{Z}}'\hat{\boldsymbol{\Omega}}_n^{-1}\ddot{\mathbf{Z}})^{-1}\ddot{\mathbf{Z}}'\hat{\boldsymbol{\Omega}}_n^{-1}\mathbf{y},$$

and define

$$\begin{aligned}\hat{\boldsymbol{\delta}}_n^* = \hat{\boldsymbol{\delta}}_n &- (\ddot{\mathbf{X}}'\hat{\boldsymbol{\Omega}}_n^{-1}\ddot{\mathbf{Z}}(\ddot{\mathbf{Z}}'\hat{\boldsymbol{\Omega}}_n^{-1}\ddot{\mathbf{Z}})^{-1}\ddot{\mathbf{Z}}'\hat{\boldsymbol{\Omega}}_n^{-1}\ddot{\mathbf{X}})^{-1}\nabla\mathbf{s}(\hat{\boldsymbol{\delta}}_n) \\ &\times [\nabla\mathbf{s}(\hat{\boldsymbol{\delta}}_n)(\ddot{\mathbf{X}}'\hat{\boldsymbol{\Omega}}_n^{-1}\ddot{\mathbf{Z}}(\ddot{\mathbf{Z}}'\hat{\boldsymbol{\Omega}}_n^{-1}\ddot{\mathbf{Z}})^{-1}\ddot{\mathbf{Z}}'\hat{\boldsymbol{\Omega}}_n^{-1}\ddot{\mathbf{X}})^{-1}\nabla\mathbf{s}(\hat{\boldsymbol{\delta}}_n)']\mathbf{s}(\hat{\boldsymbol{\delta}}_n).\end{aligned}$$

Then $\mathbf{D}_n^{-1/2} n^{-1/2}(\hat{\boldsymbol{\delta}}_n^* - \boldsymbol{\delta}_o) \overset{A}{\sim} N(\mathbf{0}, \mathbf{I})$, where

$\mathbf{D}_n = \text{avar}\,\hat{\boldsymbol{\delta}}_n - \text{avar}\,\hat{\boldsymbol{\delta}}_n \nabla\mathbf{s}(\boldsymbol{\delta}_o)'[\nabla\mathbf{s}(\boldsymbol{\delta}_o)\,\text{avar}\,\hat{\boldsymbol{\delta}}_n \nabla\mathbf{s}(\boldsymbol{\delta}_o)']^{-1}\nabla\mathbf{s}(\boldsymbol{\delta}_o)\,\text{avar}\,\hat{\boldsymbol{\delta}}_n,$

$\text{avar}\,\hat{\boldsymbol{\delta}}_n = (\mathbf{Q}_n'\mathbf{V}_n^{-1}\mathbf{Q}_n)^{-1}$, and $\hat{\mathbf{D}}_n - \mathbf{D}_n \xrightarrow{p} 0$, where

$$\begin{aligned}\hat{\mathbf{D}}_n \equiv \widehat{\text{avar}}\,\hat{\boldsymbol{\delta}}_n &- \widehat{\text{avar}}\,\hat{\boldsymbol{\delta}}_n \nabla\mathbf{s}(\hat{\boldsymbol{\delta}}_n)'[\nabla\mathbf{s}(\hat{\boldsymbol{\delta}}_n) \\ &\times \widehat{\text{avar}}\,\hat{\boldsymbol{\delta}}_n \nabla\mathbf{s}(\hat{\boldsymbol{\delta}}_n)']^{-1}\nabla\mathbf{s}(\hat{\boldsymbol{\delta}}_n)\,\widehat{\text{avar}}\,\hat{\boldsymbol{\delta}}_n\end{aligned}$$

and

$$\widehat{\text{avar}}\,\hat{\boldsymbol{\delta}}_n \equiv (\ddot{\mathbf{X}}'\hat{\boldsymbol{\Omega}}_n^{-1}\ddot{\mathbf{Z}}(\ddot{\mathbf{Z}}'\hat{\boldsymbol{\Omega}}_n^{-1}\ddot{\mathbf{Z}})^{-1}\ddot{\mathbf{Z}}'\hat{\boldsymbol{\Omega}}_n^{-1}\ddot{\mathbf{X}}/n)^{-1}.$$

Further, the conclusion of Theorem 4.61 holds for $\hat{\boldsymbol{\delta}}_n^*$ with respect to any constrained estimator based on any estimator allowed by the conditions of Theorem 4.57.

Proof: The properties of $\hat{\boldsymbol{\delta}}_n$ follow from Theorem 7.3 and the properties of $\hat{\boldsymbol{\delta}}_n^*$ follow from the proof of Theorem 4.60. The final result holds because the hypotheses of Theorem 4.61 are satisfied. The consistency of $\hat{\mathbf{D}}_n$ follows from Proposition 2.30.

Although this result establishes the asymptotic efficiency of $\hat{\boldsymbol{\delta}}_n^*$ with respect to any constrained (or unconstrained) consistent asymptotically normal estimator making use of instrumental variables formed as measurable functions of the elements of $\mathbf{W}_t$, the finite sample properties of this estimator are not necessarily optimal. In particular, neglecting the first m observations in constructing the pseudo-differenced model may lead to nonnegligible efficiency losses in finite samples. (See Harvey [1981, Section 6.1].)

Also of importance is the fact that the present estimator is the efficient estimator for the parameters of the pseudo-differenced model. If $\tilde{\mathbf{X}}_t$ does not contain lagged values of $\tilde{\mathbf{y}}_t$, then it can be shown that $\hat{\boldsymbol{\delta}}_n$ contains the efficient estimator for the original model. Otherwise, it turns out that $\hat{\boldsymbol{\delta}}_n$ is not as efficient as it would be if it were not necessary to estimate the elements of $\mathbf{R}$. This is because when $\tilde{\mathbf{X}}_t$ contains lagged values of $\tilde{\mathbf{y}}_t$ and $\tilde{\boldsymbol{\epsilon}}_t$ exhibits serial correlation then condition (i) of Theorem 7.1 is not satisfied.

Finally, we note that the moment restrictions imposed in (iii) and (iv) will imply restrictions on the admissible values for the elements of $\mathbf{R}_1, \mathbf{R}_2, \ldots, \mathbf{R}_m$. This is because $\tilde{\mathbf{y}}_t$ can be made to "explode" for certain values of these parameters. As a simple example, consider the model

$$\tilde{\mathbf{y}}_t = \rho_o \tilde{\mathbf{y}}_{t-1} + \eta_t.$$

If $|\rho_o| \geq 1$, assumption (iv.a) will be violated. Because the elements of $\mathbf{R}_1, \ldots, \mathbf{R}_m$ are unknown, it is convenient that the conditions we give do not require checking these parameters directly. Instead, it suffices to specify that the moment conditions of (iii) and (iv) are satisfied.

References

Harvey, A. C. [1981]. "The Econometric Analysis of Time Series." New York: Wiley.

Theil, H. [1971]. "Principles of Econometrics." New York: Wiley.

White, H. [1980]. Nonlinear regression on cross section Data, *Econometrica* **48**: 721–746.

Zellner, A. [1962]. An efficient method of estimating seemingly unrelated regressions and tests for aggregation Bias, *J. Amer. Statist. Assoc.* **58**: 348–368.

Zellner, A. and H. Theil [1962]. Three-stage least squares: simultaneous estimation of simultaneous equations, *Econometrica* **30**: 54–78.

CHAPTER VIII

Directions For Further Study

In this chapter we briefly discuss topics not covered in previous chapters and how techniques introduced in this book relate to these topics.

VIII.1 Extensions of the Linear Model

Although the results of the previous chapters cover a broad range of the possibilities of interest to economists, there is one situation that is not treated by any of our results. Specifically, the moment conditions imposed on the instrumental and explanatory variables rule out the use of time trends or other time series that grow without bound. Although there is some question as to whether models that make use of such variables are appropriate in economics (e.g., see Nelson and Plosser [1982]), it is certainly possible to develop a theory which covers many of these cases. In particular, the Markov law of large numbers (Theorem 3.7) or the McLeish law of large numbers (Theorem 3.47) can be useful in establishing consistency in models with trending explanatory or instrumental variables. In fact, consistency may happen "faster" in models with these variables because the error variance may become quite negligible in comparison to the magnitude of the regression function $\mathbf{X}_t\boldsymbol{\beta}_o$. Asymptotic normality can be established with the help of the Lindeberg or Martingale–Lindeberg central limit theorems (Theorem 5.6 or 5.24). In fact, conditions ensuring asymptotic normality in models with nonstochastic and possibly trending variables were the subject of careful attention very early on (Grenander [1954]) and there is a well-developed general theory now available (e.g., Crowder [1980]).

Another case not covered was generalized instrumental variables estimation of a linear model when the elements of $\mathbf{\Omega}_n$ are known functions of $\{\mathbf{W}_t\}$ and a finite number of unknown parameters. This situation is most easily treated in the framework of maximum likelihood estimation, which we discuss below.

VIII.2 Nonlinear Models

Throughout, we have restricted attention to models linear in the parameters, although we have allowed nonlinear restrictions among the parameters to hold. A more general model that contains many situations of interest to economists can be written as

$$\mathbf{q}_t(\mathbf{y}_t, \mathbf{X}_t, \boldsymbol{\beta}_o) = \boldsymbol{\epsilon}_t.$$

In the particular case we studied,

$$\mathbf{q}_t(\mathbf{y}_t, \mathbf{X}_t, \boldsymbol{\beta}_o) = \mathbf{y}_t - \mathbf{X}_t\boldsymbol{\beta}_0.$$

There are a variety of ways to obtain consistent and asymptotically normal estimators for $\boldsymbol{\beta}_o$. One way is analogous to the approach considered here. Suppose we have available instrumental variables $\mathbf{Z}_t$ such that $E(\mathbf{Z}_t'\boldsymbol{\epsilon}_t) = \mathbf{0}$. Then we can attempt to estimate $\boldsymbol{\beta}_o$ by solving the problem

$$\min_{\boldsymbol{\beta}} \mathbf{q}(\boldsymbol{\beta})'\mathbf{Z}\hat{\mathbf{P}}_n\mathbf{Z}'\mathbf{q}(\boldsymbol{\beta}),$$

where $\mathbf{q}(\beta)$ is the $np \times 1$ vector with tth block $\mathbf{q}_t(\mathbf{y}_t, \mathbf{X}_t, \boldsymbol{\beta})$, so

$$\mathbf{Z}'\mathbf{q}(\boldsymbol{\beta}) = \sum_{t=1}^{n} \mathbf{Z}_t'\mathbf{q}_t(\mathbf{y}_t, \mathbf{X}_t, \boldsymbol{\beta}).$$

The solution to this problem is called the generalized method of moments estimator. Its properties have been studied by Amemiya [1977], Burguete, Gallant and Souza [1982], and Hansen [1982], among others.

To establish properties analogous to those obtained here, we need somewhat more powerful tools than those given. In particular, repeated use is made of uniform laws of large numbers and the mean value theorem for random functions (e.g., see Jennrich [1969]).

VIII.3 Other Estimation Techniques

Whereas the method of instumental variables studied here is useful and computationally convenient, there are many other ways of constructing useful estimators. Primary among these is the method of maximum likelihood. In fact, if one assumes that the disturbances ϵ_t are independent and identically distributed as multivariate normal with unknown covariance matrix, then the IV estimators of Section 2, Chapter VII (hence Section 4, Chapter VII) can be shown to be asymptoticaly equivalent to the maximum likelihood estimator under general conditions. There is a broad range of situations where maximum likelihood and instrumental variables are asymptotically equivalent (see Hausman [1975] and Amemiya [1977]), although this equivalence fails for the general case of nonlinear models previously mentioned. In that case, maximum likelihood can be shown to be more efficient than instrumental variables (Amemiya [1977]).

Use of the method of maximum likelihood requires an assumption about the distribution of the errors, whereas instrumental variables does not. Thus, the method of instrumental variables is available in situations where a knowledge of the error distribution is absent or suspect. Nevertheless, maximum likelihood estimation can be conducted as if the errors have the assumed distribution, whether this assumption is valid or not. This procedure is known as *quasi-maximum likelihood estimation,* a member of the class of *M-estimators* (Huber [1967]), which contains a variety of useful and interesting estimators. By selecting an *M*-estimator appropriately, it is possible to obtain estimators that are quite robust to failure of distributional assumptions or to certain plausible kinds of data errors.

Again, the study of these estimators requires use of uniform laws of large numbers and mean value theorems for random functions. A general treatment of these estimators that also highlights the parallels with IV estimators has been given by Burguete, Gallant, and Souza [1982].

VIII.4 Model Misspecification

Throughout this book, we have maintained the assumption that the model is known to be

$$\mathbf{y}_t = \mathbf{X}_t \boldsymbol{\beta}_o + \boldsymbol{\epsilon}_t.$$

It would indeed be fortunate if the relationship between $\mathbf{X}_t$ and $\mathbf{y}_t$ were ever truly "known." Owing to the complexity of economic phenomena, it is perhaps more realistic to suppose that the relationship between $\mathbf{X}_t$ and $\mathbf{y}_t$ is unknown. In this case, a linear model such as that just given can be viewed as a convenient approximation but not necessarily as a definitive description of the relationship between $\mathbf{X}_t$ and $\mathbf{y}_t$. It then becomes important to consider questions such as "How is this approximation to be interpreted?", "What are the properties of the parameters of the approximation?", "How can the approximation be improved?", and "How can we tell if our approximation is exact?"

Recently, these questions have been given quite a bit of attention by econometricians. For a discussion that builds on the material in this book in a framework encompassing several of the extensions discussed in this chapter, the reader is referred to *Estimation, Inference, and Specification Analysis* (White [1984]).

References

Amemiya, T. [1977]. The maximum likelihood estimator and the nonlinear three-stage least squares estimator in the general nonlinear simultaneous equation model, *Econometrica* **45**: 955–968.

Burguete, J. F., Gallant, A. R., and Souza, G. [1982]. On unification of the asymptotic theory of nonlinear econometric models, *Econometric Reviews* **1**: 151–212.

Crowder, M. J. [1980]. On the asymptotic properties of least-squares estimators in autoregression, *Ann. Statis.* **8**: 132–146.

Grenander, U. [1954]. On the estimation of regression coefficients in the case of an autocorrelated disturbance, *Annals of Mathematical Statistics* **25**: 252–272.

Hansen, L. P. [1982]. Large sample properties of generalized method of moments estimators, *Econometrica* **50**: 1029–1054.

Hausman, J. A. [1975]. An instrumental variable approach to full information estimators for linear and certain nonlinear structural models, *Econometrica* **43**: 727–738.

Huber, P. J. [1967]. The behavior of maximum likelihood estimates under nonstandard conditions, *in* "Proceedings of the Fifth Berkeley Symposium on Mathematical Statistics and Probability," vol. 1. Berkeley, California: University of California Press.

Jennrich, R. I. [1969]. Asymptotic properties of nonlinear least squares estimators, *Annals of Mathematical Statistics* **40**: 633–643.

Nelson, C. R., and Plosser, C. I. [1982]. Trends and random walks in macroeconomic time series, *Journal of Monetary Economics* **10**: 139–162.

White, H. [1984]. "Estimation, Inference and Specification Analysis," New York: Cambridge University Press, forthcoming.

Solution Set

EXERCISE 2.8

Proof: Let $a_n \equiv A_n b_n$ where $A_n = [A_{nij}]$ and $b'_n = (b_{n1}, b_{n2}, \ldots, b_{nk})$. Then $a_{ni} = \Sigma_{j=1}^{k} A_{nij} b_{nj}$. Since $\{A_{nij}\}$ is $o(1)$ and $\{b_{nj}\}$ is $O(1)$, $\{A_{nij} b_{nj}\}$ is $o(1)$ by Proposition 2.7(iii). By Proposition 2.7(ii), $\{a_{ni}\}$ is $o(1)$ because it is the sum of k terms, each of which is $o(1)$. It follows that $\{a_n \equiv A_n b_n\}$ is $o(1)$.

EXERCISE 2.13

Proof: Since $\mathbf{Z}'\mathbf{X}/n \xrightarrow{\text{a.s.}} \mathbf{Q}$ and $\hat{\mathbf{P}}_n \xrightarrow{\text{a.s.}} \mathbf{P}$, it follows from Proposition 2.11 that $\det(\mathbf{X}'\mathbf{Z}\hat{\mathbf{P}}_n\mathbf{Z}'\mathbf{X}/n^2) \xrightarrow{\text{a.s.}} \det(\mathbf{Q}'\mathbf{P}\mathbf{Q})$. Since $\mathbf{Q}$ has full column rank and $\mathbf{P}$ is nonsingular by (iii), $\det(\mathbf{Q}'\mathbf{P}\mathbf{Q}) > 0$. It follows that $\det(\mathbf{X}'\mathbf{Z}\hat{\mathbf{P}}_n\mathbf{Z}'\mathbf{X}/n^2) > 0$ almost surely for all n sufficiently large, so that $(\mathbf{X}'\mathbf{Z}\hat{\mathbf{P}}_n\mathbf{Z}'\mathbf{X}/n^2)^{-1}$ exists a.s. for all n sufficiently large. Hence $\tilde{\boldsymbol{\beta}}_n \equiv (\mathbf{X}'\mathbf{Z}\hat{\mathbf{P}}_n\mathbf{Z}'\mathbf{X}/n^2)^{-1}\mathbf{X}'\mathbf{Z}\hat{\mathbf{P}}_n\mathbf{Z}'\mathbf{y}/n^2$ exists a.s. for all n sufficiently large. Given (i), $\tilde{\boldsymbol{\beta}}_n = \boldsymbol{\beta}_0 + (\mathbf{X}'\mathbf{Z}\hat{\mathbf{P}}_n\mathbf{Z}'\mathbf{X}/n^2)^{-1}\mathbf{X}'\mathbf{Z}\hat{\mathbf{P}}_n\mathbf{Z}'\boldsymbol{\epsilon}/n^2$. It follows from Proposition 2.11 that $\tilde{\boldsymbol{\beta}}_n \xrightarrow{\text{a.s.}} \boldsymbol{\beta}_0 + (\mathbf{Q}'\mathbf{P}\mathbf{Q})^{-1}\mathbf{Q}'\mathbf{P} \times \mathbf{0} = \boldsymbol{\beta}_0$ given (ii) and (iii).

EXERCISE 2.20

Proof: Since $\{\mathbf{Q}_n\}$ is $O(1)$ and $\{\mathbf{P}_n\}$ is $O(1)$, it follows from Proposition 2.16 that $\det(\mathbf{X}'\mathbf{Z}\hat{\mathbf{P}}_n\mathbf{Z}'\mathbf{X}/n^2) - \det(\mathbf{Q}_n'\mathbf{P}_n\mathbf{Q}_n) \xrightarrow{\text{a.s.}} 0$. Given (iii), it follows from Lemma 2.19 that $\{\mathbf{Q}_n'\mathbf{P}_n\mathbf{Q}_n\}$ is uniformly positive definite, so $\det(\mathbf{Q}_n'\mathbf{P}_n\mathbf{Q}_n) > \delta > 0$ for all n sufficiently large. It follows that $\det(\mathbf{X}'\mathbf{Z}\hat{\mathbf{P}}_n\mathbf{Z}'\mathbf{X}/n^2) > \delta/2 > 0$ almost surely for all n sufficiently large. Hence $\tilde{\boldsymbol{\beta}}_n = (\mathbf{X}'\mathbf{Z}\hat{\mathbf{P}}_n\mathbf{Z}'\mathbf{X}/n^2)^{-1}\mathbf{X}'\mathbf{Z}\hat{\mathbf{P}}_n\mathbf{Z}'\mathbf{y}/n^2$ exists almost surely for all n sufficiently large. Given (i), $\tilde{\boldsymbol{\beta}}_n = \boldsymbol{\beta}_0 + (\mathbf{X}'\mathbf{Z}\hat{\mathbf{P}}_n\mathbf{Z}'\mathbf{X}/n^2)^{-1}\mathbf{X}'\mathbf{Z}\hat{\mathbf{P}}_n\mathbf{Z}'\boldsymbol{\epsilon}/n^2$. Given (ii) and (iii) it follows from Proposition 2.16 that $\tilde{\boldsymbol{\beta}}_n - (\boldsymbol{\beta}_0 + (\mathbf{Q}_n'\mathbf{P}_n\mathbf{Q}_n)^{-1}\mathbf{Q}_n'\mathbf{P}_n \times \mathbf{0}) \xrightarrow{\text{a. s.}} \mathbf{0}$, that is $\tilde{\boldsymbol{\beta}}_n \xrightarrow{\text{a. s.}} \boldsymbol{\beta}_0$.

Exercise 2.22

Proof:

(i) Since $\{a_n\}$ is $O_{\text{a.s.}}(n^\lambda)$ and $\{b_n\}$ is $O_{\text{a.s.}}(n^\mu)$ there exist nonstochastic $O(1)$ sequences $\{c_n\}$ and $\{d_n\}$ such that $n^{-\lambda}a_n - c_n \xrightarrow{\text{a. s.}} 0$ and $n^{-\mu}b_n - d_n \xrightarrow{\text{a. s.}} 0$. Given that $\{c_n\}$, $\{d_n\}$ are $O(1)$, c_n and d_n are contained in a compact set $C \equiv [-\Delta, \Delta]$ for all n sufficiently large. By Proposition 2.16, $n^{-\lambda}a_n n^{-\mu}b_n - c_n d_n = n^{-(\lambda+\mu)}a_n b_n - c_n d_n \xrightarrow{\text{a. s.}} 0$, and since $\{c_n d_n\}$ is $O(1)$ by Proposition 2.7, $\{a_n b_n\}$ is $O_{\text{a.s.}}(1)$. Next consider $\{a_n + b_n\}$. Since $n^{-\delta}|n^{-\lambda}a_n - c_n| \leq |n^{-\lambda}a_n - c_n|$ it follows that if $\{a_n\}$ is $O_{\text{a.s.}}(n^\lambda)$ then $\{a_n\}$ is $O_{\text{a.s.}}(n^{\lambda+\delta})$ for $\delta \geq 0$. (Note that $\{n^{-\delta}c_n\}$ is $O(1)$.) Hence there exist $O(1)$ sequences $\{e_n\}$, $\{f_n\}$ such that $n^{-\kappa}a_n - e_n \xrightarrow{\text{a. s.}} 0$ and $n^{-\kappa}b_n - f_n \xrightarrow{\text{a. s.}} 0$. By Proposition 2.16, $n^{-\kappa}a_n + n^{-\kappa}b_n - (e_n + f_n) = n^{-\kappa}(a_n + b_n) - (e_n + f_n) \xrightarrow{\text{a. s.}} 0$ so that $\{a_n + b_n\}$ is $O_{\text{a.s.}}(n^\kappa)$.

(ii) Given $n^{-\lambda}a_n \xrightarrow{\text{a. s.}} 0$ and $n^{-\mu}b_n \xrightarrow{\text{a. s.}} 0$, it follows immediately from Proposition 2.16 that $n^{-\lambda}a_n n^{-\mu}b_n = n^{-(\lambda+\mu)}a_n b_n \xrightarrow{\text{a. s.}} 0$. Now $n^{-\delta}|n^{-\lambda}a_n| \leq |n^{-\lambda}a_n|$ for $\delta \geq 0$ so that $\{a_n\}$ is $o_{\text{a.s.}}(n^{\lambda+\delta})$ if it is $o_{\text{a.s.}}(n^\lambda)$. Hence $n^{-\kappa}a_n \xrightarrow{\text{a. s.}} 0$ and $n^{-\kappa}b_n \xrightarrow{\text{a. s.}} 0$, and by Proposition 2.16, $n^{-\kappa}a_n + n^{-\kappa}b_n = n^{-\kappa}(a_n + b_n) \xrightarrow{\text{a. s.}} 0$.

(iii) By definition, $n^{-\lambda}a_n - c_n \xrightarrow{\text{a. s.}} 0$ and $n^{-\mu}b_n \xrightarrow{\text{a. s.}} 0$, where $\{c_n\}$ is $O(1)$, and hence, interior to a compact set $C = [-\Delta, \Delta]$ for all n sufficiently large. Since $\{d_n \equiv 0\}$ is also $O(1)$, $n^{-\lambda}a_n n^{-\mu}b_n - c_n \times 0 = n^{-(\lambda+\mu)}a_n b_n \xrightarrow{\text{a. s.}} 0$ by Proposition 2.16. Consider $\{a_n + b_n\}$. Clearly, if $\{b_n\}$ is $o_{\text{a.s.}}(n^\mu)$, then $\{b_n\}$ is $O_{\text{a.s.}}(n^\mu)$. It follows from (i) that $\{a_n + b_n\}$ is $O_{\text{a.s.}}(n^\kappa)$.

Exercise 2.29

Proof: The proof is identical to that of Exercise 2.13 except that Proposition 2.27 is used instead of Proposition 2.11 and convergence in probability replaces convergence almost surely.

EXERCISE 2.32

Proof: The proof is identical to that of Exercise 2.20 except that Proposition 2.30 is used in place of Proposition 2.16 and convergence in probability replaces convergence almost surely.

EXERCISE 2.35

Proof:

(i) Let $\{c_n\}$, $\{d_n\}$ be O(1) sequences such that $n^{-\lambda}a_n - c_n \xrightarrow{p} 0$ and $n^{-\mu}b_n - d_n \xrightarrow{p} 0$. Since c_n, d_n are interior to the compact set $C \equiv [-\Delta, \Delta]$ for all n sufficiently large it follows from Proposition 2.30 that $n^{-\lambda}a_n n^{-\mu}b_n - c_n d_n = n^{-(\lambda+\mu)}a_n b_n - c_n d_n \xrightarrow{p} 0$ so that $\{a_n b_n\}$ is $O_p(n^{\lambda+\mu})$. Next consider $\{a_n + b_n\}$. Since $n^{-\delta}|n^{-\lambda}a_n - c_n| \leq |n^{-\lambda}a_n - c_n|$ for $\delta \geq 0$, it follows that if $\{a_n\}$ is $O_p(n^\lambda)$ then $\{a_n\}$ is $O_p(n^{\lambda+\delta})$. Hence, there are O(1) sequences $\{e_n\}$, $\{f_n\}$ such that $n^{-\kappa}a_n - e_n \xrightarrow{p} 0$ and $n^{-\kappa}b_n - f_n \xrightarrow{p} 0$. By proposition 2.30, $n^{-\kappa}a_n + n^{-\kappa}b_n - (e_n + f_n) = n^{-\kappa}(a_n + b_n) - (e_n + f_n) \xrightarrow{p} 0$, so that $\{a_n + b_n\}$ is $O_p(n^\kappa)$. (Recall that $\{e_n + f_n\}$ is O(1) by Proposition 2.7.)

(ii) We have $n^{-\lambda}a_n \xrightarrow{p} 0$, $n^{-\mu}b_n \xrightarrow{p} 0$. It follows from Proposition 2.30 that $n^{-\lambda}a_n n^{-\mu}b_n = n^{-(\lambda+\mu)}a_n b_n \xrightarrow{p} 0$ so that $\{a_n b_n\}$ is $o_p(1)$. Consider $\{a_n + b_n\}$. Since $\{a_n\}$, $\{b_n\}$ are $o_p(n^\kappa)$, we again apply Proposition 2.30 and $n^{-\kappa}a_n + n^{-\kappa}b_n = n^{-\kappa}(a_n + b_n) \xrightarrow{p} 0$.

(iii) By definition, $n^{-\lambda}a_n - c_n \xrightarrow{p} 0$ and $n^{-\mu}b_n \xrightarrow{p} 0$, where $\{c_n\}$ is O(1). Also $\{d_n \equiv 0\}$ is O(1), so that Proposition 2.30 applies and $n^{-\lambda}a_n n^{-\mu}b_n - c_n \times 0 = n^{-(\lambda+\mu)}a_n b_n \xrightarrow{p} 0$. Consider $\{a_n + b_n\}$. Since $\{b_n\}$ is also $O_p(n^\mu)$, it follows from (i) that $\{a_n + b_n\}$ is $O_p(n^\kappa)$.

EXERCISE 3.6

Proof: We verify the conditions of Exercise 2.13. Given (ii), the elements of $\{\mathbf{Z}_t'\boldsymbol{\epsilon}_t\}$ and $\{\mathbf{Z}_t'\mathbf{X}_t\}$ are i.i.d. sequences by Proposition 3.3. The elements of $\{\mathbf{Z}_t'\boldsymbol{\epsilon}_t\}$ and $\{\mathbf{Z}_t'\mathbf{X}_t\}$ have finite expected absolute value given (iii.b) and (iv.a). By Theorem 3.1,

$$\mathbf{Z}'\boldsymbol{\epsilon}/n = n^{-1}\sum_{t=1}^{n}\mathbf{Z}_t'\boldsymbol{\epsilon}_t \xrightarrow{\text{a.s.}} \mathbf{0}$$

and

$$\mathbf{Z}'\mathbf{X}/n = n^{-1} \sum_{t=1}^{n} \mathbf{Z}_t'\mathbf{X}_t \xrightarrow{\text{a. s.}} \mathbf{Q},$$

finite with full column rank. Since (iv.c) is also given, the conditions of Exercise 2.13 are satisfied and the result follows.

EXERCISE 3.13

Proof: By Minkowski's inequality,

$$\begin{aligned} E\left|\sum_{h=1}^{p} \mathbf{X}_{thi}\boldsymbol{\epsilon}_{th}\right|^{1+\delta} &\leq \left[\sum_{h=1}^{p} (E|\mathbf{X}_{thi}\boldsymbol{\epsilon}_{th}|^{1+\delta})^{1/(1+\delta)}\right]^{1+\delta} \\ &< \left[\sum_{h=1}^{p} \Delta^{1/(1+\delta)}\right]^{1+\delta} \\ &= p^{1+\delta}\Delta \\ &\equiv \Delta'. \end{aligned}$$

EXERCISE 3.14

Proof: We verify the conditions of Theorem 2.18. By Proposition 3.10, $\{\mathbf{X}_t'\boldsymbol{\epsilon}_t\}$ and $\{\mathbf{X}_t'\mathbf{X}_t\}$ are independent sequences with elements satisfying the moment condition of Corollary 3.9 given (iii.b), (iv.a), and using the results of Corollary 3.12 and Exercise 3.13. It follows from Corollary 3.9 that

$$\mathbf{X}'\boldsymbol{\epsilon}/n = n^{-1} \sum_{t=1}^{n} \mathbf{X}_t'\boldsymbol{\epsilon}_t \xrightarrow{\text{a. s.}} \mathbf{0}$$

and

$$\mathbf{X}'\mathbf{X}/n - \mathbf{M}_n = n^{-1} \sum_{t=1}^{n} \mathbf{X}_t'\mathbf{X}_t - \mathbf{M}_n \xrightarrow{\text{a. s.}} \mathbf{0}.$$

$\mathbf{M}_n$ is O(1) given (iv.a) as a consequence of Jensen's inequality and the Cauchy–Schwartz inequality. To show this, consider the i, jth element of M_n,

$$n^{-1} \sum_{t=1}^{n} \sum_{h=1}^{p} E(\mathbf{X}_{thi}\mathbf{X}_{thj}).$$

Now

$$\begin{aligned}\left| n^{-1} \sum_{t=1}^{n} \sum_{h=1}^{p} E(\mathbf{X}_{thi}\mathbf{X}_{thj}) \right| &\leq n^{-1} \sum_{t=1}^{n} \sum_{h=1}^{p} |E(\mathbf{X}_{thi}\mathbf{X}_{thj})| \\ &\leq n^{-1} \sum_{t=1}^{n} \sum_{h=1}^{p} E|\mathbf{X}_{thi}\mathbf{X}_{thj}| \\ &\leq n^{-1} \sum_{t=1}^{n} \sum_{h=1}^{p} (E|\mathbf{X}_{thi}|^2)^{1/2}(E|\mathbf{X}_{thj}|^2)^{1/2} \\ &< n^{-1} \sum_{t=1}^{n} \sum_{h=1}^{p} \Delta' \\ &= p\Delta' < \infty\end{aligned}$$

given (iv.a). Hence, the conditions of Theorem 2.18 are satisfied and the result follows.

EXERCISE 3.38

Proof: We verify the conditions of Exercise 2.13. Given (ii), $\{\mathbf{Z}_t'\boldsymbol{\epsilon}_t\}$ and $\{\mathbf{Z}_t'\mathbf{X}_t\}$ are stationary ergodic sequences by Proposition 3.36, with elements having finite expected absolute values given (iii.b) and (iv.a). By the ergodic Theorem 3.34,

$$\mathbf{Z}'\boldsymbol{\epsilon}/n = n^{-1} \sum_{t=1}^{n} \mathbf{Z}_t'\boldsymbol{\epsilon}_t \xrightarrow{\text{a. s.}} \mathbf{0}$$

and

$$\mathbf{Z}'\mathbf{X}/n = n^{-1} \sum_{t=1}^{n} \mathbf{Z}_t'\mathbf{X}_t \xrightarrow{\text{a. s.}} \mathbf{Q},$$

finite with full column rank. Since (iv.c) is also given, the conditions of Exercise 2.13 are satisfied and the result follows.

EXERCISE 3.51

Proof: We verify the conditions of Theorem 2.18. Given (ii), $\{\mathbf{X}_t'\boldsymbol{\epsilon}_t\}$ and $\{\mathbf{X}_t'\mathbf{X}_t\}$ are mixing sequences with $\phi(m)$ of size $r/(2r-1)$,

$r \geq 1$, or $\alpha(m)$ of size $r/(r-1)$, $r > 1$, by Proposition 3.50. Given (iii.b) and (iv.a) the elements of $\{\mathbf{X}_t'\boldsymbol{\epsilon}_t\}$ and $\{\mathbf{X}_t'\mathbf{X}_t\}$ satisfy the moment condition of Corollary 3.48 by Minkowski's inequality and the Cauchy–Schwartz inequality. It follows that $\mathbf{X}'\boldsymbol{\epsilon}/n \xrightarrow{\text{a.s.}} \mathbf{0}$ and $\mathbf{X}'\mathbf{X}/n - \mathbf{M}_n \xrightarrow{\text{a.s.}} \mathbf{0}$. $\mathbf{M}_n$ is O(1) by Jensen's inequality given (iv.a). Hence the conditions of Theorem 2.18 are satisfied and the result follows.

EXERCISE 3.53

(i) The following conditions are sufficient:

(a) $\mathbf{y} = \alpha\mathbf{y}_{-1} + \beta\mathbf{x} + \boldsymbol{\epsilon}$, $|\alpha| < 1$, $|\beta| < \infty$;
(b) $\{(\mathbf{y}_t, \mathbf{x}_t)'\}$ is a mixing sequence with $\phi(m)$ of size $r/(2r-1)$, $r \geq 1$, or $\alpha(m)$ of size $r/(r-1)$, $r > 1$;
(c) (1) $E(\mathbf{x}_{t-j}\boldsymbol{\epsilon}_t) = 0$, $j = 0, 1, 2, \ldots$ and all t;
(2) $E(\boldsymbol{\epsilon}_t\boldsymbol{\epsilon}_{t-j}) = 0$, $j = 1, 2, 3, \ldots$ and all t;
(d) (1) $E|\mathbf{x}_t^2|^{r+\delta} < \Delta < \infty$ and $E|\boldsymbol{\epsilon}_t^2|^{r+\delta} < \Delta < \infty$ for some $0 < \delta \leq r$ and all t;
(2) $\mathbf{M}_n \equiv E(\mathbf{X}'\mathbf{X}/n)$ has det $\mathbf{M}_n > \gamma > 0$ for all n sufficiently large, where $\mathbf{X} \equiv (\mathbf{y}_{-1}, \mathbf{x})$.

First, we verify the hint (see Laha and Rohatgi [1979, p. 53]). We are given that

$$\sum_{t=1}^{\infty} (E|Z_t|^p)^{1/p} < \infty.$$

By Minkowski's inequality for finite sums,

$$E\left|\sum_{t=1}^{n} |Z_t|\right|^p \leq \left(\sum_{t=1}^{n} (E|Z_t|^p)^{1/p}\right)^p$$

for all $n \geq 1$. Hence

$$\lim_{n\to\infty} E\left|\sum_{t=1}^{n} |Z_t|\right|^p \leq \lim_{n\to\infty}\left(\sum_{t=1}^{n} (E|Z_t|^p)^{1/p}\right)^p = \left(\sum_{t=1}^{\infty} (E|Z_t|^p)^{1/p}\right)^p$$

by continuity of the function $g(x) \equiv x^p$. Applying Fatou's Lemma (Laha and Rohatgi [1979, p. 49]),

$$\begin{aligned}
E\left|\sum_{t=1}^{\infty} Z_t\right|^p &= E\left|\lim_{n\to\infty}\sum_{t=1}^{n} Z_t\right|^p \\
&\le E\left|\lim_{n\to\infty}\sum_{t=1}^{n} |Z_t|\right|^p \\
&\le \lim_{n\to\infty} E\left|\sum_{t=1}^{n} |Z_t|\right|^p \\
&\le \left(\sum_{t=1}^{\infty} (E|Z_t|^p)^{1/p}\right)^p,
\end{aligned}$$

which is the desired result.

Next, we verify the conditions of Exercise 3.51. First $\{(\mathbf{y}_t, \mathbf{x}_t)'\}$ mixing implies $\{(\mathbf{X}_t, \boldsymbol{\epsilon}_t)'\} \equiv \{(\mathbf{y}_{t-1}, \mathbf{x}_t, \boldsymbol{\epsilon}_t)'\}$ is mixing and of the same sizes given (a) and (b) by Theorem 3.49.

Next, by repeated substitution we can write $\mathbf{y}_t$ as

$$\mathbf{y}_t = \beta \sum_{j=0}^{\infty} \alpha^j \mathbf{x}_{t-j} + \sum_{j=0}^{\infty} \alpha^j \boldsymbol{\epsilon}_{t-j}$$

so that

$$\mathbf{y}_{t-1}\boldsymbol{\epsilon}_t = \beta \sum_{j=0}^{\infty} \alpha^j \mathbf{x}_{t-j-1}\boldsymbol{\epsilon}_t + \sum_{j=0}^{\infty} \alpha^j \boldsymbol{\epsilon}_{t-j-1}\boldsymbol{\epsilon}_t.$$

Given (c), we can interchange the summation and expectation operators by Proposition 3.52. Hence

$$\begin{aligned}
E(\mathbf{y}_{t-1}\boldsymbol{\epsilon}_t) &= \beta \sum_{j=0}^{\infty} \alpha^j E(\mathbf{x}_{t-j-1}\boldsymbol{\epsilon}_t) \\
&\quad + \sum_{j=0}^{\infty} \alpha^j E(\boldsymbol{\epsilon}_{t-j-1}\boldsymbol{\epsilon}_t) = 0
\end{aligned}$$

given (c). Therefore

$$\begin{aligned}
E(\mathbf{X}_t'\boldsymbol{\epsilon}_t) &\equiv (\mathbf{E}(\mathbf{y}_{t-1}\boldsymbol{\epsilon}_t), \\
&\quad \mathbf{E}(\mathbf{x}_t\boldsymbol{\epsilon}_t))' = \mathbf{0}
\end{aligned}$$

so that condition (iii.a) of Exercise 3.51 is satisfied.

Now consider condition (iii.b). By the Cauchy–Schwartz inequality,

$$\begin{aligned}
E|\mathbf{x}_t\boldsymbol{\epsilon}_t|^{r+\delta} &\le (E|\mathbf{x}_t^2|^{r+\delta} E|\boldsymbol{\epsilon}_t^2|^{r+\delta})^{1/2} \\
&< \Delta < \infty
\end{aligned}$$

given (d.1). Further,

$$E|\mathbf{y}_{t-1}\boldsymbol{\epsilon}_t|^{r+\delta} \le (E|\mathbf{y}_{t-1}^2|^{r+\delta} E|\boldsymbol{\epsilon}_t^2|^{r+\delta})^{1/2}$$
$$< (\Delta'\Delta)^{1/2} < \infty$$

provided $E|\mathbf{y}_{t-1}^2|^{r+\delta} < \Delta' < \infty$ for some Δ'. To show this, we write $\mathbf{y}_t$ as above and apply Minkowski's inequality:

$$E|\mathbf{y}_t^2|^{r+\delta} = E\left|\beta \sum_{j=0}^{\infty} \alpha^j \mathbf{x}_{t-j} + \sum_{j=0}^{\infty} \alpha^j \boldsymbol{\epsilon}_{t-j}\right|^{2(r+\delta)}$$
$$\le |\beta| \sum_{j=0}^{\infty} |\alpha|^j [(E|\mathbf{x}_{t-j}|^{2(r+\delta)})^{1/2(r+\delta)}$$
$$+ (E|\boldsymbol{\epsilon}_{t-j}|^{2(r+\delta)})^{1/2(r+\delta)}]^{2(r+\delta)}$$
$$< \left[2|\beta|\Delta^{1/2(r+\delta)} \sum_{j=0}^{\infty} |\alpha|^j\right]^{2(r+\delta)}$$
$$= [2|\beta|\Delta^{1/2(r+\delta)}/(1-|\alpha|)]^{2(r+\delta)} < \infty$$

if and only if $|\alpha| < 1$ where we have again used Proposition 3.52 to pass the expectation operator through the summation operator. Therefore (a), (d.1) ensure that (c.2) is satisfied. We have also shown that (d.1) is satisfied, and since (d.2) is assumed, the conditions of Exercise 3.51 hold and the OLS estimate of (α, β) will be consistent.

(ii) Consider the following model:

$$\mathbf{y}_t = \alpha_0 \mathbf{y}_{t-1} + \boldsymbol{\epsilon}_t$$
$$\boldsymbol{\epsilon}_t = \rho_0 \boldsymbol{\epsilon}_{t-1} + \mathbf{v}_t,$$

where we assume

$$E(\mathbf{y}_{t-1}\mathbf{v}_t) = 0, \qquad E(\mathbf{y}_{t-1}\boldsymbol{\epsilon}_{t-1}) = E(\mathbf{y}_t\boldsymbol{\epsilon}_t),$$

and

$$E(\boldsymbol{\epsilon}_t^2) = \mathrm{var}(\boldsymbol{\epsilon}_t) = \sigma_0^2.$$

Then $\mathbf{X}_t \equiv \mathbf{y}_{t-1}$, $\beta_0 \equiv \alpha_0$, and from chapter I we know that

$$E(\mathbf{X}_t'\boldsymbol{\epsilon}_t) \equiv E(\mathbf{y}_{t-1}\boldsymbol{\epsilon}_t) = \sigma_0^2\rho_0/(1 - \rho_0\alpha_0).$$

Therefore, if $\sigma_0^2 \ne 0$ and $\rho_0 \ne 0$, condition (iii.a) of Exercise 3.51 is violated.

EXERCISE 3.78

Proof: We verify the moment condition of Theorem 3.77. Since $E|Z_t|^{2r} < \Delta < \infty$ for all t, it follows that

$$\sum_{t=1}^{\infty} E|Z_t|^{2r}/t^{1+r} < \sum_{t=1}^{\infty} \Delta/t^{1+r}$$

$$= \Delta \sum_{t=1}^{\infty} 1/t^{1+r} < \infty$$

since $\Sigma_{t=1}^{\infty} 1/t^{1+r} < \infty$ for any $r > 0$. The result follows from Theorem 3.77.

EXERCISE 3.80

Proof: We verify the conditions of Exercise 2.20. First, note that $\mathbf{Z}'\boldsymbol{\epsilon}/n = n^{-1} \Sigma_{h=1}^{p} \mathbf{Z}_h'\boldsymbol{\epsilon}_h$, where $\mathbf{Z}_h$ is the $n \times l$ matrix with rows $\mathbf{Z}_{th}$ and $\boldsymbol{\epsilon}_h$ is the $n \times 1$ error vector with elements $\boldsymbol{\epsilon}_{th}$. By assumption (iii.a), $\{\mathbf{Z}_{thi}\boldsymbol{\epsilon}_{th}, \mathfrak{F}_t\}$ is a martingale difference sequence. Given (iii.b), the moment conditions of Exercise 3.78 are satisfied so that $n^{-1} \Sigma_{t=1}^{n} \mathbf{Z}_{thi}\boldsymbol{\epsilon}_{th} \xrightarrow{\text{a. s.}} 0$, $h = 1, \ldots, p$, $i = 1, \ldots, l$, and therefore $\mathbf{Z}'\boldsymbol{\epsilon}/n \xrightarrow{\text{a. s.}} \mathbf{0}$ by Proposition 2.11.

Next, Proposition 3.50 ensures that $\{\mathbf{Z}_t'\mathbf{X}_t\}$ is a mixing sequence given (ii), which satisfies the conditions of Corollary 3.48 given (iv.a). It follows from Corollary 3.48 that $\mathbf{Z}'\mathbf{X}/n - \mathbf{Q}_n \xrightarrow{\text{a. s.}} \mathbf{0}$, and $\mathbf{Q}_n$ is $O(1)$ given (iv.a) by Jensen's inequality. Hence the conditions of Exercise 2.20 are satisfied and the result follows.

EXERCISE 4.18

Proof: Let V be $k \times k$ with eigenvalues $\lambda_1, \ldots, \lambda_k$. Since V is real and symmetric it can be diagonalized by

$$V = Q'DQ,$$

where $D = \text{diag}(\lambda_1, \ldots, \lambda_k)$ is the matrix with the eigenvalues of V along its diagonal and zeros elsewhere, and Q is an orthogonal matrix that has as its rows the standardized eigenvectors of V corresponding to $\lambda_1, \ldots, \lambda_k$. Furthermore, since V is positive (semi) definite its eigenvalues satisfy $\lambda_i > (\geq)\ 0$, $i = 1, \ldots, k$. Hence, defining

$$D^{1/2} \equiv \text{diag}(\lambda_1^{1/2}, \ldots, \lambda_k^{1/2}),$$

we can define the sqaure root of V as

$$V^{1/2} = Q'D^{1/2}Q.$$

Then

$$(V^{1/2})' = Q'(D^{1/2})'(Q')'$$
$$= Q'D^{1/2}Q$$
$$= V^{1/2}$$

so that $V^{1/2}$ is symmetric. Also, for any $x \in \mathbb{R}^k$, $x \neq 0$, the quadratic form

$$x'Q'D^{1/2}Qx = (Qx)'D^{1/2}(Qx)$$

is strictly positive (nonnegative) because $\lambda_i > (\geq)\ 0$, $i = 1, \ldots, k$. Hence, $V^{1/2}$ is positive (semi) definite. Finally,

$$V^{1/2}V^{1/2} = Q'D^{1/2}QQ'D^{1/2}Q$$
$$= Q'D^{1/2}D^{1/2}Q$$

since Q is orthogonal

$$= Q'DQ = V.$$

EXERCISE 4.19

Proof: If $Z \sim N(\mathbf{0}, V)$ it follows from Example 4.12 that

$$V^{-1/2}Z \sim N(V^{-1/2} \times \mathbf{0},\ V^{-1/2}VV^{-1/2}),$$

that is

$$V^{-1/2}Z \sim N(\mathbf{0}, \mathbf{I})$$

since

$$V^{-1/2}VV^{-1/2} = V^{-1/2}V^{1/2}V^{1/2}V^{-1/2} = \mathbf{I}.$$

EXERCISE 4.26

Proof: Since $\mathbf{Z}'\mathbf{X}/n - \mathbf{Q}_n \xrightarrow{p} \mathbf{0}$ where $\mathbf{Q}_n$ is finite and has full column rank for all n sufficiently large and $\hat{\mathbf{P}}_n - \mathbf{P}_n \xrightarrow{p} \mathbf{0}$ where $\mathbf{P}_n$ is finite and nonsingular for all n sufficiently large, it follows from Proposition 2.30 that

$$\mathbf{X}'\mathbf{Z}\hat{\mathbf{P}}_n\mathbf{Z}'\mathbf{X}/n^2 - \mathbf{Q}_n'\mathbf{P}_n\mathbf{Q}_n \xrightarrow{p} \mathbf{0}.$$

Also since $\mathbf{Q}_n'\mathbf{P}_n\mathbf{Q}_n$ is nonsingular for all n sufficiently large by Lemma 2.19 given (iii), $(\mathbf{X}'\mathbf{Z}\hat{\mathbf{P}}_n\mathbf{Z}'\mathbf{X}/n^2)^{-1}$ and $\tilde{\boldsymbol{\beta}}_n$ exist in probability. Given

(i) and the existence of $(\mathbf{X}'\mathbf{Z}\hat{\mathbf{P}}_n\mathbf{Z}'\mathbf{X}/n^2)^{-1}$,

$$\sqrt{n}(\tilde{\boldsymbol{\beta}}_n - \boldsymbol{\beta}_0) = (\mathbf{X}'\mathbf{Z}\hat{\mathbf{P}}_n\mathbf{Z}'\mathbf{X}/n^2)^{-1}(\mathbf{X}'\mathbf{Z}/n)\hat{\mathbf{P}}_n n^{-1/2}\mathbf{Z}'\boldsymbol{\epsilon}.$$

Hence, given (ii),

$$\begin{aligned}\sqrt{n}(\tilde{\boldsymbol{\beta}}_n - \boldsymbol{\beta}_0) &- (\mathbf{Q}_n'\mathbf{P}_n\mathbf{Q}_n)^{-1}\mathbf{Q}_n'\mathbf{P}_n n^{-1/2}\mathbf{Z}'\boldsymbol{\epsilon}\\ &= [(\mathbf{X}'\mathbf{Z}\hat{\mathbf{P}}_n\mathbf{Z}'\mathbf{X}/n^2)^{-1}(\mathbf{X}'\mathbf{Z}/n)\hat{\mathbf{P}}_n\\ &\quad - (\mathbf{Q}_n'\mathbf{P}_n\mathbf{Q}_n)^{-1}\mathbf{Q}_n'\mathbf{P}_n]\mathbf{V}_n^{1/2}\mathbf{V}_n^{-1/2}n^{-1/2}\mathbf{Z}'\boldsymbol{\epsilon}\end{aligned}$$

exists in probability for n large enough. Premultiplying by $\mathbf{D}_n^{-1/2}$ yields

$$\begin{aligned}\mathbf{D}_n^{-1/2}\sqrt{n}(\tilde{\boldsymbol{\beta}}_n - \boldsymbol{\beta}_0) &- \mathbf{D}_n^{-1/2}(\mathbf{Q}_n'\mathbf{P}_n\mathbf{Q}_n)^{-1}\mathbf{Q}_n'\mathbf{P}_n n^{-1/2}\mathbf{Z}'\boldsymbol{\epsilon}\\ &= \mathbf{D}_n^{-1/2}[(\mathbf{X}'\mathbf{Z}\hat{\mathbf{P}}_n\mathbf{Z}'\mathbf{X}/n^2)^{-1}(\mathbf{X}'\mathbf{Z}/n)\hat{\mathbf{P}}_n - (\mathbf{Q}_n'\mathbf{P}_n\mathbf{Q}_n)^{-1}\mathbf{Q}_n'\mathbf{P}_n]\\ &\quad \cdot \mathbf{V}_n^{1/2}\mathbf{V}_n^{-1/2}n^{-1/2}\mathbf{Z}'\boldsymbol{\epsilon}.\end{aligned}$$

Now $\mathbf{V}_n^{-1/2}n^{-1/2}\mathbf{Z}'\boldsymbol{\epsilon} \overset{A}{\sim} N(\mathbf{0}, \mathbf{I})$ given (ii) and

$$\begin{aligned}\mathbf{D}_n^{-1/2}[\mathbf{X}'\mathbf{Z}\hat{\mathbf{P}}_n\mathbf{Z}'\mathbf{X}/n^2)^{-1}(\mathbf{X}'\mathbf{Z}/n)\hat{\mathbf{P}}_n\\ - (\mathbf{Q}_n'\mathbf{P}_n\mathbf{Q}_n)^{-1}\mathbf{Q}_n'\mathbf{P}_n]\mathbf{V}_n^{1/2}\end{aligned}$$

is $o_p(1)$ since $\mathbf{D}_n^{-1/2}$ and $\mathbf{V}_n^{1/2}$ are $O(1)$ given (ii) and (iii) and

$$(\mathbf{X}'\mathbf{Z}\hat{\mathbf{P}}_n\mathbf{Z}'\mathbf{X}/n^2)^{-1}(\mathbf{X}'\mathbf{Z}/n)\hat{\mathbf{P}}_n - (\mathbf{Q}_n'\mathbf{P}_n\mathbf{Q}_n')^{-1}\mathbf{Q}_n'\mathbf{P}_n$$

is $o_p(1)$ given (iii) by Proposition 2.30. Hence, by Lemma 4.6,

$$\mathbf{D}_n^{-1/2}\sqrt{n}(\tilde{\boldsymbol{\beta}}_n - \boldsymbol{\beta}_0) - \mathbf{D}_n^{-1/2}(\mathbf{Q}_n'\mathbf{P}_n\mathbf{Q}_n)^{-1}\mathbf{Q}_n'\mathbf{P}_n n^{-1/2}\mathbf{Z}'\boldsymbol{\epsilon} \xrightarrow{p} \mathbf{0}.$$

By Lemma 4.7, $\mathbf{D}_n^{-1/2}\sqrt{n}(\tilde{\boldsymbol{\beta}}_n - \boldsymbol{\beta}_0)$ has the same limiting distribution as $\mathbf{D}_n^{-1/2}(\mathbf{Q}_n'\mathbf{P}_n\mathbf{Q}_n)^{-1}\mathbf{Q}_n'\mathbf{P}_n n^{-1/2}\mathbf{Z}'\boldsymbol{\epsilon}$. We find the asymptotic distribution of this random vector by applying Corollary 4.24 with $\mathbf{A}_n' \equiv (\mathbf{Q}_n'\mathbf{P}_n\mathbf{Q}_n)^{-1}\mathbf{Q}_n'\mathbf{P}_n$ and $\boldsymbol{\Gamma}_n \equiv \mathbf{D}_n$, which immediately yields

$$\mathbf{D}_n^{-1/2}(\mathbf{Q}_n'\mathbf{P}_n\mathbf{Q}_n)^{-1}\mathbf{Q}_n'\mathbf{P}_n n^{-1/2}\mathbf{Z}'\boldsymbol{\epsilon} \overset{A}{\sim} N(\mathbf{0}, \mathbf{I}).$$

Since (ii), (iii) and (iv) hold, $\hat{\mathbf{D}}_n - \mathbf{D}_n \xrightarrow{p} \mathbf{0}$ as an immediate consequence of Proposition 2.30.

EXERCISE 4.33

Proof: Given that $\hat{\mathbf{V}}_n - \mathbf{V}_n \xrightarrow{p} \mathbf{0}$ and $\ddot{\mathbf{V}}_n - \mathbf{V}_n \xrightarrow{p} \mathbf{0}$, it follows from Proposition 2.30 that $(\hat{\mathbf{V}}_n - \ddot{\mathbf{V}}_n) - (\mathbf{V}_n - \mathbf{V}_n) = \hat{\mathbf{V}}_n - \ddot{\mathbf{V}}_n \xrightarrow{p} \mathbf{0}$. It immediately follows from Proposition 2.30 that $\mathcal{W}_n - \mathcal{LM}_n \xrightarrow{p} 0$.

EXERCISE 4.34

Proof: From the solution to the constrained minimization problem we know that

$$\ddot{\boldsymbol{\lambda}}_n = 2(\mathbf{R}(\mathbf{X}'\mathbf{X}/n)^{-1}\mathbf{R}')^{-1}(\mathbf{R}\hat{\boldsymbol{\beta}}_n - \mathbf{r})$$

and applying the hint,

$$\ddot{\boldsymbol{\lambda}}_n = 2(\mathbf{R}(\mathbf{X}'\mathbf{X}/n)^{-1}\mathbf{R}')^{-1}\mathbf{R}(\mathbf{X}'\mathbf{X}/n)^{-1}\mathbf{X}'(\mathbf{y} - \mathbf{X}\ddot{\boldsymbol{\beta}}_n)/n.$$

Now $\mathbf{y} - \mathbf{X}\ddot{\boldsymbol{\beta}}_n = \mathbf{y} - \mathbf{X}_1\ddot{\boldsymbol{\beta}}_{1n} - \mathbf{X}_2\ddot{\boldsymbol{\beta}}_{2n} = \mathbf{y} - \mathbf{X}_1\ddot{\boldsymbol{\beta}}_{1n} = \ddot{\boldsymbol{\epsilon}}$ so that

$$\ddot{\boldsymbol{\lambda}}_n = 2(\mathbf{R}(\mathbf{X}'\mathbf{X})^{-1}\mathbf{R}')^{-1}\mathbf{R}(\mathbf{X}'\mathbf{X})^{-1}\mathbf{X}'\ddot{\boldsymbol{\epsilon}}/n.$$

Partitioning $\mathbf{R}$ as $[\mathbf{0}:\mathbf{I}_q]$ and $\mathbf{X}'\mathbf{X}$ as

$$\mathbf{X}'\mathbf{X} = \begin{bmatrix} \mathbf{X}_1'\mathbf{X}_1 & \mathbf{X}_1'\mathbf{X}_2 \\ \mathbf{X}_2'\mathbf{X}_1 & \mathbf{X}_2'\mathbf{X}_2 \end{bmatrix}$$

and applying the formula for a partitioned inverse gives

$$\mathbf{R}(\mathbf{X}'\mathbf{X})^{-1}\mathbf{R}' = (\mathbf{X}_2'(\mathbf{I} - \mathbf{X}_1(\mathbf{X}_1'\mathbf{X}_1)^{-1}\mathbf{X}_1')\mathbf{X}_2)^{-1}$$

and

$$\mathbf{R}(\mathbf{X}'\mathbf{X})^{-1}\mathbf{X}' = (\mathbf{X}_2'(\mathbf{I} - \mathbf{X}_1(\mathbf{X}_1'\mathbf{X}_1)^{-1}\mathbf{X}_1')\mathbf{X}_2)^{-1}\mathbf{X}_2'(\mathbf{I} - \mathbf{X}_1(\mathbf{X}_1'\mathbf{X}_1)^{-1}\mathbf{X}_1').$$

Hence by substitution

$$\begin{aligned}\ddot{\boldsymbol{\lambda}}_n &= 2\mathbf{X}_2'(\mathbf{I} - \mathbf{X}_1(\mathbf{X}_1'\mathbf{X}_1)^{-1}\mathbf{X}_1')\ddot{\boldsymbol{\epsilon}}/n \\ &= 2\mathbf{X}_2'\ddot{\boldsymbol{\epsilon}}/n\end{aligned}$$

since $\ddot{\boldsymbol{\epsilon}} = (\mathbf{I} - \mathbf{X}_1(\mathbf{X}_1'\mathbf{X}_1)^{-1}\mathbf{X}_1')\mathbf{y}$ and $\mathbf{I} - \mathbf{X}_1(\mathbf{X}_1'\mathbf{X}_1)^{-1}\mathbf{X}_1'$ is idempotent.

EXERCISE 4.35

Proof: Substituting $\hat{\mathbf{V}}_n = \ddot{\sigma}_n^2(\mathbf{X}'\mathbf{X}/n)$ into the Lagrange multiplier statistic of Theorem 4.32 yields

$$\mathcal{LM}_n = n\ddot{\boldsymbol{\lambda}}_n'\mathbf{R}[\ddot{\boldsymbol{\epsilon}}'\ddot{\boldsymbol{\epsilon}}/n(\mathbf{X}'\mathbf{X}/n)]^{-1}\mathbf{R}'\ddot{\boldsymbol{\lambda}}_n/4.$$

From Exercise 4.34, $\ddot{\boldsymbol{\lambda}}_n = 2\mathbf{X}_2'\ddot{\boldsymbol{\epsilon}}/n$ under $H_0: \boldsymbol{\beta}_2 = \mathbf{0}$. Substituting this into the above expression and rearranging gives

$$\mathcal{LM}_n = n\ddot{\boldsymbol{\epsilon}}'\mathbf{X}_2\mathbf{R}(\mathbf{X}'\mathbf{X})^{-1}\mathbf{R}'\mathbf{X}_2'\ddot{\boldsymbol{\epsilon}}/\ddot{\boldsymbol{\epsilon}}'\ddot{\boldsymbol{\epsilon}}.$$

Recalling that $\mathbf{X}_2\mathbf{R} = (\mathbf{0}:\mathbf{X}_2)$ and $\ddot{\boldsymbol{\epsilon}}'\mathbf{X}_1 = \mathbf{0}$ we can write

$$\ddot{\boldsymbol{\epsilon}}'\mathbf{X}_2\mathbf{R} = \ddot{\boldsymbol{\epsilon}}'(\mathbf{0}:\mathbf{X}_2) = \ddot{\boldsymbol{\epsilon}}'(\mathbf{X}_1:\mathbf{X}_2) = \ddot{\boldsymbol{\epsilon}}'\mathbf{X},$$

which upon substitution immediately yields the result.

EXERCISE 4.40

Proof: We are given that $s(\boldsymbol{\beta}) = \boldsymbol{\beta}_3 - \boldsymbol{\beta}_1\boldsymbol{\beta}_2$. Hence $\nabla s(\boldsymbol{\beta}) = (-\boldsymbol{\beta}_2, -\boldsymbol{\beta}_1, 1)$. Substituting $s(\hat{\boldsymbol{\beta}}_n)$ and $\nabla s(\hat{\boldsymbol{\beta}}_n)$ into the Wald statistic of Theorem 4.39 yields

$$\mathcal{W}_n = n(\hat{\boldsymbol{\beta}}_{3n} - \hat{\boldsymbol{\beta}}_{1n}\hat{\boldsymbol{\beta}}_{2n})^2/\hat{\Gamma}_n,$$

where

$$\hat{\Gamma}_n = (-\hat{\boldsymbol{\beta}}_{2n}, -\hat{\boldsymbol{\beta}}_{1n}, 1)(\mathbf{X}'\mathbf{X}/n)^{-1}\hat{\mathbf{V}}_n(\mathbf{X}'\mathbf{X}/n)^{-1}(-\hat{\boldsymbol{\beta}}_{2n}, \hat{\boldsymbol{\beta}}_{1n}, 1)'.$$

Note that $\mathcal{W}_n \overset{A}{\sim} \chi_1^2$ in this case.

EXERCISE 4.41

Proof: The Lagrange multiplier statistic is motivated by the constrained minimization problem

$$\min_{\boldsymbol{\beta}} (\mathbf{y} - \mathbf{X}\boldsymbol{\beta})'(\mathbf{y} - \mathbf{X}\boldsymbol{\beta})/n \qquad \text{s.t.} \qquad s(\boldsymbol{\beta}) = \mathbf{0}.$$

The Lagrangian for the problem is

$$\mathcal{L} = (\mathbf{y} - \mathbf{X}\boldsymbol{\beta})'(\mathbf{y} - \mathbf{X}\boldsymbol{\beta})/n + s(\boldsymbol{\beta})'\boldsymbol{\lambda}$$

and the first order conditions are

$$\partial\mathcal{L}/\partial\boldsymbol{\beta} = 2(\mathbf{X}'\mathbf{X}/n)\boldsymbol{\beta} - 2\mathbf{X}'\mathbf{y}/n + \nabla s(\boldsymbol{\beta})'\boldsymbol{\lambda} = \mathbf{0}$$
$$\partial\mathcal{L}/\partial\boldsymbol{\lambda} = s(\boldsymbol{\beta}) = \mathbf{0}.$$

Setting $\hat{\boldsymbol{\beta}}_n = (\mathbf{X}'\mathbf{X}/n)^{-1}\mathbf{X}'\mathbf{y}/n$ and taking a mean value expansion of $s(\boldsymbol{\beta})$ around $\hat{\boldsymbol{\beta}}_n$ gives

$$\partial\mathcal{L}/\partial\boldsymbol{\beta} = 2(\mathbf{X}'\mathbf{X}/n)(\boldsymbol{\beta} - \hat{\boldsymbol{\beta}}_n) + \nabla s(\boldsymbol{\beta})'\boldsymbol{\lambda} = \mathbf{0}$$
$$\partial\mathcal{L}/\partial\boldsymbol{\lambda} = s(\hat{\boldsymbol{\beta}}_n) + \nabla\bar{s}(\boldsymbol{\beta} - \hat{\boldsymbol{\beta}}_n) = \mathbf{0},$$

where $\nabla\bar{s}$ is the $q \times k$ Jacobian of s with ith row evaluated at a mean value $\bar{\boldsymbol{\beta}}_n^{(i)}$. Premultiplying the first equation by $\nabla\bar{s}(\mathbf{X}'\mathbf{X}/n)^{-1}$ and substituting $-s(\hat{\boldsymbol{\beta}}_n) = \nabla\bar{s}(\boldsymbol{\beta} - \hat{\boldsymbol{\beta}}_n)$ gives

$$\ddot{\boldsymbol{\lambda}}_n = 2[\nabla\bar{s}(\mathbf{X}'\mathbf{X}/n)^{-1}\nabla s(\ddot{\boldsymbol{\beta}}_n)']^{-1}s(\hat{\boldsymbol{\beta}}_n).$$

Thus, following the procedures of Theorems 4.32 and 4.39 we might propose the statistic

$$\mathcal{LM}_n = n\ddot{\boldsymbol{\lambda}}_n'\hat{\boldsymbol{\Lambda}}_n^{-1}\ddot{\boldsymbol{\lambda}}_n,$$

where

$$\hat{\Lambda}_n \equiv 4(\nabla \bar{s}(\mathbf{X}'\mathbf{X}/n)^{-1}\nabla s(\ddot{\beta}_n)')^{-1}\nabla s(\hat{\beta}_n)(\mathbf{X}'\mathbf{X}/n)^{-1}\ddot{\mathbf{V}}_n$$
$$\times (\mathbf{X}'\mathbf{X}/n)^{-1}\nabla s(\hat{\beta}_n)'(\nabla \bar{s}(\mathbf{X}'\mathbf{X}/n)^{-1}\nabla s(\ddot{\beta}_n)')^{-1}.$$

The statistic above, however, is not very useful because it depends on generally unknown mean values and also on the unconstrained estimate $\hat{\beta}_n$. An asymptotically equivalent statistic replaces $\nabla\bar{s}$ by $\nabla s(\ddot{\beta}_n)$ and $\hat{\beta}_n$ by $\ddot{\beta}_n$:

$$\mathcal{LM}_n = n\ddot{\lambda}_n'\hat{\Lambda}_n^{-1}\ddot{\lambda}_n,$$

where

$$\ddot{\lambda}_n = 2[\nabla s(\ddot{\beta}_n)(\mathbf{X}'\mathbf{X}/n)^{-1}\nabla s(\ddot{\beta}_n)']^{-1}s(\ddot{\beta}_n)$$

and

$$\hat{\Lambda}_n = 4(\nabla s(\ddot{\beta}_n)(\mathbf{X}'\mathbf{X}/n)^{-1}\nabla s(\ddot{\beta}_n)')^{-1}\nabla s(\ddot{\beta}_n)$$
$$\times (\mathbf{X}'\mathbf{X}/n)^{-1}\ddot{\mathbf{V}}_n(\mathbf{X}'\mathbf{X}/n)^{-1}\nabla s(\ddot{\beta}_n)'(\nabla s(\ddot{\beta}_n)(\mathbf{X}'\mathbf{X}/n)^{-1}\nabla s(\ddot{\beta}_n)')^{-1}.$$

To show that $\mathcal{LM}_n \overset{A}{\sim} \chi_q^2$ under H_0 we note that $\mathcal{LM}_n$ differs from $\mathcal{W}_n$ only in that $\ddot{\mathbf{V}}_n$ is used in place of $\hat{\mathbf{V}}_n$ and $\ddot{\beta}_n$ replaces $\hat{\beta}_n$. Since $\ddot{\beta}_n - \hat{\beta}_n \xrightarrow{p} \mathbf{0}$ and $\ddot{\mathbf{V}}_n - \hat{\mathbf{V}}_n \xrightarrow{p} \mathbf{0}$ under H_0 given the conditions of Theorem 4.25 it follows from Proposition 2.30 that

$$\mathcal{LM}_n - \mathcal{W}_n \xrightarrow{p} 0$$

given that $\nabla s(\beta)$ is continuous. Hence $\mathcal{LM}_n \overset{A}{\sim} \chi_q^2$ by Lemma 4.7.

EXERCISE 4.42

Proof: First consider testing the hypothesis $\mathbf{R}\beta_0 = \mathbf{r}$. Analogous to Theorem 4.31 the Wald statistic is

$$\mathcal{W}_n \equiv n(\mathbf{R}\tilde{\beta}_n - \mathbf{r})'\hat{\Gamma}_n^{-1}(\mathbf{R}\tilde{\beta}_n - r) \sim \chi_q^2$$

under H_0, where

$$\hat{\Gamma}_n \equiv \mathbf{R}\hat{\mathbf{D}}_n\mathbf{R}'$$
$$= \mathbf{R}(\mathbf{X}'\mathbf{Z}\hat{\mathbf{P}}_n\mathbf{Z}'\mathbf{X}/n^2)^{-1}(\mathbf{X}'\mathbf{Z}/n)\hat{\mathbf{P}}_n\hat{\mathbf{V}}_n\hat{\mathbf{P}}_n(\mathbf{Z}'\mathbf{X}/n)$$
$$\times (\mathbf{X}'\mathbf{Z}\hat{\mathbf{P}}_n\mathbf{Z}'\mathbf{X}/n^2)^{-1}\mathbf{R}'.$$

To prove $\mathcal{W}_n$ has an asymptotic χ_q^2 distribution under H_0, we note that

$$\mathbf{R}\tilde{\beta}_n - \mathbf{r} = \mathbf{R}(\tilde{\beta}_n - \beta_0)$$

so

$$\boldsymbol{\Gamma}_n^{-1/2}\sqrt{n}(\mathbf{R}\tilde{\boldsymbol{\beta}}_n - \mathbf{r}) = \boldsymbol{\Gamma}_n^{-1/2}\mathbf{R}\sqrt{n}(\tilde{\boldsymbol{\beta}}_n - \boldsymbol{\beta}_0),$$

where

$$\boldsymbol{\Gamma}_n = \mathbf{R}(\mathbf{Q}_n'\mathbf{P}_n\mathbf{Q}_n)^{-1}\mathbf{Q}_n'\mathbf{P}_n\mathbf{V}_n\mathbf{P}_n\mathbf{Q}_n(\mathbf{Q}_n'\mathbf{P}_n\mathbf{Q}_n)^{-1}\mathbf{R}'.$$

It follows from Corollary 4.24 that $\boldsymbol{\Gamma}_n^{-1/2}\mathbf{R}\sqrt{n}(\tilde{\boldsymbol{\beta}}_n - \boldsymbol{\beta}_0) \overset{A}{\sim} N(\mathbf{0}, \mathbf{I})$ so that $\boldsymbol{\Gamma}_n^{-1/2}\sqrt{n}(\mathbf{R}\tilde{\boldsymbol{\beta}}_n - \mathbf{r}) \overset{A}{\sim} N(\mathbf{0}, \mathbf{I})$. Since $\hat{\mathbf{D}}_n - \mathbf{D}_n \xrightarrow{p} \mathbf{0}$ from Exercise 4.26 it follows that $\hat{\boldsymbol{\Gamma}}_n - \boldsymbol{\Gamma}_n \xrightarrow{p} \mathbf{0}$ by Proposition 2.30. Hence $\mathcal{W}_n \sim \chi_q^2$ by Theorem 4.30.

We can derive the Lagrange multiplier statistic using a constrained minimization approach:

$$\min_{\boldsymbol{\beta}} (\mathbf{y} - \mathbf{X}\boldsymbol{\beta})'\mathbf{Z}\hat{\mathbf{P}}_n\mathbf{Z}'(\mathbf{y} - \mathbf{X}\boldsymbol{\beta})/n^2 \qquad \text{s.t.} \qquad \mathbf{R}\boldsymbol{\beta} = \mathbf{r}.$$

The first-order conditions are

$$\partial\mathcal{L}/\partial\boldsymbol{\beta} = 2(\mathbf{X}'\mathbf{Z}\hat{\mathbf{P}}_n\mathbf{Z}'\mathbf{X}/n^2)\boldsymbol{\beta} - 2(\mathbf{X}'\mathbf{Z}/n)\hat{\mathbf{P}}_n\mathbf{Z}'\mathbf{y}/n + \mathbf{R}\boldsymbol{\lambda} = 0$$

$$\partial\mathcal{L}/\partial\boldsymbol{\lambda} = \mathbf{R}\boldsymbol{\beta} - \mathbf{r} = \mathbf{0},$$

where $\boldsymbol{\lambda}$ is the vector of Lagrange multipliers. It follows that

$$\ddot{\boldsymbol{\lambda}}_n = 2(\mathbf{R}(\mathbf{X}'\mathbf{Z}\hat{\mathbf{P}}_n\mathbf{Z}'\mathbf{X}/n^2)^{-1}\mathbf{R}')^{-1}(\mathbf{R}\tilde{\boldsymbol{\beta}}_n - \mathbf{r})$$

$$\ddot{\boldsymbol{\beta}}_n = \tilde{\boldsymbol{\beta}}_n - (\mathbf{X}'\mathbf{Z}\hat{\mathbf{P}}_n\mathbf{Z}'\mathbf{X}/n^2)^{-1}\mathbf{R}'\ddot{\boldsymbol{\lambda}}_n/2.$$

Hence, analogous to Theorem 4.32, $\mathcal{LM}_n \equiv n\ddot{\boldsymbol{\lambda}}_n'\hat{\boldsymbol{\Lambda}}_n^{-1}\ddot{\boldsymbol{\lambda}}_n \sim \chi_q^2$ under H_0, where

$$\hat{\boldsymbol{\Lambda}}_n \equiv 4(\mathbf{R}(\mathbf{X}'\mathbf{Z}\hat{\mathbf{P}}_n\mathbf{Z}'\mathbf{X}/n^2)^{-1}\mathbf{R}')^{-1}\mathbf{R}(\mathbf{X}'\mathbf{Z}\hat{\mathbf{P}}_n\mathbf{Z}'\mathbf{X}/n^2)^{-1}(\mathbf{X}'\mathbf{Z}/n)\hat{\mathbf{P}}_n$$
$$\times \ddot{\mathbf{V}}_n\hat{\mathbf{P}}_n(\mathbf{Z}'\mathbf{X}/n)(\mathbf{X}'\mathbf{Z}\hat{\mathbf{P}}_n\mathbf{Z}'\mathbf{X}/n^2)^{-1}\mathbf{R}'(\mathbf{R}(\mathbf{X}'\mathbf{Z}\hat{\mathbf{P}}_n\mathbf{Z}'\mathbf{X}/n^2)^{-1}\mathbf{R}')^{-1}$$

and $\ddot{\mathbf{V}}_n$ is computed under the constrained regression such that $\ddot{\mathbf{V}}_n - \mathbf{V}_n \xrightarrow{p} \mathbf{0}$ under H_0. If we can show that $\mathcal{LM}_n - \mathcal{W}_n \xrightarrow{p} 0$, then we can apply Lemma 4.7 to conclude $\mathcal{LM}_n \overset{A}{\sim} \chi_q^2$. Note that $\mathcal{LM}_n$ differs from $\mathcal{W}_n$ in that $\ddot{\mathbf{V}}_n$ is used in place of $\hat{\mathbf{V}}_n$. Since $\ddot{\mathbf{V}}_n - \hat{\mathbf{V}}_n \xrightarrow{p} \mathbf{0}$ under H_0, it follows from Proposition 2.30 that $\mathcal{LM}_n - \mathcal{W}_n \xrightarrow{p} 0$.

Next, consider the nonlinear hypothesis $s(\boldsymbol{\beta}_0) = \mathbf{0}$. The Wald statistic is easily seen to be

$$\mathcal{W}_n \equiv ns(\tilde{\boldsymbol{\beta}}_n)'\hat{\boldsymbol{\Gamma}}_n^{-1}s(\tilde{\boldsymbol{\beta}}_n),$$

where

$$\hat{\boldsymbol{\Gamma}}_n^{-1} \equiv \nabla s(\tilde{\boldsymbol{\beta}}_n)\hat{\mathbf{D}}_n\nabla s(\tilde{\boldsymbol{\beta}}_n)'$$

and $\hat{\mathbf{D}}_n$ is given in Exercise 4.26. The proof that $\mathcal{W}_n \overset{A}{\sim} \chi_q^2$ under H_0 is identical to that of Theorem 4.39 except that $\tilde{\boldsymbol{\beta}}_n$ replaces $\hat{\boldsymbol{\beta}}_n$, $\hat{\mathbf{D}}_n$ is appropriately defined, and the results of Exercise 4.26 are used in place of those of Theorem 4.25.

The Lagrange Multiplier statistic can be derived in a manner analogous to Exercise 4.41, and the result is that the Lagrange multiplier statistic has the form of the Wald statistic with the constrained estimates $\ddot{\boldsymbol{\beta}}_n$ and $\ddot{\mathbf{V}}_n$ replacing $\hat{\boldsymbol{\beta}}_n$ and $\hat{\mathbf{V}}_n$. Thus

$$\mathcal{LM}_n = n\ddot{\boldsymbol{\lambda}}_n'\hat{\boldsymbol{\Lambda}}_n^{-1}\ddot{\boldsymbol{\lambda}}_n,$$

where

$$\ddot{\boldsymbol{\lambda}}_n = 2[\nabla s(\ddot{\boldsymbol{\beta}}_n)(\mathbf{X}'\mathbf{Z}\hat{\mathbf{P}}_n\mathbf{Z}'\mathbf{X}/n^2)^{-1}\nabla s(\ddot{\boldsymbol{\beta}}_n)']^{-1}s(\ddot{\boldsymbol{\beta}}_n)$$

and

$$\begin{aligned}\hat{\boldsymbol{\Lambda}}_n = {} & 4[\nabla s(\ddot{\boldsymbol{\beta}}_n)(\mathbf{X}'\mathbf{Z}\hat{\mathbf{P}}_n\mathbf{Z}'\mathbf{X}/n^2)^{-1}\nabla s(\ddot{\boldsymbol{\beta}}_n)']^{-1}\\ & \times \nabla s(\ddot{\boldsymbol{\beta}}_n)(\mathbf{X}'\mathbf{Z}\hat{\mathbf{P}}_n\mathbf{Z}'\mathbf{X}/n^2)^{-1}(\mathbf{X}'\mathbf{Z}/n)\hat{\mathbf{P}}_n\ddot{\mathbf{V}}_n\hat{\mathbf{P}}_n(\mathbf{Z}'\mathbf{X}/n)\\ & \times (\mathbf{X}'\mathbf{Z}\hat{\mathbf{P}}_n\mathbf{Z}'\mathbf{X}/n^2)^{-1}\nabla s(\ddot{\boldsymbol{\beta}}_n)'[\nabla s(\ddot{\boldsymbol{\beta}}_n)\\ & \times (\mathbf{X}'\mathbf{Z}\hat{\mathbf{P}}_n\mathbf{Z}'\mathbf{X}/n^2)^{-1}\nabla s(\ddot{\boldsymbol{\beta}}_n)']^{-1}.\end{aligned}$$

Now $\ddot{\mathbf{V}}_n - \hat{\mathbf{V}}_n \xrightarrow{p} \mathbf{0}$ and $\nabla s(\ddot{\boldsymbol{\beta}}_n) - \nabla s(\hat{\boldsymbol{\beta}}_n) \xrightarrow{p} \mathbf{0}$ given $\nabla s(\boldsymbol{\beta})$ is continuous. It follows from Proposition 2.30 that $\mathcal{LM}_n - \mathcal{W}_n \xrightarrow{p} 0$ so that $\mathcal{LM}_n \overset{A}{\sim} \chi_q^2$ by Lemma 4.7.

EXERCISE 4.46

Proof: We assume the conditions of Theorem 4.25 are satisfied. Then Proposition 4.45 tells us that the asymptotically efficient estimator is

$$\begin{aligned}\boldsymbol{\beta}_n^* &= (\mathbf{X}'\mathbf{X}\hat{\mathbf{V}}_n^{-1}\mathbf{X}'\mathbf{X})^{-1}\mathbf{X}'\mathbf{X}\hat{\mathbf{V}}_n^{-1}\mathbf{X}'\mathbf{y}\\ &= (\mathbf{X}'\mathbf{X})^{-1}\hat{\mathbf{V}}_n(\mathbf{X}'\mathbf{X})^{-1}\mathbf{X}'\mathbf{X}\hat{\mathbf{V}}_n^{-1}\mathbf{X}'\mathbf{y}\\ &= (\mathbf{X}'\mathbf{X})^{-1}\mathbf{X}'\mathbf{y}\\ &= \hat{\boldsymbol{\beta}}_n.\end{aligned}$$

EXERCISE 4.47

Proof: We assume that the conditions of Exercise 4.26 are satisfied. In addition, we assume $\tilde{\sigma}_n^2(\mathbf{Z}'\mathbf{Z}/n) - \sigma_0^2\mathbf{L}_n \xrightarrow{p} \mathbf{0}$ so that $\hat{\mathbf{V}}_n = \tilde{\sigma}_n^2(\mathbf{Z}'\mathbf{Z}/n)$. (This will follow from a law of large numbers.) Then the conditions of Proposition 4.45 are satisfied and it follows that the asymptotically efficient estimator is

$$\beta_n^* = (\mathbf{X}'\mathbf{Z}(\tilde{\sigma}_n^2(\mathbf{Z}'\mathbf{Z}/n))^{-1}\mathbf{Z}'\mathbf{X})^{-1}\mathbf{X}'\mathbf{Z}(\tilde{\sigma}_n^2(\mathbf{Z}'\mathbf{Z}/n))^{-1}\mathbf{Z}'\mathbf{y}$$
$$= (\mathbf{X}'\mathbf{Z}(\mathbf{Z}'\mathbf{Z})^{-1}\mathbf{Z}'\mathbf{X})^{-1}\mathbf{X}'\mathbf{Z}(\mathbf{Z}'\mathbf{Z})^{-1}\mathbf{Z}'\mathbf{y}$$
$$= \tilde{\beta}_{2SLS}.$$

EXERCISE 4.55

Proof: By definition,

$$\tilde{\boldsymbol{\epsilon}}_{th} = \sum_{\tau=1}^{n}\sum_{g=1}^{p} \mathbf{c}_{t\tau hg}\boldsymbol{\epsilon}_{\tau g}.$$

Hence

$$E(\tilde{\boldsymbol{\epsilon}}_{th}|\tilde{\mathbf{W}}_{th}) = \sum_{\tau=1}^{n}\sum_{g=1}^{p} E(\mathbf{c}_{t\tau hg}\boldsymbol{\epsilon}_{\tau g}|\tilde{\mathbf{W}}_{th})$$
$$= \sum_{\tau=1}^{n}\sum_{g=1}^{p} \mathbf{c}_{t\tau hg}E(\boldsymbol{\epsilon}_{\tau g}|\tilde{\mathbf{W}}_{th})$$

since $\mathbf{c}_{t\tau hg}$ is measurable with respect to $\sigma(\tilde{\mathbf{W}}_{th})$. Further, since

$$\sigma(\tilde{\mathbf{W}}_{th}) = \bigwedge_{\{1\le\tau\le n,\, 1\le g\le p:\, \mathbf{c}_{t\tau hg}\ne 0\}} \sigma(\mathbf{W}_{\tau g})$$

and therefore $\sigma(\tilde{\mathbf{W}}_{th}) \subset \sigma(\mathbf{W}_{\tau g})$, it follows from Proposition 3.63 that $E(\boldsymbol{\epsilon}_{\tau g}|\tilde{\mathbf{W}}_{th}) = 0$ given $E(\boldsymbol{\epsilon}_{\tau g}|\mathbf{W}_{\tau g}) = 0$. Hence

$$E(\tilde{\boldsymbol{\epsilon}}_{th}|\tilde{\mathbf{W}}_{th}) = 0.$$

Next,

$$E(\tilde{\mathbf{Z}}'\tilde{\boldsymbol{\epsilon}}\tilde{\boldsymbol{\epsilon}}'\tilde{\mathbf{Z}}/n) = n^{-1}\sum_{t=1}^{n}\sum_{\tau=1}^{n}\sum_{h=1}^{p}\sum_{g=1}^{p} E(\tilde{\mathbf{Z}}'_{th}\tilde{\boldsymbol{\epsilon}}_{th}\tilde{\boldsymbol{\epsilon}}_{\tau g}\tilde{\mathbf{Z}}_{\tau g})$$
$$= n^{-1}\sum_{t=1}^{n}\sum_{\tau=1}^{n}\sum_{h=1}^{p}\sum_{g=1}^{p} E[E(\tilde{\mathbf{Z}}'_{th}\tilde{\boldsymbol{\epsilon}}_{th}\tilde{\boldsymbol{\epsilon}}_{\tau g}\tilde{\mathbf{Z}}_{\tau g}|\tilde{\mathbf{W}}_{th}, \tilde{\mathbf{W}}_{\tau g})]$$
$$= n^{-1}\sum_{t=1}^{n}\sum_{\tau=1}^{n}\sum_{h=1}^{p}\sum_{g=1}^{p} E[\tilde{\mathbf{Z}}'_{th}E(\tilde{\boldsymbol{\epsilon}}_{th}\tilde{\boldsymbol{\epsilon}}_{\tau g}|\tilde{\mathbf{W}}_{th}, \tilde{\mathbf{W}}_{\tau g})\tilde{\mathbf{Z}}_{\tau g}]$$
$$= n^{-1}\sum_{t=1}^{n}\sum_{\tau=1}^{n}\sum_{h=1}^{p}\sum_{g=1}^{p} E[\tilde{\mathbf{Z}}'_{th}\omega_{t\tau hg}\tilde{\mathbf{Z}}_{\tau g}]$$

defining $\omega_{t\tau hg} \equiv E(\tilde{\boldsymbol{\epsilon}}_{th}\tilde{\boldsymbol{\epsilon}}_{\tau g}|\mathbf{W}_{th}, \mathbf{W}_{\tau g})$. Setting $\omega_{t\tau} \equiv [\omega_{t\tau thg}]$ and $\Omega_n \equiv$

$[\omega_{t\tau}]$ gives

$$E(\tilde{\mathbf{Z}}'\tilde{\boldsymbol{\epsilon}}\tilde{\boldsymbol{\epsilon}}'\tilde{\mathbf{Z}}/n) = n^{-1}\sum_{t=1}^{n}\sum_{\tau=1}^{n} E(\tilde{\mathbf{Z}}_t'\omega_{t\tau}\tilde{\mathbf{Z}}_\tau)$$
$$= E(\tilde{\mathbf{Z}}'\boldsymbol{\Omega}_n\tilde{\mathbf{Z}}/n).$$

The result follows upon showing that $\boldsymbol{\Omega}_n = \mathbf{C}_n\mathbf{C}_n'$. Consider a typical element of $\boldsymbol{\Omega}_n$,

$$\omega_{t\tau hg} = E(\tilde{\boldsymbol{\epsilon}}_{th}\tilde{\boldsymbol{\epsilon}}_{\tau g}|\tilde{\mathbf{W}}_{th}, \tilde{\mathbf{W}}_{\tau g})$$
$$= \sum_{\theta=1}^{n}\sum_{\gamma=1}^{p}\sum_{\psi=1}^{n}\sum_{\lambda=1}^{p} E(\mathbf{c}_{t\theta h\gamma}\mathbf{c}_{\tau\psi g\lambda}\boldsymbol{\epsilon}_{\theta\gamma}\boldsymbol{\epsilon}_{\psi\lambda}|\tilde{\mathbf{W}}_{th}, \tilde{\mathbf{W}}_{\tau g})$$
$$= \sum_{\theta=1}^{n}\sum_{\gamma=1}^{p}\sum_{\psi=1}^{n}\sum_{\lambda=1}^{p} \mathbf{c}_{t\theta h\gamma}\mathbf{c}_{\tau\psi g\lambda}E(\boldsymbol{\epsilon}_{\theta\gamma}\boldsymbol{\epsilon}_{\psi\lambda}|\tilde{\mathbf{W}}_{th}, \tilde{\mathbf{W}}_{\tau g})$$

since $\mathbf{c}_{t\theta h\gamma}$ and $\mathbf{c}_{\tau\psi h\lambda}$ are each measurable with respect to $\sigma(\tilde{\mathbf{W}}_{th}, \tilde{\mathbf{W}}_{\tau g})$. We are given that

$$E(\boldsymbol{\epsilon}_{\theta\gamma}\boldsymbol{\epsilon}_{\psi\lambda}|\mathbf{W}_{\theta\gamma}, \mathbf{W}_{\psi\lambda}) = 1, \qquad \theta = \psi, \qquad \gamma = \lambda,$$
$$E(\boldsymbol{\epsilon}_{\theta\gamma}\boldsymbol{\epsilon}_{\psi\lambda}|\mathbf{W}_{\theta\gamma}, \mathbf{W}_{\psi\lambda}) = 0, \qquad \theta \neq \psi, \qquad \gamma \neq \lambda.$$

Also, whenever $\mathbf{c}_{t\theta h\gamma} \neq 0$ we have $\sigma(\mathbf{W}_{th}) \subset \sigma(\tilde{\mathbf{W}}_{\theta\gamma})$; similarly, whenever $\mathbf{c}_{\tau\psi g\lambda} \neq 0$ we have $\sigma(\tilde{\mathbf{W}}_{\tau g}) \subset \sigma(\mathbf{W}_{\psi\lambda})$. It follows that $\sigma(\tilde{\mathbf{W}}_{th}, \tilde{\mathbf{W}}_{\tau g}) = \sigma(\tilde{\mathbf{W}}_{th}) \vee \sigma(\tilde{\mathbf{W}}_{\tau g}) \subset \sigma(\mathbf{W}_{\theta\gamma}) \vee \sigma(\mathbf{W}_{\psi\lambda}) = \sigma(\mathbf{W}_{\theta\gamma}, \mathbf{W}_{\psi\lambda})$ whenever $\mathbf{c}_{t\theta h\gamma} \neq 0$ and $\mathbf{c}_{\tau\psi g\lambda} \neq 0$. By Proposition 3.63,

$$E(\boldsymbol{\epsilon}_{\theta\gamma}^2|\tilde{\mathbf{W}}_{th}, \tilde{\mathbf{W}}_{\tau g}) = 1, \qquad \theta = \psi, \qquad \gamma = \lambda,$$
$$E(\boldsymbol{\epsilon}_{\theta\gamma}\boldsymbol{\epsilon}_{\psi\lambda}|\tilde{\mathbf{W}}_{th}, \tilde{\mathbf{W}}_{\tau g}) = 0, \qquad \theta \neq \psi, \qquad \gamma \neq \lambda,$$

whenever $\mathbf{c}_{t\theta h\gamma} \neq 0$ and $\mathbf{c}_{\tau\psi g\lambda} \neq 0$. Hence

$$\omega_{t\tau hg} = \sum_{\theta=1}^{n}\sum_{\gamma=1}^{p} \mathbf{c}_{t\theta h\gamma}\mathbf{c}_{\tau\theta g\gamma},$$

which is the inner product of the (t, h) row of $\mathbf{C}_n$ and the (τ, g) column of $\mathbf{C}_n'$, that is the typical element of $\mathbf{C}_n\mathbf{C}_n'$.

EXERCISE 4.56

Proof: From the hint we can express $\mathbf{Z}_{th}^*$ as

$$\mathbf{Z}_{th}^* = \sum_{\tau=1}^{n}\sum_{g=1}^{p} \mathbf{c}_{\tau t g h}\tilde{\mathbf{Z}}_{\tau g}.$$

We note that $\mathbf{c}_{\tau tgh}\tilde{\mathbf{Z}}_{\tau g}$ is measurable with respect to $\sigma(\tilde{\mathbf{W}}_{\tau g})$ so that $\mathbf{Z}^*_{th}$ is measurable with respect to

$$\mathcal{G}_{th} = \bigvee_{\{1\leq\tau\leq n, 1\leq g\leq p:\ \mathbf{c}_{\tau tgh}\neq 0\}} \sigma(\tilde{\mathbf{W}}_{\tau g}).$$

Since

$$\sigma(\tilde{\mathbf{W}}_{\tau g}) = \bigwedge_{\{1\leq\psi\leq n, 1\leq\lambda\leq p:\ \mathbf{c}_{\tau\psi g\lambda}\neq 0\}} \sigma(\mathbf{W}_{\psi\lambda})$$

it follows that whenever $\mathbf{c}_{\tau tgh} \neq 0$, $\sigma(\tilde{\mathbf{W}}_{\tau g}) \subset \sigma(\mathbf{W}_{th})$. Since $\mathcal{G}_{th}$ is the smallest σ-field containing the union of σ-fields each of which is contained in $\sigma(\mathbf{W}_{th})$, it follows that $\mathcal{G}_{th} \subset \sigma(\mathbf{W}_{th})$, so that $\mathbf{Z}^*_{th}$ is measurable with respect to $\sigma(\mathbf{W}_{th})$.

EXERCISE 4.59

Proof: Observe that

$$\begin{aligned}\sqrt{n}(\boldsymbol{\beta}^{**}_n - \boldsymbol{\beta}^*_n) = &-(\mathbf{X}'\mathbf{Z}\hat{\mathbf{P}}_n\mathbf{Z}'\mathbf{X}/n^2)^{-1}\nabla s(\boldsymbol{\beta}^*_n)' \\ &\times [\nabla s(\boldsymbol{\beta}^*_n)(\mathbf{X}'\mathbf{Z}\hat{\mathbf{P}}_n\mathbf{Z}'\mathbf{X}/n^2)^{-1}\nabla s(\boldsymbol{\beta}^*_n)']^{-1}\sqrt{n}s(\boldsymbol{\beta}^*_n).\end{aligned}$$

Now, under the conditions of Exercise 4.26, $\mathbf{Z}'\mathbf{X}/n$, $\hat{\mathbf{P}}_n$ and $\nabla s(\boldsymbol{\beta}^*_n)$ are all $O_p(1)$ and have full rank for all n sufficiently large. Thus, if we can show that $\sqrt{n}s(\boldsymbol{\beta}^*_n) \xrightarrow{p} 0$, it will follow from Exercise 2.35 and Proposition 2.30 that $\sqrt{n}(\boldsymbol{\beta}^{**}_n - \boldsymbol{\beta}^*_n) \xrightarrow{p} \mathbf{0}$. Consider a mean value expansion of $s(\boldsymbol{\beta}^*_n)$ about the true parameter value $\boldsymbol{\beta}_0$:

$$\begin{aligned}\sqrt{n}s(\boldsymbol{\beta}^*_n) &= \sqrt{n}s(\boldsymbol{\beta}_0) + \nabla\bar{s}\sqrt{n}(\boldsymbol{\beta}^*_n - \boldsymbol{\beta}_0) \\ &= \nabla\bar{s}\sqrt{n}(\boldsymbol{\beta}^*_n - \boldsymbol{\beta}_0)\end{aligned}$$

since $s(\boldsymbol{\beta}_0) = \mathbf{0}$, where $\nabla\bar{s}$ is the Jacobian of s evaluated at mean values between $\boldsymbol{\beta}^*_n$ and $\boldsymbol{\beta}_0$. This can be rewritten as

$$\sqrt{n}s(\boldsymbol{\beta}^*_n) = \nabla\bar{s}\tilde{\mathbf{A}}_n\sqrt{n}(\tilde{\boldsymbol{\beta}}_n - \boldsymbol{\beta}_0),$$

where

$$\begin{aligned}\tilde{\mathbf{A}}_n = \mathbf{I} - &(\mathbf{X}'\mathbf{Z}\hat{\mathbf{V}}_n^{-1}\mathbf{Z}'\mathbf{X}/n^2)^{-1}\nabla s(\tilde{\boldsymbol{\beta}}_n)' \\ &\times [\nabla s(\tilde{\boldsymbol{\beta}}_n)(\mathbf{X}'\mathbf{Z}\hat{\mathbf{V}}_n^{-1}\mathbf{Z}'\mathbf{X}/n^2)^{-1}\nabla s(\tilde{\boldsymbol{\beta}}_n)']^{-1}\nabla\bar{s}.\end{aligned}$$

Now $\sqrt{n}(\tilde{\boldsymbol{\beta}}_n - \boldsymbol{\beta}_0)$ is $O_p(1)$ by Lemma 4.5 under the conditions of Exercise 4.26. Since $\nabla\bar{s} \xrightarrow{p} \nabla s(\boldsymbol{\beta}_0)$, $\nabla s(\tilde{\boldsymbol{\beta}}_n) \xrightarrow{p} \nabla s(\boldsymbol{\beta}_0)$, $\mathbf{Z}'\mathbf{X}/n$ is $O_p(1)$ and $\hat{\mathbf{V}}_n$ is $O_p(1)$, it follows from Proposition 2.30 that $\nabla\bar{s}\tilde{\mathbf{A}}_n \xrightarrow{p} \mathbf{0}$, where we let $b_n(\omega) \equiv (\mathbf{Z}'\mathbf{X}/n,\ \hat{\mathbf{V}}_n,\ \nabla\bar{s},\ \nabla s(\tilde{\boldsymbol{\beta}}_n))'$ and $\mathbf{c}_n \equiv (\mathbf{Q}_n,\ \mathbf{V}_n,\ \nabla s(\boldsymbol{\beta}_0),\ \nabla s(\boldsymbol{\beta}_0))'$. Hence, by Exercise 2.35,

$$\sqrt{n}s(\boldsymbol{\beta}_n^*) = \nabla\bar{s}\tilde{\mathbf{A}}_n\sqrt{n}(\tilde{\boldsymbol{\beta}}_n - \boldsymbol{\beta}_0) \xrightarrow{p} \mathbf{0}$$

and the result follows.

EXERCISE 5.4

Proof: We verify the conditions of Exercise 4.26. To apply Theorem 5.2, let $Z_t \equiv \boldsymbol{\lambda}'\mathbf{V}^{-1/2}\mathbf{Z}_t'\boldsymbol{\epsilon}_t$, where $\boldsymbol{\lambda}'\boldsymbol{\lambda} = 1$ and consider $n^{-1/2} \sum_{t=1}^n \boldsymbol{\lambda}'\mathbf{V}^{-1/2}\mathbf{Z}_t'\boldsymbol{\epsilon}_t = n^{-1/2} \sum_{t=1}^n Z_t$. The summands Z_t are i.i.d. by Proposition 3.2 given (ii) with $E(Z_t) = 0$ given (iii.a) and $\text{var}(Z_t) = \boldsymbol{\lambda}'\mathbf{V}^{-1/2}\mathbf{V}\mathbf{V}^{-1/2}\boldsymbol{\lambda} = 1$ given (iii.b) and (iii.c). Therefore $n^{-1/2} \sum_{t=1}^n Z_t = n^{-1/2} \sum_{t=1}^n \boldsymbol{\lambda}'\mathbf{V}^{-1/2}\mathbf{Z}_t'\boldsymbol{\epsilon}_t = \boldsymbol{\lambda}'\mathbf{V}^{-1/2}n^{-1/2}\mathbf{Z}'\boldsymbol{\epsilon} \overset{A}{\sim} N(0,\ 1)$ by Theorem 5.2. It follows from Proposition 5.1 that $\mathbf{V}^{-1/2}n^{-1/2}\mathbf{Z}'\boldsymbol{\epsilon} \overset{A}{\sim} N(\mathbf{0}, \mathbf{I})$ since if $\mathcal{Y} \sim N(\mathbf{0}, \mathbf{I})$ then $\boldsymbol{\lambda}'\mathcal{Y} \sim N(0, 1)$. $\mathbf{V}$ is $O(1)$ given (iii.b) and nonsingular given (iii.c). It follows from Theorem 3.1 and Theorem 2.24 that $\mathbf{Z}'\mathbf{X}/n - \mathbf{Q} \xrightarrow{p} \mathbf{0}$ given (ii), (iv.a), and (iv.b). Since the remaining conditions of Exercise 4.26 are satisfied by assumption, the result follows.

EXERCISE 5.5

Proof: Given the conditions of Exercise 5.4 it follows that

$$\mathbf{V} = n^{-1} \sum_{t=1}^{n} E(\boldsymbol{\epsilon}_t^2\mathbf{Z}_t'\mathbf{Z}_t) = E(\boldsymbol{\epsilon}_t^2\mathbf{Z}_t'\mathbf{Z}_t).$$

Now

$$\begin{aligned} E(\boldsymbol{\epsilon}_t^2\mathbf{Z}_t'\mathbf{Z}_t) &= E(E(\boldsymbol{\epsilon}_t^2\mathbf{Z}_t'\mathbf{Z}_t|\mathbf{Z}_t)) \\ &= E(E(\boldsymbol{\epsilon}_t^2|\mathbf{Z}_t)\mathbf{Z}_t'\mathbf{Z}_t) \\ &= \sigma_0^2\mathbf{E}(\mathbf{Z}_t'\mathbf{Z}_t) \equiv \sigma_0^2\mathbf{L}. \end{aligned}$$

Hence $\mathbf{V} = \sigma_0^2\mathbf{L}$. It follows from Exercise 4.47 that the efficient IV estimator chooses $\mathbf{P} = \mathbf{V}^{-1}$ to yield the two stage least squares estimator,

$$\tilde{\boldsymbol{\beta}}_{2SLS} = (\mathbf{X}'\mathbf{Z}(\mathbf{Z}'\mathbf{Z})^{-1}\mathbf{Z}'\mathbf{X})^{-1}\mathbf{X}'\mathbf{Z}(\mathbf{Z}'\mathbf{Z})^{-1}\mathbf{Z}'\mathbf{y}.$$

The natural estimator for $\mathbf{V}$ is $\hat{\mathbf{V}}_n = \tilde{\sigma}_n^2(\mathbf{Z}'\mathbf{Z}/n)$, where $\tilde{\sigma}_n^2 = (\mathbf{y} - \mathbf{X}\tilde{\boldsymbol{\beta}}_{2SLS})'(\mathbf{y} - \mathbf{X}\tilde{\boldsymbol{\beta}}_{2SLS})/n$. The conditions of Exercise 5.4 are not quite strong enough to ensure $\hat{\mathbf{V}}_n$ is consistent for $\mathbf{V}$. In addition we need

(i′) $E|\boldsymbol{\epsilon}_t^2| < \infty$

(ii′) (a) $E|\mathbf{Z}_{ti}^2| < \infty, \quad i = 1, \ldots, l;$

(b) $E|X_{tj}^2| < \infty$, $j = 1, \ldots, k$;
(c) $\mathbf{L} \equiv \mathbf{E}(\mathbf{Z}_t'\mathbf{Z}_t)$ is nonsingular.

Note that (ii′.a) and (ii′.b) together imply (iv.a) by the Cauchy–Schwartz inequality.

We show that $\mathbf{Z}'\mathbf{Z}/n \xrightarrow{p} \mathbf{L}$ and $\tilde{\sigma}_n^2 \xrightarrow{p} \sigma_0^2$. Consider $\mathbf{Z}'\mathbf{Z}/n = n^{-1} \sum_{t=1}^n \mathbf{Z}_t'\mathbf{Z}_t$. Since $\{\mathbf{Z}_t'\mathbf{Z}_t\}$ is an i.i.d. sequence given (ii), it follows that $\mathbf{Z}'\mathbf{Z}/n \xrightarrow{p} \mathbf{L}$ by Theorem 3.1 and Theorem 2.24 given (ii′.a). Next consider $\tilde{\sigma}_n^2 = n^{-1}(\boldsymbol{\epsilon} - \mathbf{X}(\tilde{\boldsymbol{\beta}}_{2SLS} - \boldsymbol{\beta}_0))'(\boldsymbol{\epsilon} - \mathbf{X}(\tilde{\boldsymbol{\beta}}_{2SLS} - \boldsymbol{\beta}_0)) = \boldsymbol{\epsilon}'\boldsymbol{\epsilon}/n - 2(\tilde{\boldsymbol{\beta}}_{2SLS} - \boldsymbol{\beta}_0)'\mathbf{X}'\boldsymbol{\epsilon}/n + (\tilde{\boldsymbol{\beta}}_{2SLS} - \boldsymbol{\beta}_0)'\mathbf{X}'\mathbf{X}/n(\tilde{\boldsymbol{\beta}}_{2SLS} - \boldsymbol{\beta}_0)$. Now $\tilde{\boldsymbol{\beta}}_{2SLS} - \boldsymbol{\beta}_0 \xrightarrow{a.s.} \mathbf{0}$. The elements of $\mathbf{X}_t'\boldsymbol{\epsilon}_t$ have finite expected absolute value given (i′) and (ii′.b). Hence $\mathbf{X}'\boldsymbol{\epsilon}/n$ is $O_{a.s.}(1)$ by Theorem 3.1. Similarly, $\mathbf{X}_t'\mathbf{X}_t$ has finite expected absolute value given (ii′.b). Since $\{\mathbf{X}_t'\mathbf{X}_t\}$ is an i.i.d. sequence it follows from Theorem 3.1 that $\mathbf{X}'\mathbf{X}/n$ is $O_{a.s.}(1)$. Therefore $-2(\tilde{\boldsymbol{\beta}}_{2SLS} - \boldsymbol{\beta}_0)\mathbf{X}'\boldsymbol{\epsilon}/n \xrightarrow{p} \mathbf{0}$ and $(\tilde{\boldsymbol{\beta}}_{2SLS} - \boldsymbol{\beta}_0)'\mathbf{X}'\mathbf{X}/n(\tilde{\boldsymbol{\beta}}_{2SLS} - \boldsymbol{\beta}_0) \xrightarrow{p} 0$ by Theorem 2.24 and Proposition 2.30. Finally, consider $\boldsymbol{\epsilon}'\boldsymbol{\epsilon}/n = n^{-1} \sum_{t=1}^n \boldsymbol{\epsilon}_t^2$. Now $\{\boldsymbol{\epsilon}_t^2\}$ is an i.i.d. sequence given (ii) with finite expected absolute value given (i′). It follows from Theorem 3.1 that $n^{-1} \sum_{t=1}^n \boldsymbol{\epsilon}_t^2 - E(\boldsymbol{\epsilon}_t^2) = n^{-1} \sum_{t=1}^n \boldsymbol{\epsilon}_t^2 - \sigma_0^2 \xrightarrow{a.s.} 0$. Hence $\hat{\mathbf{V}}_n - \mathbf{V} = \tilde{\sigma}_n^2(\mathbf{Z}'\mathbf{Z}/n) - \sigma_0^2\mathbf{L} \xrightarrow{p} \mathbf{0}$ by Proposition 2.30. Given that $\sigma_0^2 > 0$ and $\mathbf{L}$ is nonsingular it follows from Proposition 2.30 that $\hat{\mathbf{P}}_n - \mathbf{P} = \hat{\mathbf{V}}_n^{-1} - \mathbf{V}^{-1} = (\sigma_n^2(\mathbf{Z}'\mathbf{Z}/n))^{-1} - (\sigma_0^2\mathbf{L})^{-1} \xrightarrow{p} \mathbf{0}$. This completes the exercise.

Exercise 5.9

Proof: For an identically distributed sequence $\{Z_t\}$ with $E(Z_t) = \mu$, $\text{var}(Z_t) = \sigma^2 < \infty$, the Lindeberg condition reduces to

$$\lim_{n\to\infty} \sigma^{-2} \int_{(z-\mu)^2 > \epsilon n \sigma^2} (z - \mu)^2 \, dF(z) = 0.$$

Now

$$\begin{aligned}
&\sigma^{-2} \int_{(z-\mu)^2 > \epsilon n \sigma^2} (z - \mu)^2 \, dF(z) \\
&= \sigma^{-2}\left(\sigma^2 - \int_{(z-\mu)^2 \le \epsilon n \sigma^2} (z - \mu)^2 \, dF(z)\right) \\
&= \sigma^{-2}\left(\sigma^2 - \int_{-\infty}^{\infty} 1_{[(z-\mu)^2 \le \epsilon n \sigma^2]} (z - \mu)^2 \, dF(z)\right),
\end{aligned}$$

where $1_{[(z-\mu)^2 \le \epsilon n \sigma^2]}$ is the indicator function. If we can show the integral converges to σ^2 the result will follow immediately. Let $g_n(z) \equiv 1_{[(z-\mu)^2 \le \epsilon n \sigma^2]}(z-\mu)^2$. Then $\{g_n(z)\}$ is a nondecreasing sequence for any z and $\lim_{n\to\infty} g_n(z) = (z-\mu)^2$. Next we apply the Monotone Convergence Theorem (see Rao [1973, p. 135]):

$$\lim_{n\to\infty} \int_{-\infty}^{\infty} g_n(z)\, dF(z) = \int_{-\infty}^{\infty} \lim_{n\to\infty} g_n(z)\, dF(z)$$
$$= \int_{-\infty}^{\infty} (z-\mu)^2\, dF(z) = \sigma^2.$$

Hence

$$\lim_{n\to\infty} \sigma^{-2} \int_{(z-\mu)^2 > \epsilon n \sigma^2} (z-\mu)^2\, dF(z) = \sigma^{-2}(\sigma^2 - \sigma^2) = 0$$

and the result follows.

EXERCISE 5.12

Proof: We verify the conditions of Theorem 4.25. To apply Theorem 5.11, let $Z_{nt} \equiv \lambda' \mathbf{V}_n^{-1/2} \mathbf{X}_t' \boldsymbol{\epsilon}_t$ and consider $n^{-1/2} \sum_{t=1}^n \lambda' \mathbf{V}_n^{-1/2} \mathbf{X}_t' \boldsymbol{\epsilon}_t = n^{-1/2} \sum_{t=1}^n Z_{nt}$. The summands Z_{nt} are independent by Proposition 3.2(b) given (ii), with $E(Z_{nt}) = 0$ given (iii.a), and $\bar{\sigma}_n^2 \equiv \text{var}(\sqrt{n} Z_n) = \lambda' \mathbf{V}_n^{-1/2} \text{var}(n^{-1/2} \mathbf{X}' \boldsymbol{\epsilon}) \mathbf{V}_n^{-1/2} \lambda = \lambda' \mathbf{V}_n^{-1/2} \mathbf{V}_n \mathbf{V}_n^{-1/2} \lambda = 1$ given (iii.c). By (iii.b) $E|Z_{nt}|^{2+\delta}$ is uniformly bounded (apply Minkowski's inequality). Hence, $n^{-1/2} \sum_{t=1}^n Z_{nt} = n^{-1/2} \sum_{t=1}^n \lambda' \mathbf{V}_n^{-1/2} \mathbf{X}_t' \boldsymbol{\epsilon}_t = \lambda' \mathbf{V}_n^{-1/2} n^{-1/2} \mathbf{X}' \boldsymbol{\epsilon} \overset{A}{\sim} N(0, 1)$ and therefore $\mathbf{V}_n^{-1/2} n^{-1/2} \mathbf{X}' \boldsymbol{\epsilon} \overset{A}{\sim} N(\mathbf{0}, \mathbf{I})$ by Proposition 5.1.

Assumptions (ii), (iv.a), and (iv.b) ensure that $\mathbf{X}'\mathbf{X}/n - \mathbf{M}_n \xrightarrow{p} \mathbf{0}$ by Corollary 3.9 and Theorem 2.24. Given (iv.a) $\mathbf{M}_n$ is O(1) and uniformly positive definite given (iv.b). Since (v) also holds, the result follows from Theorem 4.25.

EXERCISE 5.17: The following conditions are sufficient:

(i′) (a) $\mathbf{y} = \beta_1 \mathbf{y}_{-1} + \beta_2 \mathbf{y}_{-2} + \boldsymbol{\epsilon}$;
(b) $-1 < \beta_2 < 1$;
$\beta_2 - \beta_1 < 1$;
$\beta_1 + \beta_2 < 1$;

(ii′) (a) $\{\boldsymbol{\epsilon}_t\}$ is a stationary, ergodic sequence;
(b) $\{\boldsymbol{\epsilon}_t, \mathfrak{F}_t\}$ is a martingale difference sequence, where $\mathfrak{F}_t = \sigma(\ldots, \boldsymbol{\epsilon}_{t-1}, \boldsymbol{\epsilon}_t)$;

(iii′) (a) $E(\epsilon_t^2|\mathfrak{F}_{t-1}) = \sigma^2 > 0$.
(b) $E|\epsilon_t|^4 < \infty$.

We verify the conditions of Theorem 5.16. Given (ii′.a), $\{(\mathbf{X}_t, \epsilon_t)\} \equiv \{(\mathbf{y}_{t-1}, \mathbf{y}_{t-2}, \epsilon_t)'\}$ is a stationary ergodic sequence by Theorem 3.35, so condition (ii) is satisfied. Since $\mathbf{y}_{t-j}, \mathbf{j} = 1, 2$, depends only on past ϵ_t, $E(\mathbf{y}_{t-j}\epsilon_t) = E(E(\mathbf{y}_{t-j}\epsilon_t|\mathfrak{F}_{t-1})) = E(\mathbf{y}_{t-j}E(\epsilon_t|\mathfrak{F}_{t-1})) = 0$ given (ii′.b) by Proposition 3.52. It follows from Proposition 3.63 that $E(\mathbf{X}_t'\epsilon_t|\mathfrak{F}_{t-m}) = \mathbf{0}$, $m \geq 1$, so that condition (iii.a) is satisfied. The model given in (i′.a) is an AR(2) time series model and condition (i′.b) is the familiar stationarity condition that the zeros of the polynomial $1 - \beta_1\mathbf{z} - \beta_2\mathbf{z}^2$ lie outside the unit disk. Given (i′b) we can write $\mathbf{y}_t$ as an infinite moving average,

$$\mathbf{y}_t = \sum_{j=0}^{\infty} \mathbf{c}_j \epsilon_{t-j},$$

where $\mathbf{c}_j = (|\beta_2|^{1/2})^j \mathbf{a}(j)$ and $|\mathbf{a}(j)| < \Delta < \infty$ for all $j \geq 0$ (see Dhrymes [1980, pp. 394–395].) Since $|\beta_2| < 1$ it follows that $\Sigma_{j=0}^{\infty} |\mathbf{c}_j| < \infty$. Note that $E|\mathbf{y}_{t-1}\epsilon_t|^2 \leq (E|\mathbf{y}_{t-1}|^4)^{1/2}(E|\epsilon_t|^4)^{1/2}$ by the Cauchy–Schwartz inequality. Hence, if we can show $E|\mathbf{y}_t|^4 < \infty$, then condition (iii.b) is verified. Now by Minkowski's inequality (see Exercise 3.53),

$$\begin{aligned} E|\mathbf{y}_t|^4 &= E\left|\sum_{j=0}^{\infty} \mathbf{c}_j\epsilon_{t-j}\right|^4 \\ &\leq \left(\sum_{j=0}^{\infty} |\mathbf{c}_j|\,(E|\epsilon_{t-j}|^4)^{1/4}\right)^4 \\ &< \left(\Delta^{1/4}\sum_{j=0}^{\infty} |\mathbf{c}_j|\right)^4 < \infty. \end{aligned}$$

Next,

$$\begin{aligned} \mathbf{V}_n \equiv \operatorname{var}(n^{-1/2}\mathbf{X}'\epsilon) &= n^{-1}\sum_{t=1}^{n} E(\epsilon_t^2\mathbf{X}_t'\mathbf{X}_t) \\ &+ n^{-1}\sum_{\tau=1}^{n-1}\sum_{t=\tau+1}^{n} [E(\epsilon_t\epsilon_{t-\tau}\mathbf{X}_t'\mathbf{X}_{t-\tau}) + E(\epsilon_t\epsilon_{t-\tau}\mathbf{X}_{t-\tau}'\mathbf{X}_t)], \end{aligned}$$

where $\mathbf{X}_t = (y_{t-1}, \mathbf{y}_{t-2})$. Now

$$\begin{aligned} E(\epsilon_t\epsilon_{t-\tau}\mathbf{X}_t'\mathbf{X}_{t-\tau}) &= E(E(\epsilon_t\epsilon_{t-\tau}\mathbf{X}_t'\mathbf{X}_{t-\tau}|\mathfrak{F}_{t-1})) \\ &= E(E(\epsilon_t|\mathfrak{F}_{t-1})\epsilon_{t-\tau}\mathbf{X}_t'\mathbf{X}_{t-\tau}) = 0 \qquad \text{for} \quad \tau > 0, \end{aligned}$$

given (ii′.b). Also

$$\begin{aligned} E(\boldsymbol{\epsilon}_t^2 \mathbf{X}_t' \mathbf{X}_t) &= E(E(\boldsymbol{\epsilon}_t^2 \mathbf{X}_t' \mathbf{X}_t | \mathfrak{F}_{t-1})) \\ &= E(E(\boldsymbol{\epsilon}_t^2 | \mathfrak{F}_{t-1}) \mathbf{X}_t' \mathbf{X}_t) \\ &= \sigma^2 \mathbf{E}(\mathbf{X}_t' \mathbf{X}_t) = \sigma^2 \mathbf{M} \end{aligned}$$

given (iii′.a). Note we have used the stationarity of $\{\boldsymbol{\epsilon}_t\}$. Therefore det $\mathbf{V}_n > \delta > 0$ if and only if det $\mathbf{M} > 0$. It can be shown that (see, e.g., Granger and Newbold [1977, ch. 1])

$$E(\mathbf{y}_t^2) = \sigma^2 (1 - \beta_2)[(1 + \beta_2)((1 - \beta_2)^2 - \beta_1^2)]^{-1}$$

and

$$E(\mathbf{y}_t \mathbf{y}_{t-1}) = \sigma^2 \beta_1 [(1 + \beta_2)(1 - \beta_2)^2 - \beta_1^2)]^{-1}.$$

Hence

$$\mathbf{M} = \frac{\sigma^2}{(1 + \beta_2)[(1 - \beta_2)^2 - \beta_1^2]} \begin{pmatrix} (1 - \beta_2) & \beta_1 \\ \beta_1 & (1 - \beta_2) \end{pmatrix}$$

and det $\mathbf{M} \neq 0$ if and only if $(1 - \beta_2)^2 - \beta_1^2 \neq 0$. Thus condition (i′.b) ensures the existence and nonsingularity of $\mathbf{M}$ so that (iii.c) and (iv.b) are satisfied.

Finally, consider condition (iii.d). Given (ii′.b), $\mathcal{R}_{0ij} = 0$ for $j > 0$. For $j = 0$, $\mathcal{R}_{0ij} = E(\mathbf{y}_{-i} \boldsymbol{\epsilon}_0 | \mathfrak{F}_0) = \mathbf{y}_{-i} \boldsymbol{\epsilon}_0$, $i = 1, 2$. So $\text{var}(r_{0i0}) = E((\mathbf{y}_{-i} \boldsymbol{\epsilon}_0)^2) \leq E(\mathbf{y}_{-i}^4)^{1/2} E(\boldsymbol{\epsilon}_0^4)^{1/2} < \infty$ and $\Sigma_{j=0}^{\infty} \text{var}(\mathcal{R}_{0ij})^{1/2} = \text{var}(\mathcal{R}_{0i0})^{1/2} < \infty$. Therefore the conditions of Theorem 5.16 are satisfied and the result follows.

EXERCISE 5.18

Proof: We verify the conditions of Exercise 4.26. The proof that $\mathbf{V}_n^{-1/2} n^{-1/2} \mathbf{Z}' \boldsymbol{\epsilon} \stackrel{A}{\sim} N(\mathbf{0}, \mathbf{I})$ is identical to proving that $\mathbf{V}_n^{-1/2} n^{-1/2} \mathbf{X}' \boldsymbol{\epsilon} \stackrel{A}{\sim} N(\mathbf{0}, \mathbf{I})$ in Theorem 5.16 with $\mathbf{Z}$ replacing $\mathbf{X}$ everywhere.

Next, $\mathbf{Z}'\mathbf{X}/n - \mathbf{Q} \xrightarrow{p} \mathbf{0}$ by Theorem 3.34 given (ii), (iv.a), and (iv.b), where $\mathbf{Q}$ is finite with full column rank. Since the conditions of Exercise 4.26 are satisfied, it follows that

$$\mathbf{D}_n^{-1/2} \sqrt{n} (\tilde{\boldsymbol{\beta}}_n - \boldsymbol{\beta}_0) \stackrel{A}{\sim} N(\mathbf{0}, \mathbf{I}),$$

where

$$\mathbf{D}_n \equiv (\mathbf{QPQ})^{-1} \mathbf{Q}' \mathbf{P} \mathbf{V}_n \mathbf{P} \mathbf{Q} (\mathbf{Q}' \mathbf{P} \mathbf{Q})^{-1}.$$

Since $\mathbf{D}_n - \mathbf{D} \to \mathbf{0}$ it follows that

$$\mathbf{D}^{-1/2}\sqrt{n}(\tilde{\boldsymbol{\beta}}_n - \boldsymbol{\beta}_0) - \mathbf{D}_n^{-1/2}\sqrt{n}(\tilde{\boldsymbol{\beta}}_n - \boldsymbol{\beta}_0)$$
$$= (\mathbf{D}^{-1/2}\mathbf{D}_n^{-1/2} - \mathbf{I})\mathbf{D}_n^{-1/2}\sqrt{n}(\tilde{\boldsymbol{\beta}}_n - \boldsymbol{\beta}_0) \xrightarrow{p} \mathbf{0}$$

by Lemma 4.6. Therefore, by Lemma 4.7, $\mathbf{D}^{-1/2}\sqrt{n}(\tilde{\boldsymbol{\beta}}_n - \boldsymbol{\beta}_0) \overset{A}{\sim} N(\mathbf{0}, \mathbf{I})$.

EXERCISE 5.20

Proof: We verify the conditions of Theorem 4.25. First we apply Theorem 5.19 and Proposition 5.1 to show that $\mathbf{V}^{-1/2}n^{-1/2}\mathbf{X}'\boldsymbol{\epsilon} \overset{A}{\sim} N(\mathbf{0}, \mathbf{I})$. Consider $\boldsymbol{\lambda}'\mathbf{V}^{-1/2}n^{-1/2}\mathbf{X}'\boldsymbol{\epsilon} = n^{-1/2}\sum_{t=1}^{n} \boldsymbol{\lambda}'\mathbf{V}^{-1/2}\mathbf{X}_t'\boldsymbol{\epsilon}_t$. By Theorem 3.49, $\{\boldsymbol{\lambda}'\mathbf{V}^{-1/2}\mathbf{X}_t'\boldsymbol{\epsilon}_t\}$ is a mixing sequence with either $\phi(m)$ or $\alpha(m)$ of size $r'/(r'-1)$, $r' > 1$, given (ii). Further, $E(\boldsymbol{\lambda}'\mathbf{V}^{-1/2}\mathbf{X}_t'\boldsymbol{\epsilon}_t) = 0$ given (iii.a), and application of Minkowski's inequality gives $E(|\boldsymbol{\lambda}'\mathbf{V}^{-1/2}\mathbf{X}_t'\boldsymbol{\epsilon}_t|^{2r'}) < \Delta < \infty$ for all t given (iii.b). Letting

$$\begin{aligned}\sigma_{a,n}^2 &\equiv \operatorname{var}\left(n^{-1/2}\sum_{t=a+1}^{a+n} \boldsymbol{\lambda}'\mathbf{V}^{-1/2}\mathbf{X}_t'\boldsymbol{\epsilon}_t\right)\\ &= \boldsymbol{\lambda}'\mathbf{V}^{-1/2}\operatorname{var}\left(n^{-1/2}\sum_{t=a+1}^{a+n} \mathbf{X}_t'\boldsymbol{\epsilon}_t\right)\mathbf{V}^{-1/2}\mathbf{X}\\ &= \boldsymbol{\lambda}'\mathbf{V}^{-1/2}\mathbf{V}_{a,n}\mathbf{V}^{-1/2}\boldsymbol{\lambda}\end{aligned}$$

we have $\bar{\sigma}_{a,n} \to 1$ uniformly in a given (iii.c). It follows from Theorem 5.19 that $n^{-1/2}\sum_{t=1}^{n} \boldsymbol{\lambda}'\mathbf{V}^{-1/2}\mathbf{X}_t'\boldsymbol{\epsilon}_t = \boldsymbol{\lambda}'\mathbf{V}^{-1/2}n^{-1/2}\mathbf{X}'\boldsymbol{\epsilon} \overset{A}{\sim} N(0,1)$. Hence, by Proposition 5.1, $\mathbf{V}^{-1/2}n^{-1/2}\mathbf{X}'\boldsymbol{\epsilon} \overset{A}{\sim} N(\mathbf{0}, \mathbf{I})$.

Now

$$\mathbf{V}_n^{-1/2}n^{-1/2}\mathbf{X}'\boldsymbol{\epsilon} - \mathbf{V}^{-1/2}n^{-1/2}\mathbf{X}'\boldsymbol{\epsilon} = (\mathbf{V}_n^{-1/2}\mathbf{V}^{1/2} - \mathbf{I})\mathbf{V}^{-1/2}n^{-1/2}\mathbf{X}'\boldsymbol{\epsilon} \xrightarrow{p} \mathbf{0}$$

because $\mathbf{V}_n^{-1/2}\mathbf{V}^{1/2} - \mathbf{I}$ is $o(1)$ (hence $o_p(1)$) by Definition 2.3 and $\mathbf{V}^{-1/2}n^{-1/2}\mathbf{X}'\boldsymbol{\epsilon} \overset{A}{\sim} N(\mathbf{0}, \mathbf{I})$, which allows application of Lemma 4.6. It follows from Lemma 4.7 that

$$\mathbf{V}_n^{-1/2}n^{-1/2}\mathbf{X}'\boldsymbol{\epsilon} \overset{A}{\sim} N(\mathbf{0}, \mathbf{I}).$$

Next, $\mathbf{X}'\mathbf{X}/n - \mathbf{M}_n \xrightarrow{p} \mathbf{0}$ by Corollary 3.48 and Theorem 2.24 given (iv.a). Given (iv.a) $\mathbf{M}_n$ is $O(1)$ and $\det \mathbf{M}_n > \delta > 0$ for all n sufficiently large given (iv.b). Hence, the conditions of Theorem 4.25 are satisfied and the result follows.

EXERCISE 5.21: The following conditions are sufficient:

(i′) (a) $\mathbf{y} = \beta_1 \mathbf{y}_{-1} + \beta_2 \mathbf{x} + \boldsymbol{\epsilon}$;
(b) $|\beta_1| < 1, |\beta_2| < \infty$;

(ii′) $\{(\mathbf{y}_t, \mathbf{x}_t)'\}$ is a mixing sequence with either $\phi(m)$ of size $r'/(r'-1)$, $r' > 1$, or $\alpha(m)$ of size $r'/(r'-1)$, $r' > 1$, where $r' = r + \delta$ for some $r \geq 1$ and $\delta > 0$;

(iii′) (a) $E(\boldsymbol{\epsilon}_t) = 0$ for all t;
(b) $E|\boldsymbol{\epsilon}_t|^{4r'} < \Delta < \infty$ for all t;
(c) $E(\boldsymbol{\epsilon}_t \boldsymbol{\epsilon}_{t-j}) = 0, j = 1, 2, \ldots$, and for all t;
(d) $\mathbf{V}_{an} \equiv \text{var}(n^{-1/2} \sum_{t=a+1}^{a+n} \mathbf{X}_t' \boldsymbol{\epsilon}_t)$ where $\mathbf{X}_t \equiv (\mathbf{y}_{t-1}, \mathbf{x}_t)$, $\mathbf{V}_n \equiv \mathbf{V}_{0n}$ and there exists $\mathbf{V}$ nonsingular such that $\mathbf{V}_{an} - \mathbf{V} \to \mathbf{0}$ as $n \to \infty$ uniformly in a;

(iv′) (a) $|\mathbf{x}_t| < \Delta < \infty$ for all t;
(b) $\mathbf{M}_n \equiv E(\mathbf{X}'\mathbf{X}/n)$ has $\det \mathbf{M}_n > \delta > 0$ for all n sufficiently large.

We verify the conditions of Exercise 5.20. Since $\boldsymbol{\epsilon}_t = \mathbf{y}_t - \beta_1 \mathbf{y}_{t-1} - \beta_2 \mathbf{x}_t$, it follows from Theorem 3.49 that $\{(\mathbf{X}_t, \boldsymbol{\epsilon}_t)'\} = \{(\mathbf{y}_{t-1}, \mathbf{x}_t, \boldsymbol{\epsilon}_t)'\}$ is mixing with either $\phi(m)$ of size $r'/(r'-1)$, $r' > 1$, or $\alpha(m)$ of size $r'/(r'-1)$, $r' > 1$, given (ii′). Thus, condition (ii) of Exercise 5.20 is satisfied.

Next consider condition (iii). Now $E(\mathbf{x}_t \boldsymbol{\epsilon}_t) = \mathbf{x}_t E(\boldsymbol{\epsilon}_t) = 0$ given (iii′.a). Also, by repeated substitution we can express $\mathbf{y}_t$ as

$$\mathbf{y}_t = \beta_2 \sum_{j=0}^{\infty} \beta_1^j \mathbf{x}_{t-j} + \sum_{j=0}^{\infty} \beta_1^j \boldsymbol{\epsilon}_{t-j}$$

so that by Proposition 3.52 $E(\mathbf{y}_{t-1} \boldsymbol{\epsilon}_t) = 0$ given (iii′.a) and (iii′.c). Hence, $E(\mathbf{X}_t' \boldsymbol{\epsilon}_t) = (E(\mathbf{y}_{t-1} \boldsymbol{\epsilon}_t), E(\mathbf{x}_t \boldsymbol{\epsilon}_t))' = \mathbf{0}$ so that (iii.a) is satisfied. Turning to condition (iii.b) we have $E|\mathbf{x}_t \boldsymbol{\epsilon}_t|^{2r'} = |\mathbf{x}_t|^{2r'} E|\boldsymbol{\epsilon}_t|^{2r'} < \Delta' < \infty$ given (iii′.b). Also $E|\mathbf{y}_{t-1} \boldsymbol{\epsilon}_t|^{2r'} \leq (E|\mathbf{y}_{t-1}|^{4r'})^{1/2} (E|\boldsymbol{\epsilon}_t|^{4r'})^{1/2}$ by the Cauchy–Schwartz inequality. Since $E|\boldsymbol{\epsilon}_t|^{4r'} < \Delta < \infty$ given (iii′.b), it only remains to be shown that $E|\mathbf{y}_t|^{4r'} < \infty$. Applying Minkowski's inequality (see Exercise 3.53),

$$\begin{aligned} E|\mathbf{y}_t|^{4r'} &= E\left|\beta_2 \sum_{j=0}^{\infty} \beta_1^j \mathbf{x}_{t-j} + \sum_{j=0}^{\infty} \beta_1^j \boldsymbol{\epsilon}_{t-j}\right|^{4r'} \\ &< \left[|\beta_2| \Delta \sum_{j=0}^{\infty} |\beta_1|^j + \Delta^{1/4r'} \sum_{j=0}^{\infty} |\beta_1|^j\right]^{4r'} \\ &= [(|\beta_2|\Delta + \Delta^{1/4r'})/(1 - |\beta_1|)]^{4r'} < \infty \end{aligned}$$

if and only if $|\boldsymbol{\beta}_1| < 1$. Therefore, $E|\mathbf{y}_{t-1}\boldsymbol{\epsilon}_t|^{2r'} < \infty$ given (i′) and (iv′.a) so that condition (iii.b) is satisfied. It remains to verify condition (iv.a). Now $E|\mathbf{x}_t^2|^{r+\delta} = |\mathbf{x}_t|^{2(r+\delta)} < \Delta^{2(r+\delta)}$ given (iv.a) and $E|\mathbf{y}_t^2|^{r+\delta} < \infty$ as shown above. Hence, all conditions of Exercise 5.20 are satisfied so that the OLS estimate of $(\boldsymbol{\beta}_1, \boldsymbol{\beta}_2)$ will be consistent and asymptotically normal.

EXERCISE 5.26

Proof: First, we apply Corollary 5.25 and Proposition 5.1 to show that $\mathbf{V}_n^{-1/2}n^{-1/2}\mathbf{Z}'\boldsymbol{\epsilon} \overset{A}{\sim} N(\mathbf{0}, \mathbf{I})$. Given (iii′.a), $\{\mathbf{Z}_t'\boldsymbol{\epsilon}_t\}$ is a martingale difference sequence with $\text{var}(n^{-1/2}\mathbf{Z}'\boldsymbol{\epsilon}) = \mathbf{V}_n$ finite by (iii′.b) with $\det(\mathbf{V}_n) > \delta > 0$ for all n sufficiently large given (iii′.c). Hence, consider $\lambda'\mathbf{V}_n^{-1/2}n^{-1/2}\mathbf{Z}'\boldsymbol{\epsilon} = n^{-1/2}\ \Sigma_{t=1}^n\ \lambda'\mathbf{V}_n^{-1/2}\mathbf{Z}_t'\boldsymbol{\epsilon}_t$. Expressing $\lambda'\mathbf{V}_n^{-1/2}\mathbf{Z}_t'\boldsymbol{\epsilon}_t$ as $\Sigma_{h=1}^p\ \Sigma_{i=1}^k\ \tilde{\lambda}_{in}\mathbf{Z}_{thi}\boldsymbol{\epsilon}_{th}$, it follows from the additivity of conditional expectations that

$$E(\lambda'\mathbf{V}_n^{-1/2}\mathbf{Z}_t'\boldsymbol{\epsilon}_t|\mathfrak{F}_{t-1}) = \sum_{h=1}^{p}\sum_{i=1}^{k}\tilde{\lambda}_{in}E(\mathbf{Z}_{thi}\boldsymbol{\epsilon}_{th}|\mathfrak{F}_{t-1}) = 0$$

since $E(\mathbf{Z}_{thi}\boldsymbol{\epsilon}_{th}|\mathfrak{F}_{t-1}) = 0$ given (iii.a). Applying Minkowski's inequality yields

$$\begin{aligned}
E|\lambda'\mathbf{V}_n^{-1/2}\mathbf{Z}_t'\boldsymbol{\epsilon}_t|^{2(r+\delta)} &= E\left|\sum_{h=1}^{p}\sum_{i=1}^{k}\tilde{\lambda}_{in}\mathbf{Z}_{thi}\boldsymbol{\epsilon}_{th}\right|^{2(r+\delta)} \\
&\le \left[\sum_{h=1}^{p}\sum_{i=1}^{k}\lambda_{in}(E|\mathbf{Z}_{thi}\boldsymbol{\epsilon}_{th}|^{2(r+\delta)})^{1/2(r+\delta)}\right]^{2(r+\delta)} \\
&< \left[\Delta\sum_{h=1}^{p}\sum_{i=1}^{k}\Delta^{1/2(r+\delta)}\right]^{2(r+\delta)} < \infty
\end{aligned}$$

given (iii′.b). Now

$$\begin{aligned}
\bar{\sigma}_n^2 &= \text{var}(\lambda'\mathbf{V}_n^{-1/2}n^{-1/2}\mathbf{Z}'\boldsymbol{\epsilon}) \\
&= \lambda'\mathbf{V}_n^{-1/2}\text{var}(n^{-1/2}\mathbf{Z}'\boldsymbol{\epsilon})\mathbf{V}_n^{-1/2}\lambda = 1
\end{aligned}$$

for all n sufficiently large. Next consider $n^{-1}\ \Sigma_{t=1}^n\ \mathbf{X}'\mathbf{V}_n^{-1/2}\mathbf{Z}'\boldsymbol{\epsilon}_t\boldsymbol{\epsilon}_t'\mathbf{Z}_t\mathbf{V}_n^{-1/2}\lambda$. Since $\{\mathbf{Z}_t'\boldsymbol{\epsilon}_t\boldsymbol{\epsilon}_t'\mathbf{Z}_t\}$ is a mixing sequence with either $\phi(m)$ of size $r/(2r-1)$, $r \ge 1$, or $\alpha(m)$ of size $r/(r-1)$, $r > 1$, by Theorem 3.49, it follows that $n^{-1}\ \Sigma_{t=1}^n\ \mathbf{Z}_t'\boldsymbol{\epsilon}_t\boldsymbol{\epsilon}_t'\mathbf{Z}_t - \mathbf{V}_n \xrightarrow{p} \mathbf{0}$ given (iii′.b). By Proposition 2.30,

$$n^{-1}\sum_{t=1}^{n}\lambda'\mathbf{V}_n^{-1/2}\mathbf{Z}_t'\boldsymbol{\epsilon}_t\boldsymbol{\epsilon}_t'\mathbf{Z}_t\mathbf{V}_n^{-1/2}\lambda-\lambda'\mathbf{V}_n^{-1/2}\mathbf{V}_n\mathbf{V}_n^{-1/2}\lambda$$

$$=n^{-1}\sum_{t=1}^{n}\lambda'\mathbf{V}_n^{-1/2}\mathbf{Z}_t'\boldsymbol{\epsilon}_t\boldsymbol{\epsilon}_t'\mathbf{Z}_t\mathbf{V}_n^{-1/2}\lambda-1\xrightarrow{p}0.$$

Hence, the sequence $\{\lambda'\mathbf{V}_n^{-1/2}\mathbf{Z}_t'\boldsymbol{\epsilon}_t\}$ satisfies the conditions of Corollary 5.25, and it follows that $\lambda\mathbf{V}_n^{-1/2}n^{-1/2}\sum_{t=1}^{n}\mathbf{Z}_t'\boldsymbol{\epsilon}_t=\lambda'\mathbf{V}_n^{-1/2}n^{-1/2}\mathbf{Z}'\boldsymbol{\epsilon}\overset{A}{\sim}N(0,1)$. By Proposition 5.1, $\mathbf{V}_n^{-1/2}n^{-1/2}\mathbf{Z}'\boldsymbol{\epsilon}\overset{A}{\sim}N(\mathbf{0},\mathbf{I})$.

Now, given (ii′), (iv.a), and (iv.b), $\mathbf{Z}'\mathbf{X}/n-\mathbf{Q}_n\xrightarrow{p}\mathbf{0}$ by Corollary 3.48 and Theorem 2.24. The remaining results follow as before.

EXERCISE 6.2

Proof: The following conditions are sufficient:

(i) $\mathbf{y}=\mathbf{X}\boldsymbol{\beta}_0+\boldsymbol{\epsilon}$;

(ii) $\{(\mathbf{Z}_t,\mathbf{X}_t,\boldsymbol{\epsilon}_t)'\}$ is a mixing sequence with either $\phi(m)$ of size $r/(2r-1)$, $r\geq 1$, or $\alpha(m)$ of size $r/(r-1)$, $r>1$;

(iii) (a) $E(\mathbf{Z}_{tgi}\boldsymbol{\epsilon}_{th}|\mathfrak{F}_{t-1})=0$ for all t, where $\{\mathfrak{F}_t\}$ is adapted to $\{\mathbf{Z}_{tgi}\boldsymbol{\epsilon}_{th}\}$, $g,h=1,\ldots,p$, $i=1,\ldots,l$;

(b) $E|\mathbf{Z}_{tgi}\boldsymbol{\epsilon}_{th}|^{2(r+\delta)}<\Delta<\infty$ and $E|\boldsymbol{\epsilon}_{th}|^{2(r+\delta)}<\Delta<\infty$ for some $0<\delta\leq r$, $g,h=1,\ldots,p$, $i=1,\ldots,l$, and all t;

(c) $E(\boldsymbol{\epsilon}_t\boldsymbol{\epsilon}_t'|\mathbf{Z}_t)=\sigma_0^2\mathbf{I}_p$, $t=1,\ldots,n$;

(iv) (a) $E|\mathbf{Z}_{thi}|^{2(r+\delta)}<\Delta<\infty$ and $E|\mathbf{X}_{thj}|^{2(r+\delta)}<\Delta<\infty$ for some $\delta>0$, $h=1,\ldots,p$, $i=1,\ldots,l$, $j=1,\ldots k$, and all t;

(b) $\mathbf{Q}_n\equiv E(\mathbf{Z}'\mathbf{X}/n)$ has full column rank uniformly in n for all n sufficiently large;

(c) $\mathbf{L}_n\equiv E(\mathbf{Z}'\mathbf{Z}/n)$ has $\det\mathbf{L}_n>\delta>0$ for all n sufficiently large.

Given conditions (i)–(iv), the asymptotically efficient estimator is

$$\tilde{\boldsymbol{\beta}}_n=\tilde{\boldsymbol{\beta}}_{2SLS}=(\mathbf{X}'\mathbf{Z}(\mathbf{Z}'\mathbf{Z})^{-1}\mathbf{Z}'\mathbf{X})^{-1}\mathbf{X}'\mathbf{Z}(\mathbf{Z}'\mathbf{Z})^{-1}\mathbf{Z}'\mathbf{y}$$

by Exercise 4.47. First consider $\mathbf{Z}'\mathbf{Z}/n$. Now $\{\mathbf{Z}_t'\mathbf{Z}_t\}$ is a mixing sequence with the same size as $\{(\mathbf{Z}_t,\mathbf{X}_t,\boldsymbol{\epsilon}_t)'\}$ by Proposition 3.50. Hence, by Corollary 3.48, $\mathbf{Z}'\mathbf{Z}/n-\mathbf{L}_n=n^{-1}\sum_{t=1}^{n}\mathbf{Z}_t'\mathbf{Z}_t-n^{-1}\sum_{t=1}^{n}E(\mathbf{Z}_t'\mathbf{Z}_t)\xrightarrow{a.s.}\mathbf{0}$ given (iv.a) and $\mathbf{Z}'\mathbf{Z}/n-\mathbf{L}_n\xrightarrow{p}\mathbf{0}$ by Theorem 2.24.

Next consider

$$\begin{aligned}\tilde{\sigma}_n^2 &\equiv (np)^{-1}(\mathbf{y} - \mathbf{X}\tilde{\boldsymbol{\beta}}_n)'(\mathbf{y} - \mathbf{X}\tilde{\boldsymbol{\beta}}_n)\\ &= (\boldsymbol{\epsilon} - \mathbf{X}(\tilde{\boldsymbol{\beta}}_n - \boldsymbol{\beta}_0))'(\boldsymbol{\epsilon} - \mathbf{X}(\tilde{\boldsymbol{\beta}}_n - \boldsymbol{\beta}_0))/np\\ &= \boldsymbol{\epsilon}'\boldsymbol{\epsilon}/np - 2(\tilde{\boldsymbol{\beta}}_n - \boldsymbol{\beta}_0)'\mathbf{X}'\boldsymbol{\epsilon}/np + (\tilde{\boldsymbol{\beta}}_n - \boldsymbol{\beta}_0)'(\mathbf{X}'\mathbf{X}/n)(\tilde{\boldsymbol{\beta}}_n - \boldsymbol{\beta}_0)/p.\end{aligned}$$

Since the conditions of Exercise 3.80 are satisfied, it follows that $\tilde{\boldsymbol{\beta}}_n - \boldsymbol{\beta}_0 \xrightarrow{\text{a.s.}} 0$. Also, $\mathbf{X}'\boldsymbol{\epsilon}/n$ is $O_{\text{a.s.}}(1)$ by Corollary 3.48 given (ii), (iii.b), and (iv.a). Hence $(\tilde{\boldsymbol{\beta}}_n - \boldsymbol{\beta}_0)\mathbf{X}'\boldsymbol{\epsilon}/n \xrightarrow{p} \mathbf{0}$ by Exercise 2.22 and Theorem 2.24. Similarly, $\{\mathbf{X}_t'\mathbf{X}_t\}$ a mixing sequence with size given in (ii) with elements satisfying the moment condition of Corollary 3.48 given (iv.a), so that $\mathbf{X}'\mathbf{X}/n$ is $O_{\text{a.s.}}(1)$ and therefore $(\tilde{\boldsymbol{\beta}}_n - \boldsymbol{\beta}_0)'(\mathbf{X}'\mathbf{X}/n)(\tilde{\boldsymbol{\beta}}_n - \boldsymbol{\beta}_0) \xrightarrow{p} 0$. Finally, consider

$$\boldsymbol{\epsilon}'\boldsymbol{\epsilon}/np = p^{-1}\sum_{h=1}^{p} n^{-1}\sum_{t=1}^{n} \epsilon_{th}^2.$$

Now for any $h = 1, \ldots, p$, $\{\epsilon_{th}^2\}$ is a mixing sequence with $\phi(m)$ of size $r/(2r-1)$, $r \geq 1$, or $\alpha(m)$ of size $r/(r-1)$, $r > 1$. Since $\{\epsilon_{th}^2\}$ satisfies the moment condition of Corollary 3.48 given (iii.b) and $E(\epsilon_{th}^2) = \sigma_0^2$ given (iii.c), it follows that

$$n^{-1}\sum_{t=1}^{n}\epsilon_{th}^2 - n^{-1}\sum_{t=1}^{n}E(\epsilon_{th}^2) = n^{-1}\sum_{t=1}^{n}\epsilon_{th}^2 - \sigma_0^2 \xrightarrow{p} 0, \qquad h = 1, \ldots, p.$$

Hence, $\boldsymbol{\epsilon}'\boldsymbol{\epsilon}/np \xrightarrow{p} \sigma_0^2$, and it follows that $\tilde{\sigma}_n^2 \xrightarrow{p} \sigma_0^2$ by Exercise 2.35.

Exercise 6.6

Proof: The proof is analogous to that of Theorem 6.3, and again we explicitly consider the case $p = 1$ for simplicity. We decompose $\hat{\mathbf{V}}_n - \mathbf{V}_n$ as follows:

$$\begin{aligned}\hat{\mathbf{V}}_n - \mathbf{V}_n = n^{-1}\sum_{t=1}^{n}\epsilon_t^2\mathbf{Z}_t'\mathbf{Z}_t - n^{-1}\sum_{t=1}^{n}E(\epsilon_t^2\mathbf{Z}_t'\mathbf{Z}_t)\\ - 2n^{-1}\sum_{t=1}^{n}(\tilde{\boldsymbol{\beta}}_n - \boldsymbol{\beta}_0)'\mathbf{X}_t'\epsilon_t\mathbf{Z}_t'\mathbf{Z}_t\\ + n^{-1}\sum_{t=1}^{n}(\tilde{\boldsymbol{\beta}}_n - \boldsymbol{\beta}_0)'\mathbf{X}_t'\mathbf{X}_t(\tilde{\boldsymbol{\beta}}_n - \boldsymbol{\beta}_0)\mathbf{Z}_t'\mathbf{Z}_t.\end{aligned}$$

Now $\{\epsilon_t^2\mathbf{Z}_t'\mathbf{Z}_t\}$ is a mixing sequence with either $\phi(m)$ of size $r/(2r-1)$, $r \geq 1$, or $\alpha(m)$ of size $r/(r-1)$, $r > 1$, given (ii) with elements satisfying the moment condition of Corollary 3.48 given (iiib). Hence

$$n^{-1}\sum_{t=1}^{n}\epsilon_t^2 Z_t' Z_t - n^{-1}\sum_{t=1}^{n}E(\epsilon_t^2 Z_t' Z_t)\xrightarrow{p}0.$$

The remaining terms converge to zero in probability as in Theorem 6.3, where we now use results on mixing sequences in place of results on stationary, ergodic sequences. For example, by the Cauchy–Schwartz inequality,

$$\begin{aligned}E|X_{t\kappa}Z_{ti}Z_{tj}\epsilon_t|^{r+\delta} &\le E(|X_{t\kappa}Z_{ti}|^{2(r+\delta)})^{1/2}E(|Z_{tj}\epsilon_t|^{2(r+\delta)})^{1/2}\\ &< \Delta < \infty\end{aligned}$$

given (iii.b) and (iv.a). Since $\{X_{t\kappa}Z_{ti}Z_{tj}\epsilon_t\}$ is a mixing sequence with size given in (ii) and it satisfies the moment condition of Corollary 3.48, it follows that

$$n^{-1}\sum_{t=1}^{n}XZ_{ti}Z_{tj}\epsilon_t - n^{-1}\sum_{t=1}^{n}E(X_{t\kappa}Z_{ti}Z_{tj}\epsilon_t)\xrightarrow{p}0.$$

Since $\tilde{\beta}_n - \beta_0 \to \mathbf{0}$ under the conditions given, we have

$$n^{-1}\sum_{t=1}^{n}(\tilde{\beta}_n - \beta_0)' X_t'\epsilon_t Z_t' Z_t \xrightarrow{p}\mathbf{0}$$

by Exercise 2.35. Finally, consider the third term. The Cauchy–Schwartz inequality gives $E|X_{t\kappa}X_{t\lambda}Z_{ti}Z_{tj}|^{r+\delta} < \infty$ so that

$$n^{-1}\sum_{t=1}^{n}X_{t\kappa}X_{t\lambda}Z_{ti}Z_{tj} - n^{-1}\sum_{t=1}^{n}E(X_{t\kappa}X_{t\lambda}Z_{ti}Z_{tj})\xrightarrow{p}0$$

by Corollary 3.48. Thus the third term vanishes in probability and application of Exercise 2.35 yields $\hat{V}_n - V_n \xrightarrow{p}\mathbf{0}$.

Exercise 6.7

Proof: The proof is immediate from Exercise 5.27 and Exercise 6.6.

Exercise 6.8

Proof: Conditions (i)–(iv) ensure that Exercise 6.6 holds for $\tilde{\beta}_n$ and $\hat{V}_n - V_n \xrightarrow{p}\mathbf{0}$. Next set $\hat{P}_n = \hat{V}_n^{-1}$ in Exercise 6.7. Then $P_n = V_n^{-1}$ and the result follows.

EXERCISE 6.12

Proof: Analogously to Theorem 6.9, consider

$$(n-\tau)^{-1}\sum_{t=\tau+1}^{n}\boldsymbol{\epsilon}_t\boldsymbol{\epsilon}_{t-\tau}\mathbf{Z}_t'\mathbf{Z}_{t-\tau}-(n-\tau)^{-1}\sum_{t=\tau+1}^{n}E(\boldsymbol{\epsilon}_t\boldsymbol{\epsilon}_{t-\tau}\mathbf{Z}_t'\mathbf{Z}_{t-\tau})$$

$$-(n-\tau)^{-1}\sum_{t=\tau+1}^{n}(\tilde{\boldsymbol{\beta}}_n-\boldsymbol{\beta}_0)'\mathbf{X}_t'\boldsymbol{\epsilon}_{t-\tau}\mathbf{Z}_t'\mathbf{Z}_{t-\tau}$$

$$-(n-\tau)^{-1}\sum_{t=\tau+1}^{n}(\tilde{\boldsymbol{\beta}}_n-\boldsymbol{\beta}_0)'\mathbf{X}_{t-\tau}'\boldsymbol{\epsilon}_t\mathbf{Z}_t'\mathbf{Z}_{t-\tau}$$

$$+(n-\tau)^{-1}\sum_{t=\tau+1}^{n}(\tilde{\boldsymbol{\beta}}_n-\boldsymbol{\beta}_0)\mathbf{X}_t'\mathbf{X}_{t-\tau}(\tilde{\boldsymbol{\beta}}_n-\boldsymbol{\beta}_0)\mathbf{Z}_t'\mathbf{Z}_{t-\tau}.$$

We can proceed exactly as in Theorem 6.3 to show that each term above converges to zero in probability. Note that Theorem 3.49 is invoked to guarantee the summands are mixing sequences with size given in (ii), and the Cauchy-Schwartz inequality is used to verify the moment condition of Corollary 3.48. For example, given (ii) $\{\boldsymbol{\epsilon}_t\boldsymbol{\epsilon}_{t-\tau}\mathbf{Z}_t'\mathbf{Z}_{t-\tau}\}$ is a mixing sequence with either $\phi(m)$ of size $r'/(2r'-1)$, $r'\geq 1$, or $\alpha(m)$ of size $r'/(r'-1)$, $r'>1$, with elements satisfying the moment condition of Corollary 3.48 given (iii.b). Hence

$$(n-\tau)^{-1}\sum_{t=\tau+1}^{n}\boldsymbol{\epsilon}_t\boldsymbol{\epsilon}_{t-\tau}\mathbf{Z}_t'\mathbf{Z}_{t-\tau}-(n-\tau)^{-1}\sum_{t=\tau+1}^{n}E(\boldsymbol{\epsilon}_t\boldsymbol{\epsilon}_{t-\tau}\mathbf{Z}_t'\mathbf{Z}_{t-\tau})\xrightarrow{p}\mathbf{0}.$$

The remaining terms can be shown to converge to zero in probability in a manner similar to Theorem 6.3.

EXERCISE 6.13

Proof: Immediate from Theorem 5.23 and Exercise 6.12.

EXERCISE 6.14

Proof: Conditions (i)-(iv) ensure that Exercise 6.12 holds for $\tilde{\boldsymbol{\beta}}_n$ and $\hat{\mathbf{V}}_n-\mathbf{V}_n\xrightarrow{p}\mathbf{0}$. Next set $\hat{\mathbf{P}}_n=\hat{\mathbf{V}}_n^{-1}$ in Exercise 6.13. Then $\mathbf{P}_n=\mathbf{V}_n^{-1}$ and the result follows.

EXERCISE 7.4

Proof: Because $\hat{\boldsymbol{\epsilon}}_t=\tilde{\boldsymbol{\epsilon}}_t-\tilde{\mathbf{X}}_t(\tilde{\boldsymbol{\beta}}_n-\boldsymbol{\beta}_0)$, we have

$$\begin{aligned}
\hat{\boldsymbol{\Sigma}}_{\gamma n} - \boldsymbol{\Sigma}_\gamma &= (n_\gamma/n)^{-1} n^{-1} \sum_{t=1}^{n} \mathbf{d}_{\gamma t} \hat{\boldsymbol{\epsilon}}_t \hat{\boldsymbol{\epsilon}}_{t'} - \boldsymbol{\Sigma}_\gamma \\
&= (n_\gamma/n)^{-1} n^{-1} \sum_{t=1}^{n} \mathbf{d}_{\gamma t}\, \tilde{\boldsymbol{\epsilon}}_t \tilde{\boldsymbol{\epsilon}}_t' - \boldsymbol{\Sigma}_\gamma \\
&\quad - (n_\gamma/n)^{-1} n^{-1} \sum_{t=1}^{n} \mathbf{d}_{\gamma t} \tilde{\mathbf{X}}_t (\tilde{\boldsymbol{\beta}}_n - \boldsymbol{\beta}_0) \tilde{\boldsymbol{\epsilon}}_t' \\
&\quad - (n_\gamma/n)^{-1} n^{-1} \sum_{t=1}^{n} \mathbf{d}_{\gamma t} \tilde{\boldsymbol{\epsilon}}_t (\tilde{\boldsymbol{\beta}}_n - \boldsymbol{\beta}_0)' \tilde{\mathbf{X}}_t' \\
&\quad + (n_\gamma/n)^{-1} n^{-1} \sum_{t=1}^{n} \mathbf{d}_{\gamma t}\, \tilde{\mathbf{X}}_t (\tilde{\boldsymbol{\beta}}_n - \boldsymbol{\beta}_0)(\tilde{\boldsymbol{\beta}}_n - \boldsymbol{\beta}_0)' \tilde{\mathbf{X}}_t'.
\end{aligned}$$

The result will follow from Exercise 2.35 if we can show that each of the four terms above vanish in probability.

Given (i) and (ii), it follows that

$$(n_\gamma/n)^{-1} n^{-1} \sum_{t=1}^{n} \mathbf{d}_{\gamma t} \tilde{\boldsymbol{\epsilon}}_t \tilde{\boldsymbol{\epsilon}}_t' - E(n_\gamma/n)^{-1} n^{-1} \sum_{t=1}^{n} E(\mathbf{d}_{\gamma t} \tilde{\boldsymbol{\epsilon}}_t \tilde{\boldsymbol{\epsilon}}_t') \xrightarrow{p} \mathbf{0}$$

by Proposition 2.30. Now

$$\begin{aligned}
n^{-1} \sum_{t=1}^{n} E(\mathbf{d}_{\gamma t} \tilde{\boldsymbol{\epsilon}}_t \tilde{\boldsymbol{\epsilon}}_t') &= n^{-1} \sum_{t=1}^{n} E(E(\mathbf{d}_{\gamma t} \tilde{\boldsymbol{\epsilon}}_t \tilde{\boldsymbol{\epsilon}}_t' | \mathbf{W}_t)) \\
&= n^{-1} \sum_{t=1}^{n} E(\mathbf{d}_{\gamma t} E(\tilde{\boldsymbol{\epsilon}}_t \tilde{\boldsymbol{\epsilon}}_t' | \mathbf{W}_t)) \\
&= n^{-1} \sum_{t=1}^{n} E(\mathbf{d}_{\gamma t} (\boldsymbol{\Sigma}_1 \mathbf{d}_{1t} + \cdots + \boldsymbol{\Sigma}_{Gt} \mathbf{d}_{Gt})) \\
&= n^{-1} \sum_{t=1}^{n} E(\mathbf{d}_{\gamma t} \boldsymbol{\Sigma}_\gamma) \\
&= n^{-1} \sum_{t=1}^{n} E(\mathbf{d}_{\gamma t}) \times \boldsymbol{\Sigma}_\gamma \\
&= n^{-1} E\left(\sum_{t=1}^{n} \mathbf{d}_{\gamma t} \right) \times \boldsymbol{\Sigma}_\gamma \\
&= E(n_\gamma/n) \times \boldsymbol{\Sigma}_\gamma .
\end{aligned}$$

Hence $(n_\gamma/n)^{-1} n^{-1} \Sigma_{t=1}^{n} \mathbf{d}_{\gamma t} \tilde{\boldsymbol{\epsilon}}_t \tilde{\boldsymbol{\epsilon}}_t' - \boldsymbol{\Sigma}_\gamma \xrightarrow{p} \mathbf{0}$.

Next consider

$$n^{-1}\sum_{t=1}^{n}\mathbf{d}_{\gamma t}\tilde{\mathbf{X}}_t(\tilde{\boldsymbol{\beta}}_n-\boldsymbol{\beta}_0)\tilde{\boldsymbol{\epsilon}}_t'.$$

This can be written as the sum of k matrices with the g, hth element in the ith term ($i = 1, \ldots, k$) equal to

$$(\tilde{\beta}_{ngi}-\beta_{0gi})n^{-1}\sum_{t=1}^{n}\mathbf{d}_{\gamma t}\tilde{\mathbf{X}}_{tgi}\tilde{\boldsymbol{\epsilon}}_{th}.$$

Since $\tilde{\beta}_{ngi}-\beta_{0gi}\xrightarrow{p}0$, $g = 1, \ldots, p$, $i = 1, \ldots, k$, and $n^{-1}\sum_{t=1}^{n} d_{\gamma t}\tilde{\mathbf{X}}_{tgi}\tilde{\epsilon}_{th}$ is $O_p(1)$ for $g, h = 1, \ldots, p$, $i = 1, \ldots, k$, *it follows from Exercise 2.35 that*

$$n^{-1}\sum_{t=1}^{n}\mathbf{d}_{\gamma t}\tilde{\mathbf{X}}_t(\tilde{\boldsymbol{\beta}}_n-\boldsymbol{\beta}_0)\tilde{\boldsymbol{\epsilon}}_t'\xrightarrow{p}\mathbf{0}.$$

The third term is the transpose of the second term, so it too converges in probability to zero.

Finally, consider the last term

$$n^{-1}\sum_{t=1}^{n}\mathbf{d}_{\gamma t}\tilde{\mathbf{X}}_t(\tilde{\boldsymbol{\beta}}_n-\boldsymbol{\beta}_0)(\tilde{\boldsymbol{\beta}}_n-\boldsymbol{\beta}_0)'\tilde{\mathbf{X}}_t'.$$

This can be expressed as the sum of k^2 matrices where the g, hth element of the i, jth term ($i, j = 1, \ldots, k$) is

$$(\tilde{\beta}_{ngi}-\beta_{0gi})(\tilde{\beta}_{nhj}-\beta_{0hj})n^{-1}\sum_{t=1}^{n}\mathbf{d}_{\gamma t}\tilde{\mathbf{X}}_{tgi}\tilde{\mathbf{X}}_{thj}.$$

Since $n^{-1}\sum_{t=1}^{n}\mathbf{d}_{\gamma t}\tilde{\mathbf{X}}_{tgi}\tilde{\mathbf{X}}_{thj}$ is $O_p(1)$ for $g, h = 1, \ldots, p$, $i, j = 1, \ldots, k$, given (iv), it follows that

$$n^{-1}\sum_{t=1}^{n}\mathbf{d}_{\gamma t}\tilde{\mathbf{X}}_t(\tilde{\boldsymbol{\beta}}_n-\boldsymbol{\beta}_0)(\tilde{\boldsymbol{\beta}}_n-\boldsymbol{\beta}_0)'\tilde{\mathbf{X}}_t'\xrightarrow{p}\mathbf{0}.$$

It now follows from Exercise 2.35 that $\hat{\boldsymbol{\Sigma}}_{\gamma n}-\boldsymbol{\Sigma}_\gamma\xrightarrow{p}\mathbf{0}$.

References

Dhrymes, P. [1980]. "Econometrics." New York: Springer-Verlag.

Granger, C. W. J., and P. Newbold [1977]. "Forecasting Economic Time Series." New York: Academic Press.

Laha, R. G., and V. K. Rohatgi [1979]. "Probability Theory." New York: Wiley.

Rao, C. R. [1973]. "Linear Statistical Inference and Its Applications." New York: Wiley.

Index

L

M

N

O

P

S

T

U

V

W

ECONOMIC THEORY, ECONOMETRICS, AND MATHEMATICAL ECONOMICS

Consulting Editor: Karl Shell

UNIVERSITY OF PENNSYLVANIA
PHILADELPHIA, PENNSYLVANIA

Franklin M. Fisher and Karl Shell. **The Economic Theory of Price Indices: *Two Essays on the Effects of Taste, Quality, and Technological Change***

Luis Eugenio Di Marco (Ed.). **International Economics and Development: *Essays in Honor of Raúl Presbisch***

Erwin Klein. **Mathematical Methods in Theoretical Economics: *Topological and Vector Space Foundations of Equilibrium Analysis***

Paul Zarembka (Ed.). **Frontiers in Econometrics**

George Horwich and Paul A. Samuelson (Eds.). **Trade, Stability, and Macroeconomics: *Essays in Honor of Lloyd A. Metzler***

W. T. Ziemba and R. G. Vickson (Eds.). **Stochastic Optimization Models in Finance**

Steven A. Y. Lin (Ed.). **Theory and Measurement of Economic Externalities**

David Cass and Karl Shell (Eds.). **The Hamiltonian Approach to Dynamic Economics**

R. Shone. **Microeconomics: *A Modern Treatment***

C. W. J. Granger and Paul Newbold. **Forecasting Economic Time Series**

Michael Szenberg, John W. Lombardi, and Eric Y. Lee. **Welfare Effects of Trade Restrictions: *A Case Study of the U.S. Footwear Industry***

Haim Levy and Marshall Sarnat (Eds.). **Financial Decision Making under Uncertainty**

Yasuo Murata. **Mathematics for Stability and Optimization of Economic Systems**

Alan S. Blinder and Philip Friedman (Eds.). **Natural Resources, Uncertainty, and General Equilibrium Systems: *Essays in Memory of Rafael Lusky***

Jerry S. Kelly. **Arrow Impossibility Theorems**

Peter Diamond and Michael Rothschild (Eds.). **Uncertainty in Economics: *Readings and Exercises***

Fritz Machlup. **Methodology of Economics and Other Social Sciences**

Robert H. Frank and Richard T. Freeman. **Distributional Consequences of Direct Foreign Investment**

Elhanan Helpman and Assaf Razin. **A Theory of International Trade under Uncertainty**

Edmund S. Phelps. Studies in Macroeconomic Theory, Volume 1: *Employment and Inflation.* Volume 2: *Redistribution and Growth*

Marc Nerlove, David M. Grether, and José L. Carvalho. Analysis of Economic Time Series: *A Synthesis*

Thomas J. Sargent. Macroeconomic Theory

Jerry Green and José Alexander Scheinkman (Eds.). General Equilibrium, Growth and Trade: *Essays in Honor of Lionel McKenzie*

Michael J. Boskin (Ed.). Economics and Human Welfare: *Essays in Honor of Tibor Scitovsky*

Carlos Daganzo. Multinomial Probit: *The Theory and Its Application to Demand Forecasting*

L. R. Klein, M. Nerlove, and S. C. Tsiang (Eds.). Quantitative Economics and Development: *Essays in Memory of Ta-Chung Liu*

Giorgio P. Szegö. Portfolio Theory: *With Application to Bank Asset Management*

M June Flanders and Assaf Razin (Eds.). Development in an Inflationary World

Thomas G. Cowing and Rodney E. Stevenson (Eds.). Productivity Measurement in Regulated Industries

Robert J. Barro (Ed.). Money, Expectations, and Business Cycles: *Essays in Macroeconomics*

Ryuzo Sato. Theory of Technical Change and Economic Invariance: *Application of Lie Groups*

Iosif A. Krass and Shawkat M. Hammoudeh. The Theory of Positional Games: *With Applications in Economics*

Giorgio Szegö (Ed.). New Quantitative Techniques for Economic Analysis

John M. Letiche (Ed.). International Economic Policies and Their Theoretical Foundations: A Source Book

Murray C. Kemp (Ed.). Production Sets

Andreu Mas-Colell (Ed.). Noncooperative Approaches to the Theory of Perfect Competition

Jean-Pascal Benassy. The Economics of Market Disequilibrium

Tatsuro Ichiishi. Game Theory for Economic Analysis

David P. Baron. The Export-Import Bank: *An Economic Analysis*

Réal P. Lavergne. The Political Economy of U. S. Tariffs: *An Empirical Analysis*

Halbert White. Asymptotic Theory for Econometricians

Thomas G. Cowing and Daniel L. McFadden. Microeconomic Modeling and Policy Analysis: *Studies in Residential Energy Demand*

ISBN 0-12-746650-9

90065

9 780127 466507